Steelhead Guide

*Fly Fishing Techniques and Strategies
for Lake Erie Steelhead*

Steelhead Guide

Fly Fishing Techniques and Strategies
for Lake Erie Steelhead

by
John Nagy

Illustrated by Jeff Wynn and Les Troyer

Great Lakes Publishing
Pittsburgh, Pennsylvania

Steelhead Guide, Fly Fishing Techniques and Strategies for Lake Erie Steelhead

Fourth Edition (Updated and Expanded)

Copyrights 1998, 2000, 2003, 2008 By John Nagy

Printed in the United States of America by Jostens Commercial Publications, State College, Pennsylvania

Published by: **Great Lakes Publishing**
606 Crysler Street
Pittsburgh, Pennsylvania 15226

All photos are by the author John Nagy except where noted.

Cover and book design by Marni Cayro.

Maps by Dwight Landis.

Illustrated by Jeff Wynn and Les Troyer.

Color insert of fly patterns photographed by Roger Bonifield Photography.

Front cover photos: Ed McCarter at the end of a battle with a spring steelhead that fell for an egg pattern (background), fall steelheader fishing just after peak run-off on a Lake Erie tributary (middle), Little Manistee steelhead that was caught on a traditional swinging presentation (bottom).

Back cover photos: Fall buck steelhead caught with Scandinavian tube fly (bottom), fly box of "Temple Dog" style tube flies (top).

All photographed steelhead in this book were released unharmed.

Library of Congress Cataloging-in-Publication Data
Nagy, John
Steelhead Guide, Fly Fishing Techniques and Strategies for Lake Erie Steelhead/
John Nagy-4th edition.
Includes bibliographical references.
Illustrated by Jeff Wynn and Les Troyer.
    p   cm.
1. Fly fishing.
2. Guide to Lake Erie tributaries.
I   Title.
SH456.2N28 2008
799.1755   2007908324 CIP
ISBN 978-0-9665172-4-8

Dedication

This book is first and foremost dedicated
to serving Jesus Christ, our Lord and Savior.

Secondly, it is dedicated to the
memory of my father, John A. Nagy,
who introduced me to the wonder of the outdoors
and the sport of fly fishing.

Acknowledgements
to the Fourth Edition

The author would like to thank the following individuals who helped in the formation of this fourth edition in one form or another: Claudia Buzsics, Marni Cayro, Mac Seaholm, Tony DiBenedetto, Jr. of T Bone Fly Fishing, Stuart Anderson of the Canadian Tube Fly Company, Lorin Riutta of Outhere Smartwear, Jack Cook of the Irish Angler, Hakan Norling, Mikael Frodin, Jack Hanrahan, Roger Bonifield, Jon Luke of Eastern Fly Fishing Magazine, Mike McCoy, Mike Durkalec of the Cleveland Metroparks and Dave Skellie of Pennsylvania Sea Grants.

A very special thanks goes to the late Yuri Shumakov who not only introduced me to the world of Scandinavian tube flies, but more importantly, taught me what it is to be a generous and thoughtful human being.

Special thanks also go out to all the dedicated guides, tyers and steelhead fly fisherman in the Lake Erie region who contributed new and innovative steelhead fly patterns to this new edition. The author would also like to thank the following individuals of the various Lake Erie fishery agencies who graciously provided me with up-to-date information, reports and data on the Lake Erie steelhead fishery: Jeff Brouncheidel (Michigan Department of Natural Resources), Kevin Kayle (Ohio Department of Wildlife), Chuck Murray (Pennsylvania Fish & Boat Commission), Jim Markham (New York State Department of Environmental Conservation) and David Gonder (Ontario Ministry of Natural Resources).

Contact Information

The author John Nagy is always interested in any comments or feedback concerning his book as well as current Lake Erie tributary fishing reports, tributary run-off conditions, fishery related news and innovative, new Lake Erie steelhead fly patterns.

He can be contacted at:

Great Lakes Publishing,
606 Crysler Street,
Pittsburgh, Pennsylvania, 15226
(412) 531-5819

Author with a Lake Erie tributary fall run steelhead.

He can be found on the Web at:

http://groups.msn.com/JohnNagySteelheadGuide/
or E-mailed at: steelheadguide@hotmail.com

Table of Contents

" But the Steelhead, with the brightness of the sea still on him, is livest of all the river's life. When you have made your cast for him, you are no longer a careless observer. As you mend the cast and work your fly well down to him through the cold water, your whole mind is with it, picturing its drift, guiding its swing, holding it where you know he will be. And when the shock of his take jars through to your forearms and you lift the rod to its bend, you know that in a moment the strength of his leaping body will shatter the water to brilliance, however dark the day."

Roderick Haig-Brown
A River Never Sleeps, 1946

Introduction

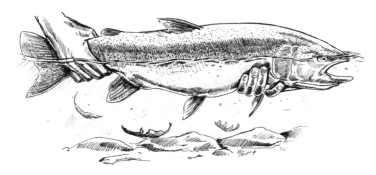

This guidebook was written to help both the novice and seasoned fly fisherman fish the tributary streams of Lake Erie for lake-run steelhead.

The Lake Erie steelhead fishery has come a long way from the 1950's when the local angler's called the Lake Erie shoreline in Pennsylvania "rainbow row." Spring stockings of domesticated rainbows (for stream trout fishing) eventually created a late winter/spring run of steelhead-size rainbows from Lake Erie into the tributaries. Local anglers enjoyed this unpublicized, spectacular fishing exclusively.

These days, Lake Erie steelhead runs, now primarily based on steelhead-strain stocks and some natural reproduction, can begin as early as September and last into April or even May. They are some of the best steelhead runs in the Great Lakes and hold their own when compared with the traditional runs of the Pacific Northwest.

Steelhead Guide, Fly Fishing Techniques and Strategies for Lake Erie Steelhead acts as your personal steelhead fly fishing guide, explaining in detail the techniques, equipment, flies, steelhead behavior, stream conditions, and weather conditions that can all combine to produce a successful Lake Erie steelhead trip. Detailed stream and road maps showing the important tributary streams of Ohio, Pennsylvania, New York, Michigan and the Canadian Province of Ontario are included. Information for each tributary, including watershed size and type, run-off rates, steelhead source, surrounding terrain, important feeders, tributary profiles and major access points are given as well. It also includes effective steelhead fly patterns, a fly selection chart and a concise steelhead run timetable.

Since many other Great Lakes tributaries have similar characteristics to the Lake Erie tributaries, this guidebook can also be useful to steelheaders who fly fish these regions as well.

Introduction *to the* Fourth Edition

The updated and expanded fourth edition of **Steelhead Guide, Fly Fishing Techniques and Strategies for Lake Erie Steelhead** has been expanded from 257 pages to 320 pages. 119 new steelhead fly patterns (including 28 hot tube flies and a new Deadly Dozen fly list) have been contributed by guides, fly tyers and steelhead fly fisherman from Ohio, Pennsylvania, New York, Michigan and Ontario. All the fly patterns include detailed recipes and comments and have been photographed in 11 fly plates and placed in the color insert section of the book including the corresponding fly pattern names. The color insert also includes 5 new color pages of steelhead photography (15 photos) taken in the Lake Erie region. An exciting new Chapter 8 on tube flies has also been added with a discussion on their history, benefits, construction and use. Additionally, detailed tube fly recipes and comments as well as tube tying material and accessory sources are included.

In another major change to the book, the Appendix section has been completely updated and expanded including the 2005 and 2006 Lake Erie Cold Water Task Group rainbow trout/steelhead stocking lists for the Lake Erie region. The Appendix also includes data taken from the 2003-2004 Pennsylvania Fish & Boat Commission Creel Analysis and Economic Impact study of Pennsylvania's Lake Erie tributary fishery, and the 2003/2004 and 2004/2005 New York State Department of Environmental Conservation Lake Erie tributary creel surveys.

Other changes to the book include updated information on the Michigan and Ontario tributaries (Chapter 10), a detailed Introduction to the Fourth Edition, an Additional Steelheader's Tips section (Chapter 9), Updated Equipment Recommendations (Chapter 6) and some revision to the original third edition text.

Finally, a little humor has been added to the book with the addition of the "Steelheader's Quiz" (Chapter 9) wherein the reader can determine if he is really a "hard-core" steelheader.

Steelhead Fishery News

Since the last edition of Steelhead Guide numerous items of importance have occurred across the Lake Erie region in regards to the steelhead fishery. The following discussion details those items by the Great Lakes Region and the specific states (including the Province of Ontario).

Great Lakes Region

In December, 2005 the Great Lakes Regional Task Force (consisting of the federal Great Lakes Inter-agency Task Force, the Council of Great Lakes Governors, the Great Lakes Initiative, the Great Lakes tribes and the Great Lakes Congressional Task Force) proposed a 15 year, $20 billion plan for cleaning up the Great Lakes. This is an effort (mandated by President Bush in 2004) to coordinate ongoing Great Lakes cleanup efforts and restoration work that has been criticized by a United States Government Accountability Office report as being "disjointed."

The plan recommends modernizing waste treatment systems, cleaning up toxic hot spots, polluted tributaries and wetlands to reduce the discharge of mercury, PCB's, dioxin, pesticides and other toxins into the Great Lakes, restoration of deteriorating animal habitats such as wetlands and enacting new federal laws (such as the National Aquatic Invasive Species Act still pending in congress) to prohibit ocean-going vessels from discharging untreated ballast water into the Great Lakes thereby introducing such non-native organisms such as zebra mussels, gobies, etc. Initial Funding for this plan in the US fiscal 2007 Federal budget will be a challenge ($300 million is hoped for) due to the devastating hurricanes of 2005 and other budget concerns.

The recent federal Great Lakes Restoration Act has approved a mass marking program for juvenile steelhead which will be managed by the Fish & Wildlife Service. The marking program will include adipose fin clippings and code wire tags (which are embedded in the nose of the steelhead and require harvesting of the fish to read the tag). The fish tracking data collected will be used to better manage salmonid fisheries in the Great Lakes. Congressional funding for the program is hoped for in 2008 with fish tracking by the various state fishery departments to begin in 2010.

Ohio

On October 26, 2006 the United States Department of Agriculture's (USDA) Animal and Plant Health Inspection Service (APHIS) banned interstate shipments of 37 species of live fish from eight Great Lakes states and also from Ontario and Quebec. The emergency edict was implemented to contain viral hemorrhagic septicemia (VHS) a saltwater virus that has found its way into the Great Lakes. In the spring of 2006, an extensive die off of yellow perch and freshwater drum was reported by the Ohio Division of Wildlife (ODW) in the central and western basins of Lake Erie. VHS has also has been identified as causing a die off of round goby and muskellunge in Lake Ontario and the St. Lawrence Seaway in 2006.

This surprise ruling by APHIS could have a severe impact on Ohio's steelhead program which depends on receiving Little Manistee steelhead fingerlings and eggs from Michigan in exchange for catfish. Kevin Kayle, Aquatic Biology Supervisor with the Ohio DOW at the Fairport Fisheries Station, says that they have already received their allotment of Little Manistee eggs and fingerlings for this year (2006) so the ruling will not impact the Ohio steelhead program immediately.

On November 14, 2006 APHIS modified its ruling by allowing several Great Lakes States including Michigan to move interstate live species of fish susceptible to VHS if they can document that the fish have tested negative for the VHS virus under existing national and international standards.

During the summers of 2002, 2003 and 2005 ODW Chief Fisheries Biologist Kevin Kayle examined the stomach contents of steelhead caught by charter boat captains in the Lake Erie Central Basin (see Figure 8.5 in Appendix E). This pilot study was part of a continuing bioenergetics analysis by the Lake Erie Cold Water Task Group to estimate the consumption of smelt and other prey fish by the main lake predators (i.e. walleye, lake trout, burbot and steelhead).

The 2002 sampling data (see Tables 5.02 and 5.03 in Appendix E) showed that the most common item in the steelhead diet was the spiny water flea followed by smelt and emerald shiners. Overall though, more than 99% of the biomass of the stomach contents was composed of fish such as smelt, white perch, emerald shiners, freshwater drum and alewife.

Rainbow smelt comprised the majority of the dry weight biomass in both 2002 and 2003, but emerald shiners were the major forage item in 2005 as smelt declined. Yellow perch were noted as occasional food items in 2003, which was a strong year class for yellow perch. Other fish, insects and invertebrate species were occasional diet items and varied by year.

The results of this study suggest that summer steelhead in the Central Basin of Lake Erie are generalists in regards to the numbers and types of food items they consumed and that their diets vary from year to year depending on the availability of forage species. However, they still obtain the majority of their energy from fish prey.

Kevin Kayle says there is also an ongoing study by the ODW surveying some of its Lake Erie steelhead tributaries for wild steelhead production and cataloging them into digital maps and GIS layers. In the future this cataloging will hopefully involve a cooperative effort with other Lake Erie agencies to develop a master map of high quality watersheds monitoring both the production and contribution ("recruitment") of wild steelhead smolts. These maps could also be used to target areas for stream improvement projects.

In early 2007 two senate bills were being reviewed in the Ohio state legislature (#351 by Senator Spada and #609 by Representative Jim McGregor) concerning the buyout of commercial netters in the Ohio waters of Lake Erie. Although the majority of fish commercially netted in Lake Erie are yellow and white perch accidental netting of walleye, smallmouth bass and steelhead occurs. The economic impact on the loss of commercial netting revenues are meager compared to the 1.8 billion dollars of economic impact sport fishing has in Ohio. These bills if passed will have a positive impact both economically and in terms of the future of the Ohio steelhead fishery and nearby fisheries in Lake Erie as well.

Ohio Governor Bob Taft on October 6, 2005 officially announced that Conneaut Creek has been given wild and scenic river status by the state. The scenic status section of the river includes 21 miles from the Ohio-Pennsylvania border to the old Penn Central Bridge or "arches" area in the City of Conneaut. The wild status section encompasses 16.4 miles from the Pennsylvania state line to Creek Road covered bridge. This designation mandates that any public project that might affect Conneaut Creek and its resources will be subject to a thorough review, ensuring that no threat is posed to the waterway, and at the same time not compromising the rights of the private property owners along the stream. The designation also gives the affected property owners a chance to participate in preservation programs which can only improve the fishery.

The collapse of the Daniels Park Dam in the spring of 2005 on the Chagrin River should allow good numbers of steelhead to run up into the upper part of the Chagrin River (although during low water periods it will still obstruct some steelhead movement). 4 miles of good public access exists for the steelheader on this upper water on the North Chagrin Reservation in Willoughby Hills, but many sections of this upper water (including the East Branch) are private and posted.

In late 2006 the Spring Ridge Club of Pennsylvania leased two sections on Conneaut Creek in Ohio (1.5 miles upstream of Creek Road Covered Bridge and a section directly downstream of Furnace Road) for its club members. The ODW considers the securing of these parcels by a private entity to be a disturbing trend and will not treat it lightly. In the future the ODW will monitor public access on Conneaut Creek and other Ohio steelhead tributaries to insure the public has adequate access to steelhead stocked with public (ODW) monies.

In 2006 an Ohio grass roots organization began asking steelheaders to sign a water access rights contact data base that will support their efforts to guarantee future public access to Ohio waterways. The data base sign-up and information on their fight can be found at http://www.flyandfloatfishing.com/stream_access.htm.

Since 2005, the Ohio DNR has been using funds obtained from the Water Resource Protection Sponsor Program (funded by the Ohio EPA in partnership with the city of Conneaut, Ohio) for purchasing conservation easements from private landowners along Conneaut Creek. The Conneaut Creek Preservation and Management Plan has identified 50 specific land parcels that are worthy of protection. These easements still allow the landowners the right to allow or deny public access. See Friends of Conneaut Creek for more details at www.friendsofconneautcreek.com.

Finally, Ohio steelheaders are reminded that in late July, 2006 a "500" year flood occurred in Northeast Ohio with the worst of the flooding in the Grand River watershed wherein the Grand reached 11 feet above flood level. The impact has changed the character of the river severely as many pools, runs, riffles and pocket water areas have been changed dramatically and flooding impacts are also evident on the nearby Chagrin and Ashtabula Rivers.

Pennsylvania

In 2006 the Pennsylvania Fish & Boat Commission (PF&BC) moved its steelhead spawning operations from the Tionesta Hatchery to the Fairview Hatchery in

Erie County. The move was prompted as result of a VHS outbreak in Lake Erie (see Ohio section on page 11). The relocation will keep steelhead in the Lake Erie drainage and prevent the possible spread of VHS (although there has been no documentation of salmonids dying off from VHS in Lake Erie so far).

The PF&BC in January, 2007 voted to temporarily ban the transport of live fish, such as emerald shiners, outside Pennsylvania's Lake Erie watershed (which encompasses Lake Erie and all the Pennsylvania tributaries). This ban will remain in place until January 2008 and will help contain the spread of the VHS virus as well as aquatic invasive species. A vote on adopting a permanent regulation is expected later in the year 2007.

Results from a 2003/2004 Creel Analysis and Economic Impact Study of the Pennsylvania Lake Erie steelhead tributary fishery by biologist Chuck Murray of the Pennsylvania Fish and Boat Commission and M. Shields of Penn State University has shown that all aspects of the steelhead fishery have improved since the last survey in 1993 including angler effort (trips), catch rate, steelhead catch and steelhead harvest (see Appendix E). The new survey of over 200,000 angler trips shows an impressive 0.630 steelhead per hour catch rate (one steelhead for every 1.6 hours fished), a harvest rate of 0.150 steelhead per angler hour (about one of every five or 22% of steelhead caught), and a catch and release rate of 78%.

The survey also showed that steelheaders are in favor of adopting a $3.00 Lake Erie stamp permit but less so if the stamp costs more. Finally, the survey showed that steelhead anglers (80% of whom reside outside of Erie County) provide a notable contribution to the local Erie economy including $9.5 million (up from $2.5 million in 1982) on trip related expenses and support 219 jobs in the Erie area.

In December, 2005, Pennsylvania's Department of Conservation and Natural Resources (DCNR) held a public meeting in regard to its preferred alternative for the development of the newly created Erie Bluffs State Park located at the Elk Creek access area. In early January, 2006 the DCNR announced its plan for future management of Erie Bluffs State Park. DCNR spokesman Michael DiBerardinis said that, "the plan is to create a nature based park that will allow visitors to experience, understand and appreciate the property's steep bluffs, rocky-cobble shore, undeveloped creek corridors and plateau." It includes proposals for the development of trail networks, lake view observation points, a small nature inn, group camping and remote/primitive camping for backpackers and paddlers. Steelhead fisherman interested in viewing the final draft of the master plan for the new park (including park map) can find it at http://www.dcnr.state.pa.us/stateparks/parks/eriebluffs.aspx

In September, 2006 the Pennsylvania Fish & Boat Commission announced that four property acquisitions will provide 8,800 feet of stream frontage for public fishing access on Elk Creek (2 properties) and Walnut and Twenty Mile Creeks (each 1 property) in Erie County, Pennsylvania. Earlier in 2006 the PF&BC helped Fairview Township purchase 3.5 acres of land near the mouth of Trout Run off Avonia Road which will provide more than 400 feet of Lake Erie shoreline fishing access. In January 2007 the PF&BC announced 3 more property purchases on Walnut Creek 1.5 miles upstream of the mouth of the creek (between Dutch and Manchester Roads) for a total of 19 acres.

All of the property acquisitions utilize money from the Lake Erie Access Improvement Program, which is funded by the Lake Erie permit fishing program begun in 2005. Mckean, Girard, Mill Creek and Northeast Townships also provided funds and took title to the 2006 property acquisitions. The PF&BC estimates that Lake Erie permit sales to reach a total of $2.5 million dollars in the next 5 years.

The Ohio Department of Natural Resources is considering a similar land acquisition program (including public easements) based on funds obtained from a fishing permit sales program. The New York State Department of Environmental Conservation (NYSDEC) has had a program in place since 1935 called Public Fishing Rights (PFR). PFR lands are permanent public easements purchased by the NYSDEC from landowners giving anglers the right to fish a stream and walk along the bank (usually a 33 foot strip on one or both banks of the stream). This right is for the purpose of fishing only and may require adjacent landowner permission to access these lands. Information on PFR lands on some of NY's Lake Erie tributaries can be found at http://www.dec.ny.gov/outdoor/32426.html

PF&BC is also developing a process and program materials for acquiring future streamside fishing easements on Pennsylvania's Lake Erie tributaries as part of the Lake Erie Access Improvement Program. In exchange for monetary compensation, easements will allow landowners to maintain title to their properties while providing permanent public fishing corridors for anglers.

Other incentives to the landowners include state liability protection for allowing anglers to fish their land under the Pennsylvania Landowner Liability Act, help with stream bank and in-stream improvements and "prioritized" law enforcement (24/7) from the state's waterways conservation officers.

In early 2007 the Pennsylvania Steelhead Association was in the process of offering maps to the public showing public fishing easements that had been obtained through the Lake Erie Access Improvement Program.

On a negative note for Pennsylvania public fishing access, the Spring Ridge Club of Pennsylvania is leasing (for one year starting in the fall of 2006) a half mile section of lower Twenty Mile Creek from a property owner. This section was posted in the past few years as a result of bad behavior by steelhead fisherman.

The PF&BC using funds from the Lake Erie Access Improvement Fund did approach the Twenty Mile creek property owner for public access prior to their commitment to the Spring Ridge Club but was turned down. The Spring Ridge Club is also leasing a section on Elk Creek (upstream of I-90) and two sections on Conneaut Creek in Ohio (1.5 miles upstream of Creek Road Covered Bridge and a section directly downstream of Furnace Road).

In 2003 the Spring Ridge Club was sued by several agencies of the state of Pennsylvania and Fly Shop owner Alan Bright for preventing public access on the Little Juniata River, a world class trout fishery in central Pennsylvania, where the club operates a section of private water for its members. In January 2007 Pennsylvania Common Pleas Judge Stewart Kurtz ruled that the Spring Ridge Club could not block public access to the Little Juniata for boating and wading since the state has ownership of the river including the streambed. This decision was based on historical evidence of navigation and trade dating from the 1700's, and the fact that it was declared a public highway by the state in 1794, 1808 and 1822.

Commenting on the decision, Pennsylvania Department of Environmental Protection Secretary Kathleen A. McGinty said that, "the court has confirmed what we have maintained throughout this process: the historically navigable waters of the Commonwealth of Pennsylvania belong to the people of the Commonwealth, and no individual or corporation has the right to restrict the public's access to these waterways. This decision affirms the state's obligation to preserve and maintain these waters for the benefit of future generations."

The Pittsburgh Post Gazette on February 5, 2007, commented that "the Little Juniata case involved a favored few with money to join a club being allowed to fish while ordinary citizens were excluded because the property owner thought that controlling the banks meant he owned the river. Thus the judge's decision upholds an important principle. This isn't Europe, with an aristocratic class enjoying special privileges. This is America, where public access is important. Woody Guthrie got it right when he sang This is Your Land. Judge Kurtz sang the same tune, just with different words." The author whole heartedly concurs with this commentary. Hopefully the ruling in this case will form a precedent for future public fishing access cases particularly with respect to the Great Lakes steelhead tributaries.

The Spring Ridge Club plans on appealing the Pennsylvania court decision (the appeal deadline is July 13, 2007). If the appeal occurs, arguments on both sides could be heard as soon as December 2007 with a ruling likely in 2008.

As of January 1, 2006 the Pennsylvania Fish & Boat Commission is requiring all charter boat captains and fishing guides working within Pennsylvania to obtain a license permit. The cost of the permit is $100 for PA residents and $400 for non-residents and will require CPR and first aid certification, a boating safety education certificate and a U.S. Coast Guard Operator License if operating a boat, as well as minimum insurance coverage. The permit also requires a Pennsylvania fishing license and a minimum age of 16 years.

In 2006 plans were in the works by a team of agencies and groups, led by the Pennsylvania Lake Erie Watershed Association (PLEWA), to restore Four Mile Creek (east of the City of Erie) to a more natural flow by removing the dam near Station Road and a concrete capped obstruction on a waterfall on the Penn State Behrend campus. With the active involvement of PLEWA, these projects are now under design, and permits are being obtained, by the PF&BC. The anticipated completion date for these projects is the summer of 2007.

Another project under discussion would remove locomotive ballast on the General Electric property from Four Mile Creek's lower reaches. Grant applications have been submitted with the assistance of the Pennsylvania Sea Grant Program to finance the installation of fish ladders on the dam and waterfall located on the Lawrence Park Golf Club property north of Route 5. These unique fish ladders (a first for Pennsylvania) will be in similar in design to those used in the Pacific Northwest and will allow steelhead migration upstream while impeding lamprey movement through them. Installation is expected in 2008 if funding is secured.

These projects will allow for steelhead migration further upstream where public fishing access exists in public parks located in Lawrence Park Township and Wesleyville Borough and the "Wintergreen Gorge" area on the Penn State Behrend property. Future public access is a possibility on the General Electric property between routes 5 and route 20. The team also plans to correct stream bank erosion caused by insufficient storm water infrastructure on a section of Trout Run (a tributary of Four Mile Creek) on the Penn State Behrend campus.

Finally, Pennsylvania Sea Grants also assisted the Erie County Conservation District in obtaining funds to complete a stream bank restoration and channelization project on the West Branch of Cascade Creek in Frontier Park (located in the City of Erie) during the summer of 2006.

New York

The big news in the state of New York is the new catch-and-release, artificial only, all-tackle sections on the Lake Erie tributaries of 18 Mile Creek and Chautauqua Creek that came into effect on October 1, 2006. The artificial only requirement refers to both flies and lures. On Chautauqua Creek the area is 1.3 miles upstream from South Gale Street Bridge to the upper water works dam which is used by Westfield for water intake. On 18 Mile Creek (Erie County, New York) the area is in the 18 Mile Creek County Park for a total of 1.6 miles excluding the South Branch. Both these areas are located in relatively hard to access/remote areas. For more detailed information refer to the 2006-2008 New York State freshwater fishing regulation book (page 22) and the New York DEC website found at www.dec.state.ny.us

Two Lake Erie Tributary Creel Survey's were completed in 2003/2004 (Year 1) and 2004/2005 (Year 2) by Jim Markham, Chief Fisheries Biologist for the New York State Department of Environmental Conservation (NYSDEC), on NY's Lake Erie tributaries (see Appendix E). The Year 1 survey showed an identical steelhead catch rate (0.630 fish/hr) to Pennsylvania's 2003/2004 creel analysis but with 3 times fewer angler hours (193,190 versus 595,584) and a higher steelhead catch and release rate of 87%.

Because overall effort was so much more in Pennsylvania, total steelhead catch numbers were substantially higher on the PA tributaries (373,329) versus the NY tributaries (115,464). A comparison to the Salmon River in Pulaski, NY (a very popular Lake Ontario steelhead tributary) showed that the NY Lake Erie tributaries had a 11 times higher steelhead catch rate in 2003. The Year 2 survey showed a decline in catch rate to 0.57 fish/hour but an increase in steelhead catch and release rate to 93%.

Cooperative angler diary data collected since 1987 by the NYSDEC and the PF&BC (see Figure 6.2 in Appendix E) has shown that catch rates by steelhead anglers in Pennsylvania and New York have steadily increased. Over that period catch rates have averaged .54 steelhead/hour with the highest catch rates recorded during the 2003 season.

Angler opinion questions in both surveys in regards to fishery management revealed that steelheaders wanted to keep the creel limit at 3 steehead but normally keep only 0 or 1 fish. Based on this information the NYSDEC feels there is no need to reduce the creel limit to fewer than 3 steelhead since catch and release is predominately practiced. Anglers also indicated that wild steelhead were an important part of their fishing experience and they were in favor of some special regulation sections on the tributaries as well as the installation of a fish passage device at the dam in Springville on Cattaraugus Creek.

Of interest regarding the Seneca Nations of Indians (SNI) lands on the Cattaraugus Creek, a high percentage of anglers (42.3%) in the survey preferred a creel limit of zero or one, a large reduction from the current creel limit of 5 fish/day on Cattaraugus Creek Reservation waters. The survey also showed that a surprising majority of anglers (80.8%) fishing SNI waters on the Cattaraugus Creek Reservation also possess a NY license in addition to the SNI fishing permit required to fish on reservation land.

On October 1, 2006 the NYSDEC increased the minimum size for salmon, steelhead and lake trout from 9 to 12 inches in New York's Lake Erie waters and tributaries. The regulation change was primarily instituted to protect NY's Lake Erie lakeshore plantings of hatchery brown trout from angler harvesting prior to their movement from the lakeshore to the main lake. Since 2002 the NYSDEC has been stocking the Lake Erie lakeshore with domesticated browns from its Rome, NY hatchery. Returns have been excellent, not only along the lakeshore (particularly Barcelona Harbor) but also in tributaries such as Chautauqua Creek, Canadaway Creek and Cattaraugus Creek. NYSDEC biologist Jim Markham says that the larger stocking size of the brown trout (8 inches plus) has undoubtedly lead to higher survival and return rates of the browns.

Jim Markham has confirmed that the Army Corp of Engineers has started the process of determining the feasibility of either installing a fish passage system on the 40-foot high, 338-foot long dam on Cattaraugus Creek at Springville, NY, or removing the dam entirely. The concept for this project was initiated by the NYSDEC when it became fundable through Army Corp of Engineers dollars. If the project turns out to be feasible, the NYSDEC will also provide matching funds for the completion of the project. The Army Corp of Engineers plans to schedule a public participation meeting in the fall of 2007 concerning the dam project.

Allowing fish to pass through the Springville Dam opens up 70 miles of water to steelhead fishing on the Cattaraugus and would likely result in significant levels of natural reproduction of steelhead due to prime spawning, nursery and feeding habitat that exists in Cattaraugus Creek and its tributaries above the dam. At the present time there is a resident population of both rainbow and browns in the Cattaraugus above the dam with wild brookies in the most remote/upper areas. This upper water also has good public access (Public Fishing Rights land) with many areas already with NYSDEC special fishing regulations in place.

The NYSDEC would prefer not to remove the Springville Dam since it provides an excellent barrier to sea lampreys. If the dam is removed, the Great Lakes Fishery Commission is recommending to the Army Corp of Engineers that a permanent sea lamprey trap be installed to reduce reproduction of sea lampreys in Cattaraugus Creek and potentially reduce the introduction of lampricides. This would improve the cost effectiveness of the sea lamprey control program already in place. The NYSDEC is also aware of both the resident and wild populations of trout in this upper water and is reviewing Michigan studies that show the impacts of steelhead runs on trout populations.

The Army Corp of Engineers is also doing a feasibility study on constructing engineered rock riffles below two low level dams located on Chautauqua Creek above the village of Westfield, NY. Besides the Army Corp, this effort is being spearheaded by a team including the city of Westfield, New York Rivers United and the US Fish & Wildlife Service. The rock riffle design will raise the water levels below the dams to more easily allow steelhead to pass over the dams into the upper gorge. The rock riffles are expected to be completed by the fall of 2009 based on expected forthcoming funding for the design and construction costs.

According to Jim Markham the NYSDEC has been doing an experimental spring stocking of 15,000 Skamania strain steelhead (surplus fish obtained from the DEC's Salmon River Hatchery) into Cattaraugus Creek in New York since 2005. The future returns of these smolt plantings will be carefully monitored by the NYSDEC (some smolts were adipose and left ventral fin clipped) to determine return rates and sizes. The hope is that this potential run, which is expected to start moving into the river in late August and September, will help supplement existing steelhead runs on the "Cat".

Jim Markham of the NYSDEC continued stream electro-shock surveys on several NY Lake Erie tributaries in order to catalog potential young-of-year (YOY) wild steelhead production. In the fall of 2005 six streams, Half-Way Brook, Grannis Creek, Derby Brook, Coon Brook, Thatcher Brook, Nigh Brook were sampled. Juvenile steelhead were caught in all of the sampled streams with Derby Brook found to be one of the best streams surveyed so far. Grannis Creek and Coon Brook were also found to have moderate potential for the production of juvenile steelhead.

The fall NYSDEC survey in 2006 (see Table J.3 in Appendix E) included the North Branch of Clear Creek, Point Peter Brook, Doty Creek, Bournes Creek and Kelley Brook. Only the North Branch of Clear Creek was considered to have an average or above stream potential for natural reproduction.

As was learned in past stream surveys deep riffle areas with large rocks or woody debris appears to be essential habitat type for juvenile trout in marginal trout streams. Trout are generally absent in marginal streams without this habitat. However, in higher quality streams such as Derby Brook, most of the juvenile and yearling trout occupy the pools, with fewer numbers of juvenile trout in the riffles.

Since 2001, 30 streams have been surveyed for wild steelhead production. Previously sampled streams bring the total number of inventoried streams by the DEC to 44 (see Tables J.1 and J.2 in Appendix E). The majority of the streams sampled showed low potential for natural reproduction. Thirteen showed moderate to high potential for producing wild steelhead. Spooner Creek, Derby Brook, The North Branch of Clear Creek (all feeders to Cattaraugus Creek) and Little Chautauqua Creek have shown the highest potential for producing wild fish. Clear Creek, Connoisarauley Creek and Coon Brook were large enough in size, despite some limitations, to produce a significant number of juvenile steelhead. 20 Mile Creek, which was surveyed by NYSDEC Region 9 Inland fisheries personnel in the summer of 2006, also showed significant production of wild juvenile steelhead.

The goal of the survey is to develop a comprehensive map of steelhead spawning waters in New York's Lake Erie tributaries, develop estimates of overall wild steelhead reproduction and identify areas to target for stream improvement to increase wild trout reproduction. Jim Markham says that in the future the NYSDEC will continue sampling the top eight "producer" tributaries in the survey to gain a better estimate of overall wild steelhead production in them.

Ohio has also been surveying some of its steelhead tributaries by cataloging streams with steelhead natural reproduction into digital maps and GIS layers.

The recent Federal Great Lakes Restoration Act has approved a mass marking program for steelhead which will be managed by the Fish & Wildlife Service. The marking program will include adipose fin clippings and code wire tags (which are embedded in the nose of the steelhead and require harvesting of the fish to read the tag). The data collected will be used to better manage salmonid fisheries in the Great Lakes. Congressional funding for the program is hoped for 2008 with Great Lakes fishery department tracking to begin in 2010.

Finally, the NYSDEC has initiated proposals banning the sale of trout eggs, banning chumming and allowing a possession limit of 1 quart of trout eggs by fisherman. These proposals, which will be preceded by a public comment period in 2007, are expected to be on the books by October, 2008.

Michigan

According to Jeff Brouncheidel of the Michigan Department of Natural Resources, about half of the 2005 spring Little Manistee steelhead plantings in the Huron River (a Lake Erie tributary) were the last steelhead fin clipped (the right pectoral) by the MDNR in that river system. Initially done to distinguish hatchery fish from wild fish, fin clipping is no longer practiced by most fishery agencies in the Lake Erie region. This last group of fin clipped steelhead (approximately 30,000 fish) by the MDNR should begin arriving in the Huron River in the fall of 2007.

The MDNR is scheduled to do a creel survey in the spring of 2007 at the fish ladder placed at the Flat Rock Dam on the Huron River. Similar surveys were done in 1999 and 2000 to evaluate the size of steelhead run as well as the fish ladder's success in passing steelhead above the dam where good fishing opportunities exist. See Appendix E for 2000 survey data.

Three fishing boardwalks have been installed 8 miles above the Flat Rock Dam in 2005. The boardwalks are located in the Lower Huron Metro Park and are each approximately 100 feet long.

Ontario

The Ontario Ministry of Natural Resources (OMNR) fishing regulations are undergoing significant changes to reflect the Ministry's new "ecological framework for fisheries management in Ontario." Ontario's fisheries will be managed on a zone basis rather than on an individual body of water basis. This approach will reduce the number of fishing divisions from 37 zones to 20 zones. The Ontario recreational fishing regulation summary book (due in 2007) will also be redesigned with better maps to make the new rules easy to understand.

Ontario has continued to do minimal stocking of steelhead since 2002 including Lake Erie shore stockings to promote a lakeshore steelhead fishery and stocking of Big Creek and Mill Creek to augment natural steelhead reproduction. The OMNR is still committed to stock far fewer steelhead than other Lake Erie fishery agencies and instead emphasizes protection and rehabilitation of steelhead habitat for steelhead natural reproduction.

Spring run hen steelhead caught on Elk Creek, PA.

Lake Erie Steelhead

Chapter 1

The substantial steelhead runs on the United States side of the Lake Erie watershed are primarily the result of the steelhead stocking programs of the Ohio Division of Wildlife, the Pennsylvania Fish and Boat Commission (including Pennsylvania's 3-C-U Trout Association), the New York State Department of Environmental Conservation and the Michigan Department of Natural Resources. On the Canadian side of the lake, relatively little stocking is done by the Ontario Ministry of Natural Resources due to a steelhead fishery that boasts 90% steelhead natural reproduction.

The lion's share of the stocking for the 2005 season was done by the Pennsylvania Fish & Boat Commission and the 3-C-U Trout Association which stocked 1,183,246 steelhead yearlings (smolts) into Pennsylvania's tributaries, averaging about 1 million over the last ten years. One million annual steelhead plantings per year may seem excessive, but according to Roger Kenyon, fisheries biologist for the Pennsylvania F&BC, this amount is necessary to compensate for walleye predation and other unpredictable factors which can result in juvenile steelhead mortality as high as 90%.

The New York Department of Environmental Conservation, the Ohio Department of Wildlife, the Michigan Department of Natural Resources and the Ontario Ministry of Natural Resources followed with 275,000, 402,827, 60,900 and 55,000 smolts stocked respectively in 2005.

For years steelhead have been classified as a sub-species of rainbow trout (Salmo gairdneri) in the genus Salmo along with Atlantic Salmon, brown trout and numerous western trout species. In 1989 the American Fisheries Society reclassified steelhead under the Pacific salmonid genus Oncorhynchus and species mykiss.

This was based on osteology and biochemistry data, which showed that steelhead are more closely related to Pacific salmon, even though they don't die

Returning fall steelhead in Trout Run, PA nursery waters.

after spawning and have the potential to be repeat spawners (polyanadromous). Many biologists feel that in the future steelhead will be further grouped as "Pacific trout" because of their polyanadromous nature.

The name steelhead seems to have two possible derivations. The most reasonable is that the name describes the characteristic blued-steel color exhibited on the backs and heads of these migratory fish. A more colorful explanation is credited to the Pacific Northwest commercial fisherman. They found it was much easier to dispatch a salmon over the head with a club versus a steelhead, whose "steel head" seemed to repel even the hardest blows.

Between 1885 and 1900, steelhead were originally transplanted from the Pacific Northwest and other Great Lakes into various Lake Erie tributary streams of Ohio, Pennsylvania, New York and Michigan. Modern Pennsylvania steelhead stocks were initially obtained from Washington State in 1961 and released in the form of fingerlings by the Pennsylvania Fish & Boat Commission into tributaries that already had some lake-run domesticated rainbows.

During the 1990's Pennsylvania also stocked Skamania steelhead received from the state of Indiana (Lake Michigan). These steelhead are a summer run strain of steelhead that begin their spawning run much earlier than Washington strain fish.

Since then, Pennsylvania uses returning Lake Erie steelhead (from the nursery waters of Trout Run and Godfrey Run) exclusively for its steelhead egg source, thereby eliminating the disease problems that have become common in West Coast steelhead.

Today's Pennsylvania steelhead, like most Great Lakes steelhead, are not a pure strain steelhead. The majority of these fish are a result of interbreeding, both intentional and unintentional, by both West Coast and Great Lakes fish hatcheries. They can best be described as a unique, naturalized strain of steelhead that has adapted very well to the ecosystem of Lake Erie. In fact, Pennsylvania steelheaders affectionately call the Pennsylvania strain of steelhead the steelhead "mutt" due to its diversified gene pool.

The New York DEC maintains its Lake Erie steelhead program through eggs obtained from returning Lake Ontario steelhead in the Salmon River, Pulaski, New York. These steelhead are originally from Washington State and are of the Chambers Creek strain.

The Ohio DOW presently stocks in its steelhead tributaries wild Little Manistee strain steelhead smots, which originally came from the McCloud River, California. They are obtained by the ODW from the Little Manistee River in Michigan (via the Michigan DNR) in the form of fertilized eggs and then raised to smolt maturity prior to stocking in the spring.

The ODW has found them superior in growth and return rates to their hatchery raised London-strain, which is actually a domesticated strain of rainbow trout. A Little Manistee-strain steelhead, after two summers in Lake Erie, averages 25 inches in length and 5-6 pounds in weight. The return rate for these fish is nearly 3 to 1 higher than for the London-strain, which is around 8%.

Spring steelhead smolt stocking by the PA Fish and Boat Commission at Legion Park on Elk Creek, PA.

London-strain fish, named after Ohio's London state fish hatchery, were originally developed to survive in warmer waters than those inhabited by a typical rainbow trout. London-strain fish plantings were discontinued temporarily in 1996 by the ODW.

In 1997 the ODW purchased a private fish hatchery at Castalia, Ohio. The ODW began operating this facility in 1999 to help supplement its Little Manistee program by at least 200,000 more steelhead annually. The source of these additional steelhead will be surplus eggs received from Pennsylvania as well as ODW breeder stocks of London strain fish, which will once again be stocked in Ohio's tributaries.

A surprising number of Pennsylvania's Washington strain steelhead start running up the tributaries in early September. This run usually peaks in November, culminating with a late winter or early spring spawn time. Such an early run could be a result of summer run genetic influence by past Skamania steelhead plantings (and interbreeding) by the Pennsylvania Fish and Boat Commission and the New York State DEC.

The Pennsylvania Fish and Boat Commission believes that by varying the time steelhead eggs are collected and fertilized for stocking purposes, they can help spread out a steelhead run over the course of the season. The Pennsylvania Fish and Boat Commission begins collecting and fertilizing eggs in December, and continues through March, resulting in juvenile steelhead of varying maturities. All these fish will be raised to yearling size and stocked the following spring.

Jason Jester with average size Pennsylvania steelhead on Elk Creek, PA.

Early April Little Manistee steelhead caught on Conneaut Creek, OH.

The Pennsylvania Fish & Boat Commission has determined that the ideal smolt size to stock in the tributaries is in the 6-8 inch range. This size smolt can more readily avoid predators like birds and walleyes and also withstand the stress of being caught by anglers in the tributaries. At the same time, planting smolts of this size range does not compromise the imprinting stage of the smolt since they have not yet chemically imprinted to any particular watershed.

Ohio's London-strain trout and Little Manistee-strain steelhead exhibit very different run and spawn times. London fish start running in October and spawn from November through January. A few will stay in the streams through spring. The Little Manistee steelhead is more of a spring run fish, starting its run in late October, with the majority of fish running and spawning from January through May. Many more Manistees than London-strain fish remain in the streams in the spring.

An angler survey conducted in April 1993-1994 by Chuck Murray and Rickalon Hoopes of the Pennsylvania Fish & Boat Commission, Lake Erie Research Unit, (see Appendix E) showed that most Pennsylvania steelhead return as three year olds (one year in the hatchery, two years in the lake) and range from 22 to 25 inches in length with a mean weight of 4.9 pounds. The occasional bigger fish range from 8 to 12 pounds although the Pennsylvania State record is a whopping 20 lbs., 3 oz.

Graduate student Bradley Thompson of Penn State University, in cooperation with the Pennsylvania Fish & Boat Commission and the Pennsylvania Steelhead

Steelheader's Tip

> Find likely steelhead lies by learning how water flow, clarity and temperature, as well as light levels, effect steelhead location in a tributary.

Association, began a two year study in 1997 on the Pennsylvania tributaries of Crooked Creek, Godfrey Run and Trout Run (see summary Table 12 in Appendix E). The purpose of the study was to describe the population structure of steelhead that spawn in these tributaries in terms of wild versus hatchery fish as well as age and sex ratios.

The study showed that the majority of male steelhead returned as stream age 2 year olds or "jacks" with the bulk of females returning as stream age 3 year olds. The percentage of return rates (as well as size) of these stream age 2 year old males was higher than any other Great Lakes study stream.

The study also showed that a larger percentage of females returned as stream age 3 and 4 year olds (including virgin and repeat spawners) when compared to males. In terms of repeat spawning, the study showed there was a larger percentage of repeat spawning females versus males (including some third and fourth time spawners) in Crooked Creek.

The faster return rates and growth rates of Lake Erie steelhead is due to the tremendous productivity possible in the Lake Erie fishery. Jeff Brouncheidel, a Biologist for the Michigan Department of Natural Resources, owes this productivity to the warmer waters of Lake Erie versus other Great Lakes like Michigan, Superior and Huron which are much colder. Studies based on scale samples and fin clippings by the Michigan Department of Natural Resources on Michigan's Huron River (a tributary to Lake Erie) have shown that most Little Manistee plantings in Lake Erie return as three year old, sexually mature fish while Little Manistee steelhead in the colder Lake Michigan typically return as four year olds to spawn.

The 3-C-U Trout Association

In 1966 Norm Ely, a local Pennsylvania waterways patrolman, felt that the modest runs of lake-run "rainbows" (as the locals called them) in several Erie County tributary streams could be increased by raising juvenile fish in raceway facilities and then releasing them as yearlings. Several sportsman's organizations became interested in this idea and formed a cooperative nursery, with the help of the Pennsylvania Fish & Boat Commission, that came to be know as the 3-C-U Trout Association.

The 3-C-U derived its name from the first letter of the second word of the names of three of the original supporting organizations. These organizations included the Gem City Outdoorsmen, the Erie County Sportsmen, the Wesleyville Conservation Club and Trout Unlimited (Northwest Chapter). Later the Erie Downriggers, SONS of Lake Erie and Pennsylvania Steelhead Association added their support.

In July 1966, a group of individuals from the fledgling 3-C-U, including Norm Ely, Bob Hetz, Jimmy Dallas and Jerry Honard seined 600 wild steelhead fry out Bear Run and Thomas Run, which are tributaries of Walnut Creek in Pennsylvania. These wild juveniles were descendents of stockings of domesticated rainbows and steelhead by the Pennsylvania Fish & Boat Commission in previous years.

To facilitate the maturation of these steelhead fry to yearling or smolt status, they were raised in a newly built, wooden raceway on a spring fed tributary of Trout Run. In the following spring of 1967, 400 of these steelhead were released into Trout Run as smolts, with 50 kept for future brood stock. In subsequent years eggs were collected from returning, wild, adult steelhead for hatchery rearing and future stockings in numerous Pennsylvania tributary streams of Lake Erie.

This program, along with the efforts of the Pennsylvania Fish & Boat Commission, formed the foundation of the modern Pennsylvania steelhead fishery program.

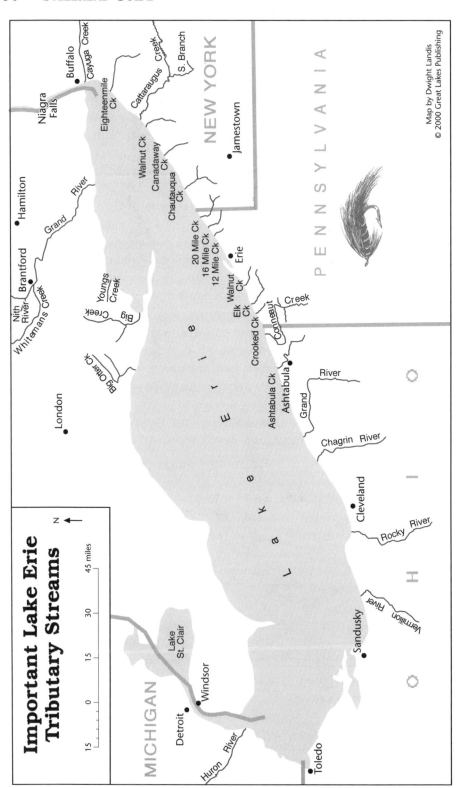

Important Lake Erie Tributary Streams

Map by Dwight Landis
© 2000 Great Lakes Publishing

The Tributaries

Chapter 2

The area on the southern shore of Lake Erie extending roughly just west of Cleveland to Buffalo has been dubbed "steelhead alley" for good reason. It contains some of the most productive steelhead tributary streams and rivers in the Great Lakes region.

Draining a watershed created by glaciers during the last ice age, most Lake Erie tributaries are relatively shallow and small in size by Pacific Northwest standards. They normally flow low and clear, and after receiving precipitation, most have a very fast run-off rate.

They can be characterized as having high gradient, predominately flash-flood type shale streambeds, with a lesser mix of rock, gravel, sand and mud areas. Stream flows during non run-off periods consist mostly of shallow runs, pools, riffles and pocket water. Classic steelhead pools of good depth and length are fairly uncommon with most existing pools averaging 2 to 5 feet in depth, depending on the water flow.

Classifying the Lake Erie tributary streams based on a number of factors is very helpful in learning their differences as well as their specific characteristics. Tables 1, 3, and 5 (at the end of this chapter) classify the Ohio, Pennsylvania and New York tributary streams according to watershed size and type, run-off rate, steelhead source, surrounding terrain and important feeder streams. Table 6a (also at the end of this chapter) profiles some of the more unique characteristics of various Lake Erie tributary streams*.

Probably the most important factor for the fly fisherman to understand is the tributary run-off rate. It is best defined as the time it takes a tributary, after reaching peak run-off from rain or melting snow, to reach fishable flows and water

See Chapter 10 for information on the Ontario and Michigan tributary streams of Lake Erie.

Dave Brown battling steelie on Elk Creek, PA near Brandy Run.

clarity (prime fishing conditions). Prime fishing conditions will be discussed in more detail in Chapter 3. Knowing when a particular tributary runs off to prime fishing conditions is crucial to consistently catching Lake Erie steelhead, especially on the southern shore.

Run-off rates vary greatly, depending on the size and characteristics of each tributary watershed. For instance, tributaries like the Grand River in Ohio and the Cattaraugus Creek in New York are very large rivers, with total watersheds of 50 and 60 miles respectively, although dams on both rivers hinder complete upstream migration. Due to their large drainage and substantial agricultural run-off, these rivers tend to drop to fishable levels and clarity much slower than other Lake Erie tributaries after rain or snow melt. It's not unusual for these rivers to take one to three weeks to become fishable after a run-off episode.

It is a good strategy to fish feeder streams to these large rivers during this period because the feeder streams clear quickly and can hold good runs of steelhead. Clear Creek on the Cattaraugus Creek and Mill Creek on the Grand River OH, are examples of this.

Medium size tributaries, such as Walnut Creek in Pennsylvania and Silver and Walnut Creeks in New York, have much shorter watersheds and usually run-off in 12 to 24 hours, depending on the amount of rain or snow melt. Smaller tributaries, like Four-Mile and Seven-Mile Creeks in northeastern Pennsylvania and Cahoon Creek in Ohio are usually fishable in 8 to 12 hours after peak run-off. Table 6b (at the end of this chapter) gives a range of ideal flow conditions for various tributary streams on the United States side of Lake Erie. For Ontario tributaries refer to Table 12 in the Ontario section of Chapter 10.

Surrounding terrain and access points vary for the Lake Erie tributaries. Some terrain is very remote like the wooded environs of Twenty-Mile Creek in Pennsylvania. Other tributaries run mostly through suburban areas such as Buffalo and Cayuga Creeks near Buffalo, New York. Elk Creek in Pennsylvania flows through a mix of remote river gorges, farmland, small towns and suburban locations.

Access to most tributaries can be difficult at times, and it takes an adventurous soul to learn where to fish them. Ohio has the best public access, with many city, metro and county parks situated along Ohio's tributaries. When access is through private land, as it frequently is, it is very important to respect landowner rights. Getting permission from the landowner prior to entering these private lands is necessary to ensure future access to the tributary streams.

Tables 2, 4 and 6 and the corresponding Ohio, Pennsylvania, and New York tributary maps (at the end of this chapter) identify the major Lake Erie tributaries and detail some of their important access points as well. Township and county maps available from the Ohio, Pennsylvania and New York Departments of Transportation and the DeLorme series of State Atlas and Gazetteers are very useful for finding other potential access points. The DeLorme maps also show topographical features. (See Appendix C for additional map sources).

Shadowy steelheaders at Rt. 5 tunnel on Twelve-Mile Creek, PA.

Terry Palmer with spring steelhead on Raccoon Creek, PA.

The original source of steelhead for each specific Lake Erie steelhead tributary is also very important to the fly fisherman. Some streams are seasonally stocked very heavily with steelhead smolts, and therefore, get excellent runs of steelhead. Examples include Elk Creek in Pennsylvania, Conneaut Creek in Ohio and the Cattaraugus Creek in New York. The steelhead smolt stocking lists in Appendix E (Table 6.1) show these popular tributaries, which over the years have been consistently stocked with smolt by the fishery departments of Lake Erie.

Other streams get smaller runs of steelhead but are not stocked with smolt. These are "stray" fish streams and examples include Arcola Creek, Huron River, Cuyahoga River and the Ashtabula River in Ohio and Big Sister Creek and Cazenovia Creek in New York. Feeder streams to the big tributary rivers mentioned earlier also can get good runs of steelhead.

Steelheader's Tip

When fishing large leeches or wooly buggers in stained water, slide a couple of plastic beads onto the tippet in front of the fly for added vibration.

Wild Steelhead of Lake Erie

Steelhead natural reproduction has been documented in numerous Lake Erie tributaries as illustrated in Figure 6.3 in Appendix E. Due to a combination of low base flows and elevated summer water temperatures wild steelhead production is limited in areas such as Pennsylvania and Ohio.

The Ohio Department of Wildlife has observed juvenile steelhead in four Ohio tributaries. Kevin Kayle of the ODW estimates that 100 wild steelhead per tributary run every season (although this is not based on any documented study). Starting in the summer of 1999 the ODW began assessments for juvenile steelhead in numerous Ohio tributaries (after a 5-year hiatus).

In 1994, the Pennsylvania Fish & Boat Commission on a number of Pennsylvania tributaries documented evidence of some natural steelhead reproduction by finding steelhead of sub-stocking length (less than 4.9 inches). These tributaries included Raccoon Creek, Crooked Creek, Elk Creek, Godfrey Run, Trout Run, Walnut Creek, Seven-Mile Creek, Eight-Mile Creek and Twelve-Mile Creek.

Brad Thompson's Population Biology study of steelhead in Pennsylvania's Crooked Creek, Godfrey Run and Trout Run (see Table 12 in Appendix E)

"Chutes" section on Walnut Creek, PA.

Daniels Park Dam on the Chagrin River, OH.
This dam collapsed in the spring of 2005. (Jerry Darkes photo)

documented the relative contribution of wild steelhead to seasonal spawning runs (fall and spring) averaged from 0 to 14%. The highest estimate was reported on Trout Run in the fall of 1997 with an estimate of 24 % wild steelhead present. The study pointed out that these estimates were lower than estimates reported for other Great Lakes tributaries due to the lack of high quality spawning and rearing habitat in the study streams.

In 1997 and 1998 the Ontario Ministry of Natural Resources accessed 33 Ontario tributary streams for juvenile steelhead density estimates. Twenty of those streams were found to contain naturally reproduced steelhead (see Table 6.3 in Appendix E). The Ontario MNR has estimated that 90% of returning steelhead in their tributaries are wild. This extraordinary percentage is not only a result of the high water quality and ideal spawning and rearing habitat in the Ontario streams, but also a direct result of their steelhead management policies over the years which has put an emphasis on naturally reproducing fish populations supported by healthy habitat over fish stocking (see Chapter 10).

A very promising example of natural steelhead reproduction in the Lake Erie watershed is Spooner Creek, a feeder stream of the Cattaraugus Creek in New York. The New York Department of Environmental Conservation completed sampling for wild juvenile steelhead in this stream in July 1995. Steelhead density estimates were approximately 1,360 fingerlings per acre. This figure compares extremely well with other Great Lakes wild steelhead streams such as the Little Manistee River in Michigan, which produced yields of 667 to 1,076 fingerling steelhead per acre for the period 1981 through 1984.

The New York DEC sampled more Cattaraugus Creek feeder streams in 1996 through 1998 with data showing additional steelhead natural reproduction. A study completed in 1999 by graduate student Mike Goehle of Buffalo State University found that 19-21% of stream running steelhead in the Cattaraugus Creek were wild fish (based on scale formation examination).

Steelheader's Tip

Avoid crowds by locating steelhead in the upper reaches of a tributary, especially in late winter and early spring.

Author hooked-up with steelhead below Creek Rd. covered bridge on Conneaut Creek, OH.

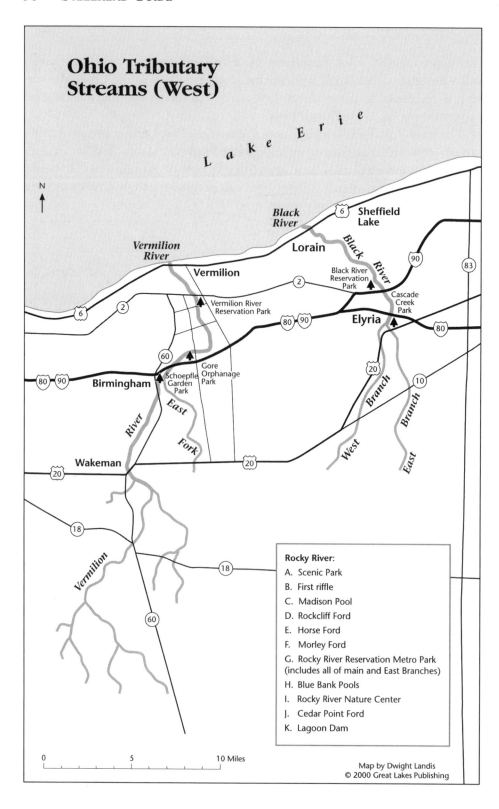

Ohio Tributary Streams (West)

N

Lake Erie

Black River
Sheffield Lake
6

Vermilion River

Lorain

Black River

Vermilion

90

83

2

Black River Reservation Park

Cascade Creek Park

Vermilion River Reservation Park

80 90

Elyria

80

6

2

60

80

20

10

80 90 Birmingham

Schoepfle Garden Park
Gore Orphanage Park

East Fork

West Branch

East Branch

River

Wakeman

20

20

18

18

Vermilion

60

Rocky River:
A. Scenic Park
B. First riffle
C. Madison Pool
D. Rockcliff Ford
E. Horse Ford
F. Morley Ford
G. Rocky River Reservation Metro Park (includes all of main and East Branches)
H. Blue Bank Pools
I. Rocky River Nature Center
J. Cedar Point Ford
K. Lagoon Dam

0   5   10 Miles

Map by Dwight Landis
© 2000 Great Lakes Publishing

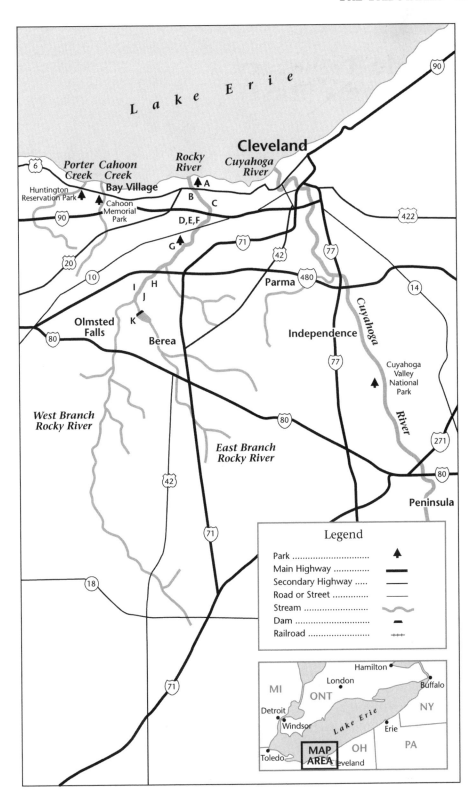

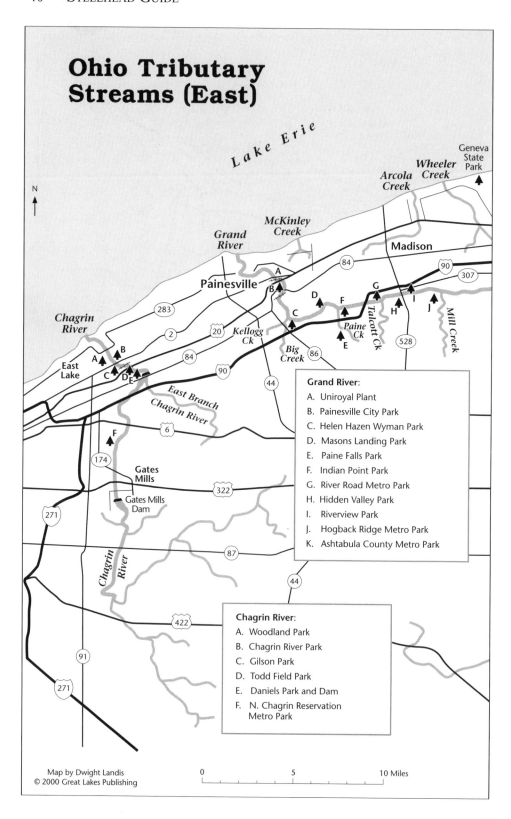

Ohio Tributary Streams (East)

Lake Erie

N

Geneva State Park

Arcola Creek

Wheeler Creek

McKinley Creek

Grand River

Madison

84

90

307

Painesville

Chagrin River

283

2

20

Kellogg Ck

East Lake

84

90

44

Big Creek

86

A
B
C
D
E
F

D

C

F

Paine Ck

E

G

Talcott Ck

H

I

J

528

Mill Creek

East Branch Chagrin River

6

F

174

Gates Mills

Gates Mills Dam

322

271

Chagrin River

87

44

422

91

271

Grand River:

A. Uniroyal Plant
B. Painesville City Park
C. Helen Hazen Wyman Park
D. Masons Landing Park
E. Paine Falls Park
F. Indian Point Park
G. River Road Metro Park
H. Hidden Valley Park
I. Riverview Park
J. Hogback Ridge Metro Park
K. Ashtabula County Metro Park

Chagrin River:

A. Woodland Park
B. Chagrin River Park
C. Gilson Park
D. Todd Field Park
E. Daniels Park and Dam
F. N. Chagrin Reservation Metro Park

Map by Dwight Landis
© 2000 Great Lakes Publishing

0   5   10 Miles

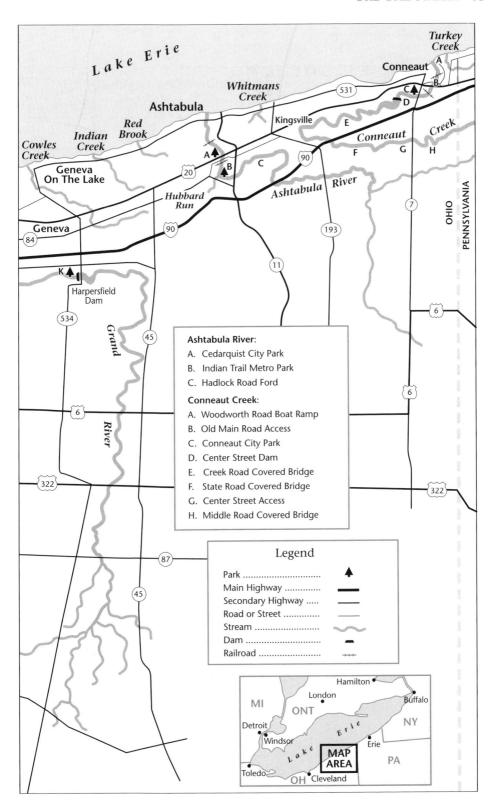

THE TRIBUTARIES 41

Turkey Creek

Conneaut

Lake Erie

Whitmans Creek

Ashtabula

531

Kingsville

E

Conneaut Creek

Red Brook

Indian Creek

Cowles Creek

Geneva On The Lake

A
B
C

F G H

90

20

90

Hubbard Run

Ashtabula River

OHIO

PENNSYLVANIA

Geneva

84

7

193

11

K

Harpersfield Dam

534

45

Grand River

6

6

322

322

Ashtabula River:
A. Cedarquist City Park
B. Indian Trail Metro Park
C. Hadlock Road Ford

Conneaut Creek:
A. Woodworth Road Boat Ramp
B. Old Main Road Access
C. Conneaut City Park
D. Center Street Dam
E. Creek Road Covered Bridge
F. State Road Covered Bridge
G. Center Street Access
H. Middle Road Covered Bridge

87

45

Legend

Park .... 🔺
Main Highway ....
Secondary Highway .....
Road or Street ....
Stream ....
Dam ....
Railroad ....

Hamilton
London
MI   ONT
Detroit
Windsor
Buffalo
NY
Erie
Lake Erie
MAP AREA
PA
Toledo   Cleveland
OH

Table 1
Ohio Tributary Information

Tributary	Watershed Size and Type*	Run-off Rate**	Steelhead Source	Surrounding Terrian	Important Feeder Streams
Vermillion River	Large, shale bottom	3-5 days	Stocked	Rural, farmland	
Rocky River	Large, shale bottom	2-3 days	Stocked	Wooded	East and West Branch
Chagrin River	Large, shale bottom	3-4 days	Stocked	Urban, wooded	East Branch
Grand River	Large, shale bottom	1 week or more	Stocked	Urban, wooded remote	Kellog, Big, Paine, Talcott and Mill Creeks
McKinley Creek	Small, shale bottom	Less than 1 day	Stray	Wooded	
Arcola Creek	Small, shale bottom	1 day	Stray	Wooded	
Wheeler Creek	Small, shale and mud bottom	1 day	Stray	Wooded	
Cowles Creek	Small, shale and mud bottom	1 day	Stray	Wooded	
Indian Creek	Small, shale and mud bottom	Less than 1 day	Stray	Wooded	
Red Brook	Small, shale bottom	Less than 1 day	Stray	Wooded	
Astabula River	Medium, shale bottom	2-3 days	Stray	Urban, wooded rural	Hubbard Run
Wittman's Creek	Small, mud bottom	Less than 1 day	Stray	Wooded	
Conneaut Creek	Large, shale bottom	3-4 days	Stocked, wild	Urban, rural, remote	
Turkey Creek	Small, shale bottom	1-2 days	Stray	Wooded	
Black River	Large, shale bottom	4-6 days	Stray	Wooded	French Creek, East & West Branches, Cascade Creek
Porter Creek	Small, shale bottom	1-2 days	Stray	Wooded	
Cahoon Creek	Small, shale bottom	Less than 1 day	Stray	Wooded	
Cuyhoga River	Large, shale bottom	1 week or more	Stray	Urban, rural	Tinker's Mill

*See Chapter 2 and 3 for discussion of run-off rates, prime conditions and watershed size.
**Time to reach prime fishing conditions after average run-off episode from rain or snow-melt

Table 2
Ohio Tributary Access Points

Tributary	Major Access Points*
Vermillion River	**Vermillion River Reservation Metro Park** (which contains **Mill Hollow and Bacon Woods Metro Parks**) is accessed via Rt. 2, North Ridge Road and Vermillion Road, **Gore Orphanage Metro Park** is accessed via Sperry and Gore Orphanage Roads, **Schoepfle Garden Metro Park** is accessed via Market Street in Birmingham, OH.
Rocky River	**Rocky River Reservation Metro Park** (including Morley, Horse, Rockcliff and Cedar Point River Fords. Also, 1st riffle, Madison Pool and Blue Bank Pool), Valley Parkway, Detroit Rd., Loraine Rd. Brookpark Rd., Rocky River Nature Center, Cedar Point Rd. EAST BRANCH: **Rocky River Reservation Metro Park,** Ruple Rd., Spafford Rd., Valley Parkway, Lagoon Dam, Berea Water Fall. WEST BRANCH: Lewis Rd., Bagley Rd.
Chagrin River	**Woodland City Park, Chagrin River Park, Gilson Park, Todd Field Park, Daniel's Park** & Dam, Pleasant Valley Rd, **Northern Chagrin Reservation Metro Park,** Rt. 174, Gates Mills Dam. EAST BRANCH: **Daniels Park.**
Grand River	Rt. 535 (Uniroyal Plant), **Painesville City Park,** Rt. 84, **Helen Hazen Wyman Metro Park** (also Kellog & Big Creeks), **Mason's Landing Metro Park, Indian Point Metro Park** (also Paine Creek), Blair Rd., **River Road Metro Park, Hidden Valley Metro Park** (also Talcott Creek), **Riverview Metro Park, Hogback Ridge Metro Park** (also Mill Creek), **Brandt Rd, Ashtabula County Metro Park,** Harpersfield Rd., Harpersfield Dam.
McKinley Creek	Lake Rd to lake.
Arcola Creek	Vrooman Rd. to lake (**Arcola Creek Metro Park),** Cunningham Rd, Rt., 20.
Wheeler Creek	Lake Rd. to lake (**Geneva State Park),** Maple Ave.
Cowles Creek	Rt. 534 to lake (**Geneva State Park),** New London Rd.
Indian Creek	Rt. 531 to lake.
Red Brook	Small section south of Rt. 531 (remainder posted).
Ashtabula River	**Cedarquist City Park,** Tannery Hill Rd, **Indian Trail Park** (also Hubbard Run), State Road, Hadlock Rd. river ford.
Wittman's Creek	Rt. 531 to lake.
Conneaut Creek	Woodworth Rd. boat ramp, "Arches" area, Old Main Rd. access, Rt. 7, **Conneaut City Park,** Center Street Dam, Keefus Rd., Creek Road Covered Bridge, Kingsbury Rd., State Rd, Horton Rd., Wetmore Rd, Center St. access, Rt. 7 (crosses twice), Middle Rd., Furnance Rd.
Turkey Creek	Old Lake Rd. to lake, Childs State Line Rd.
Black River	Black River Reserv. Metro Park (contains **Days Dam, Burr Oak and High Meadows Metro Parks**) is accessed via 31st St., East River Rd. and Ford Rd. French Creek is accessed via **French Creek Reserv.** West & East Branches, Cascade Creek are accessed via **Cascade Creek Park** in Elyria, OH.
Porter Creek	**Huntington Reservation Metro Park** is accessed via Rt. 6 and Porter Creek Dr. in Bay Village, OH.
Cahoon Creek	**Cahoon Memorial Park** is accessed via Rt. 6 and Cahoon Rd. in Bay Village, OH.
Cuyahoga River	**Cuyahoga Valley National Park** (which has access at **Rockside Rail Station, Canal Visitor Center,** Tinkers Creek Rd., **Alexander's Mill, Station Rd. Bridge,** Clover Leaf Parkway) is accessed via Canal Rd. and Riverview Rd. between Independence and Peninsula, Oh.

*Access points listed for each tributary start near the lakeshore and progress inland. Also access tributary waters adjacent to I-90 and railroad trestles *(Conrail, Norfolk & Western)* on some tributaries where possible and legal. On private land, fisherman should secure the landowner's permission before accessing tributaries.

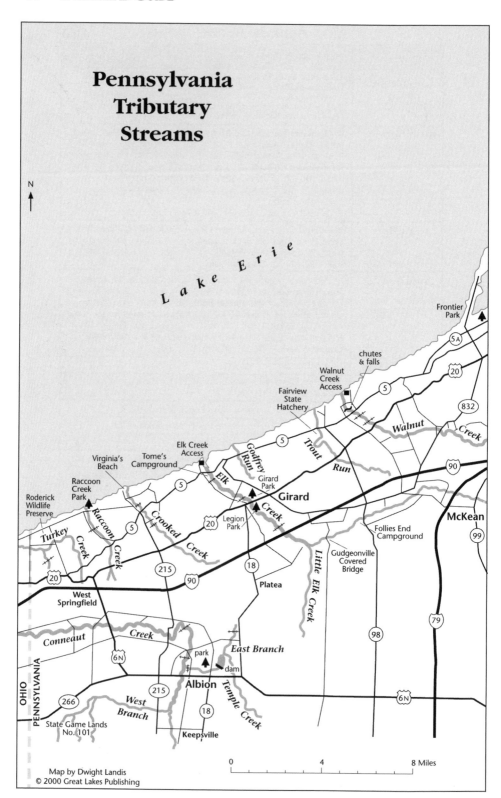

Pennsylvania Tributary Streams

N

Lake Erie

Frontier Park

5A

chutes & falls

Walnut Creek Access

20

Fairview State Hatchery

5

832

Walnut   *Creek*

Elk Creek Access

Godfrey Run

5

Trout   *Run*

90

Virginia's Beach

Tome's Campground

Girard Park

Raccoon Creek Park

Roderick Wildlife Preserve

Elk

5

Girard

McKean

Raccoon   *Creek*

20

Legion Park

Creek

Follies End Campground

99

Turkey   *Creek*

5

Crooked   *Creek*

20

Gudgeonville Covered Bridge

215

90

18

Little Elk Creek

West Springfield

20

Platea

98

79

6N

Conneaut   *Creek*

park

East Branch

OHIO

PENNSYLVANIA

215

Albion

dam

6N

266

West Branch

18

Temple Creek

State Game Lands No. 101

Keepsville

0   4   8 Miles

Map by Dwight Landis
© 2000 Great Lakes Publishing

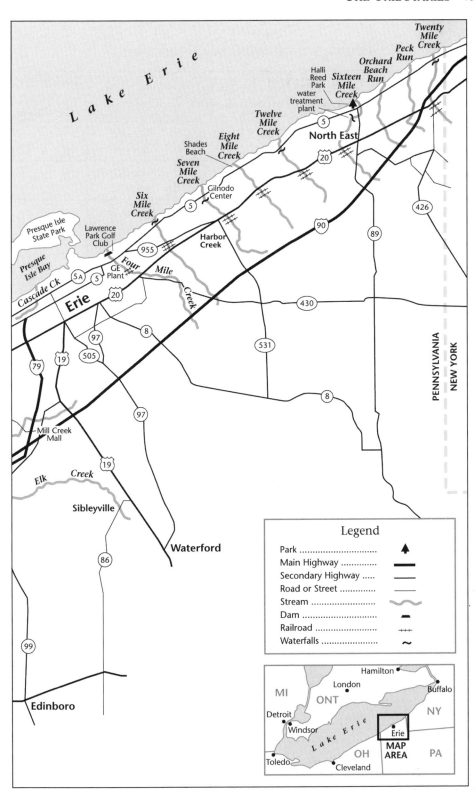

Table 3
Pennsylvania Tributary Information

Tributary	Watershed Size and Type*	Run-off Rate**	Steelhead Source	Surrounding Terrian	Important Feeder Streams
Turkey Creek	Small, brushy, mud bottom	1-2 days	Stray	Wooded, remote	
Raccoon Creek	Small, brushy, mud bottom	1-2 days	Stocked, wild	Wooded, remote	
Crooked Creek	Medium, brushy, mud bottom	2-3 days	Stocked, wild	Wooded, remote	
Conneaut Creek	Large, mud &, shale bottom	3-4 days	Stocked, wild	Wooded, remote, farmland	East Branch, West Branch
Elk Creek	Large, shale bottom	1-2 days	Stocked, wild	Wooded, remote, farmland	Little Elk Creek
Godfrey Run	Nursery waters				
Trout Run	Nursery waters				
Walnut Creek	Medium, shale bottom	1 day	Stocked, wild	Wooded, remote	
Cascade Creek	Small, mud & shale bottom	Less than 1 day	Stray	Urban	
4-Mile Creek	Small, shale bottom	Less than 1 day	Stocked	Rural	
7-Mile Creek	Small, shale bottom	Less than 1 day	Stocked, wild	Rural	
8-Mile Creek	Small, shale bottom	Less than 1 day	Stray, wild	Rural	
12-Mile Creek	Small, shale bottom	Less than 1 day	Stocked	Rural	
16-Mile Creek	Small, shale bottom	Less than 1 day	Stocked	Rural	
Orchard Beach Run	Nursery waters				
Peck Run	Small, brushy, shale bottom	Less than 1 day	Stocked	Rural	
20-Mile Creek	Medium, shale bottom	1-2 days	Stocked, wild	Wooded, remote	

* See Chapters 2 and 3 for discussion of run-off rates, prime conditions and watershed size.
** Time to reach prime fishing conditions after average run-off episode from rain or snow-melt.

Table 4
Pennsylvania Tributary Access Points

Tributary	Major Access Points*
Turkey Creek	Childs Rd., State Line Rd. **(Roderick Wildlife Preserve/State Game Lands 314).**
Raccoon Creek	Rt. 5 to lake **(Racoon Creek Park),** Elmwood Home Rd.
Crooked Creek	Conrail trestle to lake, Happy Valley Rd., Rt. 20.
Conneaut Creek	CONNEAUT CREEK: Griffey Rd. to PA state line, Rt. 6N, McKee Rd., West Cherry Hill Rd., Carter Rd. EAST BRANCH: West Cherry Hill Rd., **Albion Park,** and Bessemer Dam. WEST BRANCH: Knapp Rd., Barney Rd.
Elk Creek	Rt. 5 to Lake **(Elk Creek Access),** Whitman's Rd., **Girard Boro Park,** old Rt. 20, **Legion Park,** Bessemer and Lake Erie R.R. trestle, Tannery Rd., Beckman Rd., Sterratania Rd., Rt. 98, I-79.
Godfrey Run	Nursery waters. Excellent shoreline fishery.
Trout Run	Nursery waters. Excellent shoreline fishery.
Walnut Creek	Manchester Rd. to lake **(Walnut Creek Access),** Rt. 5, Conrail trestle, Rt.20 **(Walnut Creek Gun Club),** Millfair Rd., old Rt. 832, Zimmerly Rd., I-79, Mill Creek Mall
Cascade Creek	Alternate Rt. 5 to lake **(Frontier Park** and Niagra Pier).
4-Mile Creek	Dam below Rt. 5 to lake (Lawrence Park Golf Course and Fishing Club).
7-Mile Creek	Waterfall below Rt. 5 to lake (Gilnodo Center). Walk in only.
8-Mile Creek	Rt. 5 to lake.
12-Mile Creek	Waterfall above Rt. 5 to lake.
16-Mile Creek	**Helli Reed Park,** waterfall above Rt. 5 and Rt. 89 to lake, Mill St. in Northeast, Wellington St.
Orchard Beach Run	Nursery waters.
Peck Run	Waterfall above Rt. 5 to lake.
20-Mile Creek	Rt. 5 to lake, abandoned iron bridge above Rt. 5, Middle Rd., Hertzel Rd. Pond (Gorge Area), Gulf Rd., Gay Rd.

*Access points listed for each tributary start near the lakeshore and progress inland. Also access tributary waters adjacent to I-90 and railroad trestles *(Conrail, Norfolk, Western and Bessemer)* on some tributaries where possible and legal. On private land, fisherman should secure the landowner's permission before accessing tributaries.

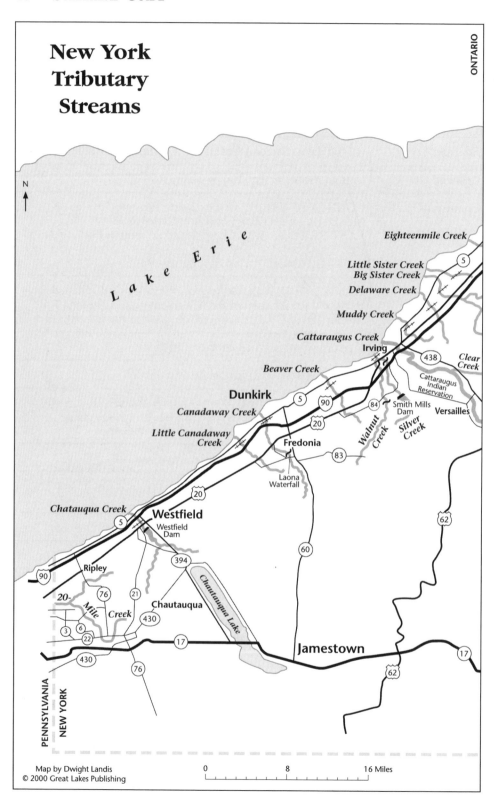

New York Tributary Streams

ONTARIO

N

Lake Erie

Eighteenmile Creek

Little Sister Creek
Big Sister Creek

Delaware Creek

Muddy Creek

Cattaraugus Creek
Irving

5

438

Clear Creek

Beaver Creek

Cattaraugus
Indian
Reservation

Dunkirk

5

90

84

Smith Mills
Dam

Versailles

Canadaway Creek

20

Walnut Creek

Silver Creek

Little Canadaway
Creek

Fredonia

83

Laona
Waterfall

20

Chatauqua Creek

Westfield

62

5

Westfield
Dam

90

Ripley

394

60

20-

76

21

Chautauqua

Chautauqua Lake

Mile Creek

430

3

6

17

Jamestown

17

22

430

62

76

PENNSYLVANIA
NEW YORK

Map by Dwight Landis
© 2000 Great Lakes Publishing

0   8   16 Miles

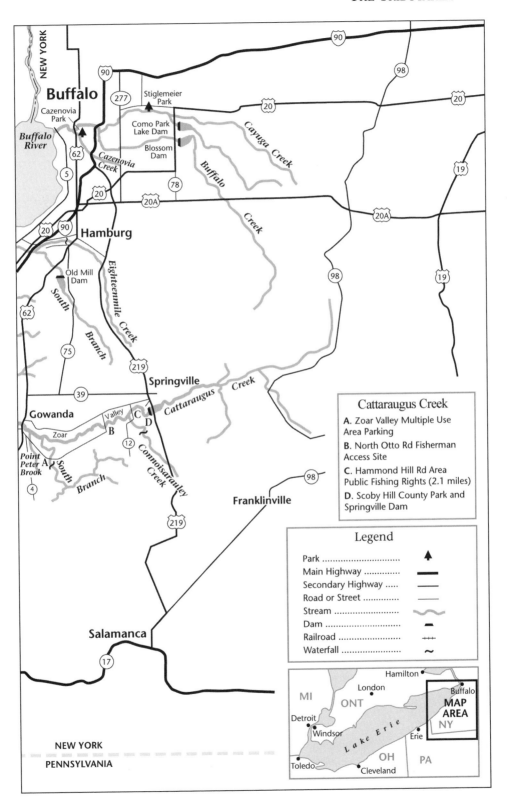

Cattaraugus Creek

A. Zoar Valley Multiple Use Area Parking

B. North Otto Rd Fisherman Access Site

C. Hammond Hill Rd Area Public Fishing Rights (2.1 miles)

D. Scoby Hill County Park and Springville Dam

Legend

Park	▲
Main Highway	━
Secondary Highway	—
Road or Street	—
Stream	∿
Dam	▬
Railroad	+++
Waterfall	~

Table 5
New York Tributary Information

Tributary	Watershed Size and Type*	Run-off Rate**	Steelhead Source	Surrounding Terrian	Important Feeders
Chautauqua Creek	Medium, shale bottom	1-2 days	Stocked	Wooded, remote	
Walnut Creek	Medium, shale bottom	1 day	Stocked	Rural, remote	
Canadaway Creek	Medium, shale bottom	1-2 days	Stocked	Urban, rural	
Beaver Creek	Small, shale bottom	Less than 1 day	Stray, wild	Rural	
20-Mile Creek	Medium, shale bottom	1-2 days	Stocked, wild	Wooded, remote	
Silver Creek	Medium, shale bottom	1 day	Stocked	Rural, remote	
Cattaraugus Creek	Large, gravel and shale bottom	1 week or more	Stocked, wild	Rural, remote	Clear Creek, Point Peter Brook, South Branch Cattaraugus
Muddy Creek	Small, mud bottom	1-2 days	Stray, wild	Rural	
Delaware Creek	Small, mud bottom	1-2 days	Stocked	Rural, remote	
Big Sister Creek	Medium, shale bottom	1-2 days	Stray	Rural, remote	
Little Sister Creek	Small, mud bottom	1 day	Stray	Rural, remote	
18-Mile Creek	Large, shale bottom	1-2 days	Stocked	Rural, remote	South Branch 18-Mile Creek
Buffalo Creek	Medium, shale bottom	2-3 days	Stocked	Urban, rural	
Cayuga Creek	Medium, shale bottom	2-3 days	Stocked	Urban, rural	
Cazenovia Creek	Small, shale bottom	1-2 days	Stray	Urban, rural	

* See chapter 2 and 3 for discussion of run-off rates, prime conditions and watershed size.
** Time to reach prime fishing conditions after average run-off episode from rain or snow-melt.

Table 6
New York Tributary Access Points

Tributary	Major Access Points*
Chautauqua Creek	Rt. 5 to Lake, North Gale St., Holly St., Rt. 20, South Gale St., Westfield Dam (above North Gale St. are **public parking areas and public fishing rights upstream to Westfield dam).**
20-Mile Creek	Rt. 3, Irish Rd., Rt. 9, Rt. 76, Rt. 22.
Canadaway Creek	Rt. 5 to lake, Willow Rd., Madison St., Rt. 20, Laona Water Fall.
Beaver Creek	Rt. 5 to lake, Rt. 82, Rt. 20.
Silver Creek	Jackson St. at mouth, Rt. 5/20, Hanover Rd., Smith Mills Dam.
Walnut Creek	Rt. 5, Rt. 20, King Rd., Rt. 39.
Cattaraugus Creek	Rt. 5/20, gravel pits (above and below I-90), Rt. 438, Buffalo Rd., Burning Spring Rd., CATTARAUGUS INDIAN RESERVATION: (between lake and Gowanda, except for south bank between lake and north of I-90 as well as Versailles area), Point Peter Rd., Valentine Flats Rd., Gowanda-Zoar Valley Rd., North Otto Road **(DEC fisherman access site),** Hammond Hill Rd. **(2.1 miles of public fishing rights)**, Scoby Road **(Scoby Hill County Park** and Springville Dam). Clear Creek: Rt. 438, Taylor Hollow Rd. (downstream of this road are Indian Reservation waters). Connoisarauley Creek: Hammond Hill Rd., waterfall 2 miles above Hammond Hill Rd. bridge. South Branch Cattaraugus: Point Peter Rd., Forty Rd., waterfall 100 yards above **DEC Zoar Valley Multiple Use Area** parking at west end of Forty Rd.
Muddy Creek	Lake Shore Rd to lake, Rt. 5.
Delaware Creek	Lake Shore Rd. to lake, Rt. 5.
Big Sister Creek	Lake Shore Rd. to lake, Rt. 5.
Little Sister Creek	Lake Shore Rd. to lake, Rt. 5.
18-Mile Creek	Lake Shore Rd. to lake, Rt. 5, South Creek Rd., Versailles Rd., Rt. 20, North Creek Rd., Lakeview Rd., Rt. 75 SOUTH BRANCH: Belknap Rd., Bley Rd., Rt. 62, Jennings Rd., E. Church Rd., Old Mill Dam
Buffalo Creek	Rt. 240/16, Rt. 277, Borden Rd., Rt. 20/78, N Blossom Rd., Dam above N. Blossom Rd.
Cayuga Creek	Rt. 354, Rt. 277, Como Park Blvd., **Stiglemeier Park,** Borden Rd., Rt. 20/78, Rt. 20, **Como Park** Lake Dam.
Cazenovia Creek	**Cazenovia Park** (South Buffalo), Rt. 240/16.

*Access points listed for each tributary start near the lakeshore and progress inland. Also access tributary waters adjacent to I-90 and railroad trestles *(Conrail, Norfolk, Western and Buffalo Southern)* on some tributaries where possible and legal. On private land, fisherman should secure the landowner's permission before accessing tributaries. Cattaraugus Indian Reservation requires a seperate license, see Appendix C.

Table 6a
Tributary Profiles
OHIO

Tributary	Comments
Vermillion River	Runs much cleaner than other Ohio tributaries. Mill Hollow Park and the Birmingham area provide good access for the steelheader. Upper reaches are very remote and scenic, have good public park access and contain excellent steelhead holding water.
Black River	In addition to a spring run of Little Manistee steelhead it also gets a small September run of king salmon (apparently wild fish). Metroparks provide good public access. Waterfalls at Cascade Creek Park in the City of Elyria, OH stop upstream steelhead migration.
Porter Creek	Clears in 1-2 days, looks very similar to 4-Mile Creek in PA.
Cahoon Creek	Spring fed tributary that is a good alternative when the Rocky River is high. Runs clear most of the time.
Rocky River	The Rocky River runs through the western Cleveland metro area and is easily accessed via the Rocky River Reservation Park. It is a meandering type stream of low to moderate gradient, which contains numerous abandoned river fords that provide ideal steelhead holding water. Even at low levels it seems to still maintain a green tint.
Cuyahoga River	Cuyahoga Valley National Park south of Cleveland provides excellent public access. Gets good run of stray steelhead.
Chagrin River	Located very close to the city of Cleveland and therefore gets intense fishing pressure. Takes 3-4 days to run-off to fishable levels and clarity. When steelhead jump the Daniels Park Dam at Willoughby excellent fishing can exist all the way to the dam at Gates Mills.
Grand River	Approximately 50 miles of fishable water is available on this tributary from the lake to Harpersfield, OH (where the dam is located). After run-off, it can take a week or more to reach fishable levels and even then it typically runs stained. Big, bright flies work best, and light tippets are not normally necessary due to the turbidity. When it is running high, feeders like Mill, Big and Paine Creek can be excellent. It can easily be floated in a canoe or pontoon boat and numerous Lake County Metro Parks provide excellent public access. Studded felt or corkers are highly recommended to wade the slippery, broken rock streambed of this big Ohio tributary. Above 400 CFS the wading gets treacherous. Lower reaches of the Grand clear before upper sections. Very fertile, containing good populations of golden stoneflies and green caddis larvae also impressive freshwater mussel population.
Arcola, Wheeler and Cowles Creeks	Good alternatives when bigger Ohio tributaries are high and muddy. Lower reaches are very slow and swampy.
Ashtabula River	A sleeper of a steelhead tributary (due to it's past reputation as a polluted body of water in its lower reaches). Run-off rate is 1 day behind PA's Elk Creek.
Conneaut Creek	A larger version of PA's Elk Creek that gets an excellent run of Little Manistee steelhead in March and April. Upper, remote reaches (around PA border) contain flatter gradient water, with heavily wooded banks, and mud and sand bottom. Can be floated with a canoe or pontoon boat in higher flows. Very fertile, containing good populations of golden stoneflies and green cadis larvae.

Table 6a
Tributary Profiles
PENNSYLVANIA

Tributary	Comments
Turkey, Raccoon and Crooked Creeks	Have mud and sand streambed areas in addition to shale. Crooked Creek can tend to run silty (even at fishable levels) due to run-off from farm fields.Very small and brushy with lots of fallen timber. Use shorter rods for easier casting and heavier tippets (3X or better) to prevent steelies from going into wood and undercuts. At low water, fish right up against logs and bank undercuts. Beware of smolts, especially on Raccoon and Crooked Creeks. Upper sections of Raccoon Creek run through State Game Lands 314. Turkey Creek drains portions of the Roderick Wildlife Preserve. These tribs fish best in winter and early spring.
Conneaut Creek	By late November/early December steelhead begin arriving in both the east and west branches of Conneaut Creek (including temple run) as well as the main branch in southern Erie County, providing good steelheading with very little fishing pressure. The upper waters of Conneaut Creek run more silty than other PA tributaries due to agricultural run-off. The West Branch watershed drains State Game Lands 101, providing good public access.
Elk Creek	This is the largest of the PA tributaries and is a classic Lake Erie tributary "spate" stream. After rain or snow-melt, it can quickly become high and muddy, but within a day or two can clear nicely. With adequate run-off flows steelhead can move very quickly upstream on this tributary due to lack of any major obstructions. Low, clear water conditions require small flies and light tippets. Elk Creek Access Area (near the lakeshore) provides excellent steelheading during low water periods, due to its deep holding water.
Walnut Creek	Gets large steelhead run, especially in the fall. Steelhead tend to concentrate from just above Manchester bridge (at "chutes" and falls) to the lake during low-water periods. PA Fish & Boat Commission "project waters" in this area provide excellent steelhead holding water but are usually crowded. High run-off flows help steelies to run as far as Mill Creek Mall.
Cascade Creek	Located in the City of Erie. It can be fishable when other tribs are "blown out." In early March (after lake ice-out) northern pike run up into it's lower reaches out of Presque Isle Bay.
4 and 7-Mile Creeks	Clear up in less than 12 hours after run-off. A dam and waterfall on 4-Mile (Lawrence Park Golf Club) and a waterfall (just south of Route 5) on 7-Mile prevent upstream steelhead migration.
8-Mile Creek and Peck Run	Last resort tributaries when everything else is high and muddy on the East side of Erie.
12-Mile Creek	Gets a lot of pressure due to excellent steelhead runs. Waterfall just above Route 5 bridge stops most steelhead migration.
16-Mile Creek	Clears very fast after run-off (less than 12 hours) and lower portions are less susceptible to freezing, due to warm water discharge from waste-water treatment plant. Pool below waterfall (located one mile from lake, south of Route 89) provides good holding water for steelhead but is passable in higher flows.
20-Mile Creek	The biggest of Pennsylvania's East side tributaries. Excellent public access exists north of Route 5 bridge to lake. Passable waterfall below iron bridge (south of Route 5) provides good staging area for migrating steelhead. Higher flows move steelies above falls where excellent remote style fishing can be enjoyed (I 90 and Rt. 20 gorge areas).

Table 6a
Tributary Profiles
NEW YORK

Tributary	Comments
Chautauqua Creek	Always gets good numbers of steelhead. Remote fishing is available below Westfield Dam.
Canadaway Creek	Runs through town of Fredonia, falls at Laona prevent any upstream steelhead migration.
Walnut and Silver Creeks	Good choices when Cattaraugus Creek is high and off-color (located only a few miles south). But drop to low, clear conditions (after rain/snow-melt) very quickly creating a small window of opportunity.
Cattaraugus Creek	The biggest of New York's tributaries, it has 50 miles of fishable water from the lake to the dam at Springville, NY. After run-off, it is not unusual for the "Cat" to take a week to reach fishable levels and decent water clarity. In a dry fall, it maintains a good base flow (due to it's watershed size and spring sources) while most other tributaries are literally bone dry. Lower part of river requires a Cattaraugus Indian Reservation fishing license. The Cat typically freezes over during the winter months and can consistently run high and stained in late winter, early spring. Provides great opportunity to catch wild (naturally reproduced) steelhead. In higher flows, floatable in a canoe or pontoon boat.
Little Sister and Big Sister Creeks	Best fished during higher flows. Not much public access.
18-Mile Creek	Runs off faster than Cattaraugus Creek. The South Branch can be fishable when the main branch is high and off-color. Public access is becoming a problem on this tributary.
Cazenovia Creek	Cazenovia Park in south Buffalo provides good access to this tributary (waterfall is located here).
Buffalo Creek	Another tributary easily accessible from south Buffalo.
Cayuga Creek	Good public access up to Como Park Lake and Dam in Lancaster, NY.

Steelheader's Tip

Experienced steelheaders are aware of the excellent fishing (and uncrowded conditions) that can occur on the smaller Lake Erie tributaries on "high water days." Due to their quick run-off characteristics these tributaries are usually fishable much faster than most fisherman anticipate.

Table 6b

Tributary Ideal Water Flow Data Table

(for United States tributaries)

Tributary	Ideal Flow (cubic feet per second)*	Watershed Size (square miles)
Brandy Run (tributary of Elk Creek, PA which will rise and fall quicker than the much bigger Elk Creek)	6-10	4.45
Grand River (OH)	250-400	685
Chagrin River (OH)	150-350	267
Vermillion River (OH)	100-200	262
Huron River (OH)	150-250	371
Cuyahoga River (OH)	250-350	151
Sandusky River (OH)	150-250	1,251
Rocky River (OH) USGS River Gage on this river also records water temperature data.	150-250	294
Cayuga Creek (NY)	200-600	96.4
Cazenovia Creek (NY)	200-300	135
Buffalo Creek (NY)	200-300	142
Cattaraugus Creek (NY)	230-500	436

*Range of ideal flow conditions for most steelhead techniques. Higher flows are more conducive to swinging and heavy nymphing methods. Water clarity is normally good at these levels, but off- color conditions can occur even at lower flows. Fall flows (from rain run-off) are usually more stained than winter/spring flows due to summer silt buildup. Run-off flows as a result of snow-melt are usually clearer due to slower melt effect. Only a limited number of Lake Erie tributary streams have operating river gages to measure flow. Real time water flow and stage data (cubic feet per second or feet) for the United States tributaries is available at the United States Geological Survey web site: http://water.usgs.gov/realtime.html

A hardy steelheader enjoying January
stream conditions on Walnut Creek, PA.

Weather *and* Stream Conditions

Chapter 3

Lake Erie's tributary streams, particularly on the southern shore, normally run low and clear due to poor groundwater flow. They are also very dependent on run-off from rain or melting snow. This run-off is what initiates fresh runs of steelhead from the lake, "energizes" old fish, brings the tributaries up to more fishable levels, creates more holding lies for migrating steelhead and helps steelhead migration further upstream.

At peak run-off levels most tributaries are a muddy torrent with few fishing opportunities. As stream levels drop, the water clarity improves and prime fishing conditions are reached. Prime fishing conditions, or more specifically, prime run-off conditions, occur as stream flows become more fishable (lower water levels and current flows) and the water color takes on a green tint. This tint is a result of suspended clay particles that are continually eroding from the shale and clay strata that are characteristic of most Lake Erie watersheds.

Steelhead are easier to catch in this type of water because their visibility is limited. They can see your fly offering, but not too clearly. These ideal conditions do not last long and can vary in length from only several hours to a few days depending on the amount of run-off flow, ongoing weather conditions, water table levels, and the run-off characteristics of that particular tributary watershed (see Tables 1, 3 and 5 in Chapter Two and also the Tributary Ideal Flow Data Table on page 55).

Prime fishing conditions are so important to the seasoned steelheader that he becomes a "weather junkie," studying local weather forecasts and seeking up-to-date stream conditions from tackle shops and local fishermen. With accurate weather information and stream conditions, the steelheader can predict prime conditions for a particular tributary, or tributaries, and get on the water with the odds in his favor. Appendix A lists local tackle shops, weather and stream flow data information sources for the Lake Erie region.

High water on Sixteen-Mile Creek, PA.

Prime fishing conditions do not guarantee fishable water all the time. Other circumstances can play havoc with a steelheader on a Lake Erie tributary stream. For example, during the later part of October, leaf-clogged streams can make drifting a fly almost impossible. This condition usually lasts for only a few weeks as most leaves are gone by early November.

The accumulation of summer silt in the tributaries can be a problem in September, October, and even November if late summer or early fall rains do not flush out the tributaries sufficiently. The result often means a muddy, murky run-off even when water flows are down to fishable levels.

By late December stream ice can become a problem. Initially, skim ice or slush will form nightly, but break up by mid-morning usually leaving open, fishable water by noon. During severe winters, a complete ice-up can occur in a stream, but

Steelheader's Tip

Monitor weather and stream conditions in order to predict "prime" or favorable conditions for a particular tributary.

George Dowling navigating morning slush-flows on Walnut Creek, PA.

Ice-up on lower Walnut Creek, PA.

mid-winter thaws usually break this up and provide some periods of open water.

Severe winters can also cause ice-jams to form at the lower ends of the tributaries, particularly when the Lake Erie shoreline freezes. These ice jams can act as barriers, blocking fresh runs of steelhead from moving up the tributaries during the winter months. Mid-winter thaws once again are the only cure to breakup these obstructions. Anchor or streambed ice forms when stream temperatures drop to 32 degrees F. This phenomenon is further encouraged by a lack of ground cover such as snow or ice, resulting in the super-cooling of stream flows. Since anchor ice formation seems to develop inconsistently on streambeds (depending on the speed of the current flow and streambed type) areas free of anchor ice will exist.

Spring not only brings the peak of the steelhead run, but also the timely run of the Lake Erie sucker. This usually occurs after the lake's winter ice layer breaks up and melts (normally early March). During the sucker run, the best steelhead pools and runs are often taken over by suckers, making finding and hooking a steelhead nearly impossible. Since suckers dislike really fast flows the steelheader should target the fastest runs and chutes in a tributary to avoid suckers.

During the spring, steelhead are easily visible and are either on their spawning beds or in a pre-spawn mode located near them. To prevent catching suckers at this time avoid blind fishing and target visible steelhead. Since suckers do not run nearly as far upstream as steelhead, they can usually be avoided altogether if you fish far enough upstream from the lake.

Smolt stockings can be a real problem on some tributaries in the spring. This is also true, to a lesser extent, in the fall when limited stockings of younger juvenile steelhead or fingerlings are made. If you are really patient you can work through the smolt, twenty-five casts with twenty-five smolt, and eventually hook an adult steelhead! You are probably better off avoiding specific areas of tributaries that receive smolt stocking and concentrating on smolt free zones. This strategy will also reduce smolt mortality rates and help ensure future steelhead runs.

A sure sign of spring is the arrival of the sucker.

Often the most annoying of problems to deal with on Lake Erie tributaries are the crowds of other fishermen. Holes that attract crowds are typically near the lake, are relatively deep, with good holding water for large numbers of fish, and receive early runs of fresh fish just after peak run-off. Action can be fast and furious with courtesy and ethics sometimes taking a back seat to sportsmanship. You shouldn't rule out these areas completely,

Fly caught yearling steelhead or smolt.

Crowded conditions on lower Walnut Creek, PA.

A solitary steelheader on middle section of Elk Creek, PA.

Spring snow squall on Ashtabula River, OH.

especially late in the day, during nasty weather, on holidays and during the buck season. During these periods they can frequently be vacant of fishermen.

The Pennsylvania tributaries are the most popular, and at times, the most crowded of Lake Erie's tributary streams. This is undoubtedly a result of excellent steelhead runs and the variety of steelhead streams Pennsylvania has to offer. The Ohio and New York tributaries have lesser steelhead runs than Pennsylvania and are therefore less crowded. Nevertheless, steelheaders who target the Ohio and New York tributary regions will be pleasantly surprised by good runs of steelhead, good public access (especially in Ohio) and plenty of water to fish.

Steelheader's Tip

Rubbing lip balm on rod guides will prevent your guides from freezing in sub-freezing air temperatures.

A fall run "chromer" leaps the falls on 16-Mile Creek, PA. (Jack Hanrahan photo)

Steelhead Behavior

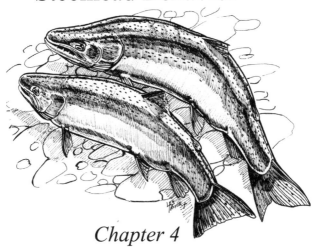

Chapter 4

By mid-September, when lake shore temperatures drop to 68 degrees F. and the days or "photo periods" become shorter, steelhead begin entering the tributaries. With the help of cool fall rains and run-off, ideally 54 degrees F. or less, the fish begin a pre-spawn migration or "run" upstream, entering the confining and rather intimidating environment of a Great Lakes tributary.

Very light sensitive in the pre-spawn mode and keenly aware of possible predators, Lake Erie steelhead quickly look for resting and holding water that also provides cover, using the streambed maze of shale ledges, chutes, pockets and pools created by erosion over the seasons. They are also very attracted to dark colored stream bottoms and will hold in these areas since their grayish-black backs are easily concealed there. Man-made structures provide another source for cover as well as areas for resting and holding. These include road and railroad bridge piers and tunnels, river fords, dams and retaining or break walls. The fly fisherman who knows all of these areas intimately improves his or her chances of finding and catching Lake Erie steelhead.

The rather small confines of the Lake Erie tributaries also cause steelhead to be very wary, making light tippets and drag-free drifts along the stream bottom (particularly in colder flows) critical for the fly fisherman. This type of steelhead behavior is what really defines Great Lake steelheading (and specifically Lake Erie steelheading) and sets it apart from the Pacific Northwest approach in both technique and equipment. Effective steelheading techniques and equipment will be discussed in detail in Chapters Five and Six.

Steelhead behavior in the tributaries is greatly affected by four factors: water flow, water clarity, light levels and water temperature.

Rt. 5 bridge tunnel on Walnut Creek, PA provides good cover for steelhead especially during low, water conditions.

Cedar Point river ford on Rocky River, OH is a man-made structure which forces steelhead to pause on their upstream migration.

Water Flow and Clarity

Steelhead use water flow as cover just as bass use structure in a lake for cover. During higher stream flows, certain runs and pools of a tributary provide good cover since their depth prevents light penetration and provides concealment. These same areas will hold fewer fish as water levels drop, not only as a result of decreased water depth, but also because the water surface texture becomes more flat as stream levels fall. Steelhead feel much more secure under shallow, broken or riffled water than in deeper, flat water. This behavior is especially true in clear water conditions.

Water clarity, or the lack of it, is used by steelhead for cover purposes. The early stage of a tributary run-off episode usually brings stained water, and steelhead can be found in very shallow water at this time. A steelhead can feel quite safe in one foot of stained water, but not in four feet of clear, flat water. Fishing fast, shallow runs and pocket water during high, stained stream flows can be very productive. This is especially true in the fall and early spring when water temperatures are warm (40 degrees F. or higher).

As run-off flows become less turbid, steelhead will gradually move to deeper and deeper water. These conditions are the prime fishing conditions discussed earlier in Chapter Three. At this stage, a steelhead feels very secure and water levels have dropped to both fishable and wadable levels. With increased water clarity steelhead become very cooperative fly takers.

Stream levels vary tremendously during a run-off episode. At the extreme of flood stage, steelhead not only seek relief from torrential currents, but also look for water that is relatively free of debris such as leaves, heavy silt and branches, etc. Current breaks located at inside bends, along stream banks, behind large rocks or dead falls and inside back eddies, help to filter the water of debris and will attract steelhead. Steelhead usually do not run far in the debris filled water of flood stage, especially if it is cold (less than 37 degrees F.), because heavy silt and organic debris irritates their gills.

Steelheader's Tip

In the winter, when steelhead locate in slow pool tail-outs and eddies usually along edges, the right-angle-floating-indicator technique is very productive.

As water flows begin to drop below flood stage to high and eventually moderate levels, the water becomes cleaner and steelhead start to run more readily. These reduced flows also allow a steelhead to move out into the main current areas of the stream and hold in the current breaks of pools, riffles and runs.

Reading Surface Water

As discussed earlier, steelhead after entering a tributary seek cover from light and predators by locating in deeper water or using water surface texture. They also look for resting and holding areas during their upstream migration, which usually means locating in current breaks created from both natural and man-made structures.

Current breaks in a stream flow create reductions in the main current speed that can vary greatly. The lower end of a pool where the streambed levels out provides a current break and a comfortable resting-place for a steelhead. At the beginning of the pool tail-out, where the streambed starts to rise, even slower currents can be found. This is because the current is being deflected and dispersed upward, and to a lesser extent to the sides, making it slow down for a short distance. If you look carefully, you can see that the water starts to rise slightly here due to the deflection of the current. As the streambed levels out again (at the lower end of the pool

A broken piece of the old Center St. Dam on Conneaut Creek,
OH provides a prime resting and holding area for steelhead.

tail-out) the current picks up in speed very quickly, creating a faster but rather shallow flow of water. (See Figure 4.0 on page 70).

The changing texture of the water surface directly shows where subsurface current breaks are located. In a classic stream/pool scenario the water surface becomes less broken as it progresses from heavy riffles at the head of the pool to gentle riffles at the pool's end, indicating an obvious drop in current speed. This can be thought of as a surface horizontal current break, which continually changes (in terms of water surface texture and current speed) as you move downstream.

This gradual drop in current speed is directly related to the friction caused by the streambed gradient on the current flow. At the upper part of the pool tail-out, the surface texture becomes very flat, indicating some of the slowest current in the pool. Figure 4.0 shows where these water surface texture changes occur in a typical stretch of stream flow as well as corresponding steelhead holding locations.

Another important variation in current speed occurs from the surface horizontal current break to the streambed. (See Figure 4.0a on page 71). Again, due to the friction of the streambed, the current speed on the surface is much faster than the current speed near the bottom, where slower subsurface horizontal current breaks exist. Steelhead are aware of this difference and like to hold on the bottom especially in colder stream flows. This current speed difference cannot be detected by any surface texture variations, but nonetheless is an important difference to be aware of especially when executing dead-drifting techniques. (See Chapter 5 for discussion on short-line nymphing techniques.)

Similar current breaks occur vertically along ledges and drop-offs and also form as a result of friction. Figure 4.0a illustrates both horizontal and vertical current breaks and how they vary (in terms of current speed) depending on the depth of the water, distance from vertical ledges and the angle of the streambed gradient.

Looking for changes in water surface texture, or reading the surface water, will help you locate prime subsurface holding areas that would otherwise be very difficult to discern. Look for variations of these surface texture changes in deeper runs, adjacent to pool back eddies, in extended riffle areas, behind large

Steelheader's Tip

In the winter, 90% of the steelhead are found in 10% of the water — deep pool tail-outs, deeper runs and eddies due to the cold water temperatures.

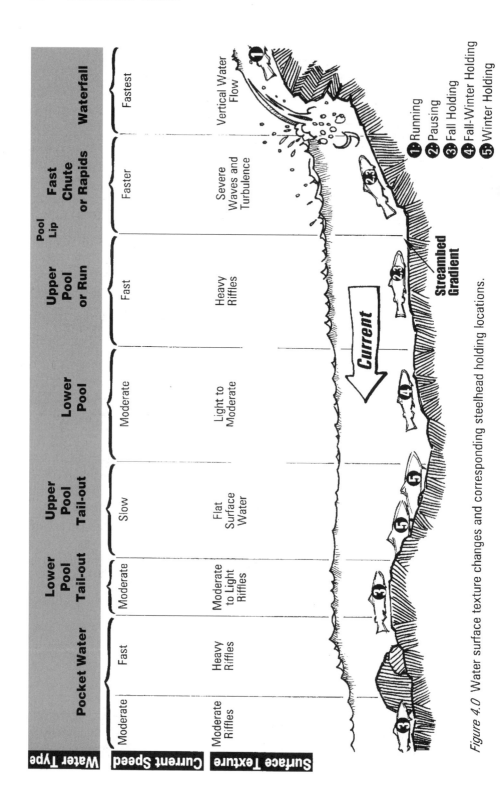

Figure 4.0 Water surface texture changes and corresponding steelhead holding locations.

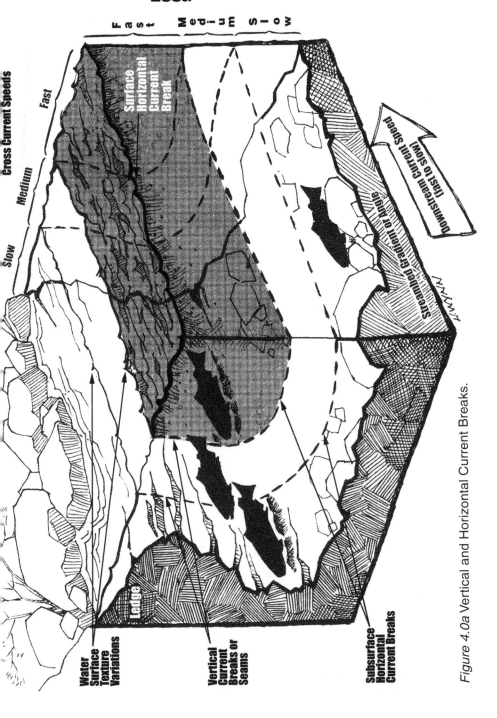

Figure 4.0a Vertical and Horizontal Current Breaks.

rocks and along shale ledges. Man-made structures and snags such as bridge abutments and log jams can also create surface texture changes that clearly indicate the location of current breaks.

Daily Light Levels

Daily light levels will influence a steelhead's choice of cover. Ideal light conditions occur on overcast, cloudy days, as well as during the early morning or late evening. These conditions give steelhead a sense of security because of their aversion to bright light, and they will venture into areas such as shallow runs and pockets, as well as shallow pool tail-outs. Steelhead will also take a fly much better when light levels are low, especially when the tributaries are flowing low and clear.

Water Temperature Effects

The final and probably most important factor affecting steelhead behavior in a tributary are fluctuations in water temperature. These temperature changes not only occur on a daily basis, but seasonally as well.

Daily water temperature changes have the most noticeable effect on steelhead behavior in the winter when morning water temperatures often dip below 36 degrees F. and bottom out at 32 degrees F. Steelhead in these ice water temperatures become very lethargic, and often get a case of "lock jaw," taking few fly offerings. As morning air temperatures increase, stream temperatures follow,

Bob Camel takes a water temperature on Elk Creek, PA.

causing steelhead to gradually become more active. Noon and early afternoon is usually the best time of the day for winter steelheading.

Seasonal water temperature changes also have a tremendous effect on where a steelhead will locate itself once in a tributary stream. As the seasons and tributary temperatures change, steelhead will seek current breaks that they can comfortably hold and rest in depending on the water temperature. This behavior is directly related to the fact that steelhead are a cold-blooded species and that their metabolism decreases as water temperatures fall. As this occurs, steelhead become less active and more lethargic and will lose their ability to hold in faster currents. Figures 4.0 (on page 70) and 4.1 (on pages 74 & 75) clearly illustrate these seasonal location changes.

In September and early October, the water temperatures of Lake Erie's tributary streams run above 45 degrees F. These warm water temperatures make steelhead very active and aggressive. They tend to hold in the heads of pools near the pool lip, where current speeds are faster, as well as fast chutes, pocket water, fast runs and the lower ends of pool tail-outs. At this time steelhead are very aggressive and will often move for a fly and take it very hard.

In late October and early November, steelhead become less active as stream temperatures cool to between 38 to 45 degrees F. This is the fall-to-winter transition period for steelhead, when they avoid holding in very fast water, and can be found instead in middle sections of pools, pocket water and moderate runs.

December marks the arrival of winter steelheading as stream temperatures drop to between 32 to 37 degrees F. Steelhead become very inactive as a result of these frigid water temperatures and prefer slow current areas. Prime-winter holding locations include the slow moving tail-out section of deep sloping pools, slow pool back eddies and slack water areas or "slicks" located adjacent to current edges created by shale ledges and drop-offs. Winter is the most challenging time to catch steelhead, because flies literally have to be put on the noses of these fish, often with multiple casts and subtle variations in drift.

Steelheader's Tip

A good rule of thumb is to fish edges, tail-outs and pockets during high water and to fish deep areas and broken or riffled water during low water periods.

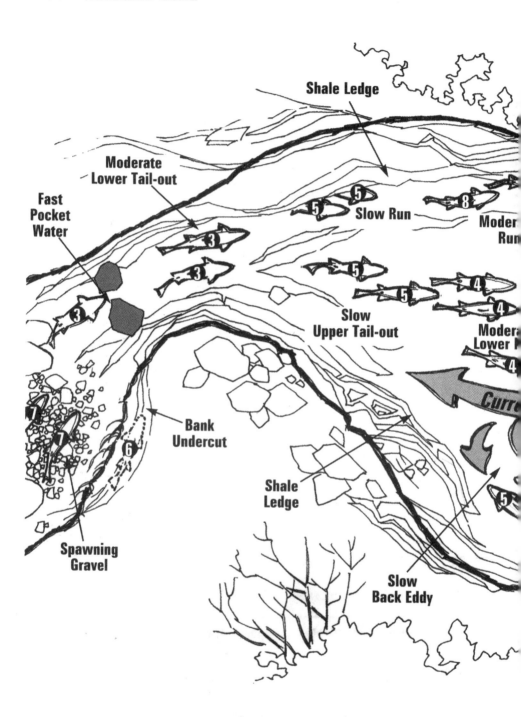

Figure 4.1 Seasonal water temperature changes and corresponding steelhead holding locations.

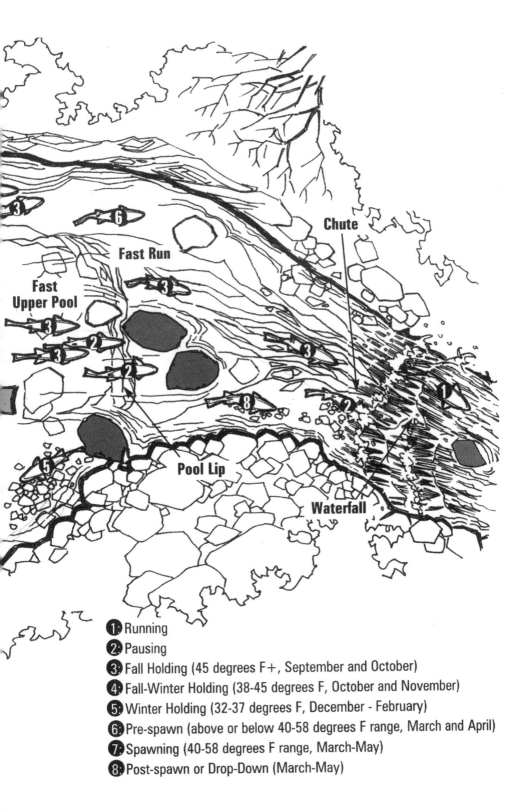

1: Running
2: Pausing
3: Fall Holding (45 degrees F+, September and October)
4: Fall-Winter Holding (38-45 degrees F, October and November)
5: Winter Holding (32-37 degrees F, December - February)
6: Pre-spawn (above or below 40-58 degrees F range, March and April)
7: Spawning (40-58 degrees F range, March-May)
8: Post-spawn or Drop-Down (March-May)

*Mark DeCarlo with a beauty from the Zoar Valley on Cattaraugus Creek, NY.
(Mark DeCarlo photo)*

In late February, when stream temperatures begin to rise over 40 degrees F., and periods of daylight increase, steelhead begin moving from their winter locations to shallow gravel riffles. The majority of steelhead are now found in the upper halves or headwaters of the tributaries. This is where good spawning areas with ideal water flow, depth and gravel, can usually be found. Really for the first time since entering the tributaries, steelhead are readily visible to the fly fisherman, as they begin digging their spawning redds and commence their spawning rituals.

Post-spawn steelhead are usually very thin from wintering over in the tributaries and also show some signs of wear from actual spawning. These fish are sometimes referred to as "drop-down" steelhead because of their movement down the tributaries toward Lake Erie after spawning.

Drop-down steelhead, after expending a lot of energy in spawning, have voracious appetites, and often take flies with abandon. They prefer to hold in slower current areas of deep pools and runs. A cold, wet spring can keep drop-down fish in the tributaries into late April and sometimes early May.

The Lake Erie Steelhead Run

Lake Erie steelhead begin their spawning run up the tributaries when their genetic code initiates this urge as well as when photo-periods (daily light level duration's) are right.

Fall/winter run Washington strain steelhead, particularly the naturalized strain of Pennsylvania steelhead, usually begin staging at the tributary mouths in late August when photo-periods become shorter. They start running upstream in good numbers by mid-to-late September when run-off flows are adequate and stream temperatures have cooled to below 55 degrees F. Low water can delay this migration if fall rains and run-off are limited. The peak of the run usually occurs in November.

Steelhead that have just entered a tributary stream from Lake Erie are called fresh-run or "bright fish". Their back coloration varies from blued-steel to green with a strikingly contrasting mint-silver color below the lateral line. The bellies of the females are almost entirely white, while the males tend to be somewhat darker. Fresh steelhead can easily conceal themselves in their surroundings since their silver and white sides act as mirrors reflecting the image of the streambed beneath them.

As adult steelhead become closer to their spawning time, they gradually undergo physiological changes related to their maturing gonads or reproductive organs. Specifically the male or "buck" steelhead grow a kype (a hooked protrusion at the end of the lower jaw), along with rosy red cheeks and sides, heavily spotted backs and a general charcoal overcast to their appearance.

The females or "hen" steelhead develop lightly spotted, bluish green backs and a dirty silver, slightly pink/purple coloration on their sides. They also develop large bellies indicating a growing supply of steelhead eggs.

Steelhead keep running up a tributary, pausing at only large obstructions like dams, river fords, waterfalls or fast, high gradient chutes, as long as stream temperatures are in the 40 to 54 degrees F. range and run-off provides for easy

Steelheader's Tip

Avoid over playing a steelhead by using a steelhead-size landing net with cotton netting, which is less damaging to the fish than synthetic netting.

Male and female steelhead (top and bottom respectively).
Both are still in pre-spawn phase. Note large belly on female
indicating that she has not "dropped" her eggs yet.

*Author with fresh run steelhead
at mouth of Sixteen-Mile Creek, PA.*

passage. Steelhead in the run mode are generally scattered, occasionally porpoising to the surface as they run upstream. While they are running they normally won't take flies well unless they switch to a pausing or holding mode.

Tributary running steelhead typically go into a holding mode as stream flows drop to lower levels (after a run-off episode from rain or snow melt). When water temperatures consistently begin to drop below 38 degrees F., during the winter months of late December through early March, steelhead will also tend to hold in pods or groups of fish in the winter holding areas described earlier.

It is not unusual for Lake Erie steelhead to drop temporarily back down to the lake during low water periods and then resume their upstream migration when water levels rise. This is especially true if they are in close proximity to the lakeshore.

Upstream movement continues during the winter months, but it is more of a slow-run or methodical movement. This type of movement continues until stream temperatures get above 40 degrees F. and the photo-periods begin to lengthen. These conditions, along with good spring run-off and ice-out of the lake, initiate the fast paced spring spawning run which ordinarily begins by early March. Spawning begins as soon as the stream temperatures reach the 40 to 58 degrees F. range. If stream temperatures suddenly drop below or rise above these ideal spawning temperatures, pre-spawn steelhead will stage in close proximity to the spawning beds at stream bank undercuts, lips of pools, heads of runs, pocket water, as well as nearby snags.

Author battling steelhead 25 miles from the lake on upper Elk Creek, PA.

After spawning, steelhead gradually drop down to the lake. Most fish are gone from the southern shore tributaries of Lake Erie by late April or early May. The steelhead run timetable (Table 7 on page 81) shows how a Lake Erie steelhead run (Pennsylvania's strain) progresses from the initial staging to the drop down phase in an average climatic year. Understanding the progression of a steelhead run allows the steelheader to more closely predict steelhead movements as well as probable locations to look for them.

Steelheader's Tip

A much heavier tippet can be used when swinging a fly since the steelhead will only see the fly on the downstream swing.

Table 7
Steelhead Run Timetable

Run Mode	Conditions	Tributary Location	Months
Lake Shore Staging/Early Fall Running	Lake shore temperatures drop to 68 degrees F, shorter photo periods, tributary temperatures above 50 degrees F.	Staging at tributary mouths and extreme lower half of tributaries.	Late August-September.
Fall Running/Holding	Tributary temperatures between 38-54 degrees F with good water flow. Leaf drop occurs last week of Oct.	Moving up to the middle reaches of tributaries, located in fast runs, pools and pocket water.	Mid September-Mid December, with peak in November.
Fall/Winter Drop Down Movement	Extreme low water conditions.	Temporary movement from lower half of tributaries to lake.	September-February.
Winter Holding	Tributary temperatures between 32-37 degrees F, lake freezes.	In middle to upper half of tributaries, located in slow pools, tail-outs and eddies.	Late December-Mid March.
Slow Run Winter Movement	Gradually increasing tributary temperatures to the upper 30's degree F range.	Slow run movement to upper half of tributaries.	Late December-Mid March.
Spring Running	Tributary temperatures increasing over 40 degrees F, ice-out begins on lake. Suckers start running also, smolt stockings begin.	Running to upper half of tributaries to spawning beds.	Early March-Mid April.
Pre-Spawn Steelhead	Suddenly dropping or increasing tributary temperatures above or below ideal spawning range of 40-58 degrees F.	Staging in holding areas adjacent to spawning beds.	Early March-Mid April.
Spawning Steelhead	Tributary temperatures between 40-58 degrees F, longer photo periods.	In middle to upper half of tributaries, located in shallow gravel riffles.	Mid March-Late April.
Drop Down Movement	Spawned out steelhead.	Moving down to mouth of tributaries, located in moderate runs and pools.	Mid March-Late April.

Fly fisherman landing a steelhead at Legion Park on Elk Creek, PA.

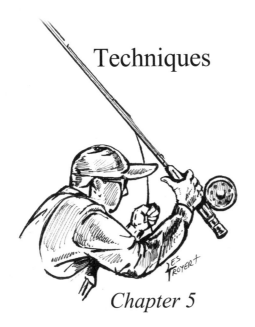

Techniques

Chapter 5

As stated earlier, the tributary streams of Lake Erie are very unique. These scenic and at times remote streams are characteristically small in size and normally run low and clear and are heavily dependent from rain or snow-melt run-off to get them up to fishable flows. Their stream bottoms are composed mostly of eroded and broken shale, making holding lies very definable to the experienced fly fisherman.

The confining nature of these tributaries makes Lake Erie steelhead very wary after they enter them in the fall. They become sensitive to light and seek any kind of cover they can find, often holding along shale ledges or in shale cuts or troughs. As a result they also become very conscious of current speed and drag, especially as water temperatures drop in late October. This requires the fly fisherman to refine his techniques and modify his equipment to achieve often crucial drag-free drifts.

A drag-free drift is simply defined as drifting your fly on the stream bottom at the same speed as the bottom current. Depending on stream flows this is most effectively accomplished by using a short-line nymphing technique such as either bottom-bouncing or the right-angle-floating-indicator technique. Both of these methods (also known as high-stick-nymphing) emphasize wading into position and the use of long fly rods, long leaders, a short length of fly line and high rod position to achieve drag-free fly drifts on the stream bottom.

Short-Line Bottom-Bouncing

In high to medium run-off flows, short-line bottom-bouncing is very effective in methodically covering the bottom and hooking steelhead (especially in shallow runs and pocket water). When steelhead seem to have their noses dug in the streambed gravel, bottom-bouncing will hook fish that you couldn't catch while using a floating indicator. This technique is very easy to do in the typically small and shallow Erie tributaries. It is best accomplished by wading within two or three rods length's of a steelhead lie and positioning yourself directly in front of where you think the steelhead is located. This area is called the "target zone."

Begin by casting your fly line and leader upstream of the target zone. You will immediately notice that a downstream "belly" develops in the fly line and leader due to the pull of the current. This belly prevents the fly and split-shot from sinking quickly to the bottom and drifting at the same speed as the bottom current. To counteract this effect (at this point fly rod is relatively low to the water) immediately flip your fly line and leader upstream to form an upstream belly. This simple technique is called an upstream mend and is illustrated in Figure 5.0 on page 85. This mend is very important since it ensures that the fly and split-shot will be on the bottom and drifting naturally through the target zone. If a tuck cast is used when initially casting upstream, your fly will sink even quicker. This is achieved by sharply checking or stopping your cast on the forward stroke causing the fly to tuck under the leader before it enters the water.

As the fly begins to drift downstream towards the target zone, begin to lift the rod tip to get all of the fly line out of the water to achieve an all leader drift (See Figure 5.1 on page 86). Follow your leader's drift downstream with your rod tip. When the fly enters the target zone, it is important to maintain a tight line to feel the bottom, so that you can detect any strikes or changes in drift. Maintaining a tight line is accomplished by raising the rod tip even higher, and with the left hand (if you're right handed), pulling on the fly line thereby shortening the length of the fly line and leader below the rod tip.

Another way to maintain a tight fly line and leader is to make sure you have at least a 3 to 7 feet of fly line below the rod tip as you drift through the target zone. This length provides enough weight to balance the weight of the fly and split-shot, resulting in a much better feel for bottom contact and strike detection.

Long fly rods, up to $10^{1/2}$ feet in length, enable you to control longer leaders and more fly line below the rod tip without fly line interference during the drift. Long rods also make it easier to fish deep runs and pools at greater distances when bottom-bouncing with a tapered floating line and a long leader.

Having all leader below the rod tip to the water creates slack, making it very difficult to detect strikes and control the line. If you have all fly line below the rod tip, you have the opposite case of fly line in the water, which can provide interference when a critical drag-free drift is needed.

Drag is more pronounced with a weight-forward line than with a triangle-taper line, because the heavy taper of the weight-forward line is close to the butt of the leader.

As the fly passes through the target zone, drop your rod tip and let some fly line out with your left hand. Doing this will allow a longer drag-free drift, extending the length of your target zone. Through the entire drift, try to follow the leader with your rod tip, rotating your torso as you do so. You can also walk downstream below the extended target zone to lengthen your drift even farther.

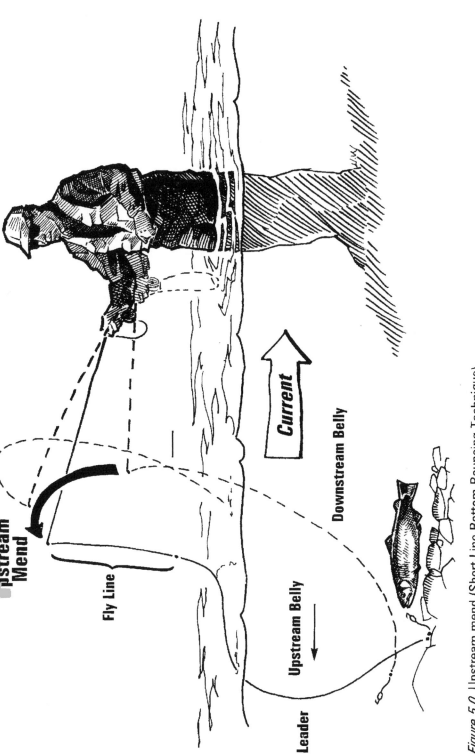

Figure 5.0 Upstream mend (Short-Line-Bottom-Bouncing Technique).

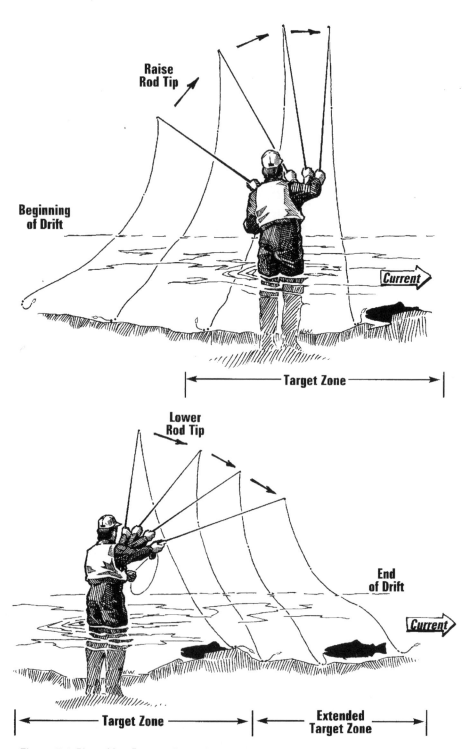

Figure 5.1 Short-Line-Bottom-Bouncing Technique sequence.

The amount of split-shot and its exact placement on the leader changes depending on whether or not you are using a weighted fly. It also varies according to stream flow, clarity, depth and bottom type. A fast moving, shale-bottomed stream, with a sharply uneven bottom, often requires that you keep your split-shot within 6 to 12 inches of the fly to reach steelhead that are holding tightly along small cuts, ledges or below sharp drop-offs. Smooth gravel runs with relatively uniform depths and flows allow you to place your split shot up to 36 inches from the fly and still keep your fly on the bottom, at fish level.

Remember that the closer you keep your split-shot to the fly when bottom-bouncing the more likely you are apt to spook a fish, especially in clear flows. Off-color stream flows allow for closer split-shot placement to the fly due to the reduced visibility of the steelhead. Some steelheader's believe that split-shot makes too much noise when bouncing along the bottom and prefer to use rubber coated shot or slinkies (to be discussed later in this chapter).

A mini-tip or head that is custom made from a sinking shooting head (see Chapter 6) can be used instead of split-shot when bottom-bouncing. Mini-tips constructed in a variety of lengths and sink rates allow the steelheader to match the varying water conditions encountered on the tributaries. They are typically incorporated into the leader using an interlocking loop system and practically eliminate any streambed snagging common with split-shot use. This type of rig can also be fine-tuned by adding very small amounts of soft-shot to the leader.

There are no regulation requirements for the allowable split-shot to fly distance in the Ohio and Pennsylvania tributaries of southern Lake Erie. This is not true in the New York Lake Erie tributaries (see regulations in Appendix B) and other areas of the Great Lakes such as Lake Michigan. In these areas a legacy of both legal and illegal snagging has been a scourge hard to eliminate. Therefore minimum split-shot to fly distance requirements were established on certain streams to discourage this unethical technique.

Weighted flies often work better than unweighted flies because they get to the bottom more quickly, requiring less manipulation of your line and leader to get a deep drift. If flies are weighted too heavily, though, they won't drift drag-free and will hang up on the stream bottom. A good system is to weight your flies by adding

Steelheader's Tip

Tying steelhead flies with a thinner profile will help them sink faster due to the reduced resistance they provide as they sink.

metallic bead-heads, lead wire under-wrappings or brass or copper ribbing and later add enough split-shot to your leader to get your fly on the bottom and still drift drag-free. If split-shot is added on to the leader with a weighted fly (which at times may not be required) it allows you to "back-off," or move away the shot from the fly. This is advantageous because split-shot placed too close to the fly can spook fish. This is especially true when bottom-bouncing in clear, slow current flows.

An alternative to weighting flies is to use heavy wire hooks (2X or 3X strong wire) or larger than normal hooks (use a #8 or #10 hook for a size #12 fly pattern). The slight weight addition provided by these hooks helps keep a fly more consistently on the bottom, especially in faster, deeper stream flows. Any fly can also easily be weighted by threading a metal bead-head or cone-head onto the tippet. The bead-head or cone-head will then slide down to the tippet/fly knot connection above the fly.

Tying flies with a smaller profile will help them sink faster. For instance, a stonefly pattern tied with a thin, compact abdomen sinks through the water much quicker than a fly constructed with a thicker, more bulky abdomen. This is a result of the reduced resistance a thinner profile fly provides as it descends through the water column.

Using tandem flies when bottom-bouncing can sometimes increase a steelheader's hook-up success, especially if you can keep both flies drifting naturally on the bottom. An in-line rig (see Figure 5.2 on page 89) with flies of contrasting pattern and size often works best. Identical tandem flies are also effective. A good example is a weighted wooly bugger or stonefly for the trailer or point fly at the end of the tippet. An egg pattern, the top or dropper fly, is located 6-18 inches above the point fly with some split-shot secured 6 to 36 inches above it on the leader.

Another way of adding split-shot is to cut the leader above the dropper fly and re-tie it with a blood or surgeon's knot. Clinch knot a separate tag of tippet material about 4 inches long to the leader above the blood knot. If you place your split shot on this tag, it will slide off when snagged, preventing the loss of both flies (see Figure 5.2 on page 89).

Slinkies are also useful for adding weight to a bottom-bouncing rig. Slinkies are pieces of parachute cord filled with varying amounts of split shot and melted closed at both ends. Slinkies are secured to the leader by a snap swivel. A barrel swivel tied into the leader prevents the slinky from sliding down on the fly. Since the slinky slides on the leader, a steelhead feels very little of the split-shot weight during a take. They are also very snag resistant when drifting over rocky streambeds.

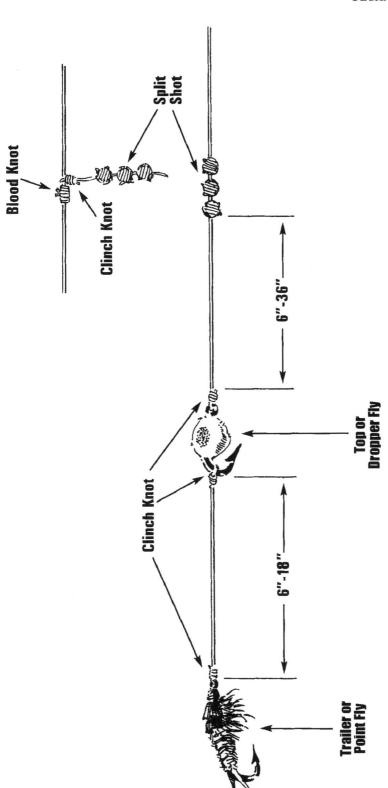

Figure 5.2 Tandem Fly Rig for Short-Line-Bottom-Bouncing Technique. *
*Note: Use of more than one hook is prohibited in NY. See regulations in Appendix B

"Chucking and Ducking" Technique

The "Chucking and Ducking" technique is a bottom-bouncing method popular in the Lake Michigan tributary rivers. Under certain conditions it has limited application in the Lake Erie tributaries as well. It is very effective in dead-drifting flies along the stream bottom in deep, fast runs that are fairly wide, have very specific steelhead holding areas or slots and are not easily approached by safe wading. It is also effective in higher run-off flows.

Conventional bottom bouncing with a long tapered leader and a tapered floating fly line (like a weight forward or even triangle taper) has its limits in deeper flows, particularly at longer distances. Invariably what happens with long casts is that a substantial part of the front taper of the fly line will make contact with the water when trying to penetrate a deep run or casting to reach a slot which is not easily waded to.

The floating taper section will tug and pull on the leader and fly to the point where even extensive mending does not prevent fly line interference with the drifting fly thus preventing a true drag-free drift along the stream bottom. The solution is to replace the tapered fly line with a thin diameter running line, a leader that has a very minimal, if any, taper and a substantial amount of weight, usually in the form of "slinkies".

The thin running line, available in both floating and intermediate densities, and level leader easily penetrate the deepest flows at long distances with very little interference on the drift. The use of heavy weight gets the fly down immediately, especially in faster currents.

The trick, or problem, is to fly cast this type of rig. A stiffer, faster fly rod is required to cast the heavy rig back and forth. The casting motion is hardly a smooth operation due to the thin, light weight running line which does very little to "load" the fly rod and allow a traditional back and forth casting motion. The forward cast is more like a "chuck" with the steelheader "ducking" to keep his head low to prevent being hit behind the head – hence the name.

Chucking and ducking is undoubtedly an effective technique under the right circumstances, but certainly takes away the fluid motion of fly casting. This technique also has the potential to cause arm and shoulder pain/soreness if done for long periods.

Right-Angle-Floating-Indicator Technique

Another short-line nymphing technique, which is both effective and controversial, is the right-angle-floating-indicator technique. Fly fishing purists may scoff at this approach, but it seems tailor-made for the ice water steelhead of late fall and winter. These sluggish fish seek slow current areas and hug current breaks along shale ledges and also hold in slow moving pools, eddies and tail-outs.

Catching them requires precise presentations with flawless drag-free drifts since the fish rarely move for a fly during this time of the year. Conventional short-line-bottom-bouncing can be very difficult in these conditions due to the lack of any substantial current to drift your fly properly. A floating indicator is also ideal for covering stream flows of shallow to moderate depth (2 to 5 feet) that have consistent bottom structure.

The right-angle-floating-indicator technique works well with longer leaders (versus bottom-bouncing) in the $10^{1/2}$ to 14 foot range and a buoyant floating indicator, such as a little corkie. A little corkie is a brightly painted styrofoam ball with a center hole that allows your leader to pass through. Inserting a tooth-pick into the corkie secures it to the leader. The water current speed will dictate the exact corkie size; 3/4, 5/8, 1/2 and 3/8-inch diameters seem to cover most situations. The corkie should be placed on the leader at the approximate depth of the water being fished.

Set the corkie on the leader a little deeper than you think the water is prior to your first cast. If it hesitates or stops on the drift shorten the corkie to fly distance until the float drifts without any hang-ups.

To keep the fly just above the stream bottom (especially in medium to faster flows), an amount of split-shot which varies according to current flow, is placed

Winter steelheader with a long fly rod reaching out into the ice water flows of 20-Mile Creek, PA. (Jack Hanrahan photo)

within 3 to 6 inches of an unweighted fly. This may seem too close at first, but if your float is correctly placed on the leader, bottom-hugging steelhead will only see the fly during the drift because the leader is vertical in the water, as shown in Figure 5.3 (below). If a weighted fly is used the split-shot can be moved farther up the leader.

The little corkie floats so well that it suspends the fly just above the bottom as it drifts downstream. This suspended fly creates a right angle in the leader, hence the name. As before, wade into position and pick a likely target zone. Your target zone will be much longer than in bottom-bouncing because you can achieve a much longer drift. Next, cast the fly line upstream of the target zone and immediately throw an upstream mend in the line to keep the float from getting ahead of the fly that is sinking to the bottom. (See Figure 5.4 on page 93).

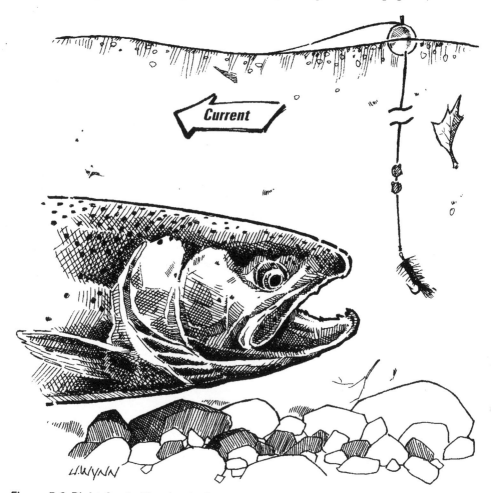

Figure 5.3 Right-Angle-Floating-Indicator Rig.

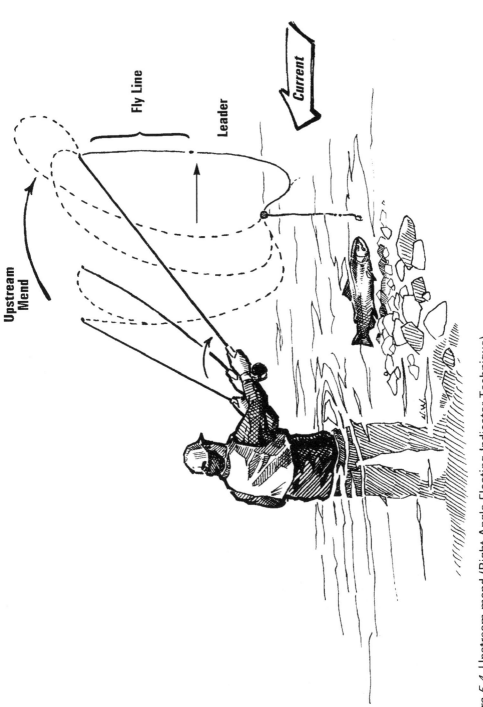

Figure 5.4 Upstream mend (Right-Angle-Floating-Indicator Technique).

At this point, in fast to medium currents, it is important to keep in mind that the surface current speed where the float is, is faster than the bottom current speed where the fly is. This effect is due to the friction of the streambed and is especially noticeable at mid-stream where the current is faster. It is also much more pronounced in deeper flows.

To compensate for this, a method developed by Canadian float fisherman called "checking" the float is used. Canadian float fisherman are able to achieve near perfect drag-free drifts for long distances using specially designed floats, free spool reels, monofilament line, long rods and line control techniques such as checking.

Checking involves intermittently stopping the floating indicator with the rod tip as it drifts through the target zone and keeping it slightly behind or inline vertically with the fly. This prevents the float from pulling the fly off the bottom and dragging it downstream in an unnatural manner (see Figure 5.5 on page 95).

Long fly rods are excellent tools for reaching out to check a float in current flows. By keeping the rod tip of these rods slightly behind and following the float as it drifts through the target zone, you are always in a position for checking as needed. More checking is required in faster currents particularly if the water flow is deep. By watching the speed of the float (and resulting hook-ups) you can determine the amount of checking necessary. In very slow currents, little or no checking is required.

A good indication of whether your fly is drifting properly through the target zone in this method is to watch the toothpick that is inserted in the little corkie. If the toothpick is in the upright position in relation to the water surface this means that the corkie and fly are roughly in alignment vertically. This will assure that the corkie is not "bossing" the fly by pulling it off the bottom and dragging it faster than the bottom current. If the toothpick is off-vertical and pointing downstream, you should check the corkie to get the fly drifting properly on the bottom. (See Figure 5.6 on page 96). It is to be noted that a large difference between the speed of the surface and bottom currents will require more shot usage (and a bigger float) to keep the fly down near the stream bottom.

Steelheader's Tip

Reading the surface water (by looking for changes in the water surface texture) will help you locate subsurface current breaks and potential steelhead holding areas.

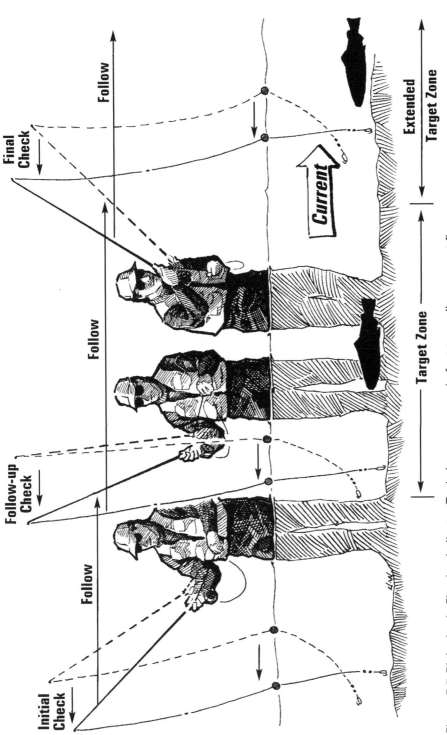

Figure 5.5 Right-Angle-Floating-Indicator-Technique sequence in fast to medium current flows. Slow current flows require little or no checking at all.

When drifting your fly through the target zone, try to keep only your leader in contact with the water to prevent your fly line from interfering with your float. Reach out and lift the fly line off the water, holding the rod tip high above your shoulders. Also, to extend the drift even longer, wade downstream tending to the float as it works its way down. Doing so can produce almost flawless, drag-free drifts of your fly just above the bottom, for very long distances.

An alternative setup in the right-angle-floating-indicator technique (RAFIT) would place the floating indicator on the leader at greater than the depth of the water. The split-shot is then placed 6-18 inches above the fly depending on the current flow. The faster the current, the closer the shot placement to the fly. This method works especially well with beginners since it requires fewer floating indicator adjustments, less mending and float checking as well as less split-shot usage. A smaller float can be used in this method since the float (really acting more like a strike indicator now) does not suspend the fly like in the RAFIT and is not influenced as much with surface currents.

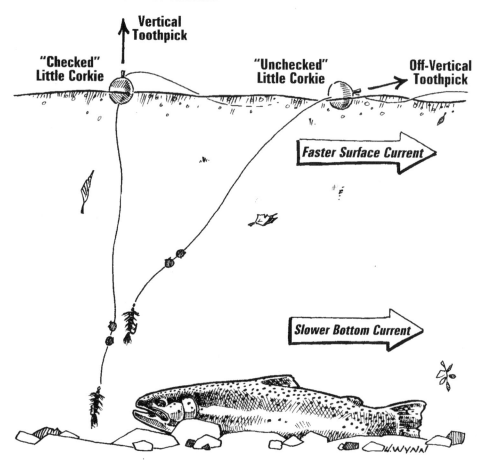

Figure 5.6 Little Corkie, split shot and fly position (checked and unchecked).

Because this setup is not a precise way of fishing (you are not fishing the exact depth of the water) you tend to lose contact with your fly and at times can miss strikes. You can also get more bottom snags with as well as unintentionally snagged fish.

A tandem fly rig is very effective in the right-angle-floating-indicator technique.* A productive setup would have an egg pattern, like a glo-ball or sucker spawn, attached to the end of the leader as the top or dropper fly. A smaller size point or trailer fly (like a bead-head nymph) is then tied below it with a 4-12 inch section of tippet. When the water is stained, keeping the flies close together in this rig will ensure that a steelhead will see both flies at the same time during the drift.

The floating indicator to fly distance (trailer fly) is set on the leader at approximately the depth of the water. Split-shot is normally placed 3 to 6 inches above the dropper fly in medium to fast flows. In faster flows an additional amount of shot can be placed between the tandem flies to keep the trailer fly down.

More often than not a steelhead will be attracted to the larger egg pattern, especially in stained water, but take the smaller trailer fly instead. Caution should be taken while attempting to unhook a steelhead with a tandem fly rig. You can easily hook yourself with the second fly if the fish suddenly thrashes about.

Nymphs like the hare's ear, prince, tellico, black stonefly or any caddis imitation work well as trailer flies especially when a metal bead is incorporated

An assortment of floating indicators along with nymphs and egg patterns.

Use of more than one hook is prohibited in NY. See regulations in Appendix B.

into the fly. During the low, ice-water flows of winter, steelhead will often locate in back eddies adjacent to pools and dams. Here current flows are directed upstream and can sometimes come to a complete stop, resulting in only a stationary suspension of your fly below the floating indicator. If this happens, try dragging your fly along the bottom by slowly moving the indicator with your rod tip in the direction of the current eddy. This can also be done when bottom-bouncing. This is not a snagging technique, but a gentle movement of the fly to mimic the force of the current.

Both bottom-bouncing and the right-angle-floating-indicator techniques are very precise methods of fly fishing. They require that the fly fisherman be keenly aware of the depth of the water being fished and fish location, as well as maintaining a tight line to feel the bottom and detect strikes. Combined with long fly rods, long leaders, small flies and minimal split-shot usage (often very little is required) these methods are very effective.

More on Floating Indicator Fishing

The challenge for the fly fisherman when using a floating indicator rig is to compensate for the effect of the faster surface current (versus the current near the stream bottom) on his floating indicator by slowing it down in some way. This is especially true when using the right-angle floating-indicator technique (described previously starting on page 90). Slowing the floating indicator down will ensure that the fly is drifting naturally on or near the stream bottom where the steelhead are.

Slowing the float indicator keeps the float from getting ahead of the fly, which can pull it off the bottom and make it move faster than the bottom current. As discussed earlier in this chapter this can be accomplished in a number of ways including the following: (1) by initially mending the line and leader upstream, (2) checking the float with the rod tip during the drift, (3) going to larger floating indicators to compensate for faster surface currents versus bottom currents and (4) adding more split-shot depending on the current flow and the size of the float used.

There is another approach to slowing the float down which eliminates or at least minimizes the amount of mending and checking necessary to get the proper fly drift. This involves placing the split-shot along the leader (between the float and the fly) at different locations and in various sizes to compensate for the surface and bottom current speeds. The Canadian float fishermen have perfected this concept in order to achieve the long, flawless drag-free drifts they are famous for.

In fast tributary flows placing the shot within 3 to 6 inches of the fly will get it down quickly through the fast surface currents (see Figure 5.6a on page 99). This shot placement is called "drop shot" or "down-weighting" and is very effective on the fast, high gradient tributaries of Lake Erie.

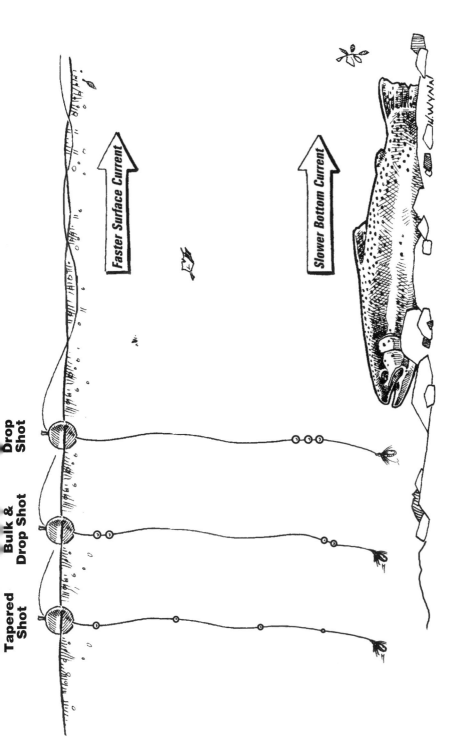

Figure 5.6a Shot placement options when using the Right-Angle-Floating-Indicator-Technique.

Not as much shot is actually needed near the fly to keep it on or near the bottom in the slower bottom currents, but more is needed near the float, where the faster surface currents are, to slow the float down and prevent it from interfering with the fly drifting near the bottom. Shot placement just below the float is called "bulk shot" and is also illustrated in Figure 5.6a. The bulk shot is heavier than the drop shot and is ideally placed within a few inches below the float.

In medium to slow current flows, all that is needed is to place the shot at or at some point below the half way point between the float and the fly since slower surface currents have a lesser effect on the float during these conditions. This shot placement can best be described as "backed-off" drop shot due to its placement further up the leader away from the fly. Some checking and mending may still be needed with this method.

Another more advanced approach is to stagger various size shot in different locations along the leader between the float and the fly. When bigger shot sizes are located near the float to slow it down and smaller sizes (in evenly spaced increments) are placed toward the fly it is called "tapering" the shot. This shot arrangement is illustrated in Figure 5.6a. Drop shot can also be arranged in a tapered manner depending on the current speed.

Soft shot is ideal to use when staggering shot because it is available in the smallest of sizes (often called "dust shot") for fine adjustments on the leader. Soft shot is usually sized using an English system with SSG, AAA, AB, BB, #1, #4, #6 and #8 the available size range (going from large to small sizes). For comparison purposes the Gremlin brand BB size is equivalent to the English BB size.

It is important to use enough shot on your leader in order to correctly "balance" the float size being used. This will ensure that the float is sensitive enough to detect fly and shot contact with the stream bottom, and more importantly, any subtle steelhead takes. Not enough shot makes a slack leader below the float and a subsequent loss of sensitivity to a strike.

What the fly fisherman is trying to do with all these shot placement arrange-ments (along with the other described adjustments) is to keep the float slightly behind or inline vertically with the fly as it is drifting downstream just above the bottom. When this is accomplished, a steelhead will ideally only see the fly drifting naturally toward it, with the tippet and any shot above or slightly behind the fly.

It is important to note that when a bigger or weighted fly is used (incorporating a heavier hook, bead head, metal ribbing, lead wraps, etc.) less shot is needed to get the fly down. Also, the shot can be moved further up the leader away from the fly which helps prevent spooking fish in clearer flows.

The number and size of shot actually used and placement on the leader depends on the float size used, current flows and depth as well as the fly being used. It is best learned on the tributary stream by experimentation, trial, and error. Typically the heaviest shot size needed is BB down to size #6.

Fly casting any rig with spaced shot arrangement and a float can be a recipe for disaster resulting in "bird's nests" and tangles. Certain adjustments can be made to minimize these occurrences.

First, use a heavier, stiffer mono for the tippet section between the float and fly. Going up to a stiffer 2X or 3X size may reduce your hook-up rate but will avoid a lot of headaches.

Next, when using a drop shot/bulk shot system keep the distance between the heavier bulk shot and the smaller drop shot twice the distance from the drop shot to the fly (the bottom fly in a tandem rig). If the two were equidistant, you'd have a bola effect when casting with annoying and time-wasting tangles the result.

Finally, it is important to cast these rigs with a much more open casting loop and a slower fly casting motion. Slower casting allows the back cast to straighten out completely before starting the forward casting stroke reducing possible tangles. Using a soft, slower action fly rod (versus a stiffer blank) allows for a smoother, less jerky operation when casting split-shot which helps to minimize tangles.

Traditional Fly Fishing Techniques

In recent years swinging wet flies such as spey flies and soft hackles (and even dry flies), in the traditional manner downstream, is becoming more popular on many of the bigger Lake Erie tributaries such as the Grand Rivers in Ohio and Ontario and the Cattaraugus Creek in New York. This popularity is due both to the effectiveness of this technique and an appreciation of the traditional methods of fly fishing for Atlantic salmon and steelhead as done in the Canadian Provinces and the Pacific Northwest.

Traditional swinging fly techniques are best accomplished with stiffer, faster fly rod blanks primarily for lifting and mending floating lines, heavy sink tip lines and sinking leaders. One-handed fly rods up to 10 feet long, in 7 and 8 fly line weights, have the sufficient lengths necessary for the line, leader and fly control on the downstream swing. Traditional double-handed rods or spey rods, in 11-14 foot lengths, have great application in covering a lot of water easily on some of the big Lake Erie tributaries.

The basic downstream swinging technique can use various types of fly lines, leaders and weight systems depending on how you want to present the fly (surface or subsurface) as it swings downstream. These can include: 1.) A floating line and leader for swinging or "skating" dry flies. 2.) A floating line and leader for swinging lightly dressed wet flies just under the surface which has traditionally been called "greased-lining." 3.) A floating line with split-shot added to the butt of the leader for faster flows. 4.) A floating line with a sinking leader. 5.) A floating line in combination with a leader that incorporates a mini-tip or head. 6.) A standard sink-tip line.

Sink-tip lines, sinking leaders and mini-lead heads of various sink rates can be used to get flies down at or near the stream bottom, depending on the current speed and water depth. Traditionally split-shot is not used in the wet fly swinging technique. Weighting systems are well up from the fly to keep from possibly spooking and snagging fish. Leaders used are relatively short, with simple 3-6 feet leaders for sink tip lines and 9 feet leaders for floating lines. Longer leaders (up to 12 feet) are used with lightly dressed wet flies and in dry fly swinging or skating techniques.

There are many variations to the wet fly swinging technique. An effective wet fly swinging technique for steelhead (see Figure 5.7 on page 103) begins by starting at the head of a pool and casting across and slightly downstream. To get the fly to begin sinking quickly, throw an initial upstream mend (flipping the line upstream). At this point it is important to keep your fly line relatively straight as it drifts downstream by making more upstream mends with the fly line. This will prevent a downstream belly from forming in the line and also reduce the "swimming" speed of the fly as it swings down-and-across likely steelhead lies. As the fly moves down-

Swinging flies on the lower Grand River, Ontario for fall steelhead.
(John Valk photo)

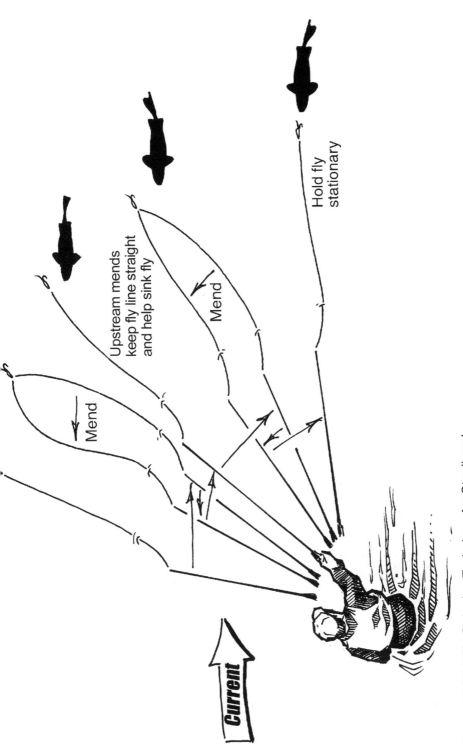

Upstream mends keep fly line straight and help sink fly

Mend

Mend

Hold fly stationary

Current

Figure 5.7 Wet Fly Swinging Technique for Steelhead.

Mike Prairie with fresh fall hen that took a "waking" orange Bomber on Cattaraugus Creek. (Mike Prairie photo)

stream, allow the fly line to lead your rod tip in that direction, all the while maintaining tension on the fly line.

Changing the tension on the fly line, by line mending and rod control, can increase or decrease the swimming speed of the fly as well as get the fly to sink shallower or deeper. Follow-up upstream mends have the effect of putting slack in the fly line (reducing tension) and making the fly not only go slower but deeper. Lifting the fly line straight up with your rod tip and then letting the line drop will also have the same effect.

The speed of a fly during the swing can be easily slowed or speeded up by rod control. In faster currents it is important to slow the fly down so the steelhead has not only enough time to see it but also to respond to it. By pointing the tip of the rod at a position behind the fly as it is swinging downstream you can slow the fly down. This rod position will keep the fly under a more moderate tension (and speed) in these fast currents.

In the slow currents of pool tail-outs, the fly must at times be forcefully led with the rod (through the swing) to keep the fly moving and prevent it from sinking too fast. Multiple downstream mends of the fly line are also helpful in increasing the swimming speed of a fly across slower currents.

To methodically cover a pool after you have made your initial swing with the fly, lengthen your subsequent casts in increments of a foot or so until you have satisfactory covered a desired section of water. Next, take a few steps downstream and begin the entire sequence again.

In warmer water conditions (mid 40's and higher), steelhead are more aggressive and will move actively to the sides or upward to take a swinging fly. As the water temperatures get colder (low 40's and upper 30's) they tend to stay put on the bottom where you want to target your swinging fly. At the end of the swing hold the fly stationary for a few seconds. Steelhead will often follow a fly on the swing and take it just after it stops or after it is dangled for awhile.

The downstream swinging or skating technique, with waking dry flies such as bombers or stimulators, is without question the most exciting way to hook a steelhead. In this technique you are trying to create a disturbance or wake on the surface of the water that will trigger a natural feeding response in the steelhead. The technique begins by initially casting slightly downstream and slowly skating the fly sideways on its downstream drift. The more upstream line mending that is done as the fly swings downstream, the slower the fly will go. Controlling the lateral speed of the fly is important since going too fast can spook fish and doesn't mimic the natural movement of insects. Varying the speed of the fly will also make the presentation more life-like.

Using a riffle-hitch connection to the fly can increase the waking effect of the dry fly in this technique. This second connection is made after the fly is initially tied to the tippet by making two half hitches (with the tippet) behind the tippet/fly knot. The half hitches can be placed either to the side of the fly or underneath it, which has the added effect of helping the fly ride on the surface.

On some of the Ontario tributaries, like the Grand River and it's feeder Whiteman's Creek, waking dry flies is very effective in imitating the movement of emerging and adult caddis on the water surface (see southern Ontario tributaries in Chapter 10).

The key factors to consider when using a traditional downstream swinging technique effectively are water temperatures and water types, as well as fishing pressure. In the Lake Erie region steelhead respond better to a swinging wet fly in

Steelheader's Tip

When bottom-bouncing flies, periodically lift the rod tip to "hop" the fly. This will keep the fly moving and cut down on hang-ups and snags on the stream bottom.

Another fall chromer on the "Cat" that took a
Ken's Beady Zonker on a traditional downstream swing

water temperatures above 40 degrees F. and above 48 degrees F. for dry flies. This means the fall months of September, October and November and the spring months of April, May and June (Ontario) are the best times. Below 40 degrees F., dead-drift techniques become the mainstay for catching ice water steelhead that are in a pre-spawn, holding pattern.

Steelhead also take swung flies much more actively in water which has not been disturbed heavily by fishing activity. This means that the traditionalist fly fisherman may have to hike to remote areas of tributaries to find undisturbed steelhead.

Swinging a fly downstream (especially subsurface) also requires a special type of water type to be consistently effective. Wide gravel runs and long pools, with large tail-outs, that have even depths (3-6 feet) and moderate flows are ideal. In this type of water a fly can be effectively fished down-and-across in a precise and methodical manner in front of holding steelhead. The problem is that most Lake Erie tributaries do not have these characteristics, but are more like shallow trout streams with narrow, fast runs, short pools and uneven shale streambeds that have sharp ledges and chutes. This type of water (which has been described by some as "short drift" water) is most effectively fished with a short-line nymphing technique such as either bottom-bouncing or the right-angle-floating-indicator technique.

Spring Steelhead Techniques and Strategies

A good strategy when fly fishing the Erie tributaries in the spring is to concentrate on the upper halves of these streams or their feeders. The majority of spring steelhead will be found here because of the presence of ideal spawning riffles. Spawning activity can also occur very close to the lake in some of the smaller tributaries.

If a tributary has an impassable upstream barrier like a dam or waterfall, spring steelhead will stack up below it. These areas will hold a concentration of pre-spawn, spawning and spawned-out steelhead.

Usually spring steelhead fly fishing requires locating spawning areas. Ideal spawning areas are riffles that are 1 to 4 feet deep which contain dark colored gravel bottoms. Next to these areas are usually deeper runs, pockets, or pools that harbor pre-spawn fish and spawning fish that have been scared off their beds.

Prior to spawning, a female steelhead moves into a spawning area and digs out a redd. She does this by turning on her side and making powerful upsweeps of her tail in the gravel. The current washes away loose gravel, forming a saucer-shaped hole that will hold the eggs. Males are attracted by this digging activity and begin competing for spawning rights, with the largest and most heavily kyped males winning out.

Spawning female steelhead digging out a redd in a spawning riffle.
Note dark colored male below her.

They use their superior power and large kypes (hooked lower jaws) to drive inferior males from the redd. After the female drops her eggs, about 20 percent of what she is carrying, the dominant male fertilizes them.

Sometimes one, or possibly two, sub-dominant males will also participate. The female will then move immediately upstream to begin making another redd. The displaced gravel from this redd covers the previously fertilized eggs downstream. The female continues this process until she is spawned out.

When you are fly fishing a spawning bed there are several things to keep in mind. If you don't notice any spawning activity on the bed itself, fish the adjacent deep-holding areas. These areas often hold pre-spawn or spooked spawning steelhead.

Fishing on the redds has a simple strategy. Fish for the males or "bucks". They are easy to distinguish from the females, or "hens," because they are almost black, while the females are lighter in color and tend to blend in with the stream bottom and current flow. If you catch the female first, the males will quickly scatter. These aggressive males are very territorial. They are not actually feeding, but they will chase flies to dominate the redd.

Before fishing, position yourself slightly upstream and to the side of the redd. If the water is less than 2 feet deep you have to be concerned about the fish seeing you. Avoid detection by keeping a low profile by crouching, or if necessary, getting on your knees. Locating yourself next to the redd with brush and trees to your back and wearing drab clothing can also help conceal your presence.

Next, cast your fly far enough above the redd so that it can reach stream bottom as it drifts through the redd. Mend your line to maintain a dead drift and keep a tight line so you are able to quickly set the hook. When a male takes your fly he will usually only snap at it, then quickly spit it out. So watch your fly carefully as it drifts through the redd, and set the hook at the appropriate time. If water visibility is good, you should be able to target a specific male. If you do hook a female, you will notice that their takes are much more deliberate.

Steelheader's Tip

Look for dark areas in shallow runs and pocket water. Steelhead often hide there, using their grayish-black backs as concealment.

Greg Senyo with a January buck steelhead that was caught on a Blue Wiggle Stone (Greg Senyo photo).

A tandem fly rig (see Figure 5.2 on page 89) of a large streamer or wooly bugger (size 4 or 6) as the trailer fly, with a smaller egg pattern or nymph as the top fly, works well when drifted over a redd.* Spawning steelhead can become intimidated by the larger fly and will move away from it (usually toward you) as it is drifting downstream. When it makes this move it will quickly encounter the egg pattern or nymph which is drifting behind the larger fly. This smaller fly is moving toward a more inside position (where the steelhead has moved) and is often taken by the steelhead.

Drifting two smaller tandem flies over the redds is also very effective especially when spawning steelhead seem to be moving constantly on the redds. If a moving steelhead doesn't intercept the trailer fly he will more than likely encounter the top fly as it drifts or swings over another area of the redd. To ensure that the steelhead sees at least one of these flies adjust the distance between the two flies on the leader to correspond with the approximate side to side movement of the fish.

Use of more than one hook is prohibited in NY. See regulations in Appendix B.

Ken Seremet connected with a steelhead on lower Elk Creek, PA.

Another technique is to stand directly upstream of the redd, without spooking the fish, and drop the fly right down onto the noses of the steelhead. You can sweep the fly back and forth in front of the fish or just hold it stationary. Amazingly, this technique can induce some tremendous strikes from spawning steelhead (especially males).

In off-color flows it will be difficult to see the fish on their spawning beds. This is usually the result of spring run-off that causes high, turbid water, or a spawning bed with a dark bottom. You can often spot the brighter females, as they turn on their sides and shake their tails. This action gives off flashes of silver in clear water and gold in murky water. Wearing polarized sunglasses on bright days is a tremendous help in seeing these flashes. Mentally mark this spot in the stream and fish to areas just downstream where the males will be holding.

Steelheader's Tip

Drag-free drifts are best accomplished by wading into position and reaching out with your fly rod to mend and control your leader/fly line. In other words, use your "legs and arms" (versus fly casting at long distances) to achieve drag-free drifts.

Steelhead comes to the net on the Grand River, OH. (Jerry Darkes photo)

Fishing steelhead spawning beds has its proponents and detractors. In the Pacific Northwest, this practice is strongly discouraged on rivers with wild steelhead because of concern that it is very detrimental to successful spawning. On the other hand Michigan steelheaders, however, seem to have no problem with fishing on the beds, even though 50% of their fish are known to be naturally reproduced.

Most of southern Lake Erie's tributaries support steelhead runs which are based on stocking programs, not natural reproduction. So fishing on spawning beds is not harmful to the fishery. On tributaries like the Cattaraugus Creek in New York, however, a significant amount of natural reproduction is developing. Here it makes sense to stay away from the spawning beds. This will protect what someday could be a self-sustaining fishery.

The Ontario tributaries on the northern shore of Lake Erie support steelhead runs that have been estimated by the Ontario Ministry of Natural Resources to be 90% wild fish. In order to protect this wild steelhead fishery most of Ontario's tributaries are closed during the peak-spawning season. The normal open season for southern Ontario tributaries is Apr. 29 to Sept. 30 with an extended season on most of the major tributaries from Oct. 1 to Dec. 31.

Hooking, Playing and Landing a Steelhead

Hooking a steelhead successfully depends on the technique and equipment being used. When using a high-stick-nymphing technique with a long, soft action fly rod it is necessary to set the hook with a quick snap of the wrist and a forceful raising of the fly rod, upward and to the side. Ideally you want to do this in the downstream direction to avoid pulling the hook out of the steelhead's mouth. This aggressive hook set is necessary because of the give and flex in a long, soft action fly rod blank.

The takes when dead-drift nymphing are usually very subtle and soft, and difficult to detect at times, especially in cold water flows. The beginner is best advised to react and lift up on anything that may seem to be a strike, like any hesitation, stop, or movement (upstream or downstream) of his indicator. At times this could merely indicate fly/split-shot contact with the stream bottom, but it is not worth a chance of missing a real "take." It is also important not to hesitate on the strike when nymphing since a steelhead will often quickly spit out a dead-drifted fly after he senses it is not the real thing.

When bottom-bouncing without an indicator, strike detection is a combination of both watching the fly line/butt of the leader and feeling in the rod and fly line for any stops or bumps that may indicate a strike. Eventually with experience, the nymphing steelheader will develop a sort of instinctive feel or "sixth sense" for strike detection and will set the hook without any seemingly real reason.

Cattaraugus Creek, NY below Gowanda.

When swinging wet flies downstream in the traditional manner the takes are often explosive, especially in the warm tributary flows of fall and spring. Heavy tippets can be used in this technique, since the steelhead normally never sees the tippet. After feeling the strike, the fly fisherman simply raises the rod up and to the side and the steelhead will essentially hook himself. It is usually a very solid hook-up in the corner of the steelhead's mouth, particularly if the steelhead takes the fly from the side. The combination of heavy tippet and solid hook-set results in very few fish lost in this method versus nymphing techniques.

When waking or skating dry flies downstream for steelhead, it is imperative to wait after a steelhead takes the fly on the surface. Don't strike immediately when you see the steelhead take the fly as you're taught when dead-drifting dry flies upstream for trout because invariably you will pull it out of the fish's mouth.

Waiting allows the steelhead to turn down with the fly in his mouth and enables the fly fisherman to set the hook after he feels tension or a pull in his line. Striking to the side will also help to hook the steelhead in the side of the mouth in this technique.

Sharp hooks with offset points and medium sized barbs allow for good hook penetration during hook-sets and keep hard fighting steelhead from throwing a hook. Chapter 7 discusses hook selection in more detail.

Once hooked, fall and spring steelhead often go ballistic and accelerate on a drag screaming run with a few cartwheels thrown in for good measure! To absorb these surges keep your fly rod high and immediately reel any slack onto the reel. The guides call this "getting the fish on the reel." Use the drag of the reel, setting it light enough to prevent your tippet from breaking but heavy enough to put steady pressure on the fish and slow the fish down initially.

Early in the fight, let the steelhead take out line on its runs and surges while maintaining a tight line with light to moderate pressure. Eventually the steelhead will begin to settle down. This is a signal to begin "working" the fish by applying heavy pressure. Pull the rod upward toward you and reel line in as you move the

Steelheader's Tip

Constantly fine tune fly drift (depending on water conditions) by adjusting the number of split shot used, split shot to fly distance, floating indicator to fly distance, tippet size and floating indicator size as needed. These slight changes can result in more hook-ups.

Steelheader's Tip

When you locate a good concentration of steelhead, your better off not leaving it to find "better" water. Usually, you will never find it that day.

rod down towards the fish. This is called "pumping" the fish. It is possible to reel in a steelhead using this technique, but it is very time consuming because of the size of these fish and their fighting ability. Also, fighting a steelhead in this fashion can exhaust a steelhead even to the point of death.

To more effectively work a fish, alternately turn your rod from side to side, dropping it parallel to the stream, while continuing to pump the rod. This side position of the rod will throw a steelhead off balance and cuts in half the time it takes to reel him in, and the fish will also be in much better condition upon release.

If after hooking a steelhead, it moves either downstream or upstream a great distance, it is advisable to follow the fish to avoid excessive fly line getting into the water. The more fly line in the water (especially in fast current flows) the more additional pull or drag you will have to fight. Eventually, try to move the steelhead into slower water where the current effects are minimized.

When using heavy tippet you have the option of controlling a running steelhead by using the bow created in your fly line by the force of the current. The most common scenario where this tactic is effective is when a steelhead runs downstream in a high, fast current flow and you are unable to chase it down-stream due to the deep water or an obstacle. By putting slack in your fly line and allowing it to bow downstream, you apply downstream pressure to the fish which can cause the steelhead to move back upstream toward you.

If the steelhead suddenly jumps out of the water, move your rod quickly and momentarily downward to create slack line and prevent the steelhead's sudden movements from snapping your tippet. Do not eliminate all tension, though, since this could allow the fish to throw the hook. When a fish becomes hung up around a log or snag, giving the fish slack line may be your best chance of freeing it. Slack line reduces pressure on the fish and may encourage the fish to swim out of the obstruction. With luck the fish will exit the way it entered freeing the line.

When playing a steelhead, always be aggressive. Keep steady pressure on the fish when possible and never give it the opportunity to rest. If you allow the fish to rest, it will invariably give him a second wind which could lead to a break-off or a thrown hook.

When a steelhead is close enough to be netted, bring your rod up to the vertical position. In this upright position, your rod will absorb any unexpected surges or runs. These can occur when a steelhead rubs his belly on the stream gravel or sees your net.

When you can turn the fish on it's side and move its head toward the surface, it is a signal that the fish is spent or tired and ready to be netted. Keep the net stationary in the water and guide the steelhead into the net. Use a large steelhead-size net and net the fish head first. Avoid jabbing the net at the steelhead (especially if it is still active). This sudden movement could knock the hook out of the fish's mouth or cause it to bolt suddenly.

If you don't have a net, you have the option of either beaching or tailing the steelhead. Beaching a steelhead requires a stout tippet and a shallow area of water near the shoreline that also has a relatively even bottom. By applying steady side-to-side pressure on the fish and gradually backing away from the shoreline, a spent steelhead can be pulled up onto the beach.

Tailing is the preferred method of landing larger Atlantic salmon (over 7 pounds) in many of the provinces of Canada. This method is less physically harmful than netting or beaching a fish and can also be applied to larger Lake Erie steelhead. It works well along deep banks when no net is available. Simply approach the spent steelhead with the tail pointed toward you and slowly reach down and grab below the tail with the thumb on top of the fish's rear body. The steelhead will quickly become immobilized as you lift it out of the water.

Using a wool glove insures a good grip when tailing a fish. Midstream makes a product called the Landing Hand (with retractor) which is a knotless mesh mitten that allows an angler to tail and hold a fish firmly with minimum loss of fish scales and protective slime.

Mint-silver, hen steelhead caught during a
November "run" on Elk Creek, PA.

Equipment

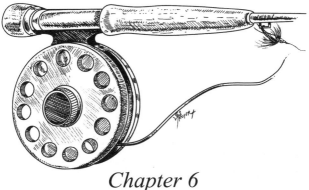

Chapter 6
Fly Rods

Experienced Lake Erie steelhead fly fishermen usually use fly rods over 9 feet in length in order to achieve the drag-free drifts that are often required to catch Lake Erie steelhead. These long fly rods allow for tremendous control when mending and manipulating your fly line and leader in the runs, pools and pocket water areas of a typical Erie tributary. Their long lengths provide a great advantage when steering fly line and long leaders around ice flows and boulders as well as when reaching over logs or iced-in shorelines. They also have soft, progressive actions that can help to protect light tippets when fighting large steelhead.

A custom-made fly rod built with a semi-noodle rod spinning blank such as St. Croix's $10^{1/2}$ foot Wild River blank, rated for 2-6 pound test line, performs very well for catching Lake Erie steelhead. The term semi-noodle probably sounds foreign to most fly fishermen and can be best defined by first understanding what a noodle rod blank is.

A true noodle rod blank has a soft, slow action and is primarily used by spin fishermen or noodle-rodders. It is manufactured in lengths up to 14 feet and it has a completely progressive action (parabolic). Parabolic means it bends from tip to butt in what noodle-rodders call the "big C." A noodle rod is ideal for shock absorption and extreme light lining (1-4 pound test line). By maintaining steady pressure when fighting a fish, this rod can easily play a big fish on light monofilament line. This can be a time consuming process, though, because of the minimal amount of pressure it can apply to a fish.

A fly rod made from a semi-noodle blank (they are presently custom made only) is not a true parabolic rod. A semi-noodle blank only flexes 75 percent of the way below the rod tip when fighting a fish. This soft rod is ideal for the steelhead fly fisher because it can handle playing large steelhead on tippets as light as 2 pound test, but at the same time apply substantial pressure to a fish. This reduces total fighting time and avoids overplaying the fish.

Playing a steelhead with custom made 10$^{1/2}$ foot fly rod on Conneaut Creek, OH.

A semi-noodle fly rod also casts a fly line relatively well because of its stiffer butt section. The St. Croix Wild River blank casts fly lines up to 5 or 6 line weights easily if you slow your casting motion down a bit and use a single-haul to increase fly line speed. It also casts split shot and floating indicators much more smoothly than most standard fly rod blanks. Being custom made, it can be fitted with an extended butt section for greater leverage for playing fish and oversized tip top and guides to prevent guide freeze-up in the winter.

If you choose a production fly rod instead of a custom built rod, look for a rod 9 feet or longer in a medium to medium-fast action. This rod is especially well suited for buffering steelhead runs and surges due to its lower modulus graphite blank, which is softer and has a slower action.

Some good production fly rod choices include the Orvis TLS (10-foot, 7-weight), the Redington Red Fly (9$^{1/2}$ and 10-foot, 6/7-weights) and Wayfarer (10-foot, 7-weight, 5 piece), the St. Croix Avid (9$^{1/2}$-foot, 7-weight), the Scott SAS Series (10-foot, 6 and 7-weight, 3 piece), the Diamondback All American (10-foot, 6/7-weight), the Sage VPS (9$^{1/2}$-foot, 6-weight), the Quarrow (10-foot, 6 and 7-weight) and the Winston WT (9$^{1/2}$-foot, 6-weight).

Scott and Thomas & Thomas offer light double-handed fly rods, which are good crossover rods that have application for both high-stick-nymphing and traditional fly swinging techniques on bigger water. Scott's rod is an ARC series 11-foot 9-inch 6-weight (4 piece) while the Thomas & Thomas is a double-handed 11-foot 7-weight (3 piece). Redington has two crossover rods in their Red Fly series that also make great nymphing rods. They include a 10$^{1/2}$-foot, 6/7-weight and an 11-foot 3-inch, 6 weight.

Pacific Bay's fly rods are also a good choice but are only available in fly rod blanks. Pacific Bay makes a 10-foot medium action, Tradition series blank in both 6 and 7 line weights and also a $10^{1/2}$-foot medium-fast action, Professional series blank (which is actually a spinning blank) which casts a 6 or 7 weight line well.

Production made western steelhead and Alaskan salmon fly rods (typically a 9-foot length for an 8 or 9-weight line) have a standard design that has limited application on the Lake Erie tributaries. These rods are typically made of high modulus graphite and have fast, stiff actions that flex only in the upper 1/4 to 1/3 of the blank.

They are designed to "punch out" 70 feet of fly line against the wind, not play big fish on light tippets. They are also too short for maximum line mending and control, which is critical for drag conscious steelhead. In addition, 8-weight fly rods (and bigger) can be a handicap when trying to achieve drag-free drifts with small flies and light tippets. This is due to the weight of the heavier fly lines that are matched with these rods. Even with constant line mending and control these heavy lines will interfere with a natural drag-free drift.

If you choose to use a stiffer, standard fly rod for Lake Erie steelhead, there is a simple way to help buffer your tippet during hook sets and sudden steelhead surges. Add 6 inches of Rio's Shock Gum leader material to the butt section of the leader. This material has a 100% stretch characteristic with the 9 lb. trout size ideal for Lake Erie steelhead. During the ice water flows of winter steelheading, shock leader material can also prevent brittle tippets from breaking prematurely.

While long, soft-action fly rods are ideal for their big fish playing ability on light tippets and achieving drag-free drifts, there are some scenarios where a standard fly rod design will perform better. For example, in extremely high, turbid flows, where bigger

Master rod builder Terry Palmer putting finishing touches on a custom Great Lakes fly rod.

flies and heavier tippet and split-shot are required, a fast high-modulus fly rod is more efficient at "chucking" large amounts of lead than a slow action fly rod. Stiffer fly rod blanks are also ideal for fly casting and mending when doing traditional downstream wet and dry fly swinging techniques (see Chapter 5).

A shorter, stiffer fly rod ($9^{1/2}$ foot or less) is also useful when steelhead move onto their spawning beds in the spring and become very territorial, aggressive and not easily spooked. This type of rod allows for faster up and down casting in close proximity to the beds while visually targeting the fish. It also handles very well the bigger flies, shorter leaders and heavier tippets that are normally used when fishing the spawning beds.

Finally, short fly rods are much more manageable than long fly rods in the extremely small, brush-lined tributaries of Lake Erie, such as Raccoon Creek in Pennsylvania and the upper reaches of some of the larger tributaries. This is also true when strictly fly fishing small pockets and narrow chutes where a short fly rod and leader would be advantageous. These short rods (whether custom or production made) should still have softer, progressive actions to protect light tippets from the surges and runs of big fish.

Fly Lines

Short-line nymphing techniques (whether bottom-bouncing or the right-angle-floating-indicator technique) can effectively be performed with a floating, triangle-taper fly line such as the Royal Wulff Products Triangle Taper fly line. Figure 6.0 (see page 121) shows the profile of a triangle taper and how it compares to other fly line tapers.

A floating triangle-taper combines the delicacy of a double-taper with the power of a weight-forward. It is especially an ideal choice for bottom-bouncing because the heavy taper of the fly line is well away from the water, which minimizes interference with fly drift, but at the same time, it can turn over split-shot easily. Double-taper fly lines can produce very delicate drifts, but do not have the power to turn over large flies, heavy split-shot or floating indicators. Weight-forward lines have plenty of power, but their heavy tapers near the butt of the leader hinder a drag-free drift. A floating triangle-taper line can also be used for the right-angle-floating-indicator-technique.

You can easily switch from the right-angle-floating-indicator technique to bottom-bouncing by making the floating indicator easier to remove from the leader. Split a little corkie on one side with a razor blade and insert two toothpicks (top and bottom) to hold it in place on the leader. This allows you to change techniques without removing the fly and split shot. This is handy when switching techniques between fast runs and slow pool tail-outs.

Running lines, which were originally designed to be attached to sinking

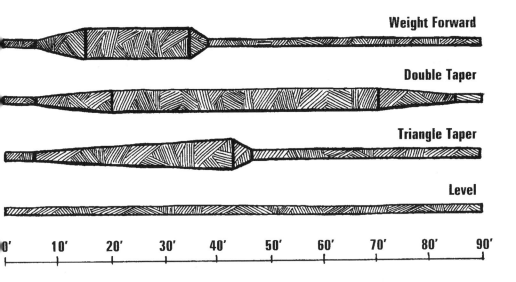

Figure 6.0 Fly Line Tapers.

shooting heads, have some useful application on the Lake Erie tributaries. These lines are available in both floating and intermediate density types, have level tapers and are available in diameters of .024 to .031 inches.

During winter tributary flows, when 90% of the steelhead are holding in tailouts and eddies, a floating running line can be used instead of a floating tapered fly line since you are likely to use floating indicators all day. This line produces little interference (drag) on the float, even at long distances.

Running lines can also be used to bottom-bounce wide, deep runs and pools, which have very specific steelhead holding areas or slots, and are not easily reached by safe wading. (See Chucking and Ducking discussion in Chapter 5). AirFlo's PolyShoot is a low stretch, low memory, excellent shooting running line that comes in an intermediate density (1.5 inches/sec.) and a thin diameter of .024 inches. It's low stretch core provides excellent strike detection and hooking ability while its slim profile and intermediate sink rate help it "cut" through the water.

Sink tip lines, sinking leaders and mini-tips or heads are very useful, when doing traditional wet fly swinging techniques (see Chapter 5) on both large Lake Erie tributaries such as the Cattaraugus Creek in New York and mid-size tributaries like Elk Creek in Pennsylvania. These sinking systems come in a variety of sink rates to match the desired depth, current flows and size of the water being fished.

The Teeny Nymph Company Tip Taper line is a 22-foot, density compensated sink tip line that is ideal for bigger water and faster flows. The front part of the tip is more heavily weighted, allowing it drop faster (with minimal line drag) along ledges, cut banks and into deep holes. The Teeny Mini-Tip line is a 5-foot sink tip

Jerry Darkes enjoying some spring steelheading on the Rocky River, OH. (Jerry Darkes photo)

which is easy to mend and doesn't get caught as much (versus longer sink tips) on rocky and uneven streambeds. This line is very effective on smaller water and more moderate flows.

Fly line companies like Rio, Airflo and Orvis now offer sink tip lines with interchangeable tips (or heads) of different densities that give the steelheader convenient versatility in depth control. An important feature of these systems are stiff loop connections that make a "non-hinging" connection between the tips and main fly line. Rio's VersiTip system comes with a floating, weight-forward Rio Wind Cutter fly line and four 15-foot tips that have a tapered design for easier turnover. It includes a floating, an intermediate, a type 3 (3 inch-per-second), and a type 4 (6-7 inch-per-second) tip. The type 3 and 4 tips are also density compensated to allow the tip to sink first.

A very popular way to swing wet flies on the Lake Erie tributaries has been to use sinking leaders and floating fly lines. This system allows for a very precise and natural presentation to steelhead holding in specific slots in pools and runs. Rio and Airflo both make sinking leaders with tungsten in a variety of densities and lengths. A good starting selection for the steelheader (in a variety of sink rates) would be an Airflo Poly leader in 5 and 10-foot lengths and a Rio Powerflex leader in 7 and 12-foot lengths.

Making your own mini-tips or heads of various lengths and sink rates allows for very precise depth control for the steelheader on the specific water that he is accustomed to fishing. Mini-tips made in the 2 to 10-foot range will cover most fishing conditions. Mini-tips are commonly made from fast sinking shooting heads which come in long 30-foot lengths like Scientific Angler's Deep Water Express, Rio's Tungsten T-14 or LC-13 lead core line. LC-13 has a braided lead core that is coated with a plastic that sinks very quickly due to its thin diameter and weight (13 grains per foot). Cortland produces a very thin (nylon braid cased) solid lead core trolling line called Kerplunk that is also ideal for making mini-tips.

By installing braided loop connectors at both ends of these custom made mini-tips, they can quickly be connected or removed from a fly line or monofilament leader. Mini-tips are usually placed at either directly between the end of a floating fly line (which also has an attached loop connector) and the butt of the leader or directly behind the tippet section of the leader.

Integrated surgeon loops can easily be made at either end of a mini-tip using Cortland's Kerplunk trolling line. First remove a few inches of the interior lead core from each end of the cut tip section (by pulling the nylon braid down and cutting the lead wire) and then use the remaining hollow nylon braid to tie the surgeon loops.

Cortland also offers a convenient Mini-Head Kit that includes 12 feet of lead core fly line and several loop connectors for assembling mini-tips in different lengths. These kits are available in 3, 6 and 9 inch-per-second sink rates.

In warm water conditions (mid 40's and higher) steelhead will at times actively move up in the water column to take a swinging fly. Here, floating fly lines in a weight forward taper design are ideal for presenting a swinging fly both subsurface and on the surface. The new specialty floating steelhead tapers incorporate an extended rear taper or "long belly" taper design which allows for easier line control and mending when swinging flies downstream. This taper is especially helpful when fishing flies at longer distances on really big water.

Leaders

Leader designs for both the short-line-bottom-bouncing and right-angle-floating-indicator techniques are pretty simple (See Figures 6.1a and 6.1b on pages 124 and 125). The idea is to initially build the butt and middle sections of the leader with a stiff monofilament or mono, such as Maxima Chameleon, in a simple taper design. This makes the leader turn over split shot and floating indicators rather easily.

The leader is then finished off with a section of flexible tippet material, such as Maxima Ultra Green, Orvis Super Strong, Rio Power Flex and Gamma Technologies Frog Hair. Orvis Super Strong, Rio Power Flex and Gamma Technologies Frog Hair are smaller in diameter and more flexible than Maxima Ultra Green, but less abrasion resistant. Using a section of Sunset Amnesia mono filament running line in the butt section is especially helpful when bottom-bouncing. This fluorescent red mono acts as a strike indicator making it easier to detect bottom contact and strikes.

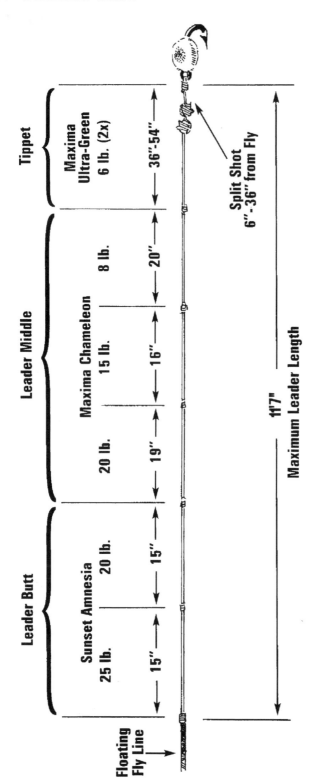

Figure 6.1a Leader Formula for Short-Line-Bottom-Bouncing Technique.*

*Note: This leader works well for a 10½ foot fly rod. For shorter fly rods, a shorter leader will function better. Subtract the rod length difference from the length of the leader (middle and tippet sections) to get the proper leader length for the rod used. For example, a 9½ foot fly rod requires 1 foot to be subtracted from the leader length.

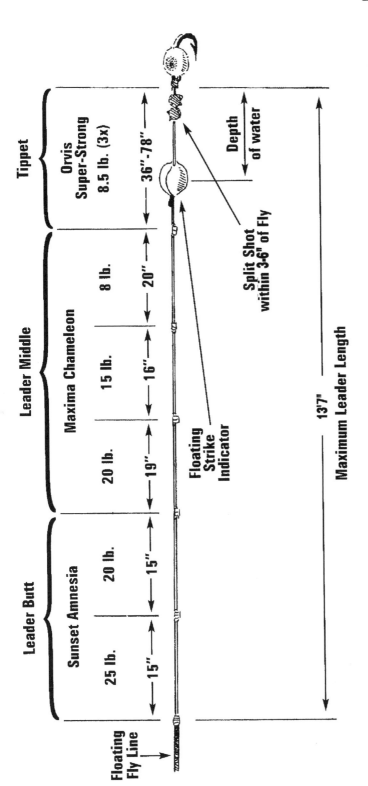

Figure 6.1b Leader Formula for Right-Angle-Floating-Indicator Technique.*

*Note: This leader works well for a 10½ foot fly rod. For shorter fly rods, a shorter leader will function better. Subtract the rod length difference from the length of the leader (middle and tippet sections) to get the proper leader length for the rod used. For example, a 9½ foot fly rod requires 1 foot to be subtracted from the leader length.

Don Mathews with a buck steelie caught on his #14 Glass Egg fly on Elk Creek, PA. (Don Mathews photo)

A leader that tapers down from a small diameter butt section like 25 or 20 pound test mono will sink much faster (when bottom-bouncing) than a leader tapered down from a larger diameter butt like 40 pound test mono.* This difference in sink rate occurs because thinner diameter mono provides less resistance in the water column as it sinks to the stream bottom (which is also true for thinner profile flies versus thicker profile flies).

Leaders tapered from mono's as thin as 10 pound test sink even faster. The problem with this leader, though, is that there is a corresponding strength or power loss when using smaller diameter butt sections. The result is a drastic reduction in the ability of the leader to turnover split-shot and weighted flies smoothly.

Due to the shallow nature of most Lake Erie tributaries extremely thin diameter leader tapers are not required. This means a leader tapered from butt sections of 25-20 pound test mono can be used on the Erie tributaries providing sufficient sink rate and at the same time maintain a large degree of leader turnover ability.

Tippet selection is very important and depends on stream conditions and the fishing technique being used. When using a floating indicator, it is advantageous to use a long tippet section of at least 3-6$^{1/2}$ feet of the more flexible variety like Orvis Super Strong, Rio Power Flex and Gamma Technologies Frog Hair. If you keep an adjustable float, like a little corkie, on this flexible, knotless section, you can easily move the corkie up and down to adjust for varying water depths. Using a flexible tippet section also makes it easier to achieve the desired right angle effect in the leader.

When strictly bottom-bouncing, normally the case when fishing high to moderate run-off flows, a stiff, more abrasion-resistant tippet material like Maxima

It is to be noted that mono pound test roughly varies proportionally to the mono diameter.

Ultra Green is recommended. This material maintains a much straighter leader during the drift, allowing better bottom detection and strike detection. Using a too soft or supple tippet material while bottom-bouncing can result in loss of bottom contact and fish takes. A bonus of using stiff tippet materials is that they are very abrasion resistant and can help to prevent break-offs due to streambed abrasion and cuts from fish gill plates and teeth.

Tippet lengths used in bottom-bouncing are shorter than the ones used in floating indicator fishing (usually 3-4$^{1/2}$ feet). As discussed in Chapter 5, this enables the fly fisherman to use the weight of the fly line (3-7 feet of fly line below the rod tip) to balance the weight of the fly and split-shot and produce a tight line.

A leader that is too long (no fly line below the rod tip) can result in a loose line, while a leader that is too short can cause the fly line to enter the water at the target zone and cause unwanted drag on the fly and split-shot.

Another point to remember about proper tippet length concerns the length of the fly rod used. Short fly rods do not handle long leaders very well and therefore require shorter leaders. The leader formulas illustrated in Figures 6.1a and 6.1b are ideal for a fly rod of 10$^{1/2}$ feet in length. For shorter fly rods, modify the leader formula as instructed at the bottom of Figures 6.1a and 6.1b.

A final note about tippet selection concerns diameter. Use the heaviest (largest diameter) tippet material allowable for the water conditions. It becomes pretty obvious to the beginner steelheader that extremely light tippets (5x diameter or less) make drag-free drifts more easily achievable with much less line and leader manipulation. These thinner diameter tippets also sink much faster than larger diameter tippets. However, very few large or trophy steelhead are landed on these flexible tippets because of their reduced tensile and knot strength and lack of abrasion resistance. Once you become skilled in drag-free drift presentations (discussed in Chapter 5), tippet diameters of 3X or 4X will be as light as you will need to go most of the time.

Steelheader's Tip

Use a piece of fluorescent red Amnesia monofilament in the butt section of your leader to act as a strike indicator.

Using a loop knot for a fly-to-tippet connection (like the open clinch knot shown in Figure 6.2 below) can be a good remedy for achieving a drag-free drift when using heavier tippets. This knot practically eliminates the influence of stiff/heavy tippets and tight knot connections on a fly by allowing the fly to move more freely in the current.

Sometimes "fish bowl" conditions exist (extremely low and clear stream flows) and you may be forced to use light tippets as a last resort. Under these conditions steelhead hook-ups can become more the norm than actual fish landed due to light tippet break-offs.

Over the years, fluorocarbon tippet materials have been introduced by most of the major tippet manufacturers. The present generation of these materials (when compared to monofilament tippet) are nearly as supple, have reduced water absorption, increased knot strength and have both greater abrasion resistance and breaking strength (some as high as 60 % stronger for a given diameter). Seaguar's Grand Max, Rio's Fluorflex Plus fluorocarbon and Gamma Technologies Frog Hair Fluorocarbon are good examples.

The most important quality of fluorocarbon is that it is markedly less visible under water (versus nylon monofilament materials) due to its lower light refraction characteristics. This invisible characteristic makes fluorocarbon tippets very effective in low, clear flows and particularly on shallow steelhead spawning beds where nylon tippet materials can spook fish.

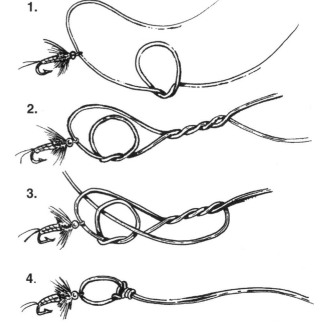

1. Put overhand knot in tippet and leave open. Insert tippet through hook eye.

2. Wrap tippet around itself 5 times.

3. Insert end of tippet through overhand knot and loop formed by twisted tippet.

4. Pinch knot at distance desired from hook eye.

Figure 6.2 Open Clinch Knot

Steelheader's Tip

More hook-ups can result in the right-angle-floating-indicator technique by tying a smaller size trailer fly (like a bead-head nymph) below a larger egg pattern. Steelhead are often attracted to the larger fly but instead will take the smaller trailer.*

Fluorocarbon does have a few drawbacks. A major concern is that it tends to get brittle in extremely cold water temperatures (low 30 degree F range). Because of this, some steelheaders will switch to nylon tippet during the cold winter months even though it may cost them some hookups in clear flows.

Fluorocarbon also tends to be a bit pricey when compared to nylon tippet materials, but there are some quality bargain brands like Ashima and Airflo's Sight Free. An option would be to buy fluorocarbon marketed for spin fisherman in large capacity spools like Seaguar's Carbon Pro fluorocarbon line. Although offering fewer diameter choices, the quality is still very good with substantial savings for the angler.

A final concern about fluorocarbon is how it impacts the environment. Obviously it is important not to discard any type of leader material along the tributary streams. This is even more critical with fluorocarbon, which takes much longer to degrade in the environment versus monofilament.

Fly Reels

Fly reel selection for fishing the Lake Erie tributaries is not as crucial as fly rod choice, but it does have a few important requirements. Some of the most important considerations are to select a fly reel with a smooth drag system that can be finely adjusted (especially on the light end) and that has a low start-up inertia. This combination of features will protect light tippets during steelhead surges and runs and also prevent backlashes when drags are set very light.

Trout reels can be used when fly fishing for Erie steelhead, but they have a few drawbacks. They are usually too light to balance the weight of the longer rod lengths typically used. Also, they generally do not have disc-drag systems with the heavy end settings that can be useful in slowing down steelhead in high run-off flows. Finally, the small spool diameters of trout reels produce slow line pickup, which

*Use of more than one hook is prohibited in NY. See regulations in Appendix B.

Guide Karl Weixlemann with a happy client on Cattaraugus Creek, NY.
(Jack Hanrahan photo)

becomes very noticeable when a hooked steelhead runs directly at you and you need to retrieve your line quickly!

Fly line backing capacity for fly reels is not important because of the relatively small size and normally shallow flows of most Lake Erie tributaries. After being hooked, most steelhead don't travel very far, except during higher run-off flows. Instead they fight in the pool or run where they were hooked. It's a good idea, though, to fill your fly reel with the maximum backing capacity. This will noticeably increase your line pick-up speed.

Some good conventional fly reel choices considering features and price include the Scientific Angler System II 7/8, the Lamson LP 3, the Orvis Battenkill Disc 7/8, the Harris Solitude III and the Teton #8-10.

Recently, many reel manufacturers have produced reels with larger inside spool or arbor diameters that are ideal for steelheading. A large arbor reel retrieves as much as two or three times more line per revolution of the spool than a conventional reel. This is an ideal feature to have when a steelhead is running directly toward you and you need to get it on the reel quickly. Large arbor reels also have slower spool rotation during a run, a smooth drag start-up (torque), less fly line coiling due to memory and provide more consistent drag pressure.

Some excellent large arbor reel choices would include the Teton Tioga #8, the Bauer M4SL or MX3, the Orvis Rocky Mountain LA 7/8 or Battenkill LA IV, the Waterworks/Lamson Litespeed #3, the Ross Big Game #4, the Harris Solitude IV, the Redington Brake-Water 7/8 and GD 7/8, the Loop Tackle Loop #2 and the Abel Reel Super #6.

Floating Indicators and Split-Shot

As discussed earlier in Chapter 5, Little Corkies are ideal indicators to use in the right-angle-floating-indicator-technique because of their excellent buoyancy, sensitivity, variety of sizes and colors available and ease of fly casting. They can be secured to the leader either using a toothpick or a rubber band.

Inserting a toothpick into the top center hole secures the Corkie and allows for adjustment by simply sliding the Corkie up or down the leader. They can also be modified for easy removal from the leader, without removing the fly and split-shot, by splitting them on one side with a razor blade prior to use. When this modification is done, it will require two toothpicks (in top and bottom holes of Corkie) for a more secure attachment to the leader.

The rubber band method for attaching a Corkie to the leader (See Figure 6.3 on page 132) involves looping the leader through the center hole, inserting a small section or rubber band and then pulling the loop down and inside the Corkie forming a true 90 degree angle in the leader. The Corkie is also adjustable on the leader with this method and can be easily removed by simply holding the Corkie and pulling on one end of the leader.

Pop Top indicators are basically Little Corkies that have a stem that points in the opposite direction of the fly and split-shot telling the fly fisherman when a drag-free drift has been achieved. When the stem is straight up, it indicates optimal dead drift of the fly (see discussion on page 94). The leader is attached to the bottom stem using a rubber sleeve, making the indicator easily adjustable.

Tipper styrofoam indicators are tear-drop shaped, making them both aero and hydro-dynamically efficient when fly casting and floating in the current. They come

Steelheader's Tip

Use the maximum amount of fly line backing in your fly reel in order to increase line pick up speed which is ideal to have when a hooked steelhead runs straight toward you.

in a variety of sizes, are easily positioned on the leader and can be removed without removing your shot and fly due to a slit and built in rubber core or "leader grabber".

Thill (now manufactured by Lindy-Little Joe, Inc.) makes two floating indicators that are ideal for right angle floating indicator fishing. They come in a variety of sizes and include the oval shaped Ice 'N Fly Special and the thinner shaped profile Mini-Shy Bite. The Ice 'N Fly Special is secured to the leader using a silicon insert and the Mini-Shy Bite uses silicone rubber sleeves. Thill classifies these indicators not only by their size but also by the amount of shot weight required to balance the float for maximum sensitivity to strike detection.

Glo-Bob makes a Styrofoam float in a $1^{1/4}$ inch size (# B2) that works great in high/fast tributary flows where heavy amounts of split-shot are needed. It comes with a lead insert that can be easily removed and replaced with a toothpick for easy fly casting.

Split-shot is available in basically two varieties. Water Gremlin makes a rounded shot with an "ear" design that is available in both lead and non-toxic forms, but in limited sizes — particularly on the small end. This split-shot is by far the most popular shot used by fly fisherman because it's easy to remove, but it has some disadvantages.

The ear design does not cast well aerodynamically. It also can cause leader spin and tangles, hang-ups on the stream bottom as well as slowing down the sink rate of the shot. Gremlin shot also comes in a bright finish which can spook a steelhead when placed close to the fly. Some steelheaders spray paint their Gremlin shot with

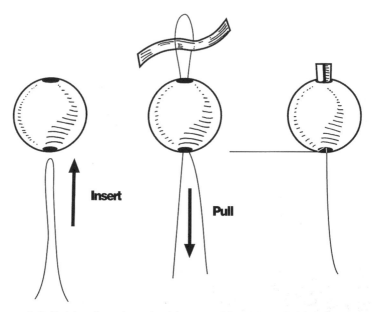

Insert

Pull

Figure 6.3 Rubber band method for attaching Little Corkie to a leader.

Tony DiBenedetto Jr. with a spring run Little Manistee steelhead.

grey auto body primer to remove this bright finish, swearing it makes a difference.

Lead, rounded shot in the ear-less form (like those manufactured by Redwing and Dinsmore) is known as English "soft shot". It's advantages are that it is made in the tiniest of sizes (also called "dust" shot), has a compact size and dark finish. This results in fast penetration through the water column and a minimal tendency to spook steelhead. Since it is very soft it does little damage to lighter tippets. Redwing's soft shot is made in Canada and is labeled as Blackbird shot.

Some of its disadvantages are that it can be difficult to remove and tends to slide down the leader, although Black Bird shot seems to hold in place much better than others.

Thill makes a double-cut soft shot (cut on both sides) that is easily removed and comes in both the lead and non-toxic forms.

Dinsmore seems to offer the ultimate shot design with a green, cushion coated, tin shot that has an ear-less, weight-forward egg shape. The list of advantages are impressive including: tapered, egg shaped profile (allowing for smoother casting), faster sink rates and fewer hang-ups. The green cushion coating prevents slippage on leaders, reduces damage to leaders, provides a low visibility appearance, has a divot for easy thumbnail removal and is non-toxic.

A recent alternative to split-shot is a soft putty made of tungsten that is non-toxic and 30 % heavier than lead. When warm, it is very pliable and can be molded to any size and applied to the leader by simply rolling it between your fingers. It hardens and secures in place on the leader immediately after coming into contact with cold water.

The issue of the effects of lead shot and sinkers on the environment has been raised in recent years. Studies have shown that discarded lead shot is often mistaken for food or grit by water birds such as ducks, geese, swans, gulls or loons.

The toxic effects of lead can cause a bird to experience tremors, an impaired ability to fly, and loss of balance. It can also have trouble feeding, nesting, mating and caring for its young.

Responding to these effects, New York State has passed legislation banning the sale of lead fishing sinkers weighing less than one-half ounce (including split-shot) beginning in 2004. This, more than likely, will be a coming trend in the Lake Erie region in the near future. In the meantime the responsible angler should voluntarily convert to non-toxic shot alternatives like tin, bismuth, steel and tungsten to help reduce the risk of lead poisoning in wildlife.

Accessories

A number of accessories are very useful to the Lake Erie steelheader. At the top of the list would have to be waders. In the fall and spring when water temperatures are above 40 degrees F., neoprene waders aren't necessary and can become hot and clammy when worn in warm air temperatures. Breathable waders are ideal at this time and can be insulated, if necessary, by wearing thermal underwear like Patagonia capilene or fleece wading pants. But during the winter steelhead months of January and February, when water temperatures can drop into the lower thirties, neoprene waders are almost mandatory. The insulation that neoprene waders provide allows you to fish comfortably all day in very cold water.

Boot foot waders are ideal for fishing in cold water all day because of the increased amount of insulating air space surrounding the foot. They also save a lot of time when getting dressed versus stocking foot waders.

Steelheader's Tip

During cold water tributary flows be prepared for "soft" steelhead takes, especially at the end of your fly's drift.

*Drift boat guide Marion Graven with a nice spring buck on the Grand River, OH.
(Marion Graven photo)*

If you plan to hike along the tributaries though, stocking foot waders (that have a separate wading shoe) are the best. Wading shoes provide great support for walking on uneven surfaces due to their better ankle support and are lighter than boot foot waders. The only drawback is that because of their tight fit they do not insulate as well as boot foot waders in very cold water. A good remedy for this is to buy a wading boot one size bigger than normal to allow for more air space and the addition of 1 or 2 pairs of insulating socks.

Chota has come out with an innovative boot foot wader (the Tellico Shoal boot foot) that combines some of the best features of both stocking foot and boot foot waders. They have incorporated into a boot foot design a QuickLace system that provides solid lateral support and a hiking boot type feel and performance.

Felt soled waders are highly recommended because of the slippery shale streambeds of the tributaries — especially in the fall and the spring due to algae growth. Studded felt soles, attachable chains and Korker type sandals give the steelheader increased traction and wear versus felt alone.

Korkers and Orvis have come up with a wading boot design with interchangeable soles to cover both wading and hiking conditions. The felt sole is ideal for all-around wading traction, the studded felt sole provides maximum traction for most slippery surfaces, the rubber lugged soles are ideal for hiking to the stream (especially in snow) and the studded rubber soles provide superior traction on extremely slippery, slimy, algae covered rocks.

Fingerless gloves keep hands warm in cold air temperatures and at the same time allow the angler to tie knots easily. They are available in wool, neoprene and synthetic fleece. Glacier Gloves makes an innovative fingerless glove design that has neoprene palms, Polartec Windbloc fleece for the backs and is fleece lined for warmth.

For extreme conditions, Grabber makes economical, air activated warmers that fit into gloves and produce 6-7 hours of heat. They also make a toe warmer design that functions in the low oxygen environment of a boot or shoe.

A layering system works well in the varied weather conditions encountered by the steelheader. A medium or heavy weight, waist-length, fleece jacket worn under a breathable, wind proof and waterproof shell is ideal. Waist-length jackets allow for wading in deeper waters, and the option to wear the shell or jacket, or both, makes it a versatile system. Some popular shell designs for the steelhead fisherman include the Patagonia SST jacket and the Simms Gore-Tex Guide jacket which is also designed to pack down and fit into the back of the fishing vest.

A steelheader's vest should be cut high at the waist for wading and should be one size larger than normal to allow wearing it over thick layers of clothing and to accommodate carrying various fly boxes and accessories. New vest designs incorporate either padding or stretch mesh built into the yoke to help the angler carry a heavy load all day while experiencing less neck and shoulder fatigue.

An alternative to the fishing vest are chest pack and creel designs such as made by William Joseph. Their Gear Bag Chest is fully adjustable, has a mega-heliport workstation and can be fitted with optional hydration bladder. The innovative William Joseph Creel distributes weight evenly and allows for easy fly casting for either right or left handed anglers. It is easily "spun" around while worn to access rear storage capability.

Vests, chest packs and creels should be stocked with various spools of leader and tippet material to rebuild leaders on the stream, floating indicators in a variety of sizes, toothpicks and a generous supply of split-shot.

Steelheader's Tip

Applying liberal amounts of hand lotion to the hands, face and even feet can help keep the extremities warm during the winter months.

A large steelhead-size net with a long, telescopic handle is highly recommended as an aid in landing a steelhead quickly, preventing fish exhaustion and possible mortality. Cotton netting is somewhat better than synthetic netting because it reduces the risk of injury to the fish.

Transporting a net this large all day can be very cumbersome. Hang it upside down by its bow (behind your vest) with a Brodin magnetic release or a Edgin clip release. This will prevent the netting from being tangled in underbrush and low tree branches when the steelheader is walking.

A net with a scale built into the handle (like the B. K. Weigh Net) is ideal for weighing steelhead quickly and also eliminating possible fish injury. The Boga Grip scale accurately weighs fish up to 15 or 30 pounds (depending on the model) by using a spring scale and pressure created by lifting the fish in its pincers jaw. The pincers also allow for easy landing and handling with no harm to the fish.

If you do not have a scale you can estimate the weight of a steelhead by taking it's length and girth measurements and later plug them into a fish weight calculation formula. (See Useful Web Sites in Appendix A). You can also estimate the weight of a steelhead, if it is at least 24 inches in length, by calculating one pound for the first 20 inches and adding one more pound for each inch over 20.

Vaseline lip balm comes in handy to prevent rod guide freeze-up in sub-freezing air temperatures by applying it liberally to the rod guides. Stanley's Ice Off paste is a non-toxic, anti-freeze paste that keeps both fly lines and guides from freezing in temperatures as low as zero degrees.

Other important accessories include surgical forceps (for easy hook removal), clippers, polarized sunglasses (for reading surface currents and textures, streambed topography and locating fish), a stream thermometer and a weatherproof camera.

Updated Equipment Recommendations

Since the third edition of Steelhead Guide many new and improved fly fishing products and equipment items have come on the market. The following are some of the more innovative and useful ones for the steelhead fisherman.

Fly Rods

Scott introduced a 10 foot 8 inch, 8 weight, 4 piece in 2007. This limited edition "concept" rod is called the Two-Hand-Assist-Special. It features a second upper grip position and a mini bottom grip to allow a second hand assist in casting. This "switch" rod can be used for either single- or double-handed casting depending on the type of cast you want to make, your position in the river, or the condition of your arm at the end of a long day!

Scott has improved their 10 foot, 4 piece SAS series of fly rods by softening their tips and beefing up the butts a bit while still maintaining the medium-fast action. Scott calls them the A2 series of fly rods. The length and action of these rods are great for "high-stick" nymphing as well as swinging flies. They are moderately priced and come in 6, 7 and 8 line weights. There is also a double handed 13 foot 8 weight, 3 piece model in the A2 series that makes a good introductory rod for the new spey caster.

The Winston BIIx 11 foot, 7 weight, 4 piece is an extremely light boron/graphite composite that performs well across a wide casting range. Some other great "cross-over" rods that can be used as a short spey rod or a "high-stick" nymphing rod include Sage's Z-Axis, 11 foot, 8 or 7 weight, 4 piece and the lighter Ultra Light Spey, 12 foot, 5 weight, 4 piece.

The Winston BIIx 10 foot, 8 weight, 4 piece is a dynamite rod for single-handed casting and swinging flies. This rod has both the power and lightness to cast sinking leaders and sink tips all day. Another single-handed option for swinging flies would be the Sage FLi, 10 foot, 7 or 8 weight.

Rajeff Sports makes an economically priced spey rod called the Echo classic. The action is medium-fast and can handle a standard spey line as well as sink tips and Skagit lines. There are four models including two 13 foot rods in 7/8 or 8/9 weights.

The newly redesigned and mid-priced Redington Red.Fly2, 10 foot, 7 or 8 weight, 4 piece and St. Croix Avid, 9 foot, 7 or 8 weight, 4 piece fly rods are ideal for both "high-stick" nymphing and swinging presentations. Orvis makes 10 foot, 7 weights in both Streamline Tip-Flex and T3 Mid-Flex models. The Streamline is bargain priced and makes a good introductory or backup steelhead rod.

Fly Reels

The Nautilus CCF large arbor fly reel features the maintenance free CCF brake system. This hybrid cork/carbon-fiber disc drag is housed in a hermetically sealed hub that is impervious to the elements and has near zero start-up inertia. The spool turns on four over-size stainless steel ball bearings delivering silky smooth performance.

The Galvan Rush R8 large arbor fly reel is a mid-priced reel with a state-of-the-art drag that was designed for the budget conscious angler. It features the same durable heat and wear resistant thermoplastic drag system as their higher-end Torque model but with a more basic spool and frame design. The Rush R10 and R12 also make good mid-priced spey reels. Another, mid-priced fly reel is the updated Orvis Battenkill large arbor. It features an ultra-large arbor design, cork-to-Rulon center disc drag, aircraft grade aluminum bar stock ventilated spool and frame and a numbered drag system.

Ross Reels offers a series of three new larger arbor fly reels that are very affordably priced with surprising quality in manufacturing tolerance, performance and sound. They include the Flystart, the Flycast and the Flywater.

Edco, Inc. has continued the "guides reel" tradition laid down by the Harris Reel Company by offering an improved version of the out of production Harris Reel called the Solitude. The Solitude reel drag system is silky smooth with multiple settings on the light end to protect light tippets, has zero start-up inertia, delivers even and consistent pressure during the fight and performs extremely well during freezing conditions. The hard corrosion-proof finish also resists common nicking and scratching.

The new Solitude design (which will come in 4 models with two available in large arbors) has a reversible drag created to facilitate right and left hand reel conversions. Also manufacturing tolerances have been tightened to improve fit between the spool and housing.

Fly lines, Leaders and Tippet Material

Royal Wulff Products has improved their classic Triangle Taper fly line by adding a hard finish coating called J3. Versus the old line, it shoots better, floats higher and stays clean and slick longer. The "dry" feel of the line minimizes resistance for longer casts.

Monic has introduced a new Red Stripe Series spey fly line. A 5 inch "red stripe" is strategically placed on the fly line as a visual indicator for proper loading of the rod on the recast. Beginners should start with the red stripe 3-4 feet into the rod. As the skill of the angler progresses the red stripe will move toward the rod tip.

An advanced spey caster might leave the red stripe outside the tip a foot or more, allowing for a very tight loop. It is available in both an easy casting short belly head or a Skagit head for turning over heavy tips and flies.

Rio's new Skagit Cheaters are a system of four short heads for converting an interchangeable tip Rio Wind Cutter spey line into a Skagit head line. The Skagit spey line was developed in the Pacific Northwest for "Skagit-style" spey casting where short, heavy sinking tips and short casting strokes allow delivery of large flies. This style of casting has become popular in the Great Lakes as well.

Airflo's new third generation Sightfree G3 fluorocarbon tippet has a significantly smaller diameter that results in impressive break-strength-to-diameter ratio. Sightfree G3 spools also come with a revolutionary new concealed cutting blade, allowing you to cut tippets to length without the use of nippers or teeth! The original Sightfree is slightly more abrasion resistant than the G3, though.

Gamma Technologies makes a fluorocarbon Great Lakes steelhead leader. The knotless leader incorporates a light, long fluorocarbon tippet section that is ideal for floating indicator fishing. This leader is smooth casting and has the power to turn over indicators, beaded flies and split-shot.

Floating Indicators, Split-Shot

Float Master has developed a new strike indicator in tear-drop and round shapes in 9 different sizes. They attach to your leader using a piece of interchangeable rubber tubing allowing for easy adjustment. They can also be easily removed or added to the leader without removing the fly or split-shot. This is a great feature when changing indicator sizes on the stream depending on the current flow. The indicators come in solid and two-tone colors including a river "camo" pattern which has a shaded grey pattern on the bottom. This is ideal for fishing clear water or to pressured fish.

The Toobies Shot System seems to have solved the problem of split-shot slipping down the tippet. The system uses a short section of clear tubing threaded onto the leader and a special Toobies Tool that pushes one or more, non-toxic, heavier-than-lead Toobies Shot into the tube snugly against the tippet. Shot is stored on a magnet on the Toobies Tool which simplifies shot handling. Another great feature of Toobies Shot is that it is virtually snag-proof when drifted along the bottom.

The Split-Shot Companion tool allows you to efficiently and safely attach and remove split-shot avoiding dental injury, sore fingers and absorption of toxic metals. To attach split-shot, place tippet in the split-shot groove with the open ends facing outward, then squeeze the tool to close. To remove split-shot, place the tool's pry end over the seam of the split-shot, swivel over the base and press down to open.

Waders, Wading Boots, Fishing Vests

Simms new ExStream Bootfoot Wader will be available to steelheaders in the fall of 2007. This is Simms' ultimate cold weather wader. Simms has paired a great fitting, comfortable Muck Boot Arctic Sport Boot, which is rated to 40 degrees below zero, with a breathable wader that uses proprietary Thermotron fabric and carbon ceramic-resin for maximum heat-retention efficiency. These components make for an extremely warm and durable wader. Other features include a flip out, zippered chest pocket with key cord, fleece-lined hand warmer pockets, and reinforced leg panels. The boot is available with a lug or felt sole and can easily be converted to a studded boot with Hard Bite studs, sold separately by Simms.

Chota has introduced a Steelheader Boot Foot Wader that is designed for cold water fishing. Some of its features include high traction rubber soles with optional case hardened steel cleats, a rugged heavy weight breathable upper, super-warm rubber boots insulated with neoprene and lined with fleece and a quick lace system (protected with unique "Lace Guards") which keeps the foot from "swimming" inside the boot. They also have articulated knees and special "vented" knee pads.

William Joseph's Dry-Namic stocking foot waders feature a waterproof center zipper opening which makes taking your waders on and off a snap. They are made with a 5 layer breathable membrane in high wear areas like the thighs and knees with the primary seams taped on both the inside and outside. They also have a seamless crotch, built-in gravel guards and front and rear waterproof pockets.

Toggs's Hellbender stocking foot waders are economically priced and include features such as articulated and reinforced 5-layer knee construction, custom chest pocket, adjustable waist straps and "no sand" attached gravel guards.

The Adventure Fly Fishing Company manufactures an all season waterproof vest that will keep you fishing on a steelhead tributary in all types of weather and wading conditions. Well designed with a multitude of innovative features that include a waterproof exterior, two large exterior 3-D dry pockets, stitched and tape sealed seams, retractor and tippet cavities and hydration bladder.

Korkers wading shoes have been redesigned for a better fit, more support and a lighter design. They feature the OmniTrax V2 interchangeable sole system which has 6 different types of soles depending on the activity. The studded Aquastealth sole incorporates high friction rubber for added durability and reduced water absorption and is ideal for scrambling trails, rock hopping and wading on slippery streambeds. Korkers new Guide Boot wading shoe with Boa Lace Technology uses stainless steel laces that are impervious to freezing. The laces can be easily tightened or loosened using a dial system with a 4-to-1 gear.

Fishpond introduced the High Country Tech Pak in 2007. This versatile carry system combines a large, full-featured fishing chest pack with a compact backpack. The two components can be worn together or separately depending upon how much gear you want to carry. The chest pack features a molded "zip-down" fly bench with replaceable foam while the back pack has a hydration bladder pocket that can hold up to a 52 oz. Fishpond water bladder.

Soft Goods

Lasava makes a Polartec under-wader liner layering system designed to get you in and out of waders with ease. Feet are built into the liners eliminating the "bunching" that occurs with regular under-gear as well as the need for socks. The Polartec fabric is tough, lightweight and comfortable. The Lasava winter layering system incorporates 3 separate layers (base, flurry and arctic layers) to keep you dry and warm while fishing in the coldest temperatures.

Patagonia has just updated their Shelled Insulator Pant. This pant is basically their R1 pant with a finished Supplex outer layer. It is light weight, super warm and can be worn casually after a day of fishing. Velcro at the ankles prevents socks from creeping.

Chota makes a Stow-A-Way fleece Flip Mitt that allows both the mitt finger covering and the thumb covering to be tucked away under the patented Stow-A-Way cuff. This great feature eliminates the "line grabbing" bulk on the back of the hand when the fingers are exposed.

William Joseph manufactures a quality Ultra-lite rain jacket that is ideal for storing in the rear cargo compartment of a fishing vest. It weighs less than 5 ounces, stows in its own case and costs less than 60 bucks!

Accessories

Orvis, Flambeau, Scientific Angler and C & F all make waterproof fly boxes that are a godsend for anglers taking accidental plunges. The problem is that not only do they keep water out but they keep it in after you insert water soaked flies back into them. This could mean rusted hooks down the road. Angling Designs Dry Tech MRT fly boxes uses a moisture absorbing, silicon gel crystal container that will soak up and store moisture from any wet flies while maintaining a constant dry humidity level in the box. After the crystals change color, indicating full absorption, insert the crystal container into the microwave for a few seconds to drive moisture away and then reinsert it into the box.

Orvis's Dropper Rig fly box stores multiple pre-tied dropper rigs until you need them on the stream. Each box holds five removable inserts, each of which holds multiple rigs. Orvis also offers a large fly box that in addition to the standard foam and compartment areas for flies has room for a dropper rig insert that snaps into place.

Keeping your hands warm has just gotten easier with the Optronics Firepod pocket hand warmer. Powered by 4 AA batteries, it can create a 150 degree F " micro-climate" in five minutes for up to 5 hours.

William Joseph has recently designed and developed the industry's first infrared point-and-shoot thermometer. Just point it at the water and in a matter of milliseconds the water temperature is displayed in degrees F or C.

Steelheader's Tip

Fly fishing in the winter is tough on fly lines particularly when you cast them through iced-over guides on your fly rod which can damage the exterior coating of the fly line. At some point this is going to happen no matter how diligent you are at keeping ice off the guides. A good strategy is to have a fly line strictly for sub-freezing conditions and keep your good lines for other times.

Steelhead egg patterns and nymphs at confluence of Brandy Run and Elk Creek, PA.

Flies

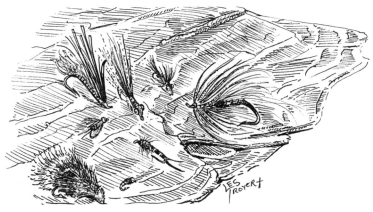

Chapter 7

Choosing fly patterns for Lake Erie steelheading is directly related to the type of water encountered and the technique used.

Traditional steelhead flies, spey flies and soft hackles are mostly designed for "swimming" downstream on the wet fly swing (see Chapter 5). This technique is most effectively used on some of the bigger Lake Erie tributaries that have wide runs, long pools, and even depths along with moderate current flows. Water temperatures can also be critical during this technique with above 40 degrees F. temperatures ideal.

The relatively small size, fast currents and shale streambed character of most Lake Erie tributaries lend themselves well to dead-drifting egg patterns and nymphs. Dead-drifting these flies using a short-line nymphing technique (see Chapter 5) allows the steelhead fly fisher to easily reach steelhead that are holding along shale ledges, below drop-offs and in streambed depressions. This method is particularly effective during cold water conditions, which is the norm for most of the season on the Erie tributaries.

Egg patterns and nymphs are specifically designed for dead-drifting and are relatively simple to tie compared to traditional flies. This is important on the Erie tributaries since many flies can be lost from break-offs. Break-offs usually result from drifting flies along the stream bottom (and the snags that inevitably occur) and the light tippets often required to catch finicky, drag conscious Erie steelhead.

Veteran Erie steelhead fly fisherman will tell you that egg patterns are usually the most effective steelhead flies. In most cases the egg pattern itself is really not that important, but variations in color, size and material density are.

In general, bright colored flies work best for steelhead because these fish are natural egg eaters. They seem to be genetically programmed to eat eggs. Even though after entering the tributaries they require no sustenance to survive, they will strike at flies out of instinct. Biologically the steelhead has adapted so that it could survive in a spawning river for several months without feeding, while living only off its body fat. This insured that the spawning run was not dependent on feeding in order to be successful. It also made certain that adult steelhead would not be competing with or eating their own offspring.

Egg patterns like glo-balls (also known as glo-bugs), scrambled eggs, blood dots and sucker spawns tied in neon colors of chartreuse, pink, orange and red are standards. Chartreuse is one of the best colors to use on the Erie tributaries especially during higher, off-color flows due to it's high visibility.

Pastel shades of these colors are also effective, especially in clear water. Steelhead find sucker spawn flies tied in pastel colors like cream are hard to resist. The sucker spawn also seems to be idiot proof because the angora yarn used to tie this fly easily gets caught in a steelhead's teeth after he takes it. This effect is similar to how velcro works. If you're slow in setting the hook with this fly, it really doesn't matter. Of course, you still have to present it properly!

Angora yarn, Glo Bug Yarn, as well as other synthetic yarn materials (readily found in yarn or craft stores), are commonly used to tie egg patterns. McFLYFOAM is a new material similar to Glo Bug Yarn except that it is very stretchable. It is easily cut into perfectly round balls, especially in very small sizes. Like angora yarn, it has a sticky or velcro characteristic to it.

Choosing the right egg pattern size and material density is very important and these choices are determined by the water conditions. Rising water levels that become off-color and eventually muddy from rain or melted snow run-off are bad news for the fly fisherman. Under these turbid water flows (less than 3 inches of water visibility) it is very hard for a steelhead to see your fly, no matter how large, colorful or flashy it may be. During these high run-off periods, you are better off moving to another stream or returning later when water conditions improve.

As stream levels slowly recede and water clarity improves somewhat (3-6 inches of water visibility), your chances of hooking a steelhead get better. Densely tied egg patterns that give an opaque profile in the water, in size #10 or larger, work well in these flows. Adding flash material like Krystal or Axxel flash to these flies makes them even more effective.

Steelheader's Tip

Use big, bright flies for high, stained water; small and natural colored flies for lower (clearer) conditions.

A good egg pattern selection is critical for success on the Lake Erie tributaries.

When water conditions are at the opposite extreme, low and clear conditions with 15 or more inches of visibility, sparsely tied flies give a softer, more translucent look. Smaller hook sizes like #16 or #18 are often necessary. It sounds incredible, but some very big steelhead have been taken on nothing more than a piece of lint on a hook that is equivalent in size to a #18 or #20 fly! When tying small patterns, though, it is best to use larger hooks to ensure secure hook sets and prevent straightened hooks. For example, tie #16 and #18 sucker spawn patterns on #14 and #16 hooks respectively.

Water flows of 7-15 inches of visibility are considered prime fishing conditions. Flies made in a variety of neon and   colors using moderate material densities (less material than used for turbid   but more than used for clear water) in sizes #12 and #14 work well at this time.

Fly pattern material densities are hard to quantify specifically for the variety of water conditions that can be encountered. Tying egg patterns of various sizes, which vary from opaque to translucent, and testing their effectiveness on the stream is the best way to learn this.

Hook selection is very important, especially when using light tippets (4X or smaller) and the soft noodle-type fly rods that are becoming very popular on the Lake Erie tributaries. Using heavy wire hooks with big barbs, like a standard steelhead or Atlantic salmon-style hook (although they sink better than standard wire hooks), can make hook sets very difficult.

The solution is to use a thinner wire, high-strength hook with a chemically sharpened point. It is important that the barb is not too small since a hard fighting steelhead can throw a hook very easily. The Dai Riki #135 hook is an ideal hook to use when light-lining. The point of this hook is also off-set, which increases its hooking ability. The Daiichi #1530 and #1120 are also good hook choices.

When tying glo-ball patterns, avoid using standard egg hooks like the Mustad #9174. These hooks have very short hook shanks (usually 3X short) that mechanically limit your ability to set the hook. Use longer shanked scud/caddis pupae hooks (1x short) or even standard wet fly hooks. The exposed hook shank of these hooks will not discourage steelhead takes, and at the same time will increase your hook-ups.

Natural fly patterns that imitate aquatic insects and bait fish such as nymphs, streamers, wooly buggers and spring wigglers are also very effective for Lake Erie steelhead. Early run fall fish just in from the lake actively chase streamer patterns and wooly buggers. This is particularly true when stream temperatures are warm (above 50 degrees F.). In the winter, Lake Erie steelhead readily take imitations of the Lake Erie Emerald Shiner, which enter the lower reaches of the tributaries beginning in late December.

The willingness of a tributary run steelhead to take natural or realistic fly patterns is undoubtedly related to former food sources that they have "imprinted" to and remember as feeding adults. During the summer of 2002 Kevin Kayle of the Ohio Department of Wildlife examined the stomach contents of 310 steelhead caught by charter boat captains in the Lake Erie Central Basin (see Introduction to the Fourth Edition and Tables 5.02, 5.03 and Figure 8.5 in Appendix E).

The results of his study suggest that summer steelhead in the Central Basin of Lake Erie are generalists in regards to the numbers and types of food items they consumed. Their diet included bythotrephes cederstroemi (spiny water flea), Asian lady beetles, chironomid (midge) larvae as well as smelt and emerald shiners.

Steelheader's Tip

Mid-day and early afternoon is the best time to fish for lethargic winter steelhead because water temperatures are usually the warmest at this time.

Wild steelhead readily imprint to food sources that they fed on as juveniles in their spawning rivers. James Johnson, a senior Aquatic Biologist for the New York Department of Environmental Conservation showed in a 1978 study that 54 % of the diet of sub-yearling steelhead in Orwell Creek (a tributary of the Salmon River in NY) consisted of aquatic insects such as mayflies, midges, caddis, ants, beetles and moth larvae.

When steelhead move onto shallow gravel runs in the spring to spawn, natural imitations again can produce. Male steelhead are very territorial and aggressive and will drive lesser males off their spawning redds. Drifting a streamer, stonefly pattern or wooly bugger over these redds will often result in ferocious strikes.

Wooly buggers and stoneflies that incorporate a fluorescent colored ball at the head of the fly (mimicking a fish egg) will trigger the protective instincts of spawning steelhead. Steelhead view these flies, commonly known as egg sucking leeches and egg sucking stones, as egg stealers and strike at them accordingly!

In low water visibility conditions, natural imitations can be made more visible and appealing to steelhead by simply adding materials with neon color and flash like Glo Bug Yarn, Crystal Chenille, Estaz, Lite Brite dubbing, Krystal Flash, Axxel Flash and Flashabou. For example, tie a hare's ear nymph with a chartreuse tag of Glo Bug Micro Yarn or a few strains of pearlescent Krystal Flash added to the tail. Spring wigglers, caddis larvae and stoneflies that are tied partially or completely with bright and flashy materials can also be effective.

Adding motion to a fly pattern will greatly increase a steelhead's strike response to that fly, especially when fished in faster currents. Materials such as philoplume, ostrich herl,

Carey Clark with spring steelhead on Big Creek, OH.

webby saddle hackle fibers, marabou and even rubber legs when added to your favorite nymph or egg pattern will provide movement that can prove irresistible to a steelhead.

Table 8 (on page 151) is a steelhead fly selection chart for the Lake Erie tributaries. Egg patterns are emphasized because they are consistently effective and easy to tie. This chart is a good starting point for fly selection, especially for beginning steelheaders.

Fly selection can be very perplexing when you are fly fishing a heavily fished piece of water on your favorite tributary. Under these conditions your normally reliable steelhead patterns lose their productivity because the fish have repeatedly seen or have been hooked by similar patterns. Trout fishers who fish "fly fishing only projects" often have similar experiences.

One solution for fussy fish is to go to a much smaller fly with a softer profile (less material). When you're dead-drifting flies this is an effective tactic and should work most of the time. The opposite tactic is to go with a very large fly, such as wooly bugger or other streamer. Stripping these flies quickly along the stream bottom sometimes excites steelhead and can initiate hard-hitting strikes.

Another approach is to use what can amicably be called a "unique" fly that off-the-wall concoction used by the sport on the other side of the stream! He's catching one on every cast! These so-called patterns have no rhyme or reason except to the steelhead on that particular day. Be creative and experiment by making your own unique patterns. These never-before-seen flies often save the day, triggering strikes from steelhead that previously had a severe case of "lockjaw."

Fly Color Selection

Selecting the most effective fly color for the conditions encountered on the stream has perplexed fly fisherman for years. Some fly fisherman have no method to their color selection and seem to break all the rules. Others believe it is greatly determined by the conditions encountered on the water, specifically the amount of available light present at the point where the fly is presented to the fish. This light

Steelheader's Tip

Any fly can be easily weighted by sliding a metal bead-head or cone-head onto the tippet in front of the fly.

Table 8
Steelhead Fly Selection Chart
Egg Patterns

Conditions	Size	Color	Material Density*
3-6 inches of water visibility	#10 or larger	Neon colors in chartreuse, pink, orange, yellow, alaskan roe. Flash and/or "glow in the dark" materials should be added. White egg patterns are excellent on brighter days in stained water.	Opaque
7-15 inches of water visibility	#12-#14	Various neon and standard colors as well as pastels and white.	Moderate
15 inches or more of water visibility	#16 or smaller	Pastels in cream, pink, peach, light blue, etc. Blue and purple work well on overcast days.	Sparse, translucent

See discussion of material density starting on page 146 of this chapter.

Nymphs, Soft Hackles, Leeches, Streamers and Spey Flies

Conditions	Size	Color
3-6 inches of water visibility	*Nymphs and soft hackles*, #6-#10 (smaller sizes can be used as trailers with bigger egg patterns or streamers). *Streamer and leeches, #4-#6* *Spey flies*, #1.5-#3 (Alec Jackson Spey Hook)	Large black, purple, brown flies. Neon colors, flash and/or glow in the dark materials should be added. White is excellent on brighter days in stained water.
7-15 inches of water visibility	*Nymphs and soft hackles*, #12-#14. *Streamers and leeches, #6-#8* *Spey flies*, #5-#7 (Alec Jackson spey hook)	Black, purple and brown as well as some lighter colored flies.
15 inches or more of water visibility	*Nymphs and soft hackles*, #12 and smaller. *Streamers and leeches, #6-#10* *Spey flies*, #7 (Alec Jackson spey hook)	Lighter/natural colored flies in olive, grey, tan, ginger. Black, purple, brown on overcast days.
Winter steelheading	See water conditions above.	Brightly colored flies, and flies with incorporated movement can "turn-on" lethargic winter steelhead.
Spawning steelhead	See water conditions above.	Red added to nymph and streamer patterns can induce territorial strikes from males.

is determined by the current overhead light conditions, water clarity and depth of water fished.

Trout and salmon have excellent color vision during daylight periods although they only see black and white at night. They can distinguish all the complimentary colors and up to 24 different color hues. What affects their ability to actually see these various visible colors is the available light conditions.

On sunny days, in clear water (1-3 feet), steelhead can see all the colors. At the same time they try to avoid intense sunlight and seek shade or deeper water. This is because a steelhead's eye doesn't filter bright light well due to its lack of eyelids and the inability of the iris of their eye to adjust to intense light as well as a human eye does.

In deeper water under the same conditions, the longer wave length colors such as red and orange become less visible (due to absorption) versus the shorter wavelength colors of yellow, green and blue. This is also true in stained water, at dusk and dawn and on partly cloudy and overcast days. Blue is the last color visible to a steelhead before nightfall and the first color it can see in the morning.

Chartreuse has been "the go-to color" for steelhead egg patterns on the Lake Erie tributaries for years. Its effectiveness (particularly during stained flows) seems to be enhanced by the green tint run-off coloration that is characteristic of most Lake Erie tributary streams. Adding a contrasting or complementary color to

Kathie Shore hooked-up with steelhead on the Cattaraugus River, NY.
(Kathie Shore photo).

chartreuse makes it even more noticeable to a steelhead. The simple half-n-half egg pattern of chartreuse and alaskan roe is an example of this.

The old axiom of "bright day, bright fly and dark day, dark fly" has been a time honored approach to fly selection over the years and has a lot of truth to it. A large black or purple leech is easily recognized by steelhead in stained water at short distances. This is also true at even further distances in low light and clearer water. This is due to the blocky profile or silhouette that a large dark fly provides under these conditions.

White streamers and sucker spawns with added flash materials also work well in stained conditions as long as there is available light to reflect off of them. But their effectiveness is reduced on overcast days and deeper water due to lack of light.

Standard orange or red colors (which are rich but subdued) can be effective on bright days and shallow or clear water flows since they are very visible to steelhead under these conditions. Like white, their effectiveness is reduced on overcast days and deeper or stained water. The exception is reds and oranges that are of the "neon" or "hot" variety, which are really another color in themselves.

Any standard color can be made more attractive and noticeable to a steelhead if it is simply made brighter than its standard color version. Hot pink, orange and yellow are good examples. This increased degree of brightness and intensity is rarely found in nature and makes them markedly more noticeable to steelhead, especially in low light conditions.

Adding some neon orange to a black leech or stonefly is an effective color combination in stained water. The bright orange is very noticeable and the black background of the fly provides a good silhouette in the murky water.

Steelhead flies incorporating some sort of red in them are very effective in inducing strikes from spawning males when they are on or near spawning redds and other females. Red duplicates the red lateral line and rosy cheeks exhibited by mature males. The theory is that a territorial male steelhead will instinctively strike out at this color thinking it is a glimpse or hint of another steelhead in the area.

Steelheader's Tip

When dead-drifting flies, use your fly rod's length to your advantage by lifting as much line and leader as possible off the water. Mend, reach out and follow the drift with the tip of your fly rod.

Steelheader's Tip

*A tiny drop of super glue on the leader can keep
a split-shot from slipping down toward the fly.*

Many times, bright flies can spook steelhead during good light conditions and clear water. The remedy is to use a dark or drab nymph, wooly bugger or spey fly in black, olive, brown, grey or dirty blonde colors which are less startling to the fish. Sucker spawns and egg patterns tied in pastel colors have the same effect.

In recent years steelheaders have been adding "glow in the dark" or phosphorescent fly tying materials to their fly patterns to attract steelhead in low light and even night time conditions. These materials will emit light for a period of time after exposure to a light source. Flow Tek, Inc. makes a glow in the dark, non-toxic, paste dressing called Aqua Glo that when applied to a fly or strike indicator gives it a bright yellow/green glow after being activated by sunlight or an artificial light.

The steelheader should not get totally locked into any fly color selection theory. Sometimes doing the exact opposite of what is normally recommended can result in some pleasantly unexpected hook-ups!

The Steelhead Strike Response

The strike response of a steelhead to a fly is triggered by a number of factors. After entering a tributary, fresh steelhead (particularly fall fish) have not been stressed from fishing pressure or variable stream conditions such as cold water temperatures and low, clear flows. Steelhead usually enter a tributary when stream flows are high and off-color giving them a sense of security. Under these conditions steelhead are much more active (especially in water temperatures above 40 degrees F.) and will energetically chase and strike flies out of curiosity and even experimentation.

Both hatchery and wild steelhead will strike at flies out of a feeding response when a familiar food form drifts their way. Adult wild steelhead often revert back to their juvenile feeding patterns taking stream aquatic insects such as caddisflies, stoneflies and mayflies (in both their nymphal and adult stages). Hatchery fish have a more genetically based response to feeding and will voraciously consume drifting fish eggs though they have no past history of eating them.

Both hatchery and wild steelhead also have a very strong feeding response toward baitfish imitations such as streamers and wooly buggers, especially after just entering the tributaries from Lake Erie. Out in the lake during the summer months, steelhead grow to impressive sizes primarily as a result of feeding on baitfish such as emerald shiners, rainbow smelt and alewives.

Steelhead that have been stressed from fishing pressure, stream conditions and spawning activity don't have much of an active strike response and have a very limited (if any) feeding response. Steelhead with this type of nonresponsive or "stale" attitude often have to be provoked and practically forced into striking.

Steelhead that have been heavily fished over or even previously caught can be activated into striking by repeatedly changing fly patterns and/or sizes. Presenting unique fly patterns and designs (something they haven't seen all day) is another good tactic. Multiple fly presentations with minor rigging changes such as shot amount and placement, tippet size, floating indicator placement, can result in subtle changes in fly drift. These changes often make all the difference with finicky steelhead.

In low, clear water steelhead feel very insecure, but will eventually take a nymph or small egg pattern if repeatedly drifted in front of their "noses." The take under these conditions is practically unnoticeable, and steelhead usually reject it quickly by spitting it out. This strike can be seen as a feeding reflex or mode of self-protection.

Winter steelhead seem to have a case of "lock-jaw" as a result of icy tributary flows slowing their metabolism and reducing their ability or interest in actively pursuing flies. Again, multiple drifts right in the face of these lethargic steelhead often can induce a strike response. Brightly colored fly patterns as well as fly patterns incorporating movement from marabou, grouse feathers, philoplume, etc. also have the effect of "turning on" winter steelhead.

As discussed earlier in this chapter, steelhead on their spawning beds are preoccupied with spawning activities and normally have a nonresponsive attitude toward flies drifting in their vicinity. But at times, spawning steelhead will strike flies if they feel it is a threat to the spawning redd. This is particularly true with the more aggressive males.

The Deadly Dozen III

These 13 fly patterns (a baker's dozen) continue an ongoing tradition of John Nagy's Steelhead Guide book series listing some of the hottest steelhead flies going in the Lake Erie region.* Specific recipes can be found in the Steelhead Fly Patterns section that follows.

1. Senyo Wiggle Stone *(nymph)* by Greg Senyo of Holland, OH.

2. Mirrored Minnow *(streamer)* by Jim Guida of Williamsville, NY.

3. Glo-Butt Greenie *(spey fly)* by John Burkhardt of Kitchener, ON.

4. Lake Erie Emerald Shiner *(tube fly)* by John Nagy of Pittsburgh, PA.

5. Blue Steel *(nymph)* by Mark DeFrank of Uniontown, PA.

6. The Weamer *(spey fly)* by Peter Charles of Hagersville, ON.

7. Grapefruit Head Leech *(leech)* by Kevin Feenstra of Newaygo, MI.

8. Bow Buster *(egg pattern)* by John Miller of Tonawanda, NY.

9. Blue Humpback Nymph *(nymph)* by Joe Gablick of Lower Burell, PA.

10. Funny Bunny Emerald Shiner *(streamer)* by Jerry Darkes of Strongsville, OH.

11. Skinny Spey *(spey fly)* by Ken Chandler of Markdale, ON.

12. Tubular Bugger *(tube fly)* by Nick Pionessa of Williamsville, NY.

13. Yarn Bubble *(egg pattern)* by Dan Walker of Belleville, MI.

* The numerical order of patterns is completely random.

Bonus brown trout caught in October on Elk Creek, PA.

Steelhead Fly Patterns
Egg Patterns

Hair Ball

Tyer: Jim Guida of Williamsville, NY.
Hook: Daiichi #1120, sizes #8-#14.
Thread: Uni-Thread, chartreuse, 8/0.
Body: Egg Glo Bug Yarn cut into dubbing, spun into a dubbing loop and then wrapped around the hook shank. Insert a piece of brite red McFly Foam (about 1/4 inch by 1/8 inch) vertically into thread of dubbing loop and Glo Bug Yarn dubbing (prior to spinning and wrapping loop) to have added effect of a center core.
Comments: Jim says that this simple egg pattern works very well in clear water as the fly is very translucent and natural looking in the water. Also try pink lady and apricot for body colors. Email Jim Guida at: jimguida@hotmail.com for step-by-step instructions.

Yarn Bubble

Tyer: Dan Walker of Egg Man Flies, Belleville, MI.
Hook: Targus #2457 (any scud type hook), sizes #8-#12.
Thread: A to 8/0, neon colors and white, 70 to 210 denier.
Bubble: Bubble is made of a strand of Oregon cheese Glo-Bug Yarn that is split (1/4 to 1/2) depending on the hook size. Tie the yarn strand onto the hook shank (starting at above the point of the hook) up to just behind the hook eye. Leave approximately 3/4 inch of yarn forward of the eye. Roll the strand of yarn onto the hook shank prior to tying in for even distribution around the shank. Next cut excess yarn that extends to the rear of the hook. Dub in nucleus on forward tie in spot (see below) and then pull yarn strand back to rear, over nucleus, to loosely form "bubble." Finish by securing yarn with thread and trimming off excess yarn. Bubble should provide full coverage over nucleus but with some translucency.
Nucleus: Deep dark red Glo Bug Yarn sheared off at inch and dubbed in to form a tiny nucleus on front part of hook shank.
Comments: Other good bubble/nucleus color combos include egg, tetra yellow or chartreuse over orange; golden nugget over cerise with chartreuse thread; orange and pink over chartreuse or cerise. Dan says that this is a good egg pattern bottom bounced in clear water fast flows or hanging below a float in slow currents. He recommends presenting the Yarn Bubble close to fish eye level, matching the current flow and depth. They tangle badly so store them stuck in foam!

Nuke Egg

Tyer: Dan Walker of Egg Man Flies, Belleville, MI.
Hook: Dai Riki #155 (any egg type hook), sizes #10-#6.
Thread: A to 8/0, neon colors and white, 70 to 210 denier.
Veil: Egg Glo Bug Yarn split (1/4 to 1/8) depending on hook size, tied in along hook shank and then doubled back toward hook bend over nucleus (see below). Trim veil length to approximately hook bend. Also cut rear portion of the yarn that was tied in along hook shank to form tail. Veil should cover nucleus sparsely so as not to obscure. Dull Yellow, yellowish white, yellowish orange, pale pinks, chartreuse, oranges are also good veil colors.
Nucleus: Dark Roe Glo Bug Yarn split very thin (1/16 to 1/32 inch depending on hook size) and wrapped to form small nucleus on top of tied in yarn. Wrap nucleus on front part of hook shank. Other bright colored Glo Bug Yarns also work well.
Comments: Nuke Eggs use less yarn and are more translucent than standard Glo Ball type patterns. Dan says to carry all the good color combos in case the fish get hot for a certain pattern.

Steelhead Ant

Tyer: Brian Emerick of FishUSA.com, Erie, PA.
Hook: Dai Riki #135, sizes #10-14.
Bead: Orange Hot Bead to match hook size.
Thread: Danville, red, 6/0.
Tail: Silver Krystal Flash.
Abdomen: Orange chenille.
Legs: White Estaz.
Comments: This fly works well in green to brown water. Omit the tail to use as the top fly on a dropper.

Super Fruit

Tyer: Craig Kopczyk of Kopczyk's Fly Sales, Milford, MI.
Hook: TMC #2488H, sizes #12-#18.
Thread: Danville, orange, 6/0.
Body: Chartreuse McFly Foam cut very short.
Halo: Wapsi salmon egg or peachy king Glo Bug Yarn. Ideal color to match is steelhead orange Glo Bug Yarn with a hint of pink in it which is custom dyed by Jay's Sporting Goods in Clare, MI (see Fly Tying Materials in Appendix D for contact info).
Comments: On small tributaries this is THE egg fly. The color combination drives them crazy!

Another Egg

Tyer: Jim Winger of Steubenville, OH.
Hook: Daiichi #1150, size#12.
Thread: Danville, pink or fluorescent orange, 6/0.
Over Body: 1/3 strand of Glo Bug Yarn.
Under Body: Tying thread.
Body: Regular Estaz (yellow or opalescent white).
Comments: I prefer to spiral the Estaz up the hook shank (1/32 inch gaps) to allow the underbody to show through and allow the Estaz to move.

Spawn Egg

Tyer: Craig Kopczyk of Kopczyk's Fly Sales, Milford, MI.
Hook: TMC #105, sizes #6-#10.
Thread: Kevlar or heavy waxed.
Body: 2 colors of McFly Foam.
Tying instructions: Start thread and wrap to the middle of the shank and then half way back over the thread towards the eye. Separate out 2 strands of each color about the width of a pencil so you have 4 strands, 2 of each color. Stack the McFly Foam strands on top of each other in alternating colors. Cut off one end straight and pinch the yarn about 1/2 from the tip. Push the yarn over the eye of the hook right through the middle of the yarn so the edge is about half way in between the barb and point and the eye of the hook. The McFly Foam will spring back making it more round. Move the thread to the front of the hook and tie off.
Comments: Ugly but very effective. Don't worry about the egg being perfectly round since it actually works better a little ragged. Best colors are yellows and pinks together.

Halo Estaz

Tyer: Craig Kopczyk of Kopczyk's Fly Sales, Milford, MI.
Hook: TMC #105, sizes #8-#10.
Thread: Danville, orange, 6/0.
Body: Estaz with contrasting color of McFly Foam.
Tying instructions: Tie in a piece of Estaz. Take a strand of McFly Foam and make 6 wraps in the middle of it. Wrap the Estaz as you would a parachute dry fly and then make one wrap of Estaz in front and tie off. Pull up the McFly Foam and cut it short.
Comments: Something different instead of the same old Estaz flies. The Estaz actually halos the whole piece of McFly foam. This fly is sparser than many other Estaz flies making it well suited for clearer water.

Egg Sucking Worm

Tyer: Bill Turner of Lewisburg, WV.
Hook: TMC #2457, sizes #12-#8.
Bead: Tungsten bead to match hook size (brass bead, bead chain eyes or mono eyes can also be used).
Thread: Danville, fluorescent red, 6/0.
Body and Tail: Chartreuse micro size Ultra Chenille (burn the tag end or tail before tying in).
Head: Orange or Chartreuse Krystal Egg pushed onto hook (over some tying wraps) and secured with super glue. Otter's Soft Egg or Orvis Reel Egg can also be used. If you don't have pre-made eggs try making a standard Glo Ball with Glo Bug Yarn or McFly Foam or just wraps of Ultra Chenille.
Comments: This is a variation of a fly originated by Joe Endy and was developed by combining two "junk" flies-the San Juan Worm and the Glo Bug. The result is a fish catching machine for both steelhead and trout!

Bow Buster

Tyer: John Miller, Tonawanda, NY.
Hook: Daiichi #1530, sizes #12-#8.
Thread: Danville, fluorescent orange, 3/0.
Tail: White artic fox or marabou.
Body: Steelhead orange Glo Bug Yarn tied in as a scrambled egg pattern (with Alaskan roe dot added to center) with chartreuse Petite Estaz wrapped through breaks in the yarn.
Comments: This fly is basically an Oak Orchard Omelette (see 3rd edition of Steelhead Guide) except with an Alaskan Roe dot added for contrast and a soft tail for movement. John says other effective yarn/ estaz color combos include pink lady and pearlescent white, chartreuse and chartreuse, white and pearlescent white, Oregon cheese and pearlescent white.

Sac Fry

Tyer: Steven Vorkapich of Brunswick, OH.
Hook: Mustad Signature C67S, sizes #8-#10.
Thread: Danville, fluorescent orange, 6/0.
Tail: Hareline white pseudo dubbing or marabou tied sparse and 4 to 6 strands of blue UV Krystal Flash or silver Flashabou.
Egg Sac: Oregon cheese Hareline dubbing small Trilobal chenille.
Eyes: 1/8 inch silver 3-D molded eyes. Apply a drop of Zap-a-Gap first then position the eyes on shank behind hook eye. Let dry then add a drop of Loon Hard Head clear finish in between the eyes.
Comments: Steven likes to swing this fly under a floating indicator just below spawning redds in deeper pools to drop-back and fresh steelhead. It is especially effective when fished in tandem with a sucker spawn (which is tied in as the top fly) where the rig gives the appearance of the sac fry chasing the sucker spawn.

Go-To

Tyer: Clyde Murray of Erie, PA
Hook: Mustad #C675 Z (wide gap), size #12
Thread: Danville, orange, 6/0.
Tail: Twice as long as hook gap, 4 strands Orange Krystal Flash.
Body: Peach Petite Estaz with peach pearl sparkle.
Comments: Clyde ties this fly on when the fishing gets tough on Elk Creek, PA.

Egg-Butted Sucker Spawn

Guide: John Nagy of Pittsburgh, PA
Hook: Daiichi #1530, sizes #12-#8.
Bead: Gold bead to match hook size.
Thread: Danville Plus, fluorescent green, 3/0 to tie egg butt. Gudebrod, white, 8/0 to tie sucker spawn body.
Tail: 2-3 strands of lime Krinkle Mirror Flash.
Body: Make a standard round Glo Bug egg with chartreuse Glo Bug Yarn to form butt at hook bend, and then tie in standard sucker spawn body with white angora yarn up to bead.
Comments: This particular color combination is especially deadly for late winter/spring run Little Manistee strain steelies. The addition of the bead helps get it down with less split-shot usage. Try it either dead-drifted alone or fished as the top fly in a tandem rig with a bead-head nymph under a floating indicator. Color combinations are endless.

Breaking Skein Glitter Fly

Tyer: Joe Montello of Andover, OH.
Hook: Mustad #3366, size #12.
Thread: Uni-Thread, peach, 6/0.
Tail: Wapsi pearl Krystal Flash (3 strands).
Body: Wapsi fluorescent orange or pearl sparkle braid ribbed with Rumpf regular white Estaz between each loop of sparkle braid.
Comments: Joe says that this fly looks like broken egg skein in the current flow. He uses it in the spring as an attractor fly (top fly) in a tandem rig with a nymph.

Nymphs

Candy Caddis

Guide: John Nagy of Pittsburgh, PA.
Hook: Dai Riki #135, sizes #16-#12.
Bead: Gold bead to match hook size.
Thread: Danville, fluorescent green, 6/0.
Body: Flat silver tinsel underbody wrapped with Spirt River chartreuse Jelly Rope plastic cord (small). For a neat body (after tying in tinsel), secure piece of Jelly Rope along hook shank with thread to bend and then proceed to wrap Jelly Rope back toward hook eye (over previous Jelly Rope). By stretching Jelly Rope as you are winding it you can control the diameter of the Rope and also help to taper the body at the hook bend.
Collar: A few wraps of purple or blue Estaz chenille trimmed to shape.
Comments: Purple and blue are under-used colors on the Lake Erie tributaries and can turn steelies on in pressured water, in dark, deep flows and during low light conditions. Jelly Rope has incredible light reflection properties resulting in rich, iridescent colors that seem to glow especially when tied over a reflective underbody. The color combos are endless for this quick-tie caddis.

Filament Caddis

Guide: John Nagy of Pittsburgh, PA.
Hook: Dai Riki #135, sizes #16-#12.
Bead: Gold bead to match hook size.
Thread: Danville, fluorescent chartreuse, 6/0.
Body: Secure piece of fluorescent jelly rope along top of hook shank ending at hook bend, wrap hook shank with silver tinsel, reverse (and stretch) jelly rope toward hook bend and secure by forming thin shell-back or "filament" over tinsel with cross-hatched thread segments. Try to minimize thread wraps so that silver tinsel shows through wraps underneath filament.
Legs: Spirit River
Head: Dub in black or peacock dubbing around legs and whip finish behind bead.
Comments: This fly has it all: movement, flash, iridescent color and a buggy look!

Santa's Helper

Tyer: Mark Kasubick of Chagrin River Gilles, Gates Mills, OH.
Hook: Daiichi #1120 (scud hook), size #10.
Bead: Gold, 1/8 inch, Spirit River Brite Bead.
Thread: Uni-Thread, black, 6/0.
Body: Chartreuse Spirit River Depth Advantage dubbing.
Rib: Red Ultra Wire, small.
Head: Black rabbit fur.
Comments: Mark has found that many of the steelhead tributaries of Northeast Ohio, such as the Grand River and Conneaut Creek, are very fertile and contain a good variety of aquatic insects including a large, uncased, bright green caddis. Mark's Santa's Helper is his imitation of that caddis and he finds it most effective during post run-off periods when fresh steelhead key in on tributary naturals.

Mean Joe Green Caddis

Guide: Mike Shultz of Michigan River Works.
Hook: Tiemco #2457 or Daiichi #1120, sizes #8-12
Thread: Uni-Thread, black, 6/0.
Body: Dubbing mix of chartreuse and green caddis Ice Dubbing.
Legs: Barred mini rubber legs (tan, olive, brown or white).
Head: Aussie possum or similar dubbing.
Comments: This fly works well during the spring run-off. Change your dubbing mix for water clarity. For dark water use more chartreuse and clear water more green caddis.

Fly Plate I

Another Egg

Hair Ball

Super Fruit

Go-To

Spawn Egg

Nuke Egg

Yarn Bubble

Halo Estaz

Egg-Butted
Sucker Spawn

Bow Buster

Breaking Skein
Glitter Fly

Steelhead Ant

Egg Sucking
Worm

Sac Fry

Candy Caddis

Blue Steel

Fresh Water Scud

Santa's Helper

Mean Joe
Green Caddis

Filament Caddis

Blue Humpback
Nymph

Spider

Purple Stinger

Rock worm

Orange Flash
P.T.

Fly Plate II

Ray's
Steelhead Brassie

Yerger
Miracle Nymph

Mini-Bug

Mink's Ear

CJ's
Salmo Slayer

60 Second
Stone

Senyo
Wiggle Stone

Chamois Pinky

Steelie
Long Legs

Lake Erie
Swinger's Hex

PF
Egg Stone

Steelie
Golden Stone

Copper Per
(PT)

Chloe Nymph

Mark's
Wiggle Hex

Steak-and-Egg

Provan's Stone

C.J.'s Mysis

Quick Shrim

Fly Plate III

Bloody Mary

Electra
Soft Hackle

Grimm Reaper

Jennings Nymph

Mallard
Minnow

Steelhead
Sparrow

PF
Flyer

Lil' Rainbow
Fluoro Fiber Minnow

Mirrored Minnow

Rainbow Runner

Funny Bunny
Emerald Shiner

Silver Side
Minnow

Marion's
Versatile Minnow

German's White Nightmare

Fly Plate IV

STS
Streamer

Doc's
Wally Bugg

Bob's Baby "Bow"

Spring
Bugger

Greg
Cat-A-K

Olive
Pipe Brush

White Bellied
Bugger

Bess's
Best Be

Funny Bunny
Sculpin

Articulated
Wooly Bugger

Senyo Sculpin

Boa Leech

Fly Plate V

Grapefruit
Head Leech

Simple Sculpin

Emulator Sculpin

Lake Erie
Goby

Black Mamba

Diablo
Cock Spey

Bead Head
Spey Bunny

The
"Grand" Illusion

Strawberry
Creme Spey

Fly Plate VI

The Weamer

Southwest Jewel

Pink Matuka Spey

Copper Grey Spey

Winter Spey

Classic Oraange Spey

Sorta Sp

Orange Peacock Spey

Senyo Spey Stone

Skinny Spey

Caroline Elizabeth Gordon

Glo-Butt Greenie

Fly Plate VII
Tube Flies

Turduken

Tubular Bugger

Foxy E.S.L.

Sashimi Shiner

Ice Bunny

Lower River Minnow

Smolten-Smelten

Chartreuse Lazer Flex

Fly Plate VIII
Tube Flies

Black Maria

*Grand River
Bunny Tube*

*Yerger Hot Bead
Tube Fly*

*Gotham
E.S.L.*

*Taylor's
River Bug*

Tail #1

Tail #2

TB's Single Egg

Tail #1

Tail #2

Fly Plate IX
Tube Flies

Tail #1

Tail #2

Frank's Jig Fly

Conehead No-Body Matuka

Tail #1

Tail #2

Furabou 1/2-Incher

Halebop

Fly Plate X
Tube Flies

*Lake Erie
Emerald
Shiner*

Sun Burst

*Red, Black
and Blue*

*Lemon
Lime*

*Pulaski
Persecutor*

Liu Snake Tube

Fly Plate XI
Tube Flies

Liu
Temple Dog Leech

Witchy Woman

Fat Boy
Slim

Steel
Flamingo

Specialty Tube Bodies

FITS
Tubing
& Cone

Shumakov
Long Range

mer Teardrop

Cook TTS

Wurm Tungsten

Loop Bottle

Fall steelheaders on middle Elk Creek, PA.

An elated Maurice Prendergast with a trophy fall Elk Creek, PA steelhead.

Spring buck steelhead with a selection of steelhead fly patterns.

Winter steelheader "high-stick nymphing" on Walnut Creek, PA. (Jack Hanrahan photo)

Trophy buck steelhead that "slammed" a Lake Erie Emerald Shiner tube fly.

Angler playing steelhead with guide "at the ready" with net. (Jack Hanrahan photo)

Steelheader "hooked-up" with a Grand River, OH steelhead.
(Jack Hanrahan photo)

Author with
Grand River, OH spr
buck steelhead.

Pontoon boat steelheader on the Grand River, OH.
(Jack Hanrahan photo)

Steelheader on a upper section of 'onneaut Creek, OH during the "down-side" of a run-off period.

Lake Erie tributary hen steelhead that fell for a Black and Blue Stonefly Nymph.

Lori Doolittle doing remote style steelheading on a Lake Erie tributary stream.

Grand River at Caledonia, ON.
(Peter Charles photo)

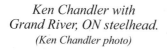

Ken Chandler with
Grand River, ON steelhead.
(Ken Chandler photo)

Wild hen steelhead comes to the net on the Grand River, ON.
(Ken Chandler photo)

Copper Pete (PT)

Tyer: Jerry Darkes of Strongsville, OH.
Hook: Daiichi #1530, sizes #10-14.
Thread: Uni-Thread, black, 6/0.
Tail: Pheasant tail fibers.
Body: Copper wire in desired colors.
Thorax: Peacock herl with pheasant tail fibers pulled over the top then tied back and trimmed as legs.
Comments: Jerry says that this fly is easy to tie, sinks well and is very durable. He uses it to bring in quick color changes for nymphs. If steelhead are not eating your nymphs, try changing color and size-in that order.

Fresh Water Scud

Guide: Bob Tomlinson.
Hook: TMC #2457 sizes #12-16.
Thread: Uni-Thread, olive, 8/0.
Tail: Dyed pheasant tail (olive or orange).
Body: Sow scud dubbing, clear body stretch.
Shell back: Clear body stretch.
Rib: Gold Ultra Wire.
Comments: Bob likes to fish this scud on a dead-drift and finds it deadly on the Rocky and Vermillion Rivers.

Purple Stinger

Guide: Steve Brugger of Lake Erie Ultimate Angler, Erie, PA.
Hook: TMC #2488H, size #14.
Bead: Purple 1/8 inch Hot Bead.
Thread: Uni-Thread, orange, 8/0.
Tail: Pink Artic Fox.
Body: Red pearl Flashabou Tinsel.
Thorax: Pink H2O Fuzzy Bug chenille material.
Wingcase: Red pearl Flashback.
Comments: Steven pulls this fly out when the fishing is tough. It is best fished dead-drifted and makes a killer dropper fly.

Orange Flash P.T.

Guide: Steve Brugger of Lake Erie Ultimate Angler, Erie, PA.
Hook: TMC #2488H, size #14.
Thread: Uni-Thread, orange, 8/0.
Tail: Orange pheasant tail fibers.
Body: Orange pheasant tail fibers.
Thorax: Orange H2O Fuzzy Bug chenille with lead under wrap.
Wingcase: Orange pheasant tail and pearl flat braid.
Comments: Steven took the original P.T. and dressed it up a bit. He added enough color to use in clear water conditions without spooking fish. It is also an excellent dropper pattern for those who like to fish tandems.

Rock Worm

Guide: Bob Tomlinson, Fairview Park, OH.
Hook: TMC #2457 sizes #12-16.
Thread: Coats and Clark Kerry Green #177.
Tying Notes: Spin thread until it is completely flat and then wrap the hook shank. Then spin thread tightly, now put your ribs in, whip finish head.
Comments: Very effective in the spring below spawning redds. Bob says to let this small rock worm drop below spawning redds where females are digging gravel and kicking up all kinds of larvae. Bob has landed steelhead as large as 14 pounds on the Rock Worm.

Minks Ear

Tyer: Brian Emerick of FishUSA.com, Erie, PA.
Hook: Dai Riki #730, sizes #12-16.
Thread: Uni-Thread, black, 8/0.
Tail: Mink guard hairs.
Abdomen: Mink under fur dubbed sparingly.
Rib: Gold wire.
Thorax: Mink under fur dubbed fuller.
Wingcase: Large gold mylar tinsel over turkey tail fibers.
Legs: Wood duck flank.
Comments: A hare's ear variation, this fly was developed by Brian over several straight days of fishing on Conneaut Creek, OH during the leaf season. The tinsel out produced plain 5 to 1.

Senyo Wiggle Stone

Guide: Greg Senyo of Jag Fly Co. and Steelhead Alley Outfitters, Holland, OH.
Thread: Black Uni-Thread, 8/0.

TAIL SECTION
Hook: Mustad #3906, sizes #12-16 (cut at bend).
Tail: 2 black goose biots.
Rib: 4 lb. mono.
Body: Black seal or rabbit dubbing.

THORAX SECTION
Hook: Daiichi #X120, sizes #10-16.
Thorax: Hare Line Ice dubbing. Blue and peacock are ideal for clear to slightly stained water. Orange, chartreuse and pink are ideal for murky water. Purple, flashback and cream also produce well.
Wingcase: Pearl Flashabou or black electrical tape.
Legs: 2 black goose biots.
Tying notes: Connect tail to thorax by forming a loop with 12 pound fire line or 8 pound fluorocarbon. Make sure to leave loop just wide enough to give tail free swimming motion.
Comments: This is Greg's go-to nymph and he carries them in numerous colors. His largest steelhead of the year is usually caught on this nymph pattern. You can impart great action to this fly at the end of a dead-drift by slowing lifting your fly rod and retrieving with short line strips and slight bounces of the rod tip.

Mini-Bug

Tyer: Clyde Murray of Folly's End Campground Fly & Tackle Shop, Erie, PA.
Hook: Mustad #C67S (wide gap), sizes #12-14.
Thread: Danville, black, 6/0.
Tail: Blue Dun floss.
Body: Gray Ultra Chenille palmered with size #14 grizzly hackle.
Shell Back: The remainder of floss pulled over body.
Comments: Fishing the shale bottomed streams of Pennsylvania can result in many lost steelhead flies. For this reason, Clyde designed this fly to be a quick-tie. He likes to fish it on a dead-drift (no indicator) as the top fly in a tandem rig with an egg pattern (12 inches apart). The natural colored Mini-Bug is very effective in clear water conditions.

Blue Humpback Nymph

Tyer: Joe Gablick of The Contented Angler, Lower Burrell, PA.
Hook: Dai Riki #135, size #12.
Thread: Danville, black, 6/0.
Tail: Black pheasant tail.
Body: Black pheasant tail.
Rib: Black Danville waxed nylon.
Bead: Spirit River blue Humpback glass bead. The off-set hole in this bead makes it position in the "humpback" on the hook shank.
Thorax: Black Ice Fur and black rabbit.
Comments: The "humpback" look to this to this nymph drives both steelhead and trout crazy!

Steak-and-Eggs

Guide: Greg Senyo of J.A.G. Fly Co., Holland, OH.
Hook: Daiichi #X120, sizes #10-14.
Thread: Uni-Thread, black, 6/0.
Tail: 2 black goose biots.
Thorax: Peacock Ice Dub.
Legs: 2 black goose biots.
Head: Any color egg yarn or McFly Foam.
Yoke or post: White or cream egg yarn and pearl Krystal Flash.
Tying notes: Tie in yoke long with Krystal Flash and hold tightly to the side with hackle pliers.
Once egg has been trimmed pull the yoke back to the top and trim leaving 1/4 inch or higher than egg
and fan out material.
Comments: Greg developed this fly for when water conditions are very low in the spring.
He likes to fish this pattern for steelhead in swift water.

Steelie Golden Stone

Tyer: Guide John Rochus of Canton, OH.
Hook: Daiichi #1720 (3XL), size #8-#14.
Thread: Light Cahill Uni-Thread, 8/0.
Bead: Gold Spirit River Brite Bead to match hook size.
Tail: Golden Stone Spirit River goose biots.

Abdomen: Yellow and brown Spirit River V-Tube, small.
Wingcase: Mottled turkey quill.
Thorax: Shimmer gold Spirit River Estaz.
Legs: Tan or yellow Spirit River Tarantula Leggs, medium.
Tying Notes: Tie the yellow V-tube down the near side of the hook and the brown V-tube down the far
side of the hook. This gives the fly a wider, flatter appearance and allows you to start the first part of the
banded abdomen with the yellow coloration. Wind the yellow and brown tubing up together creating the
alternate coloration.
Comments: John ties this nymph pattern in various sizes to match the different year classes of the
insect. He fishes it on a dead-drift on the fertile waters of the Grand River and Conneaut Creek, OH in
rocky bottomed, fast riffles and runs where the stoneflies like to hang out.

PF Egg Stone

Tyer: David Jugan of Prime Flies, Aliquippa, PA.
Hook: Daiichi #1730, sizes #10-16.
Bead: Gold bead to match hook size.
Thread: Uni-Thread, black, 6/0.
Antennae: Black goose biots.
Tail: Black goose biots.
Rib: Black Swannundaze or D Rib.
Abdomen: Black Rabbit Dubbing.
Wingcase: Three sections of turkey clipped V shape.
Legs: Black round rubber legs.
Thorax: Hareline Ice Dub or Spirit River Lite Brite.
Head Same as thorax.
Comments: David likes to fish this pattern behind an egg pattern during high water flows, in deep
pools and runs. In low, clear water situations, he ties them in #14 and #16's using angora goat dubbing
for a more subtle appearance.

Chloe Nymph

Tyer: David Jugan of Prime Flies, Aliquippa, PA.
Hook: Daiichi #1150, sizes #10-16.
Bead: Gold bead to match hook size.
Thread: Uni-Thread, tan, 6/0.
Tail: Spirit River tan micro round rubber legs.
Abdomen: Copper and yellow ultra wire.
Wingcase: Scud back.
Legs: Spirit River tan micro round rubber legs.
Thorax: Gold holographic Hareline Ice Dub or Spirit River Lite Brite.
Comments: Great fast water pattern that gets to the bottom quick. Fishes great alone or as a dropper.

Provan's Stone

Tyer: Jim Winger of Steubenville, OH.
Hook: Daichi #1270, size #10.
Thread: Uni-Thread, black, 6/0.
Tail: Round black rubber (split).
Weight: .015 lead.
Abdomen: Black petite Estaz (trimmed top and bottom).
Wing case: Bronze Flashabou (epoxied).
Thorax: Black Petite Estaz.
Tying notes: Wrap the Estaz in a spiral (approximately 1/32 inch gaps) so that the underbody shows through. This also allows the Estaz to move when fished.
Comments: This is Jim's go-to black nymph.

Spider

Tyer: Clyde Murray of Folly's End Campground Fly & Tackle Shop, Erie, PA.
Hook: Mustad #C67S (wide gap), size #12.
Thread: Danville, black, 6/0.
Tail: Twice as long as hook gap, 4 strands black peacock Krystal Flash.
Body: Black petite opalescent Estaz.
Shell Back: Olive/pearl sparkle braid.
Comments: Clyde originated this quick-tie pattern over 10 years ago. He likes to fish it on a dead-drift (no indicator) as the top fly in a tandem rig with an egg pattern (12 inches apart). Olive versions of this fly are also very effective.

60 Second Stone

Tyer: Sean Swatsky of Fly and Float Fishing, Cleveland, OH.
Hook: Daiichi #1560, sizes #10-16.
Thread: Danville, black, 6/0.
Tail: Black goose biots.
Ribbing: Copper Krystal Flash or gold wire.
Abdomen: Black Life Cycle Dubbing.
Wingcase: Black Swiss Straw.
Thorax: Black Life Cycle Dubbing.
Comments: Sean designed this stone to be simple for quick tying. He likes to fish it in riffles, runs and heads of pools. It is be deadly on cold winter days!

Quick Shrimp

Guide: Steve Brugger of Lake Erie Ultimate Angler, Erie, PA.
Hook: TMC #200R, size #12.
Thread: Uni-Thread, pink, 6/0.
Body: Pink SLF Davey Watton Dubbing.
Hackle: Pink hackle from eyes down, trimmed close.
Rib: Pink Glow Flashabou or equivalent wrapped from eyes down.
Tag: Pearl Mylar.
Eyes: Burnt mono or equivalent.
Antennae: Glow Flashabou or equivalent.
Comments: This is a good low water fly and can be dead-drifted with little twitches or swung in tailouts. Green or grey versions of this fly also produce well.

CJ's Mysis

Tyer: Craig Kopczyk of Kopczyk's Fly Sales, Milford, MI.
Hook: TMC #2487, sizes #8-12.
Eyes: Black mono.
Thread: Danville, white, 6/0.
Eyes: Black mono.
Body: White angora dubbing.
Tail: Pearl Lite Bright.
Shellback: Pearl Lite Bright.
Antennae: Pearl Lite Bright.
Rib: Mono.
Comments: Craig feels that this fly out fishes all mysis patterns out there right now and finds it very effective when fished close to the lake.

CJ's Salmo Slayer

Tyer: Craig Kopczyk of Kopczyk's Fly Sales, Milford, MI.
Hook: Daiichi #1560, size #10-14.
Thread: Danville, black, 6/0.
Tail: Purple buck tail.
Body: Medium copper wire.
Thorax: Purple antron dubbing.
Hackle: Purple saddle.
Comments: Craig developed this fly for clear water conditions. Try it when the Erie tribs have bottomed out and you will not be sorry!

Blue Steel

Tyer: Mark DeFrank of Chestnut Ridge Flies, Uniontown, PA.
Hook: Ashima # F52, sizes #8-#14.
Bead: Nickel to match hook size.
Thread: Danville, black, 6/0.
Abdomen: Peacock blue Wapsi antron dubbing.
Flashback: Pearl Hareline Mirage Sheeting.
Rib: Black Ultra Wire (small).
Hackle: Brown.
Thorax: Peacock Ice Dub in front of hackle.
Comments: During the low light conditions that exist in early morning, evening and on overcast days the color blue is very visible to steelhead due to its shorter wavelength (longer wavelength colors like red and orange become less visible due to absorption in the water). Mark says that the Blue Steel is the result of much redesign and perfecting of materials with the peacock blue dubbing and Mirage flash proving to be a very effective combo.

Ray's Steelhead Brassie

Tyer: Ray Travis of Lake Erie Ultimate Angler, Erie, PA.
Hook: TMC #2457, size #14-#16.
Thread: Chartreuse Uni-Thread, 8/0.
Underbody: Chartreuse thread wraps.
Overbody: Medium chartreuse Ultra Wire wrapped with wraps spaced to reveal underbody thread color.
Head: Chartreuse dubbing.
Notes: Other productive head/body color combinations include white/white, black/olive and black/brown.
Comments: Ray's Steelhead Brassie works well in the low, clear water of a dry fall or during the low base flows that invariably follow tributary run-off periods.

Chamois Pinky

Guide: Ken Chandler of Ken Chandler Fly Fishing Adventures, Markdale, ON
Hook: Tiemco #2487, sizes #8-14.
Thread: Uni-Thread, red, 6/0.
Body: 1/8 inch wide strip of natural chamois (4 inches long). Stretch and color with pink permanent marker.
Rib: Red larvae lace for "clitellum" bulbous section of the body.
Comments: Natural chamois, when wet, has a texture steelhead will not let go! This pattern has proven itself on many tributaries of the Great Lakes. Effective in low, clear flows as well as water with less than 18 inches of visibility. Ken says that this is a great pattern for trout and smallmouth as well.

Mark's Wiggle Hex

Tyer: Mark DeFrank of Chestnut Ridge Flies, Uniontown, PA
Hooks: Rear/Ashima #F55, size #14 and front/Ashima #F52 size #14.
Thread: Uni-Thread, tan, 8/0.
Tails: Tan marabou.
Abdomen: Dirty yellow dubbing.
Wing case: Brown Swiss straw (front and rear of the fly).
Rib: Amber Ultra Wire (small).
Gills: Tannish grey after shaft feather.
Thorax: Dirty yellow dubbing.
Hackle: Brown speckled hen back (tied in flat).
Hinge: 6 pound Fireline.
Comments: The articulated design of this fly creates an enticing movement that steelhead key on. Although Hexagenia nymphs are more common in Michigan steelhead waters this pattern has found a permanent home in Mark's fly box when fishing the Lake Erie tribs.

Lake Erie Swinger's Hex

Guide: Greg Senyo of Jag Fly Co. and Steelhead Alley Outfitters, Holland, OH.
Hook: Daiichi #1270, sizes #4-#8.
Thread: Uni-Thread, tan, 6/0.
Tail: Pink Krystal Flash and gold Flashabou.
Body: Yellow silk thread or yellow dubbing substitute.
Rib: Fine gold wire.
Wing case: Copper or bronze Swiss straw
Thorax: Pink Ice Dub or Trilobal Steelhead dubbing.
Hackle: Palmered soft hackle feather.
Eyes: Mono or black bead eyes.
Comments: Greg developed this hex pattern to have a slimmer bug profile with flashy, attractive colors and supple materials for movement. It is very effective on the swing or dead-drifted.

Yerger Miracle Nymph
Tyer: Rod Yerger of Rod Yerger Custom Flies, Lawrence, PA.
Hook: Daiichi #1530, sizes #14-#16.
Thread: Uni-Thread, black, 8/0.
Body: Black thread base covered by white rayon floss.
Rib: Fine copper wire.
Head: Black thread epoxied.
Comments: When in the water the body will turn a slimy grey when wet. Rod had been very successful fishing this simple nymph on Elk and Walnut Creeks in Pennsylvania in low, clear water. He likes to sight fish with no indicator, keeping it drifting exactly at the target fish's level. Watch any movement in the steelhead (especially the mouth) which will indicate a take.

Steelie Long Legs
Tyer: John Nagy of Pittsburgh, PA.
Hook: Daiichi #1720, sizes #10-#8.
Bead: Black bead to match hook size.
Thread: Uni-Thread, black, 8/0.
Legs: Olive Doug Swisher Incredible Legs.
Tail: Black Doug Swisher Wiggly Legs with four strands of olive Krinkle Mirror Flash. Ends of Wiggly Legs are cut uneven for natural look.
Body: Doug Swisher Peacock PLUS Dubbing. Pick out rubber legs with Velcro. For a fuller "leggy" look to the body cut up some black Wiggly Legs and add to dubbing mix.
Comments: This fly is based on Doug Swisher's Georgie Long Legs pattern. The speckled Incredible Legs have a built in "support system" allowing the use of super long legs. They don't tangle around the fly body or hook bend and provide an amazing action in the water. The Peacock Plus Dubbing contains Wiggly legs that add lots of body action as does the Wiggly Legs tail. If you want to wake up a steelhead tie this fly on! Also great for trout and smallmouth. Find Doug Swisher Fly Tying materials available on the web at www.DougSwisher.com

Soft Hackles

Mallard Minnow
Tyer: Jim Winger of Steubenville, OH
Hook: Daiichi #1720, size #8
Thread: Tan Uni-Thread, 8/0
Tail: White saddle hackle (webby part at butt of hackle)
Body: Regular opalescent pearl Estaz.
Throat: Red marabou fluff
Wing: Tip of white marabou blood feather
Collar: Natural mallard flank "folded" and wrapped.
Comments: Jim likes to fish this pattern on the swing for both steelhead and smallmouth. He finds it most effective in clear water.

Electra Soft Hackle

Guide: John Nagy of Pittsburgh, PA
Hook: Dai Riki #135, sizes #16-#8
Bead: Gold bead to match hook size.
Thread: Danville, fluorescent red, 6/0
Body: 1/8 inch gold Gudebrod Electra Metallic Hologram Braid.
Thorax: Bright orange yarn wrapped or dubbed.
Collar: 1 or 2 turns of grouse or partridge feathers.
Comments: Smaller versions of this fly work great dead-drifted in tandem with an egg pattern. Larger sizes are effective fished on the swing in the fall or late winter/early spring to active steelhead.

Jennings Nymph

Tyer: Johnny Kuehn of Angler's Roost Enterprises, Williamsville, NY
Hook: Mustad Sproat, 2XL, size #12
Thread: Danville, black, 6/0
Tag: Fine oval gold tinsel
Tail: 8-10 barbs of dark brown partridge
Body: Fluorescent chartreuse seal's fur substitute.
Rib: Gold oval tinsel
Thorax: Peacock herl
Wing: Dark brown mottled partridge, reversed, tied in by the tip.
Comments: This classic trout pattern has proven to be a winner on the Lake Erie tributaries for steelhead. Other effective body colors include natural olive, brown, tan and dark wine/claret (Peter Jennings original body color) as well as bright red, orange and cerise.

Steelhead Sparrow

Guide: John Nagy of Pittsburgh, PA.
Hook: Daiichi #1560, sizes #14-#8.
Bead: Black bead to match hook size.
Thread: Uni-Thread, olive, 8/0.
Tail: 1 or 2 dyed olive Chickabou feathers. Do not trim feathers at tie in point on hook bend, but use as an underbody for Estaz body by winding thread over feathers and hook shank toward eye of hook. Cock pheasant or grizzly marabou rump marabou feathers can also be used for tail.
Body: Fluorescent green Estaz wound on hook shank and trimmed to form body.
Collar: One turn of dyed olive cock pheasant rump hackle.
Head: One or two dyed black cock pheasant after shaft feathers tied in by butts and wound in front of collar.
Comments: This is John Nagy's steelhead variation of the classic Jack Gartside pattern which uses various feathers from a cock pheasant skin to tie a simple but deadly fly. Smaller versions of the Steelhead Sparrow work great dead-drifted in tandem with an egg pattern. Larger sizes are effective fished on the swing in the fall or late winter/early spring to active steelhead. Both the flash and movement generated in this fly are great strike triggers for steelhead.

PF Flyer

Tyer: Ray Travis of Lake Erie Ultimate Angler, Erie, PA.
Hook: Tiemco #9393, sizes #10-#8.
Thread: Uni-Thread, red, 6/0.
Body: Holographic red tinsel.
Wing: Black Polar Fiber.
Hackle: Red guinea feather.
Comments: This is Ray's favorite soft hackle for steelhead. He says another killer color combo is a silver body, white wing and natural guinea hackle.

Bloody Mary
Guide: John Nagy of Pittsburgh, PA
Hook: Daiichi #1560, sizes #14-#12
Bead: Gold bead to match hook size.
Thread: Uni-Thread, black, 8/0
Tail: 2 tan goose biots
Body: Red floss ribbed with peacock herl
Thorax: Peacock herl
Collar: 1 or 2 turns of grouse or partridge feathers.
Comments: A very popular fly in Colorado for trout that works gang busters for Erie steelhead! It is one of my "go-to" nymphs that I like to fish in tandem with an egg pattern.

Grimm Reaper
Tyer: Mark DeFrank of Chestnut Ridge Flies, Uniontown, PA
Hook: Ashima F55, sizes #8-#12
Thread: Uni-Thread, brown, 8/0
Abdomen: Gold holographic tinsel
Rib: Red Ultra Wire (small)
Hackle: Brown speckled hen back
Thorax: Black and red Spirit River Squirrel Bright Dubbing.
Comments: This is Mark's favorite fly for dead-drifting or swinging. The mottled hackle contributes to its buggy appearance while the holographic flash captures the steelhead's attention. The red wire around the tinsel also increases this fly's durability.

Streamers, Wooly Buggers, Sculpins and Leeches

Mirrored Minnow
Tyer: Jim Guida of Buffalo Outfitter's, Williamsville, NY.
Hook: Daiichi Alec Jackson #2052 (nickel) spey fly hook, size #7.
Thread: Uni-Thread, red, 8/0.
Body: Silver flashabou dubbing, spun with a dubbing loop.
Overwing: Grey zonker strip tied in at hook point then over body and tie in at front.
Beard: White marabou tied under and to hook point.
Eyes: Silver 3/16 in. holographic adhesive eyes, with coating of Loon's hard head on eyes and thread.
Comments: The Mirrored Minnow is effective for steelhead, trout and smallies. Can be fished on the swing, dead-drifted or stripped in. Visit www.cattaraugusflyshop.com for step-by-step instructions.

Funny Bunny Emerald Shiner
Tyer: Jerry Darkes of Angling Consulting Services, Strongsville, OH.
Hook: Daiichi #2220, sizes #6-#4.
Thread: Danville, Chartreuse, 6/0.
Tail: White marabou or rabbit strip.
Body: White cross-cut rabbit (wrapped) topped with a few strands of Mirror Flash
Head: Chartreuse UV Ice Dub
Tying notes: Put a little super glue on the hook shank before you wrap the cross-cut to make the fly more durable.
Comments: Jerry says that this simple shiner imitation has plenty of movement on the swing and is extremely durable. It is also killer on smallmouth and trout!

German's White Nightmare

Guide: Bill German of Steely Guide Service, Chagrin Falls, OH.
Hook: Daiichi #2220, sizes #4-#8.
Thread: Brown or white Uni-Thread, 6/0.
Body: Silver Ice Hackle (trimmed).
Wing: 1/8 inch white rabbit fur strip secured with copper wire along its length and topped with 6 strands of pearlescent Krystal Flash.
Collar: Mallard flank.
Comments: This is Bill's #1 streamer pattern for steelhead (it took a little coaxing to get it from him!). It has contributed many double-digits days for Bill when swung down-and-across with some added strips in slower moving holes. Another version of this streamer called "The Illuminator" (black rabbit strip fur and chartreuse schlappen feather for the collar) is great for stained water conditions or low light conditions.

STS Streamer

Tyer: Jim Distefanis of Canton, MI.
Hook: Mustad #3366A, size #6.
Thread: Danville, pink, tan or grey, 6/0.
Eyes: 1/8 inch silver bead chain.
Body : Pearl Flashabou wrapped flat on hook shank.
Throat: White marabou.
Under-wing: White calf tail or craft synthetic topped with a few strands of pearl Flashabou.
Over-wing: Gray marabou colored on top with green marker.
Comments: Jim developed this quick-tie pattern to imitate the Lake Erie Emerald Shiner. He likes to fish it in clearer flows in a down-and-across presentation. He recommends waiting before retrieving it since steelhead will often take it at the end of the swing.

Silver Side Minnow

Tyer: Mark DeFrank of Chestnut Ridge Flies, Uniontown, PA.
Hook: Kamasan #B820, sizes #6-#12.
Thread: Danville, olive, 6/0.
Body: Chartreuse Spirit River Depth Advantage Dubbing.
Wing: Silver holographic Ice Dub.
Overwing: 6 Peacock herls.
Comments: Mark proves with this minnow pattern that the simplest flies are usually the deadliest!

Bob's Baby "Bow"

Guide: Bob Tomlinson, Fairview Park, OH.
Hook: Daiichi #2370, size #6.
Thread: Danville, black, 6/0.
Tail: Chartreuse buck tail.
Body: Pink seals fur or Antron dubbing.
Rib: Medium flat silver tinsel.
Throat: Pink buck tail.
Wing (bottom to top): A few strands of white buck tail, pink buck tail, chartreuse buck tail and badger hair.
Cheeks: Jungle cock eyes (optional).
Comments: Very effective in the late fall and early spring. Bob says to swing this streamer across current and then let it "hang" for a few seconds before stripping it back to you.

Marion's Versatile Minnow
Guide: Marion Graven of North Coast Salmon & Steelhead, North Olmsted, OH.
Hook: Daiichi #2340, size #6.
Thread: Uni-Thread, white, 6/0.
Body: Pearl tinsel wrapped on hook shank.
Throat: Fine white buck tail and red floss.
Wing (top to bottom): 6 strands of pearl Flashabou, 2 gray or olive hackle tips, 2 silver badger hackle tips.
Eyes: 2 jungle cock nails.
Comments: Marion uses this streamer pattern for multiple species in both streams and lakes. For steelhead fishing he likes to dead-drift it in the fast water section that dumps into a deep pool or fish it on a traditional swing across current. The red throat is a great strike trigger and the black longitudinal stripe provided by the silver badger (that tapers to a point) is very natural, like a baitfish or minnow.

White Bellied Bugger
Tyer: Mark DeFrank of Chestnut Ridge Flies, Uniontown, PA.
Hook: Kamasan #B820, sizes #6-#12.
Thread: Danville, black, 6/0.
Tail: White Marabou.
Body: White chenille.
Overbody: Purple Marabou (tied in at front and extending back to tail).
Hackle: Purple.
Comments: This is Mark's interpretation of the Wooly Bugger. The white belly on this fly imitates a bait fish while the intensity of movement from the tail and hackle is sure to provoke strikes!

Articulated Wooly Bugger
Tyer: John Nagy of Pittsburgh, PA.
Hooks: Daiichi #1720 (front and rear).
Thread: Uni-Thread, hot pink, 6/0.
Bead: Pink Spirit River Hot Bead.
Legs: 4 Hareline Grizzly Barred Crazy Legs (clear/pearl flake) tied in slightly behind bead on front hook with marking side of legs showing from top and bottom of the fly.
Tails: Hot pink marabou for front and rear bodies. Use fluffy marabou for front body tail and straighter marabou for rear body tail.
Hackle: Black (front body only).
Front and read bodies: Black chenille.
Tying notes: Connect front and rear hooks by loop formed with 12 pound fire line (which is secured to rear shank of front hook under body material).
Comments: Bill Turner of Lewisburg, WV showed John Nagy this pattern on a fall guide trip on Cattaraugus Creek, NY. He said he had come across it while trout fishing in Chile. This fly is all about movement. The articulated body, marabou and rubber legs can wake up a steelhead big time! Also great for smallmouth and trout. Hot chartreuse and olive versions also work well.

Olive Pipe Brush
Tyer: Alan Carter of Ashtabula, OH.
Hook: Mustad #9674, size #8.
Bead: 1/8 inch gold bead.
Thread: Gudebrod, bright green, 3/0.
Tail: Olive Marabou topped with 2 strands of olive Mirror Flash.
Body: Crystal Mirror Flash (wrapped).
Hackle: Olive.
Comments: Alan fashioned this fly after an old Mirimichi Atlantic salmon tie by W.W. Doak. He has had great success with it on the lower part of tributaries near the lake shore drifting, swinging or stripping.

Greg's Cat-A-Killer
Guide: Greg Senyo of Jag Fly Co. and Steelhead Alley Outfitters, Holland, OH.
Hook: Daiichi #1720, size #8.
Thread: Uni-Thread, black or chartreuse, 6/0.
Tail: Chartreuse Marabou with pearl flashabou tied in on sides of tail.
Hackle: Chartreuse hen hackle.
Body: Chartreuse chenille.
Wing Case: Black Antron.
Comments: Greg developed this pattern to combine the steelhead's fascination with the color chartreuse and the most popular fly known the wooly bugger. It works extremely well on Cattaraugus Creek, NY and has been a staple for Greg there for years.

Spring Bugger
Tyer: Craig Kopczyk of Kopczyk's Fly Sales, Milford, MI.
Hook: TMC #700, sizes #8-#10.
Thread: Danville, orange, 6/0.
Tail: Burnt Orange grizzly marabou.
Body: Orange and black variegated chenille.
Hackle: Orange grizzly.
Comments: Craig says that this is a great pattern for spring steelhead especially the males.

Doc's Wally Bugger
Guide: Walter J. Myslewski, M.D. Greensburg, PA.
Hook: Mustad #79580, size #8.
Thread: Danville, white, 6/0.
Tail: White marabou.
Body: White chenille palmered with white saddle hackle.
Wing: 6 rainbow Krystal flash and 2 silver Krystal Flash strands topped with white marabou.
Head: Painted enamel eyes (black) and throat (red).
Comments: Doc developed his bugger to have a minnow like appearance. At the end of a dead-drift try twitching the fly up towards you in the current to entice more steelhead strikes. In clear water, slowly drift the fly down to just in front of a targeted steelhead and then twitch up in the current. If you see Doc on Elk Creek, PA hooked up with a steelie it's a good bet that he is using a Wally Bugger!

Senyo Sculpin
Guide: Greg Senyo of Jag Fly Co. and Steelhead Alley Outfitters, Holland, OH.
Hook: Any turn-up-eye salmon hook, sizes #8-#4.
Thread: Uni-Thread, olive, 6/0.
Tail: Reversed tied olive rabbit strip, olive Krystal Flash and rainbow Flashabou.
Body: Peacock Ice dubbing.
Gills: Barred olive marabou.
Head: Peacock Ice dubbing.
Tying notes: The head is tied in with 1/8 inch clumps of Ice dubbing starting on the top and then side-to-side and back to the top again to the eye of the hook. The head is then brushed with a wire brush and then trimmed to form a wide and flat head.
Comments: Greg developed this pattern to imitate both the native sculpins in the Lake Erie watershed and the round gobies which recently invaded Lake Erie providing a new food source for the steelhead. It is best fished deep on the swing through pools and submerged structures that steelhead tend to use as cover. Purple and flesh colored patterns (change thread, tail, gill and head colors) also are very effective.

Lake Erie Goby

Guide: Greg Senyo of Jag Fly Co. and Steelhead Alley Outfitters, Holland, OH.
Hook: Mustad #3191, size #1/0.
Thread: Uni-Thread, black, 6/0.
Tail: Olive Grizzly Marabou.
Body: Peacock, blue, emerald Ice Dub blend.
Hackle: Olive shlappen feather.
Wing: Barred mallard feather.
Head: Peacock, blue, emerald Ice Dub blend.
Eyes: Prismatic silver eyes.
Comments: Greg developed this pattern to take advantage of the Goby invasion of Lake Erie which the opportunistic steelhead has taken advantage of as a food source. Fish it on a heavy sink tip on the swing, keeping the fly on the bottom.

Simple Sculpin

Tyer: Jim Guida of Williamsville, NY.
Hook: Daiichi #472, sizes #2-#4.
Thread: Uni-Thread, brown, 8/0.
Eyes: White lead dumbbell eyes painted with black eyes tied in on top of hook shank.
Tail/Over-wing: Barred white and black rabbit strip tied in on bottom of hook shank.
Body: Amber Angora goat with some Angel Hair.
Head: Tan E-Z Bug chenille tied around lead eyes and teased out with dubbing brush. Black and olive colors also are effective.
Comments: This sculpin pattern will ride with hook up due to the positioning of dumbell eyes on the hook shank. Jim fishes it by dead-drifting it along the bottom and hopping it along slowly. It works great for both steelhead and smallmouth. Email Jim Guida at: jimguida@hotmail.com for step-by-step instructions.

Funny Bunny Sculpin

Tyer: Jerry Darkes of Angling Consultants, Strongsville, OH.
Hook: Daiichi #2220, sizes #6-#4.
Thread: Danville, olive, 6/0.
Tail: Tan or olive grizzly marabou.
Body: Golden variant or sand variant cross-cut rabbit (Hareline colors) wrapped on hook shank and trimmed flat on bottom. Top with 6 strands of copper Flashabou.
Head: Sculpin olive rams wool.
Comments: Another variation of Jerry's Funny Bunny series can also be used as a crayfish imitation. Smallmouth and trout also love this fly!

Emulator Sculpin

Guide: Kevin Feenstra of Feenstra Guide Service, Newaygo, MI.
Hook: Daiichi #2220 (4XL), size #1 (a heavy hook for fishing in heavy current). Daiichi #2461(3XL), size 1/0 or 2/0 (for a shorter, fatter version of the fly). Try sizes #6-#8 for smaller size tributaries.
Thread: Uni-Thread, tan, 6/0.
Tail: Tan grizzly marabou feathers and a few strands of copper Flashabou.
Body: Emmu feather wound tightly forward.
Hackle: Brown or olive schlappen feather.
Pectoral fins: A clump of mallard flank feather fibers tied on both sides of fly.
Head: Sunburst or grape Flashabou (extending to hook bend) followed by clump of Australian opossum fur tied with tips facing rear of hook. Roughly trim opossum fur to form head and allow for some tip fibers to form collar. Ram's wool can be substituted for opossum fur.
Comments: Developed on Michigan's Muskegon River by guide Kevin Feenstra it has also been extremely effective on the Lake Erie tributaries for steelhead in smaller sizes. Kevin likes to swing it deep and slow and finds it especially effective in the spring but will even work in the dead of winter. The takes with this big sculpin can be vicious, often with a steelie bumping the fly midway through the drift only to come around and hammer it at the end of the swing!

Boa Leech

Tyer: Jerry Darkes of Angling Consultants, Strongsville, OH.
Hook: Daiichi #1710, size #4.
Thread: Danville, black, 6/0.
Tail: Black or purple marabou.
Body: Black or purple craft store Boa Yarn (also known as Flapper Yarn or Eye Lash Yarn).
Head: Shrimp pink or fluorescent pink UV Ice Dub.
Comments: The Boa Leech fills the need for a darker bodied streamer. The head can contrast or blend with the body but Jerry favors the contrast with bright Ice Dub colors.

Grapefruit Head Leech

Guide: Kevin Feenstra of Feenstra Guide Service, Newaygo, MI.
Hook: Daiichi #2461 or equivalent 3XL streamer hook, sizes #8-2/0.
Thread: Uni-Thread, black, 6/0.
Tail: Black marabou with sparse red flash of Angel Hair or Fire Fly. Length is at least 3 times body length.
Body: Black marabou feather wound 2/3 way up hook shank (tie in by tip).
Hackle: Black, purple or olive schlappen feather wound through marabou (be careful not to bind down too many of the marabou fibers).
Collar: Large mallard flank or blue eared pheasant.
Over-wing: (top to bottom): Silver, blue and Kelly green Flashabou (to tail length).
Head: Fuchsia Cactus Chenille (large) followed by a veil of chartreuse Ice Dubbing.
Comments: This is a great fall pattern particularly during high/stained flows. Kevin likes to use big sizes in the fall and also smaller sizes in the winter. The takes on this leech are vicious, so hold on!

Bess's Best Bet

Tyer: Dan Walker of Egg Man Flies, Belleville, MI.
Hook: Daiichi #1720, size #8.
Thread: Danville, black, 6/0.
Tail: Chartreuse or steelhead orange Glo Bug Yarn.
Body: Metallic gold chenille.
Hackle: Palmered webby black saddle hackle.
Comments: Dan says that this old fly was originated by a Wisconsin guide named Bess and is a killer on the Erie tribs as well. It has three great stimuli (color, flash and movement) to trigger a strike.

Lil' Rainbow Flouro Fiber Minnow

Tyer: Ray Travis of Lake Erie Ultimate Angler, Erie, PA.
Hook: Tiemco #9395, sizes #10-#8.
Thread: Uni-Thread, olive, 6/0.
Eyes: Silver dumbbell eyes (small) tied in behind hook eye and under hook shank.
Belly: White Flouro Fiber tied in under hook shank (1 1/2 inches long for a size #8 hook).
Under tuft: Pink Polar Plus tied in under hook shank.
Wing (bottom to top): Pink Flouro Fiber, tuft of olive Polar Plus, olive Flouro Fiber, 3 or 4 strands of peacock Krystal Flash tied in behind hook eye and on top of hook shank. Wing is 1 1/2 inches long for a size #8 hook.
Comments: Ray uses this streamer pattern on the Pennsylvania tributaries when they have run-off to clean and low water conditions. Bigger streamer patterns typically send the steelies "running" the other way during these conditions but not the down-sized and sparse Lil' Rainbow!

Rainbow Runner

Tyer: Jim Guida of Williamsville, NY.
Hook: Umpqua #7999, sizes #8-#2.
Thread: Uni-Thread, black, 8/0.
Body: Pearl Lagartun Mini-Braid.
Belly: White rams wool.
Underwing: Pearl DNA Holo Fusion.
Overwing: Multi-color smolt blue or multi-color perch SLF Hank topped with 10 peacock herls.
Eyes: Silver 3/16 in. holographic adhesive eyes, with coating of Loon's hard head on eyes and thread.
Comments: Jim says that when wet the colors and shape of the multi-color SLF Hank overwing "pop out" in an unbelievable display. The Rainbow Runner is effective for steelhead, trout and smallies and can be fished on the swing, dead-drifted or stripped in. Try tying this one on a tube also.
Email Jim Guida at: jimguida@hotmail.com for step-by-step instructions.

Black Mamba

Tyer: Jeff "Bear" Andrews of Grand Ledge, MI.
Hook: 3XL streamer hook, sizes #8-#4.
Thread: Uni-Thread, black, 8/0.
Tail: Black rabbit fur strip topped with black marabou (2-3 inches long). Also tie in 4 strands of blue Krinkle Mirror Flash material along either side of tail.
Body: Black Estaz tied double thickness (leave some room at front of hook shank for collar) and palmered with black schlappen feather.
Collar: Black pheasant rump feather. Should be bigger than schlappen feather body hackle in order to form a distinctive head.
Comments: Legendary guide Jeff "Bear" Andrews of Grand Ledge, MI. originated the Black Mamba. He designed this cross between a wooly bugger and a leech to have movement, volume and flash. The dark silhouette and flash provided by this big pattern will get the attention of a steelhead quickly in heavily stained and high flows. Try fishing it in tandem with an egg or nymph pattern as well. Great pattern to tie up in a tube fly design as well.

Spey Flies

Bead Head Spey Bunny

Tyer: Alan Carter of Ashtabula, OH.
Hook: Mustad #9674, size #8.
Bead: 1/8 inch gold bead.
Thread: Uni-Thread, black, 6/0.
Tail: Purple rabbit strip topped with 2 strands of pearlescent Krystal Flash.
Body: Black cross-cut rabbit strip (wrapped).
Collar: Purple schlappen feather.
Comments: Alan has had great success with his spey bunny on the Grand River, OH during the fall. He fishes it on the swing with a 5 inches per second tip running it about 2 1/2 feet under the surface. Expect some really "smash" hook-ups with this fly!

The "Grand" Illusion

Guide: Bob Tomlinson, Fairview Park, OH.
Hook: Alec Jackson's Steelhead Irons, size #3 (1X stout, 1X short).
Thread: Danville, black, 6/0.
Tail: 4 strands each of orange, red, chartreuse and yellow buck tail.
Body: Dark green Poly Flash.
Wing: Black marabou.
Collar: Orange Guinea feather.
Comments: This is Bob's favorite fly for the Grand River, OH when the water is low and clearing. He also uses it all year round with great success as well.

Diablo Cock Spey

Guide: Marion Graven of North Coast Salmon & Steelhead, North Olmsted, OH.
Hook: Daiichi Alec Jackson Spey fly hook #2051, size #7.
Thread: Uni-Thread, red or black, 8/0.
Body (optional): Red or purple floss ribbed with silver tinsel.
Wing: 8 strands of pearl Flashabou.
Hackle: Red and purple marabou tied in by stems and wrapped a few turns (leave room for attaching eyes and making head).
Cheeks: Jungle cock.
Comments: Marion's series of spey flies are very basic and quick ties. They provide great movement, flash and color when fished on the swing. Other effective hackle colors include purple and white, black and blue as well as all black, white, blue and purple hackles.

Senyo Spey Stone

Guide: Greg Senyo of Jag Fly Co. and Steelhead Alley Outfitters, Holland, OH.
Hook: Any turn-up-eye salmon hook, sizes #8-#4.
Thread: Uni-Thread, black, 6/0.
Body: Gray rabbit dubbing and black larvae lace.
Thorax: Pearl and blue Ice Dubbing.
Wing Case: Black goose feather.
Collar: Black and blue schlappen and 2 black goose biots.
Comments: According to Greg spey flies and spey fishing are very addicting and so are dead-drifting and tying stonefly nymphs for steelhead. This fly is Greg's mixture of the two. It fishes extremely well when fished as a dropper off a marabou spey or large minnow pattern.

The Weamer

Tyer: Peter Charles, Hagersville, ON.
Hook: Daiichi #2051, sizes #3-#5.
Thread: Uni-Thread, tan, 3/0.
Tag: Medium gold mylar tinsel.
Body: 3 layers of white Uni-wool.
Hackle: Select a white marabou feather that has well separated and erect barbs. Strip on one side but leave about 1 inch of barb at the tip (tip is very fragile and cannot be stripped). Tie in feather in by tip and wrap on body stroking back barbs as wrap forward. Finish with one complete turn at the front of the body.
Underwing: 3 strands of gold Flashabou (thin, extra limp type) that is "doubled over" and "stagger cut" at diffe rent lengths. Try to avoid a squared off end when cutting.
Wing: Tan Mega Hair (goat hair) or Icelandic sheep hair.
Overwing: 2 strands of peacock herl approximately wing length.
Eyes: Small gold peel and stick eyes secured with a layer of very fine mono thread and sealed with gloss clear head cement.
Tying notes: Peter recommends not using a standard streamer hook since the low hook eye and long shank will produce a drooping fly in slow currents. He also ties a low-water version where he applies less turns of the marabou using a smaller feather, plus the wing is a bit shorter and thinner as well. For a slim profile baitfish like shiners, smelt and young trout use a thin wool body and minimal marabou body wraps. For a more "bulbous" species like a chub, collar the marabou in front of a wool ball or a raised ball of dubbing at the front of the fly. This causes the marabou to flare out with a bullet profile. This bigger profile is also beneficial when fishing the fly in heavy currents or stripping since the large "shoulders" to the fly can resist heavy water currents and "push water" when stripped in at the end of the swing. This sends out a disturbance in the water that a steelhead can sense with his lateral line.
Comments: Peter developed this fly as a cross between a spey wet fly and a streamer type pattern and thus the name "Weamer." It uses materials that move in a life-like manner even in low currents. It closely imitates the light transmitting characteristics found in a baitfish; very opaque in the head, belly and back but translucent in the rest of the body. The tan wing and gold flashabou combination has been Peter's best producer but he also varies colors to represent different baitfish species. He has caught nine species of fish on it including steelhead!

Pink Matuka Spey

Guide: Ken Chandler of Ken Chandler Fly Fishing Adventures, Markdale, ON
Hook: Partridge Bartleet, sizes #3/0-#4
Thread: Uni-Thread, red, 6/0
Tag: Flat silver Mylar (medium)
Body: White micro chenille
Rib: Gold, oval varnished French tinsel (medium)
Collar: Pink Ice Chenille (3-5 wraps)
Wing: Bright pink magnum rabbit zonker strip topped with 4-6 strands of Krystal Flash
Hackle: Pink mallard flank strip (one side, tied tip first).
Comments: Ken developed this pattern with subtle changes over a 10 year period. Can be fished with a short, fast sink tip on the swing or on a dead-drift/swing with a floating line, a long leader and a small amount of shot. A purple version of this Matuka Spey is also very effective.

Skinny Spey

Guide: Ken Chandler of Ken Chandler Fly Fishing Adventures, Markdale, ON.
Hook: Daiichi Low Water Salmon Fly Hook #2421, sizes #2-#10.
Thread: Uni-Thread, black, 8/0.
Tag: Flat silver Mylar (medium).
Body: Black antron.
Rib: Silver Mylar with gold oval tinsel.
Collar: 5-6 strands of ostrich herl tied tip first in a dubbing loop for strength.
Hackle: Sparse black burnt goose shoulder spey hackle.
Over-wing: Mallard flank (optional).
Comments: Ken says that this pattern is exceptional for low, clear conditions. He likes to fish the Skinny Spey using a floating line, a long leader and a small amount of shot on a dead-drift or swing. Try attaching a dropper fly like a small black stone, egg pattern or hare's ear nymph approximately 18 inches from the spey to give the steelhead a choice of flies. Ken recommends maintaining tension on the line, as steelhead will often pick up this fly very gently.

Orange Peacock Spey

Tyer: John Burkhardt of Natural Sports-The Fishing Store, Kitchener, ON.
Hook: Daiichi Alec Jackson Spey fly hook #2051 (also Partridge Bartleet or Talon), sizes #3-#5.
Thread: Danville, flat waxed, black, 6/0.
Tag: #14 silver Mylar.
Ribbing: #14 silver Mylar followed by XS silver oval tinsel.
Body: 2/3 orange floss, 1/3 peacock Ice Dub/black rabbit dub blend.
Hackle: Blue eared pheasant dyed black or burnt goose shoulder spey hackle (Hareline or Umpqua supplies it). John recommends soaking burnt goose hackle (the stems can be too stiff and thick for tying) in warm water for 15-20 minutes and then stripping the stems in half with a razor blade. This will facilitate much easier wrapping.
Throat: Gadwell.
Wing: Bronze mallard shoulder.
Comments: This sparse pattern produces well in clearing or clear flows and can be fished on a dry line in fast water or with light to moderate sink tips.

Steelheader's Tip

> *"It is good to remember there will be a lot more steelhead caught on a piece of yarn, than all the fanciest flies ever tied."*
> *Roger Haig-Brown*

Caroline Elizabeth Gordon

Tyer: John Burkhardt of Natural Sports-The Fishing Store, Kitchener, ON.
Hook: Daiichi Alec Jackson Spey fly hook #2051 (also Partridge Bartleet or Talon), size #1.5.
Thread: Danville, flat waxed, wine, 6/0.
Tail: Rusty red golden pheasant flank.
Tag: #14 gold Mylar.
Ribbing: #14 silver Mylar followed by XS silver or gold oval tinsel.
Body: 50/50 mix of fall brown SLF and peacock SLF dubbing for rear 2/3. For front 1/3 same dubbing mix except spun in dubbing loop.
Hackle: XL dun spey hackle (3 turns).
Wing: Bronze mallard shoulder.
Throat: Rusty red golden pheasant.
Comments: John's fishing buddy Peter Pettos has great faith in this Northwestern adaptation of the traditional Lady Caroline. This pattern has greatly influenced John's tying style and he characterizes it as "big and swimming."

Glo-Butt Greenie

Tyer: John Burkhardt of Natural Sports-The Fishing Store, Kitchener, ON.
Hook: Daiichi Alec Jackson Spey fly hook #2051 (also Partridge Bartleet or Talon), size #1.5.
Thread: Danville, flat waxed, black, 6/0.
Tag: #14 silver Mylar.
Tail: Chartreuse saddle hackle.
Butt: Chartreuse Ice Dubbing.
Ribbing: #12 gold Mylar followed by XS silver oval tinsel.
Body: Mixture of 2/3 caddis green Trilobal dub and 1/3 peacock/black Ice dub.
Hackle: XL black spey hackle.
Wing: Bronze mallard shoulder.
Throat: Gadwell.
Cheeks: Jungle Cock.
Comments: This pattern is a simple version of the poplar "Akroyd" and fish's well in off-colored water or just clearing flows (less than 1 foot of visibility). John says that it can also be tied in a hot pink variation.

Winter Spey

Tyer: Joe Gablick of The Contented Angler, Lower Burrell, PA.
Hook: Daiichi Alec Jackson Spey fly hook #2050, size #7.
Thread: Danville, white, 6/0.
Tail: Golden pheasant crest.
Tail veiling: Black and white wood duck.
Butt: Red ostrich herl.
Body: White floss (rear), white fluorescent yarn (front).
Ribbing: Fine oval silver tinsel.
Hackle: White spey hackle.
Throat: Sparse teal.
Wing: Lady Amherst center tail.
Comments: Joe likes to fish this fly in the winter when ice is on the water. Try it on a dead-drift with some shot to keep it down.

Strawberry Cream Spey

Tyer: Joe Gablick of The Contented Angler, Lower Burrell, PA.
Hook: Daiichi Alec Jackson Spey fly hook #2050, size #7.
Thread: Danville, black, 6/0.
Tail: Pearl Krystal Flash.
Body: Pink rabbit, red marabou, black rabbit.
Hackle: Long, white schlappen.
Comments: This cold weather pattern is for the hardy winter steelheaders who break tributary ice to get open water. Joe likes to dead-drift it with an occasional jigging action.

Copper Grey Spey

Tyer: Joe Gablick of The Contented Angler, Lower Burrell, PA.
Hook: Daiichi Alec Jackson Spey fly hook #2050, size #7.
Thread: Danville, red, 6/0.
Tail: Orange hen hackle.
Body: Flat copper tinsel (rear), black wool (front).
Hackle: Blue eared pheasant.
Ribbing: Copper wire over front half.
Throat: Orange saddle hackle (short).
Wing: Dyed red squirrel tail.
Comments: This dull colored pattern is very
effective in low water. Joe likes to dead-drift or
swing it early in the morning.

Classic Orange Spey

Tyer: Joe Gablick of The Contented Angler, Lower Burrell, PA.
Hook: Daiichi Alec Jackson Spey fly hook #2050, size #7.
Thread: Danville, white, 6/0 (finish fly with black head cement).
Tail: Golden pheasant tippets.
Tag: Flat gold tinsel.
Body: 1/3 orange Uni-stretch (rear) and orange wool (front).
Rib: Extra fine oval gold tinsel.
Hackle: Blue eared pheasant.
Throat: Orange dyed guinea.
Wing: Bronze mallard.
Comments: This is Joe's fall fly for low water conditions.

Sorta Spey

Tyer: Gary Selig of Mertztown, PA.
Hook: Daiichi #1530, size #4.
Thread: Uni-Thread, olive, 8/0.
Tag: Flat silver Uni-Tinsel.
Rib: Fine copper wire.
Body: 2 layers of flat silver Uni-Tinsel and wrapped with fluorescent chartreuse or pearl Lagartun Mini-Braid (lacquer or superglue tinsel before braid wrap).
Wing and throat: Fluorescent chartreuse imitation seal's fur (to body length) which helps to support hackle in water.
Hackle: Fluorescent chartreuse hen hackle and dyed black pheasant Rumph feathers.
Comments: Gary originated this pattern for Atlantic salmon fishing in New Brunswick but it has proved deadly for Great Lakes Steelhead as well. He likes to swing the fly in normal to low current flows to maintain the action of the spey hackle in the water. Fishing in faster currents could collapse the hackle like most spey patterns. Gary says if you keep this fly wet you will catch fish!

Southwest Jewel

Tyer: Ray Travis of Lake Erie Ultimate Angler, Erie, PA.
Hook: Tiemco #9395, sizes #6-#2.
Thread: Uni-Thread, purple, 6/0.
Body (rear): Green Holographic tinsel (3/4 of total body length).
Body (front): UV chartreuse Polar Chenille (1/4 of total body length).
Hackle: Turquoise marabou.
Wing (bottom to top): Krinkle Mirror Flash (same as marabou hackle length) and purple Krinkle Mirror Flash (1/2 marabou hackle length). Five strands of each color.
Comments: Ray has had some of his hardest takes while swinging this spey fly in normal to high flows. He says the steelies will either love or hate the combined color and action of this pattern!

Illustrated Egg Pattern Tying Instructions

Half-N-Half

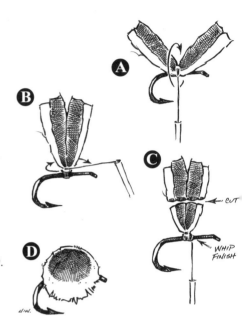

A. For a size #10 hook (Daaichi #1530), secure 3 pieces of Glo Bug Yarn (each piece 2 inches long) at center of hook shank with 2 or 3 wraps of thread. One piece of alaskan roe yarn is on top and 2 pieces of chartreuse yarn is on bottom. Use strong tying thread like 3/0 Danville plus, fluorescent red or orange.

B. Pull both pieces of Glo Bug yarn upward and wrap thread around base, working upward also (5 to 6 wraps).

C. Whip finish at base. Proceed to cut yarn by first firmly pulling Glo Bug Yarn upward and then cutting straight across with sharp scissors (approximately 3/8 inch above hook shank for size #10 hook).

D. Finished fly.

Sucker Spawn

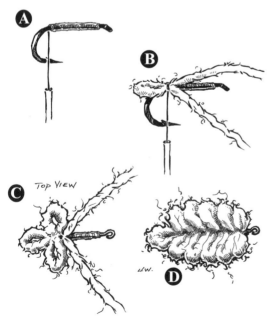

A. Wrap hook shank with multiple layers of fluorescent red thread finishing at bend. Use heavier 3/0 thread for this step (switch to fluorescent red, 6/0 thread for next steps).

B. For a size #14 hook (Dai Riki #135), take a 5 inch piece of angora yarn (use 2 strands) and fold in half. Proceed to tie in at bend making tail.

C. Begin making successive pairs of loops (on top of hook shank) starting in front of tail and working toward eye of hook (make 5 pairs of loops for a size #14 hook). Initially make loops larger than normal and then adjust to desired size by tightening up on both free ends of angora yarn simultaneously. After fifth loop pair is made, cut remaining angora yarn close to shank and build up a head with thread. Whip finish at eye.

D. Finished fly.

Scrambled Eggs

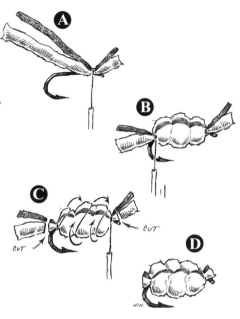

A. For a size #10 hook (Daaichi #1530), secure one piece of chartreuse Glo Bug Yarn and one piece of flame Micro Yarn (both 2 inches long with flame positioned on top) behind the hook eye. Leave some yarn in front of hook eye (1/4 inch) to form head later. Use 6/0, fluorescent red or orange tying thread.

B. Working backward toward hook bend, make 3 segments with the yarn pieces.

C. Secure thread at bend of hook (behind last segment) by making multiple wraps around hook shank. Then proceed to wrap thread back toward hook eye, diagonally wrapping thread once over each segment. Whip finish at eye. Cut remaining yarn material at bend and eye of hook to form tail and head.

D. Finished fly.

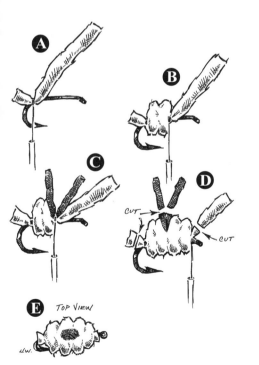

Blood Dot

A. For a size #16 hook (Dai Riki #135), take a 2 inch piece of pink lady Glo Bug Yarn and divide it (separating it length wise) so that only 25 % remains. Secure this piece of yarn at hook bend (use 6/0, fluorescent red tying thread) leaving some yarn trailing behind bend to form tail later (about 1/4 inch).

B. Working toward eye of hook, make 2 segments with yarn.

C. Immediately in front of the second segment tie in a 1/2 inch long piece of flame Micro Yarn.

D. Proceed to make 2 more segments with the yarn, working toward hook eye. Whip finish at eye and cut remaining yarn material at bend and eye of hook to form tail and head. Finish by cutting remaining flame Micro yarn piece to form dot.

E. Finished fly.

Fall hen steelhead that took a tube fly
(note tube fly has disengaged from hook during fight).

Tube Flies

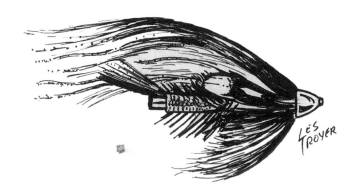

Chapter 8

The beauty and effectiveness of tube flies is slowly spreading to "in-the-know" steelheaders throughout the Great Lakes region. Very popular in Europe, tube flies were originally tied on turkey quills by Salmon fly dresser Winnie Morawski in Aberdeen, Scotland, in 1945. The turkey quills were used because salmon hooks were both expensive and scarce in post-war Britain. Winnie's design, although groundbreaking, had faults.

The hollow turkey quills were very fragile and she bound the hook shank (a snelled treble) to the inside of the quill which precluded any possible hook replacement. William Mitchell, a British doctor visiting Winnie's employer (tackle manufacturer Charles Playfair & Co.) recommended using surgical IV tubing instead of the quills which turned out to be more durable. The tube fly could now slide freely up the leader protecting the fly from any damage caused by the fish's teeth.

Since this tube fly design allowed the fly to spin unencumbered on the leader (junction tubing was not being used to secure the hook to the end of the tube as is done now) it created a problem for traditional salmon flies since it could cause them to ride improperly in the water. The solution was to tie tube fly patterns symmetrically or "in-the-round" where the wing (normally buck tail) was tied completely around the tube. This style of tying was undoubtedly influenced by Britain's Richard Waddington and his revolutionary salmon fly patterns which were tied in the round on flat wires or "Waddington shanks."

Modern tube fly designs now use short sections of flexible silicon or stiff vinyl junction tubing as a hook sleeve for attaching the hook to the tube fly; although some tube designs accept insertion of hook directly into the rear of the tube fly itself. Stiff plastic and metal tubing is also commonly used to tie tube flies today. (Note: Tube fly hooks are designed with a straight eye for direct insertion into the junction tubing connection or the tube itself. Also, the end of leader is strung through the tube fly body first and then is attached to the hook.)

More recently, Swedish tyers such as Mikael Frodin, Yuri Shumakov, Hakan Norling and Mikael Lindstrom borrowed many of the elaborate and showy British Atlantic salmon patterns that were tied on standard salmon hooks and converted them to hairwing flies (while still maintaining a standard asymmetrical design that has the wing configured above the body) using metal and plastic tubes. Tied in the classic Scandinavian "Temple Dog" style these tube flies incorporate soft materials such as Temple Dog fur and Arctic fox tail into the wing. The wings are characteristically long, tear-drop shaped and angled high and away from the body (to maximize profile and movement in the water) and have small finished heads.

For the Great Lakes steelheader, the Scandinavian Temple Dog fly design is a very effective way to construct baitfish imitations. The undulating action, size and silhouette of the Temple Dog wing are all great strike triggers for steelhead that have spent most of their lives feeding on baitfish in the Great Lakes. Coupling this design with the advantages of using a tube fly system makes it even more effective.

Some of the benefits of using a tube fly versus a standard hook design fly pattern

- The tube fly allows you to use a smaller, short shank tube hook versus a larger, long shank hook which is commonly used in long-winged streamer or traditional salmon fly designs. Heavy, long-shanked hooks can be hard to cast and will twist and bend during a fight resulting in a dislodged hook and a higher percentage of lost steelhead. Also, short shank tube fly hooks cause less injury to a fish versus the "lever-action" of a long-shank streamer hook which can gouge a much bigger wound in the fish's mouth during a long fight.

- Tube flies allow you to control the weight of the fly by changing the tube design used for the specific fly pattern. In general, plastic tubes are ideal for moderate to lower flows (although faster sinking systems and leader adjustment can effectively sink plastic bodied tube flies in faster, deeper flows). Plastic tubes with metal coneheads and metal tubes of various weights (aluminum, brass, copper, tungsten) and designs (straight diameter, Loop Bottle, Shumakov 1/2 inch, Eumer Teardrop, Wurm Tungsten) are effective for getting down in faster, deeper flows.

- After hooking a steelhead, a tube fly normally disengages from the hook and slides up the leader out of the way. This greatly extends the fishing life of the fly since it is not damaged by the steelhead's teeth during the fight and is less likely to get soaked from stream mud or sediment when the fish is landed along the stream bank. This also makes it easier to disengage the hook from a steelhead's mouth since there is clear access to the hook.

- A damaged or dull hook can easily be replaced with a new one on the stream without discarding the fly.

- Tube flies are generally more economical to tie since only a handful of hooks are needed for dozens of tube flies (although some specialty tube bodies can be expensive). This is especially true when comparing the price of tying on expensive streamer and salmon hooks versus a small quantity of small tube fly hooks.
- When necessary a tube fly gives the fly fisher the capability of easily positioning the hook point in the "up" position (like a keel fly) reducing the chances of bottom snagging. This is very helpful when fishing some of the heavier metal tube body designs. Double hooks when fished in this hooks "pointed-up" fashion seem to also make the tube fly swim better in the water and also more efficiently hook fish.
- The hook can also be adjusted to sit further back in longer tube fly patterns by using a longer tube body or extending the junction tubing connection to compensate for "short-striking" fish.
- The hook changing ability of a tube fly enables the fly fisher to easily change the hook size and design (thereby increasing or decreasing hook weight) in order to help balance the fly and make it swim level on the swing.

Conventional Tube Fly Patterns and Designs

The majority of Great Lakes tube fly patterns tied today typically use straight diameter plastic (rigid or semi-rigid variety) or metal cylindrical tubing with many using large diameter tubing which often results in bulky finished heads. The patterns tied on this tubing include the traditional British in-the-round hairwings as well as numerous Great Lakes streamer, zonker, wooly bugger, leech, steelhead wet and spey fly patterns. Even nymph and egg patterns are being tied on tubing by Great Lakes steelhead tube tyers. (see Conventional and Convertible Tube Fly Patterns).

A multitude of readily available products including cotton swabbed Q tip tubes, spray can nozzle tubing, automotive air brake line and hardware store metal tubing have been used for tubing, but the rigid plastic and metal tubing offered by HMH, Veniard and others is more commonly used due to its convenience, durability and low profile design.

Plastic versus Metal Tubing

Rigid plastic tubing is more economical than metal tubing but is not as durable particularly in colder temperatures where splitting and shattering can occur when the tube fly impacts stream rocks, etc. during casting. FlexTube by the Canadian Tube Fly Company and Veniard Slipstream plastic tubes hold up much better than most rigid plastic tubing in a broad range of temperatures.

Semi-rigid, more flexible varieties of plastic tubing (like FlexTube and Guideline FITS tubing) allow for direct hook connection into the rear of the tube without the junction tubing connection needed on metal tubing. This is a definite plus since junction tubing can have a bulky appearance, be cumbersome to use and can loosen after multiple casts if not glued or secured in place.

Tube flies tied on plastic tubing maintain a more natural "swimming action" in the current flow than straight diameter, heavy metal tubing (brass or copper) which sinks quicker but can at times get hung up on the streambed. Heavy metal tubing can also be more difficult to cast than plastic tubing with lighter single-handed fly rods although this is not normally a problem when spey casting with double-handed rods which generate more energy on the cast.

Most steelheaders feel that although straight diameter, metal bodied tubes are very effective for "getting down" in high, fast flows, plastic bodied tube flies can also be fished at these depths and flows by using the appropriate sinking system (see Chapter 5) as well as the correct leader length and at the same time keep the tube fly natural and "lively" on the swing. Tube flies with plastic tube bodies cast better though with the addition of a light conehead, bead or wire ribbing. This small amount of weight will help the leader turn-over at the end of the cast.

Conventional Tubing Manufacturer's

HMH offers plastic tubing in a 3/32 inch (.09 inch) and 1/8 inch (.125 inch) outside diameters that can be easily cut to any length. The smaller 3/32 inch size, which HMH calls "low profile" tubing, results in somewhat smaller finished heads and lower profile bodies than bigger diameter conventional tubing. The slimmer design also helps to sink tube flies faster in the water column.

After cutting this tubing (like most "raw" tubing) it is recommended that the front end be melted to form a collar which prevents any tying materials or thread from slipping off the front of the tube and facilitates a nice, neat head (although some tube tyers perform this step after tying the fly). Melting the rear of the tube can also help to secure the junction tubing connection in the rear. Although normally not a consideration (since leader material is typically tougher than most rigid plastic tubing), melting the ends of the tube may have the added benefit of smoothing the sharp edges of the tube preventing possible leader abrasion.

HMH also has pre-cut plastic tubes in lengths up to 3 inches long that have smooth, finished ends. HMH also has aluminum and heavier copper tubes which sink 2-3 times faster than aluminum tubes. HMH metal tubes are made in pre-cut lengths up to 2 1/2 inches long and have plastic liners with finished ends. Small sections of clear, soft silicon or stiff vinyl junction tubing are normally used for the hook connection with HMH tubing. Silicon junction tubing is also available in a variety of colors.

Veniard offers what it calls a Slipstream tube in a slim design for neater finished heads and slim bodies. The plastic tubes (sized regular and heavy) are pre-cut with "molded" ends. The heavy plastic tube has a double wall design and built-in hook connection capability. This soft tubing is somewhat less brittle than the HMH variety and holds up well when fished. Veniard also sells plastic lined, pre-cut aluminum and copper tubes that have finished ends. These metal tubes fish much deeper than larger diameter metal tubes due to their smaller profile in the water.

Rooney Tube Works manufactures linerless brass tubes in 1/8 inch (heavy) and 3/32 inch (light) outside diameter sizes. These affordably priced tubes are hand-made and hand polished with a guarantee to be burr-free to prevent leader chafing and fraying. They also incorporate a flare at one end to eliminate thread slippage when finishing the head of the fly. Rooney also offers pre-cut plastic tubing in various lengths.

The Canadian Tube Fly Company offers rigid plastic tubing in a 1/8 inch size (outside diameter) in 10 inch lengths. It comes individually or in a variety pack of 6 eye catching colors.

As stated earlier, short sections of silicon or vinyl junction tubing are typically used as a hook sleeve for attaching the hook to the tube fly in most conventional tube designs. Transparent FlexTube (in various colors) is ideal for junction tubing connections and adds just a hint of color to the rear of the tube fly. Custom fly tyer Rod Yerger has designed an innovative vinyl hook sleeve that is tapered to accept any size hook including both straight and oval hook eyes.

Selection of Scandinavian style steelhead tube flies.

Basic tube tying instructions and information can be found by visiting the following websites:

Global Fly Fisher (Denmark's Martin Joergensen covers the basics of tube flies with great tube diagrams): www.globalflyfisher.com/tiebetter/

TubeFlies.com (the name says it all!): www.tubeflies.com

Tying Tube Flies (tube tying and fishing basics): www.flyfisherman.com/ftb/bctubeflies/

HMH Vises (tube tying guide): www.hmhvises.com/tubeflyguide.pdf

Temple Dog Flies (tube fly pattern and fishing forum): www.templedogflies.com

The Canadian Tube Fly Company (great info on tube fly basics): www.canadiantubeflies.com/index.html

Dick Talleur's tube tying DVD's and the Mark Mandell and Les Johnson book *Tube Flies* and the Mark Mandell and Bob Kenly book *Tube Flies Two, Evolution* are excellent sources for beginning and advanced tube tying techniques and patterns. Tony Pagliei also has some informative DVD's on tying convertible tube flies. Rod Yerger's new book *"Tube Flies, A Professional's Patterns & Techniques"* is scheduled to be out in the spring of 2008. It will detail Yerger's innovative tube tying techniques and tube patterns. See Appendix C for more information on these books and DVD's.

Convertible Tube Fly Patterns

Convertible tube fly patterns are "two-part" flies that consist of a standard tube fly body or "head" and a trailing hook or "tail". By dressing the head and tail in various pattern styles and then combining them, the steelhead fly fisherman is able to adapt to any fishing situation in a matter of seconds. Michigan's Tony Pagliei has created a number of innovative convertible tube fly patterns for Great Lakes steelhead and salmon as well as for bass and trout. (See Conventional Tube Fly Patterns at the end of this chapter for some of Tony's tube patterns.)

Sunray and Snake Style Tube Patterns

The eel like sunray and snake style tube patterns were originally designed to imitate sand eels and used for sea trout and salmon fishing in the U.K. and Norway. Although eels are not an important food source for Great Lakes steelhead, these patterns work amazingly well for steelhead.

The first Sunray style tube pattern was tied by Ray Brooks on Norway's classic Atlantic salmon River Laerdal. He called it the Sunray Shadow and it is basically a variation of the Collie Dog which is the ultimate bare-bones salmon fly. Both of these slim profile flies are all about action and movement in the water due to their long, undulating and pulsating hair wings.

The Collie Dog uses Border collie hair as a wing and a flat silver tinsel body ribbed with round silver tinsel. Brook's Sunray Shadow pattern originally called for black colobus monkey hair as an over-wing and white tipped squirrel tail hair as the under-wing (1/3 over-wing length). The stiffer under-wing added wing support and helped prevent the wing from tangling with the hook. The over-wing length is about 4 inches, with the fly tied on a bare section of light-weight, clear or white, rigid plastic tubing that is slightly shorter than the under-wing. The wing is topped with 2 to 4 peacock herls.

Recent versions of Brook's fly substitute goat hair, Border collie (or other dog hair), temple dog, llama and T's Hair for the monkey hair and use white buck tail for the under-wing. The fly can also be modified by adding flash to the wing and tube body, jungle cock for the eyes and using colored tubing and different color combinations of hair in the wing. Modern Sunray patterns are commonly tied long with lengths as long as 7 inches not unheard of (see Witchy Woman tube fly pattern).

The simplicity of the Sunray style tube pattern makes it ideal for the beginner tube tyer. The original pattern was designed to be fished with a stripping retrieve, fast and near the surface, to active fish in warm flows that are low and clear. Great Lakes steelheaders can get this pattern down closer to steelhead in colder flows by using a sinking leader, a sink tip or incorporating metal cones or metal tubes (straight or bottle types) or any combination of the above into the pattern to help sink it better on the swing and strip.

Snake flies with their highly flexible bodies are popular in Wales for sea trout. They are tied with long sections of soft, braided mono covered with woven Mylar tubing. They also typically use permanently attached hooks. See www.seatroutfishing.net/flies.htm for more details on this pattern style.

Tube versions of snake flies use long pieces of small diameter, soft plastic tubing that match the length of a long wing (see Liu Snake Tube fly pattern). The long tube bodies also allow for hook placement further back on the wing for "short-strikers." Snake patterns typically incorporate a secondary wing material under the tube body as well. The Canadian Tube Fly Company markets a product called Wiggle Tube which is ideal for tying snake tube bodies. T Bone Fly Fishing has a similar product called T's Tubing.

The Scandinavian Temple Dog Style of Tying Tube Flies

The "Temple Dog" or "Fatback" style of tying Atlantic salmon or streamer fly patterns was originated by Hakan Norling of Sweden in 1986 with the goal of adding more movement to the wings of Atlantic salmon hair wing patterns, which can be best described as "stiff and lifeless".

The Temple Dog name refers to the soft fur used in tying the wings of Temple Dog style flies, which has great action not only in fast water but in slow water as well. The temple dog fur also has finely curled base fibers which provide volume or a "fat back" to the shoulder of the wing while the tips can be easily stroked into a tapered point.

Norling tied the wings of his Temple Dog patterns using the "reverse-wing-technique" where you initially tie the wing facing forward, with the trimmed wing fibers facing the rear of the fly, and then fold the wing toward the rear to achieve a high wing angle. This technique maximizes both the profile and movement of the wing particularly in fast, heavy water. Placing the tying thread tight in front of the bend formed in the wing kept the wing from "flattening" and also resulted in a smaller finished head. (It is to be noted that the wing can also be tied in the conventional way, towards the rear, as long as stiff materials are used in the collar and body hackle, tail and under-wing which all help to "lift" the wing and support a high wing angle.)

Hakan Norling tied his Temple Dog patterns on metal and plastic tubes and called them "1/2-inchers" due to the short tube bodies he used (although the completed wing length was substantially longer than the tube and hook length). The result was a dynamite combination with the benefits of a tube design and the incredible movement and silhouette of a Temple Dog style wing. Legendary Swedish Atlantic Salmon fly tyer Mikael Frodin shortly caught onto this and developed, in collaboration with Norling, the Frodin Improved Tube Fly System (FITS) for tying Temple Dog style flies.

Hakan Norling felt that the "swimming action" of a Temple Dog style tube fly could be more natural and lively on the swing with the lightest combination of conehead (or bead-head), tube weight and hook size/weight for the speed and strength of the current flow. Also, the texture of the wing hair as well as collar and body hackle must be correct for the water flow you are fishing.

The Temple Dog style wing is primarily constructed of soft, natural hair materials like temple dog fur, Arctic fox tail, Icelandic sheep hair, llama hair, T's Hair and Russian silver goat that move with a lively action in the current. Small amounts of flash material add subtle reflection, color and movement throughout the wing as well. Small amounts of stiffer materials like bucktail or T's Hair can be added to the wing (usually in the bottom layer) to provide support if needed. The wing is characteristically long (3-4 inches on average), angled high and tapered to a point over the hook, but at the same time it is broad at the shoulders as viewed from the top (tear-drop shaped).

The taper of the wing is formed by layering small amounts of hair, of different thicknesses and lengths, from bottom to top. As stated earlier, the Temple Dog fur is particularly ideal for constructing this type of wing profile since the base of the fur allows for bulk and volume at the front of the wing and then tapers nicely to form a pointed tail.

The silhouette of the wing and the movement provided by the soft wing materials make the Temple Dog fly design very effective for imitating a baitfish. Adding jungle cock cheeks to either side of the wing, suggesting eyes on a baitfish, make it even deadlier.

The wing itself is very light and translucent allowing for light penetration and reflection while absorbing very little water. The lightness of the wing in combination with a short tube hook makes the fly very easy to cast as opposed to a fly with a heavier, wind resistant, water absorbing wing like a rabbit fur strip streamer. At the same time it maintains the full baitfish silhouette.

The volume or fullness of the wing is achieved by interspersing it with sparse layers of flash material like Angel Hair, Fire Fly, Krinkle Mirror Flash, Krystal Flash, Flashabou and Gliss-n-Glow which provide a delicate support structure for the wing. Collared hackle introduced at various stages of wing development, palmered body hackle and long, stiff tails also help to support the wing. The Swedish tube tyers mentioned previously use the Temple Dog style wing as the foundation of many of their patterns with variations in the tube system.

Steelheader's Tip

To help control the sink rate of your tube fly on the swing (when using a sinking leader, mini-tip or sink tip fly line) shorten the leader to sink the tube fly quicker to less aggressive, "bottom-hugging" steelhead in colder tributary flows. Lengthen the leader to move the tube fly higher up in the water column to more active steelhead in warmer flows.

Russian-born Yuri Shumakov (who lived in Sweden and unexpectedly passed away in 2006) and Mikael Frodin realized that long-winged flies like Temple Dog style patterns can experience "hang-down" when fished on the downstream swing, especially in slower water flows. Hang-down occurs due to the weight of the long wing, rear body and hook as well as insufficient wing support from soft, sparsely tied wings causing the rear of the fly to tip downward slightly and not swim level on the swing.

Shumakov's machined brass or aluminum 1/2 inch tubes, which are a hybrid type bottle tube (see Bottle Tubes discussion), have a weight forward design to level the fly on the swing. Frodin's design uses a longer tube body in a "step tube" design that incorporates two diameters of flexible plastic tubing (FITS tubing is available in clear or fluorescent) and lightweight metal cones of different sizes and weights to balance the fly and help it sink.

For a conehead tube fly the Frodin tube design balances well with a light wire hook and is relatively easy to cast, with the lightweight metal cone providing ample weight to both turn over the leader and sink the fly (see Lake Erie Emerald Shiner tube pattern). The conehead of the Frodin design (cone has machined interior for this) also helps to cover thread wraps at the front of the fly and for a streamlined profile into the tapered Temple Dog wing. The downside to the design is purely aesthetic. The addition of the cone at the front of the fly eliminates the characteristic small, finished heads that the original Scandinavian tube patterns were known for.

Shumakov designed his 1/2 inch tubes so the finished fly would have a small, neat head (no bigger than 2mm!) due to the use of small diameter, rigid plastic tubing at the front of the fly. This eliminated the bulky and unsightly finished heads made with tying thread (especially when using larger diameter tubing) as well as

the need for metal coneheads. The small heads also seem to give additional action to Temple Dog patterns in the current flow (see Red, Black and Blue tube fly pattern). They are available in various weights and configurations for different water conditions including the Long Range, Heavy Long Range, Skittle and Summer Arrow.

Jack Cook of The Irish Angler has recently launched a 1/2 inch machined tube (another bottle tube design) as part of the Steelhead Anglers Tactical Tube System (TTS tubes). This tube design is based on Jack's experience working with Yuri Shumakov, Mikael Frodin and Henrik Anderson fly designs as well as his own very successful steelhead fly design theory. TTS tubes ride horizontally in the water and the shoulder design supports the wing perfectly. They are made in the USA in Portland, Oregon, and are available in brass (.8 grams) and aluminum (.35 grams) with brass, nickel, copper and gun metal finishes. Various colored bodies are also available. They come complete with small diameter, hard plastic liner tubing.

Bottle Tubes

Bottle tubes are available in aluminum, brass and tungsten designs. They are generally short in length and fast sinking due to their concentrated weight. As their name implies, they have a bottle shape although they can also take on other configurations. The tapered front of the bottle tube helps to streamline the fly while the small diameter of the front "collar" portion allows for a small finished head. A short section of junction tubing is typically used to make the hook connection at the rear of the bottle tube with most bottle tubes lined with small diameter plastic tubing to prevent leader abrasion.

Bottle tubes are generally more expensive than conventional metal and plastic tubing. They come in two varieties, the traditional bottle design where the fly is tied on the front collar portion of the bottle itself and the hybrid type which uses a small diameter, rigid plastic liner to tie the fly on (in front of the bottle tube). One of the advantages to the hybrid design is the ability to finish the fly with a much smaller head than is capable with a traditional bottle tube. The Shumakov 1/2-incher and the Cook TTS tubes discussed previously are hybrid type bottle tubes. See Fly Plate XI for pictures of assembled (and undressed) specialty tube bodies.

The Morrum bottle tube was one of the original metal bottle tubes and was manufactured by The Danish company The Fly Co. Named after the Morrum River in Sweden these traditional bottle tubes concentrated weight to the rear of the fly giving action and movement to the fly on the swing. The conical front end also made for a pleasing wing shape and angle and a somewhat small head. They were made in both brass and aluminum versions.

Martin Joergensen of Denmark improved this designed with a bottle tube that has a small diameter front collar with "rim" that allows for close and secure tying at the head and a small diameter rear end to fit a vinyl or silicon hook sleeve. Optional metal extension tubes can also be connected to the tube for tying longer bodied flies and increasing the weight of the tube. The French company Bidoz produces the Joergensen bottle tube in 15 and 12 mm lengths as well as the metal extensions all in aluminum and brass designs. By combining the brass and aluminum you can also control the weight balance of the tube and how the tube swims in the water.

The Swedish company Loop Tackle makes a fast sinking brass, traditional bottle tube in 1/2 inch and 5/8 inch lengths (gold or silver finishes) that are extremely heavy for their size. Like the Morrum bottle tubes, the center of balance of the Loop bottle tube is toward the rear resulting in great tail action in the fly.

Loop Bottle tubes are easy to cast and enter and leave the water quietly. Ideal for tying short, compact flies, longer winged patterns require lengthening the junction tubing to position the hook further back on these tubes. A front tapered head and a small diameter collar with a rim allowing for a smaller finished head than straight metal tubes. The front and rear tube openings on Loop bottle tubes are also beveled and polished to prevent leader abrasion.

Yuri Shumakov's 12 mm length brass and aluminum bottle tubes, which are not to be confused with his 1/2 inch hybrid bottle tubes, are engineered to ride level in the water due to three slotted machining grooves on the rear of the tube that give the tube a weight-forward weight distribution. These more traditional bottle tubes have a shorter body and are lighter than the Shumakov 1/2 inch Long Range tubes and are designed to tie on a metal neck instead of an extended plastic liner. They are lined to prevent leader abrasion and the machining grooves can also be painted with various colors to add color to the tube body.

The German company Wurm Tungsten Products makes a "micro" Tungsten Bottle Tube (97% pure tungsten and lead-free) in silver, gold, copper and gun-smoke finishes. This extremely compact but heavy tube comes in 6, 9, 12 and 15 mm lengths and is designed to use with Wurm's integrated soft external and stiff internal colored tubes. These tubes can be used in either a traditional or hybrid bottle application.

The Wurm tube system allows for tying a fly without creating bulk in the head as well as long tube bodies both of which are not possible with most bottle tube designs. Wurm tubes can also replace the weight of a cone on a conehead Temple Dog style tube fly. The advantage of this is that the small diameter Wurm tube can easily be concealed farther back on the fly under dubbing and collar hackle. This maintains the characteristically small, finished heads that Scandinavian tube flies are known for around the world (see Steel Flamingo tube fly pattern). It also balances the fly much better versus a conehead at the front of the fly.

The Canadian Tube Fly Company offers traditional brass and aluminum bottle tubes in 22 mm and 15 mm lengths that are similar to the Bidoz design except they are much heavier. This is due to a smaller center-hole design. They also have a tapered shape to allow for a smaller head, have contoured lips on both ends for the junction tubing connection in the rear of the tube and close and secure tying at the front collar of the tube.

The Finnish company Eumer manufactures a variety of brass tubes which include both traditional and hybrid bottle designs as well as designs that are a combination of the two. They come in a variety of interesting shapes including the Teardrop, Cone Tube (cone is incorporated into brass tube body) and Conehead (cone is separate from tube body) designs. The Teardrop tube (see Lemon Lime tube fly pattern) has a "tapered" shape that helps to balance the fly on the swing. Both the Teardrop and Conehead tube designs can accommodate small diameter, plastic tubing (which Eumer supplies) for reducing tying bulk and finishing with small heads. Eumer tube bodies come in a variety of sizes as well as bright colors which makes dubbing a body optional. Eumer also makes brass tubes in Ball Tube, Tag Tube and Crayfish Tube designs.

Tube tying instructions and information for specialty tube designs can be found at:

Sexy Loops (basic step-by-step instructions for tying Mikael Frodin style tube flies): www.sexyloops.com/flytying/black_and_silver.shtml

Rackelhanen Fly Fishing Magazine (detailed step-by-step instructions for tying Shumakov style tube flies by Shumakov himself, the site also includes many articles by Shumakov): http://www.rackelhanen.se/eng/10265.htm

Eumer (step-by-step instructions for tying with Eumer tube bodies, look under "tying "samples): www.eumer.com

Sea Trout Fishing (information on tying snake flies and tubes): www.seatroutfishing.net/ flies.htm

Global Fly Fisher (Denmark's Martin Joergensen covers available specialty tube designs and patterns with great tube diagrams): www.globalflyfisher.com/tiebetter/

Toni Karuvaara Fly Fishing (great inspiration for tying Scandi style tube flies!): www.karuvaaraflyfishing.com

Mikael Frodin's DVD "Modern Salmon Flies-Tying on Tubes" (detailed step-by-step instructions for tying Mikael Frodin style flies by Frodin himself, see Appendix C).

Tube Fly Hooks

As discussed earlier, one of the biggest advantages of using a tube fly design is the ability to incorporate a small, short-shanked hook into large fly patterns like streamers. The result is a marked increase in the ratio of fish hooked to fish landed and less damage to the steelhead.

In the United States most tube fly fisher's use single hooks due to local fishery regulations and also the emphasis on catch-and-release practices. In Scandinavia double hooks are very popular while in Europe trebles have traditionally been used with tube flies.

Standard straight eye egg hooks and even straight eye bait hooks and salt water hooks (which are typically heavy wire) will work as tube hooks but may not fit well into smaller diameter junction tubing or tube bodies. Thinner wire tube hooks are better suited for tubing connection and generally provide better hook penetration.

Some specialty hook models that are ideal for tube flies include: Daiichi X Point # X510, short shank salmon #2450, #1640 and #1650, Partridge Nordic Single # MM3STBN and Salar #CS14T, Owner Straight Eye-Cutting Point SSW, TMC #105, Mustad #60500, Gamakatsu #C14S and bonefish #SL11-3H and the Talon #2A-8346 tube fly hook. Hook gap, wire thickness (weight) and point design vary slightly between hook models.

Choosing the right hook size or wire thickness to "balance" a tube fly and make it swim level on the swing is an important consideration. Examples include the Talon tube fly hook which is a stout, heavy wire design while the Nordic Single and Owner SSW use lighter wire configurations.

The very strong, medium-shanked Gamakatsu bonefish hook (the short shank salmon Daiichi #2450 is a similar design) is a unique compromise between short-shanked tube hooks and longer-shanked streamer hooks. Its longer length has the ability to pick up "short-strikers" in long winged patterns with no twisting and bending while minimizing the "lever-action" effect inherent with much longer hooks. It also has a relatively light wire design which is ideal for eye insertion into tube flies as well as hook penetration.

Loop, Hywel and Partridge short shank, double tube fly hooks are very popular with Atlantic salmon fly fishers and have some advantages over single shank tube hooks.* Due to their characteristic solid hook planting (the Partridge hook points are slightly beaked for this), very little hook movement occurs during the fight resulting in minimal tissue damage.

A single hook (whether long-or-short-shanked) has "pre-releasing and re-engagement movement" during the fight which can produce more damage versus a double hook. Double tube hooks are also typically taken less deeply than single tube hooks which again results in less harm to the fish. The hook points on a Loop double are slightly closer than some other double hook models. This helps to assure both hooks are implanted during the hook set.

During colder flows it is not unusual for soft-taking steelhead to "take-and-spit" a fly on the swing. Double hooks can prevent this due to their practically "self-setting" ability when a steelhead takes a fly.

Use of more than one hook or hook point is prohibited in NY. See Regulations in Appendix B.

Conventional and Convertible Tube Fly Patterns

erger Hot Bead Tube Fly

yer: Rod Yerger of Rod Yerger Custom Flies, Lawrence, PA.
ube: Veniard Slipstream, 1 inch aluminum tube with 3/16 inch pink Hot Bead epoxied to tube.
hread: Uni-Thread, black, 8/0.
ody: Medium silver flat braid.
'ing: Black marabou, then purple marabou, then black marabou tied in the round. Each wing layer is
rogressively shorter than the first.
ides: Holographic tinsel tied in after the first black marabou wing layer.
'ook: Daiichi #X510 tube fly hook (wide gap bend, 3X short, 3X strong, straight eye), size #4 connected
▶ the rear of the fly with Yerger tapered hook sleeve or standard clear junction tubing.
omments: Rod ties this steelhead tube pattern in numerous wing color combinations including black/
lue, orange/yellow and cerise/orange. He also varies the bead color in gold, silver, copper and various Hot
ead colors. Can be dead-drifted or swung on some of the bigger tributaries. The Yerger Hot Bead finishes
ut at about 2 1/4 inches (including the Hot Bead).

:e Bunny

yer: Jerry Darkes of Angling Consulting Services, Strongsville, OH.
ube: HMH 3/32 inch, "low-profile" plastic tubing, 1 1/2 inches long.
hread: Danville, white, 6/0.
one: Nickel cone to fit tube.
ail: Light blue marabou plumes (use two for larger sizes) with 6 strands of pearl Mirror Flash mixed in.
ody: White cross cut rabbit strip.
ollar: Pearl Ice Dubbing.
'ook: Daiichi #X510 tube fly hook (wide gap bend, 3X short, 3X strong, straight eye), size #8 connected
▶ the rear of the fly with clear junction tubing.
omments: Jerry has found this simple tube tie effective for steelhead as well as smallmouth and
argemouth bass. It finishes out at about 2 1/2 inches (including conehead). For bigger flies increase the
ength of the tubing. Also go to aluminum and copper tubes for faster sink rates. Other productive color
ombos include (tail/body/collar): grey/ white/ pearl; chartreuse/white/chartreuse; olive/sand variant/root
eer or olive; black/black/black; purple/purple/fluorescent pink or shrimp.

,ower River Minnow

yer: Jim Guida of Williamsville, NY.
'ube: HMH 3/32 inch, "low-profile" copper tubing, 2 inches long.
hread: Uni-Thread, white, 8/0 or Bennechi, 12/0.
:yes: 3/16 inch Holo Eyes coated with Hard Head.
one: Nickel cone to fit tube.
ody: Pearl flat braid.
ag and throat: Pearl Blue Angel Hair.
ving: Angel Hair layered (Pearl, DNA Holo Fusion, Polar, Baitfish).
'ook: Daiichi #X510 tube fly hook (wide gap bend, 3X short, 3X strong, straight eye), size #8 connected
) the rear of the fly with clear junction tubing.
omments: Tying large wings on a standard cylindrical metal tube usually means that you end up with
. big head at the end of the tying process. Jim covers this up nicely with the use of Holo Eyes. He likes
) swing this tube on the lower part of Cattaraugus Creek, NY in the spring to both steelhead and small-
nouth. Total fly length is about 3 inches. Email Jim Guida at: jimguida@hotmail.com for step-by-step
nstructions.

'urduken

'yer: Nick Pionessa of Oak Orchard Fly Shop, Williamsville, NY.
'ube: HMH 3/32 inch, "low-profile" copper tubing, 1/2 inches long.
'hread: Uni-Thread, red, 6/0.
3ody Hackle: Orange schlappen (folded).
'lash: 4 strands of Silver Holographic Flashabou (tied in after body hackle).
'ackle: Purple marabou (folded).

Collar: Orange dyed teal or mallard.
Hook: Daiichi #2450 (short shank salmon), size #6 with transparent orange junction tubing.
Tying notes: The schlappen is tied in by the tip, folded and the entire feather is wrapped to fluffy fibers at the quill end.
Comments: This tube pattern (name comes from **tur**key, **du**ck and chick**en** feathers used to tie the fly differs from other marabou speys in that it allows the schlappen to support the center of the marabou provide contrasting color and allow the longer marabou tips to wiggle much more than other multi-marabou patterns. Nick says other top colors are black and purple, all white as well brown and olive. The Turduken finishes out at about 2 1/2 inches long.

Tubular Bugger

Tyer: Nick Pionessa of Oak Orchard Fly Shop, Williamsville, NY.
Tube: HMH 3/32 inch, "low-profile" copper or plastic tubing (1 1/4 inches).
Thread: Uni-Thread, red, 6/0.
Tail: Marabou folded and wrapped.
Body: SLF purple haze dubbing (brushed with Velcro before and after the hackle is wrapped).
Hackle: Black schlappen (3 turns to add some shoulders to fly).
Collar: Purple Guinea.
Hook: Daiichi #2450 (short shank salmon), size #6 with transparent orange junction tubing.
Tying notes: The tail is wrapped marabou which is nice and long with amazing motion. The SLF body is brushed with Velcro before and after hackle is wrapped. The hackle is folded schlappen with three turns at the front to add some shoulders.
Comments: A big silhouette tube pattern (it finishes out at about 3 1/2 inches long) that fishes well on Cattaraugus Creek, NY. Nick usually ties this pattern on a plastic tube and adds a cone or bead to the leader if he needs additional weight when fishing.

Foxy E.S.L.

Tyer: Nick Pionessa of Oak Orchard Fly Shop, Williamsville, NY.
Tube: HMH 3/32 inch, "low-profile" plastic tubing, 1 1/4 inches long.
Thread: Uni-Thread, black, 6/0.
Bead: 4/0 Scarlet Glass Bead or HMH Eggheads plastic bead (held in place by melting front of tube).
Tail: Black artic fox tail spun in dubbing loop (which creates illusion of bulk with great movement and without excess buoyancy).
Body: Fuchsia Bodi Works braid.
Wing: Black artic fox tail spun in dubbing loop.
Hook: Daiichi #2450 (short shank salmon), size #6 with transparent orange junction tubing.
Tying notes: The body braid is wound forward, tied off and remaining tag is trimmed (tube length) and pulled back and tied in again. This gives the fly a great sparkle of red that is encased in the wiggling fox tail wing. Total fly length is about 3 inches long including bead.
Comments: This tube pattern is top producer for Nick in stained water on Cattaraugus Creek, NY. Changing the tail color to contrasting color is a nice option. An all purple version of this tube fly has also produces well. Finished fly is easily 3 inches long.

Grand River Bunny Tube

Tyer: John Burkhardt of Natural Sports-The Fishing Store, Kitchener, ON.
Tube: HMH 3/32 inch, "low-profile" aluminum tubing (1/2 inch long) inserted onto HMH XS liner (1 inch long). Liner is exposed at rear of tube to eliminate the need for junction tubing. See tying notes below for assembling tube body.
Cone: Black HMH (small).
Thread: Danville, black, 6/0.
Body: Peacock SLF dubbing.
Hackle: 2-3 turns of black spey hackle, 2-3 turns of XL hot orange saddle hackle.
Wing: Black rabbit fur strip, topped and sided with pearlescent Flashabou.
Collar: Fiery red SLF spun in dubbing loop.
Hook: Daiichi #X510 tube fly hook (wide gap bend, 3X short, 3X strong, straight eye), size #8 inserted into the rear liner of the tube body.
Tying notes: Place cone at front end of liner and melt liner end to form lip against cone. Then apply crazy glue to inside of aluminum tube and insert on liner (snuggling up to rear of conehead). There should be

bout 1/4 inch of liner exposed at rear of tube which is used later to affix hook.
Comments: John says to pre-make your tube bodies ahead of time to cut down on your vise time for this relatively easy tube fly. The Grand River Bunny Tube was named for the Grand River in Ontario and finishes out at about 2 3/4 inches total length (including conehead).

Gotham E.S.L.

Tyer: Steven Wascher of Greenhurst, NY.
Tube: HMH 1/8 inch plastic tube, cut to length (1 1/2 inches) with ends melted to form small lip.
Thread: Gudebrod, black, 6/0.
Head: HMH Eggheads plastic bead (color of choice).
Body: Black Master Bright dubbing, spun in a loop, wrapped and teased out in a tapered fashion.
Wing: Black magnum rabbit strip, glued to tube with Loon Knot Sense.
Hackle: Black schlappen and natural guinea feather.
Collar: Small tuft of black Master Bright dubbing.
Hook: Daiichi #X-Point, X-510 (wide gap bend, 3X short, 3X strong, straight eye), size #4 inserted with clear junction tubing.
Comments: The Gotham E.S.L. is a rejuvenation of an old stand-by, the Egg Sucking Leech. Purple, olive and white wing/body versions also work well. Can be tied smaller with a 3/32 inch HMH tube and also with brass or aluminum tubes to match fishing conditions. The E.S.L. finishes out at about 3 1/2 inches long (including Egghead bead).

Sashimi Shiner

Tyer: Steven Wascher of Greenhurst, NY.
Tube: HMH 1/8 inch plastic tube, cut to length (1 1/4 inches) with ends melted to form small lip.
Cone: Large HMH conehead glue to tube and painted with dark olive highlights applied with sharpie marker.
Thread: Wapsi, white, UTC 210 Denier.
Body: 3 consecutive batches of Mike Martinek's Electric Sashimi polyester pearl body material tied in at the bottom, top, left and right sides of tube. The material is them pulled back and cemented with a thin penetrating cement such as Fly Tite. This process is done at the rear and center of the tube and slightly behind the conehead.
Cheeks: Small mallard breast or flank feathers tied in on each side.
Eyes: 4.5mm molded plastic 3-D stick on eyes cemented on with Zap-a-Gap.
Hook: Daiichi #X-Point, X-510 (wide gap bend, 3X short, 3X strong, straight eye), size #4 inserted with clear junction tubing.
Tying notes: Highlight top of fly (wing) with green Sharpie marker and top of junction tubing with red marker. Also, any combination of colors can be added to meet the baitfish "hatch."
Comments: Great attractor pattern for steelhead in high/stained flows. Steven recommends tying this fly in a variety of sizes and colors for varying stream flows and pressured water scenarios. Total length of the Sashimi Shiner is about 3 1/2 inches (including conehead).

Smolten-Smelten

Tyer: Steven Wascher of Greenhurst, NY.
Tube: Veniard Slipstream 1/16 inch plastic tube, cut to length (1 inch) with ends melted to form small lip.
Thread: Danville fine monofilament thread.
Body: Large pearl Mylar tinsel.
Throat: Small batch of white or clear Super Hair.
Under-wing: Small batch of pink Super Hair.
Over-wing: 6-8 strands of chartreuse Super Hair topped with 6-8 strands of olive super hair.
Eyes: Small molded plastic 3-D stick on eyes.
Finish: Pro Lac.
Hook: Daiichi #X-Point, X-510 (wide gap bend, 3X short, 3X strong, straight eye), size #8 with clear junction tubing that has been highlighted with an olive Sharpie marker.
Comments: This is one of Steven's Baitfish Series patterns (others include the Arrogant Emerald and the Baby Brown Trout) They were developed primarily for small NY Lake Erie tributaries like Chautauqua and Walnut Creeks during the fall particularly when they get low and clear and pressured from other anglers. Finishing out at about 2 1/2 inches in total length they are normally fished in a delicate fashion but can be swung in heavier water also. Adding a small pair of lead dumbbell eyes can give them a little added

weight if desired. Parr markings and spots can be added with a Sharpie marker to the Smolten-Smelten t enhance the overall appearance of the fly. The Arrogant Emerald has a white/olive/gray (throat/under wing/over-wing) Super Hair color combo and the Baby Brown Trout has a white/yellow/light brown an dark brown (throat/under-wing/over-wing) Super Hair color combo.

Black Maria

Tyer: Steven Wascher of Greenhurst, NY.
Tube: HMH 1/8 inch plastic tube, cut to length (1 1/2 inches) with front end flared.
Thread: Wapsi, black, UTC 70 Denier.
Hook: Gamakatsu #C14S, size #4 inserted into the end of the plastic tube itself.
Body: Rear half is yellow floss, front half is black floss ribbed with 5 turns of fine silver oval tinsel.
Wing: Black bucktail tied "in the round" on tube over which a natural guinea feather is wrapped. Total fl length is about 2 inches long.
Comments: This is a Ken Sawada version of an old pattern tied British tube style "in-the-round." Usin more traditional type materials, it may not be the "hottest" fly on steelhead alley these days but as Steve says "getting ripped by a fresh chromer on a traditional pattern can send us back to the roots of the sport o fly fishing and for a moment Cattaraugus Creek becomes the River Dee in Scotland!" Some of Steven' other traditional tube ties include the Black Ranger, Green Wasp and Akroyd series.

Conehead No-Body Matuka

Tyer: Tony Pagliei of T. Pags Company, East Lansing, MI.
Tube: HMH large, 1/8 inch plastic tube, cut to 1 1/2 inch length (no junction tubing). Rear of tube i colored with black marker. Melt ends to form small lip.
Thread: Gudebrod, black, 3/0.
Wings(2): Black Arctic fox fur tied in at the front (above the throat) and the rear of the tube body (both 1 inch long). Pearlescent Flashabou is tied in with front wing, along tube body, toward rear (1 3/4 inche long).
Throat: Fluorescent green Arctic fox fur (1 inch long).
Hackle collar: Black rooster saddle hackle (webby).
Conehead: Black HMH Custom Drilled Conehead (large).
Tail #1
Hook: Mustad Ultra Point #60500, size #4 or Gamakatsu C14S, size #4.
Thread: Gudebrod, fluorescent green, 3/0.
Tail: Fluorescent green Zonker rabbit strip (2-4 inches in length).
Tail #2
Hook: Mustad Ultra Point #60500, size #4 or Gamakatsu C14S, size #4.
Thread: Gudebrod, black, 3/0.
Tail: Black Arctic fox fur (1 3/4 inches long).
Comments: Convertible tube flies are standard tube flies that have the trailing hook dressed. Tony Paglie has incorporated a complete "component" concept to convertible tube flies that he calls "two-part" flies This system gives the steelheader the ability to "mix-and-match" colors and tailing material depending or the food sources and fishing conditions at hand. For example, a wooly bugger style tube fly that has marabou dressed tail can be transformed into an eelworm style fly by adding a long hackle dressed tail. The front half of the tube or "head" can also be tied in several colors and different sinking rates along with several colors of each trailing hook or "tail". The head and tail combinations can be limitless. An addec benefit of convertible tube flies is that the steelheader needs less tube patterns which means less fly boxes to carry on the steelhead tributaries. For more detailed instruction on tying Tony Pagliei's tube fly patterns see his Tying Convertible Tube Flies (Volumes 1 and 2) DVD's.

Tony's Conehead No-Body Matuka is a convertible leech tube pattern that allows the steelheader to change tail profiles and color combinations depending on the water conditions. Can also be tied in a lighter version without the conehead. This will help to suspend the fly a foot or two off the bottom especially wher using a short leader and a sink tip line. Other favorite color combinations include white/fluorescent red and purple/fluorescent orange.

Taylor's River Bug (TRB)

Tyer: Tony Pagliei of T. Pags Company, East Lansing, MI.
Tube: HMH large, 1/8 inch plastic tube, cut to 1/2 inch length with amber colored HMH junction tubing connection. Melt ends to form small lip.
Thread: Gudebrod, tan, 3/0.

egs: 2 brown, medium round, rubber filaments to match each side. Filaments are 3/4 inch long.
Tackle Collar: Dyed tan grizzly rooster saddle hackle (webby).
yes: Painted red dumbbells with black pupil in 3 sizes (1/2 oz./#4, 1/30 oz./#6, 1/40 oz./#8)
ead: Tan rabbit fur dubbing to cover dumbbell eyes and threads.

ail #1
ook: Mustad Ultra Point #60500, sizes #4-#8 or Gamakatsu C14S, size #4-#8.
hread: Gudebrod, tan, 3/0.
ail: 2 dyed tan grizzly chickabou feathers (hackled) with two brown, medium round, rubber filaments.
ilaments are 1 1/2 inches long.

ail #2
ook: Mustad Ultra Point #60500, sizes #4-#8 or Gamakatsu C14S, size #4-#8.
hread: Gudebrod, tan, 3/0.
ail: 2 dyed tan grizzly hen saddle hackles (1 1/2 inches long).
Tackle collar: Tan rooster saddle hackle (webby).
omments: Tony says that this attractor nymph/sculpin pattern can be tied utilizing different sizes of dumbbell
yes to achieve various sink rates. Drabby color combinations like rusty dun, olive, grizzly, dyed tan and
atural grizzly are very effective. Tony recommends fishing the TRB near the bottom under a strike indica-
or which allows the steelheader to drift close to structure where the typical dead-drift technique is difficult
o employ.

Frank's Jig Fly
yer: Tony Pagliei of T. Pags Company, East Lansing, MI.
ube: HMH large, 1/8 inch plastic tube, cut to 1/2 inch length with clear HMH junction tubing. Melt ends
o form small lip.
hread: Gudebrod, fluorescent orange, 3/0.
Tackle Collar: White and fluorescent cerise marabou plumes with pearlescent Flashabou (2 1/2 inches
ong). Cerise marabou is tied in first.
yes: Painted lead dumbbell eyes in 2 sizes (1/24 oz. and 1/100 oz.)
ead: Fluorescent cerise rabbit fur dubbing to cover dumbbell eyes and threads.

ail #1
ook: Mustad Ultra Point #60500, size #4.
hread: Gudebrod, fluorescent orange, 3/0.
ail: White and fluorescent cerise marabou plumes (2 1/2 inches long). White marabou is tied in first.

ail #2
ook: Partridge CS14T, size #5.
hread: Gudebrod, white, 3/0.
ail: Large, white Curly Tail from the Kreel Tackle Co.
ody: White rabbit fur dubbing.
omments: This pattern was originated by Frank Zak of New York. It is a marabou Clouser variation with
a two-tail system. Tony says that by varying the sink rate with different size dumbbell eyes, while adding a
Curly Tail, makes this a deadly convertible tube fly pattern. This is Tony's "go-to" tube fly for Great Lakes
steelhead.

Steelheader's Tip

Try a tube fly design when tying long streamers, sculpins, leeches, etc. They allow you to use a smaller, short shank hook versus a standard larger, long shank hook. Smaller tube hooks cause little harm to a steelhead and result in a high percentage of landed fish since they do not twist and bend during the fight like longer shank hooks.

TB's Single Egg
Tyer: Tony Pagliei of T. Pags Company, East Lansing, MI.
Tube: HMH large, 1/8 inch plastic tube, cut to 5/16 inch length (no junction tubing). Melt ends to form small lip.
Thread: Gudebrod, white, 3/0.
Wing: White Arctic fox fur (1 inch long).
Egg: 7 mm JigBead from Troutbeads.com.
Tail #1
Hook: Daiichi X510, size #10.
Thread: Gudebrod, white, 3/0.
Tail: Pearlescent Flashabou (1 inch long).
Tail #2
Hook: Daiichi X510, size #10.
Thread: Gudebrod, white, 3/0.
Wing: Arctic fox fur topped with pearlescent Flashabou (both 1 1/2 inches long).
Comments: According to Tony Troutbeads.com carries the best selection of American made, single egg beads in the world. The Jigbead is available from Troutbeads.com in realistic egg colors as well as brilliant fluorescent colors. This convertible tube fly allows the steelheader to change over from a single egg to a mini-Egg Sucking Leech within seconds!

Chartreuse Lazer Flex
Tyer: Stuart Anderson of the Canadian Tube Fly Company, Edmonton, Alberta.
Thread: Uni-Thread, chartreuse, 6/0.
Tube: Canadian Tube Fly Company transparent yellow Flex Tube cut to 1 3/8 inches long.
Body: Rear half, chartreuse Lazer Wrap. Front half, green seals fur or substitute palmered with green cock feather.
Hackle: Orange teal flank feather ("folded" and wrapped to extend to end of tube),
Wing (from bottom to top): Chartreuse bucktail, two chartreuse cock feathers laid flat, 8 strands of chartreuse Krystal Flash, two grizzly feathers dyed chartreuse laid flat. Wing is approximately 2 inches long.
Cheeks: Jungle Cock.
Hook: Talon #2A-8346, sizes #2-#6.
Comments: Stuart took the transparent tube idea one step further with this feather wing tube pattern. The Lazer Wrap over the transparent yellow Flex Tube body has to be seen to be believed! Flex Tube has a translucent glow, is temperature resistant and is flexible to allow for hook insertion directly into the back of the tube (no junction connection needed). The addition of the chartreuse bucktail underwing helps to support the wing in fast water.

Scandinavian Style Tube Fly Patterns

Lake Erie Emerald Shiner
Tyer: John Nagy of Pittsburgh, PA.
Tubes: Coat a small size Frodin Improved Tube System (FITS) chartreuse or clear plastic tube (1 1/2 inches long) with super glue or Loctite and insert it into a large size FITS chartreuse or clear plastic tube (1 1/4 inches long). Leave 1/2 inch of the small tube sticking out the front end of the large tube. Do not slide the small tube completely to the end of the large tube (leaving a 3/16 inch space at the end which is used as a hook holder for the eye of the tube hook later). Tie the body of the fly and under-wing on the large tube (rear tube) and use the small tube section (that extends in front) to tie collar and over-wing on. A metal cone is also slid onto this small tube. Any excess of the small tube is trimmed after the metal cone is slid on at the final tying step (see cone step below). Tying the over-wing and collar on the small tube allows for a small finished head which the cone can then cover. FITS small and large tubing is approximately .08 and .16 inches in outside diameter respectively. See Fly Plate XI for picture of assembled FITS tube body.
An alternative tube body system is to use the Candian Tube Fly Company FlexTube tubing with their small diameter plastic liner and Spirit River or Wapsi regular coneheads. These coneheads twist easily onto the soft plastic liner and are held in place by melting the plastic liner and forming small lip.
Thread: Uni-Thread, white, 8/0 or Bennechi, 12/0.
Tail: Red or orange Fluoro Fiber approximately 1 inch long and tied in at the point where the small tube ends inside the large tube. The tail should be long to blend into the wing and formed somewhat flat. Use a "doubling" technique by securing a large piece of Flouro Fiber at center of fibers, folding back, and then

ying into where the rear body starts. Finish by tapering tail to a point with scissors. The long tail supports the wing and helps to keep it from wrapping around hook.

Ribbing: Medium oval silver tinsel tied in after tail. Note: Ribbing is wound forward (clockwise) over the front and rear bodies (as well as body hackle) and secured on front of large tube after body and hackle steps below.

Rear body: Lilac Gudebrod Electra Metallic Hologram Flat Braid tinsel or Lagartun holographic silver flat braid is 3/8 inch long. Start the rear body 3/16 inch from the end of the large FITS tube. Exposed portion of tube acts as hook holder and also as a bonus colorful tag feature if colored tubing is used.

Front body: Polar Pearl Lite Brite dubbing spun in a loop and teased out with a Velcro brush (teasing step to give length and volume to dubbing is best done after body is hackled.) Dubbed body to front of large tube leaving about 1/8 inch of tube exposed. To bring out the color and transparency of the tube use less dubbing or try a dubbing with transparent properties.

Hackle: Stiff white saddle or cock neck feather palmered over the front and rear bodies which helps to support the characteristic high wing angle of this Temple Dog style fly. Stiff body hackle also helps prevent fly from tipping backward in the water ("hang-down") by providing stability. Hackle is tied in by the stem on the exposed front portion of the large tube and wound rearward and clockwise over the front and rear bodies. Hackle is secured in place by winding ribbing forward and counter-clockwise over hackle.

Under-wing layers (from bottom to top): 4 strands of silver Angel Hair, white temple dog (1 1/2 inches long and tied in thick), 4-6 strands of silver Fire Fly. The under-wing is tied on the front of large tube with length extending to just beyond the tail. Use a Velcro brush (loop side) to tease the short under fur from temple dog or arctic fox tail before tying in. Also remove any long guard hairs. When tying flash material into wing, stroke back extra material behind tie in point and tie in again. This is called "doubling" and helps to support the wing. Next "taper-cut" the flash material (including the doubled material) at different lengths. This is accomplished by holding flash material at front of the fly and cutting on a taper in one sweeping motion with scissors toward the tip of the wing. This will result in varying lengths of flash material in the wing and a more natural finish taper. The longest piece of flash material should be about 3 3/4 inches long.

Collar: White schlappen feather or saddle hackle tied on the small tube after the under-wing is finished. After wrapping feather (making sure all the fibers are at the same side of the stem by "folding" them back as you wrap the feather), stroke fibers downward and secure to allow room for over-wing. The length of the fibers should extend back to the end of the body.

Over-wing layers (from bottom to top): 4 strands of rusty olive Angel Hair, light olive temple dog (2 1/2 inches long and tied in thicker, wider and longer than the previous white temple dog layer), 4 strands of rusty olive Angel Hair, light olive Russian silver goat or equivalent (3 1/2 inches long and tied in longer and thinner than the previous light olive temple dog layer), 6 strands of silver Fire Fly (do not double). Tie the over-wing in front of the collar on the small tube. The top layer of the light olive Russian silver goat or equivalent in the over-wing should be slightly shorter than the longest flash material. Fly finishes out at about 4 inches long with conehead.

Wing tying notes: When constructing the wing on a typical Temple Dog style pattern think of it as having three distinct sections (bottom, middle and top) which in combination help to form a tear-drop shape wing. Each section may consist of more than one layer of wing material. The bottom wing section should be tied in thick but not longer than the tail. The middle section defines the volume or bulk of the wing. It is tied in wide, longer than the bottom section and also twice as thick. The top wing section is thinner and longer than the middle wing section. It is recommended to apply a small amount of super glue after tying in each wing layer for fly durability. Also spread the wing material over the top of the tube liner (over a thin base of tying thread) to reduce the thickness of the tie down area and increase the overall wing volume. Arctic fox tail, Icelandic sheep hair, llama fur, Artic Runner (Icelandic horse hair), soft Russian silver goat. T's Fur and synthetic Polar Fiber can also be used as wing material in Temple Dog style wings. Mixing these materials in layers is very effective in forming Temple Dog wings. (Often this is necessary when you have an ideal color in a certain wing material). Materials such as temple dog and Russian silver goat are ideal since they have good volume at their base (due to "micro-curling") but at the same time are soft enough to easily taper to a point (when stroked back) to form a tail. They also are fairly straight and have good length which is very important for the longer top section of the wing. Stiffer materials like bucktail, T's Hair, calf tail, squirrel tail and goat hair can be used but are best suited at the shorter, bottom wing section since they are conducive for supporting the upper wing layers.

Cheeks: Jungle Cock slightly over 1 inch long and angled up along wing. Any splits in the Jungle Cock feathers can be repaired with an application of thin head cement to both sides prior to tying in. The cement will also prevent future splitting when fishing the fly.

Cone: Medium size silver FITS cone (or 1/4 inch long Spirit River or Hareline cone) slid down on front of small FITS tube and secured with super glue to cover the base of over-wing, hackle collar, jungle cock feathers and thread wraps of small finished head. The tube is then trimmed to 1/16 inch and melted to form a small lip which also secures cone and provides a smooth non-abrading surface for your leader. Option of using a fluorescent chartreuse small FITS tube allows for lip to be colored.

To allow the cone to fit more easily on the FITS small tubing slightly widen cone opening by drilling with a 5/64 inch metal drill bit. Then remove the fly from the tube needle (see tying notes) and cut the front Fits tube to a sharply angled point. Next insert cone onto front FITS tube (twisting helps) and pull pointed tube end through cone with needle nose pliers or hemostats allowing cone to slide toward the head of the fly. Cone should have enough room on the inside to cover the head of the fly. Ideal cone has a "machined out" interior resulting in a lighter weight than standard cones and allowing tighter cone placement at the front of the fly.

Finding the right cone to fit FITS tubing (if not using FITS cones) is best done by selecting cone with the right center hole diameter and size/weight for the tubing size you are using. It is difficult to get a perfect match but your better off with a tight fit versus a loose fitting cone.

The addition of this bullet-shaped cone prevents "hang-down" (see previous tube fly text discussion) by balancing the fly in the water and keeps it swimming level on the downstream swing. Using a heavy, stiff tippet material can also prevent hang-down since it will not bend from the weight of the fly and hook but it can take away the action of the fly.

A medium size, lightweight FITS cone balances a 3 to 4 inch Frodin style fly well when using a light weight hook like the Gamakatsu bonefish hook. The sparse Temple Dog wing and lightweight cone make the Lake Erie Emerald Shiner easy to cast. The cone at the same time provides ample weight to both turn over the leader (which can be a problem with all plastic bodied tube flies) and help sink the fly.

The cone also creates a small eddy of turbulence behind the fly that prevents the wing material from "flattening out" in faster current flows and keeps it "swimming." (See Fat Boy Slim tube pattern for discussion on Turbo Cones.) Using a larger size cone may require use of a larger/heavier hook to balance the fly.

Hook: Gamakatsu #SL11-3H, size #8 standard bonefish hook (3X strong/carbon steel/tin plated). Although not a standard, short shank tube hook, this very strong, light-weight, medium-length shank hook is ideal for picking up "short-striking" steelhead without bending and twisting during a fight (which can be a problem with longer shanked hooks). The "lever-action" of this hook is also minimal versus longer shanked hooks. Secure hook to fly by inserting hook eye directly into the end of large, flexible FITS tubing. The light wire Partridge Nordic Single tube fly hook, # MM3STBN, size #8 is a good alternative. FITS tubing is designed with built in hook connection due to its semi-soft and flexible properties. No junction tubing connection is needed.

Tying notes: By tying the over-wing and collar on the small tube section you can finish with a very small head that can be covered easily with the cone. Use an inexpensive, tapered European tube fly needle (which can support two diameters of tubing at once) to hold the assembled tube in your vice.

The Irish Angler at www.irishangler.com carries the tube fly needle along with the flexible Guideline FITS plastic tubing (XS, S, M and Large) and cones (including tungsten models) that are sized to fit the FITS tubing. They also carry XL temple dog fur. FITS tubing is available in clear and black as well as fluorescent chartreuse, orange and red colors that seem to glow in low light.

The Irish Angler also supplies plastic tubing as part of their Steelhead Anglers Tactical Tube System (TTS Tubes) for Scandinavian style tube flies. It is sold in 1 meter lengths and 2 sizes (liner and rear tubing) in a variety of steelhead colors.

Comments: The Lake Erie Emerald Shiner tube fly is an imitation of a native Lake Erie minnow species called *Notropis atherinoides*. Originally very prevalent in the Lake Erie system its numbers were suppressed by expanding populations of alewives in the 1960's. Adult Emerald Shiners are rather slender, have characteristically large eyes and average 3 to 4 inches in length. They are generally silver in appearance with emerald green to silvery blue iridescent sides, silvery backs and white/silvery bellies. Young Emerald Shiners are more transparent in appearance than adults.

Although a somewhat involved tie, it is very durable and has a long fishing life due to the inherent advantages of using a tube fly design. It uses a Mikael Frodin tube system tied in the Scandinavian "Fat Back" or "Temple Dog" style where the emphasis is on a high-angled, long and tapered wing that is teardrop shaped when viewed from above. The wing also incorporates soft materials to impart movement in the water and is very sparse and translucent, maintaining its volume by interspersing small amounts of flash material in between the wing layers.

It is to be noted that the Norling reverse-wing-technique (the original wing construction technique for Temple Dog style flies) was not used since the stiff white saddle or cock neck feather palmered (counter clock-wise) over the front and rear bodies was sufficient to provide the support for a high wing angle. The jungle cock eyes and red tail add great strike triggers to the pattern. Smaller diameter FITS tubing (M, XS) and cones (XS) are ideal for constructing slimmer profiled tube bodies for lower, clearer flows. A side benefit of these lower profile tubes is that they cast somewhat easier and sink faster than larger diameter tube bodies.

I fish the Lake Erie Emerald Shiner on the swing with a Rio Versi-Tip line, a fast sinking leader like a RIO 7 foot, 5.6 or 7.0 inch per second (IPS) sink rate and a short tippet section (3 feet or less of 10 lb.) along pool or run current seams and also in pool tail-outs on some of the big Lake Erie tributaries like the Grand River in OH and Cattaraugus Creek in NY. The best conditions for this presentation are during the warmer tributary run-off of fall, late winter and early spring when steelhead are more active and aggressive. The fly works particularly well on sunny days due to its white coloration and flash that reflect sunlight. Hold on because the takes can be brutal!

For more detailed information on tying a Mikael Frodin style tube fly visit the Sexyloops website at: http://www.sexyloops.com/flytying/black_and_silver.shtml or watch Mikael Frodin's DVD "Modern Salmon Flies-Tying on Tubes" which is available from the Irish Angler at: www.irishangler.com.

Red, Black and Blue
Tyer: John Nagy, Pittsburgh, PA.
Thread: Uni-Thread, black, 8/0 or Bennechi, 12/0.
Tube: Yuri Shumakov 1/2 inch Long Range or Heavy Long Range brass tube and .07 inch (outside diameter.) hard plastic tube liner. The Jack Cook inch TTS brass tube and Eumer Teardrop tube (both have liners) can be substituted for the Shumakov tube body. Leave at least 1/2 inch of plastic liner in front of the tube for tying the fly on. Prior to inserting liner into tube slightly melt one end of liner with flame to form lip. This end of liner will snug against rear of tube after insertion into tube. After fly is tied on exposed forward extension of liner, remaining liner in front of unfinished fly head is then cut to approximately 1/16 inch and then melted to form lip. Final step is to finish head with thread up to lip of liner. Liner and tube can be mounted on a thread needle (secured in the vice jaws) that has a square eye to keep liner from rotating. HMH Vises, The Canadian Tube Fly Company, Veniard and Eumer offer inexpensive tube fly vice adapter tools that slip into the jaws of your vice and include metal pins or mandrels of different diameters for various size tubes. See Fly Plate XI for picture of assembled Shumakov tube body.
Wing layers (from bottom to top): Royal blue bucktail, 4 strands of ice blue Angel Hair, stiff black saddle or cock neck feather, 4-6 strands of blue Krinkle Mirror Flash, black temple dog, stiff black saddle or cock neck feather, 4 strands of black light Angel Hair, black temple dog, red guinea feathers, 4 strands of black light Angel Hair, black Russian silver goat or equivalent, 4 strands of purple Angel Hair, 4 black ostrich herls. Wing is tied completely on the front plastic liner. Fly finishes out at close to 3 5/8 inches long.
Wing tying notes: "Double" and "taper-cut" all flash material except for the angel hair at the top of the wing (see Lake Erie Emerald Shiner tube patterns for details). The top silver goat wing layer should be approximately 3 1/2 inches long and slightly shorter than the longest flash material which should be around 3 3/4 inches. The ostrich feathers should extend to the length of the longest flash material.

Progressively build the wing from short to long starting from the bottom. The lower layer of bucktail (1 1/2 inch long) should have good width with the middle layers of temple dog (2 1/2 inches long) having most of the bulk of the wing. The top wing layer of silver goat (3 1/2 inches long) should be thin and long. Use a dubbing brush to remove under fur from temple dog before tying in. The stiff bucktail and cock feathers in between wing layers of this Temple Dog style wing is needed for wing support since the "bodyless" Shumakov tube design does not allow for palmered body hackle or a stiff tail like in Mikael Frodin tube designs. The soft guinea feathers allow the front collar to more easily blend into wing.

Use a dubbing brush to remove under fur from temple dog and silver goat before tying in. When tying wing materials on the tube liner make sure each layer of material is tied directly onto the liner and not the previously tied in material. In addition to using minimal tying wraps, this will assure a small, neat head at the end of the tying process. Also spread the wing material over the top of the tube liner (over a thin base of tying thread) to reduce the thickness of the tie down area and increase the overall wing volume. Shumakov liked to use a surgical scalpel to cut his wing material (after secured on the tube liner) to minimize tying bulk. See Lake Erie Emerald Shiner tube pattern for more details on constructing Temple Dog style wings.
Cheeks: Jungle Cock slightly over 1 inch long and angled up along wing.
Head: Black thread wraps. Shumakov tube patterns characteristically are finished with small, neat finished heads that are no longer than 2mm in length.
Hook: Gamakatsu #SL11-3H, size #8 standard bonefish hook (3X strong/carbon steel/tin plated) connected to the rear of Long Range brass tube with flexible silicon or vinyl junction tubing (transparent blue or red colored). Transparent FlexTube (in various colors) is ideal for junction tubing connections and adds just a hint of color to the rear of the tube fly. Although not a standard, short shank tube hook, the Gamakatsu

bonefish hook is a very strong, medium length shank hook that is ideal for picking up short-striking steel-head without bending and twisting during a fight (which can be a problem with longer shanked hooks). The "lever-action" of this hook is also minimal versus longer shanked hooks. Lengthening the junction tubing connection can locate hook even further back on long-winged flies also helping with "short-strikers". The light-weight Gamakatsu bonefish hook balances well with the weight forward, inch Long Range brass tube. The light wire Partridge Nordic Single tube fly hook, # MM3STBN, size #8 is a good alternative.

Long-winged flies that use short 1/2 inch tube bodies and short shank hooks (affixed with short sections of junction tubing) can be prone to the hook tangling in the wing especially in fast water. Shumakov's 1/2 inch tubes, which don't allow for wing support from a long, angled tail or body hackle (like in the Lake Erie Emerald Shiner tube pattern) can foster this problem even more. The solution is to use a "free-swing-ing" hook by disconnecting the junction tubing from the tube body and leaving the hook eye inserted into the rear of the junction tubing. The junction tubing will keep hook riding straight behind the fly.

Tying notes: Tying the fly on the exposed forward extension of the thin diameter, hard plastic tube liner results in very little bulk in the tying process and small, finished heads (which are characteristic of Shumakov tube patterns). The longer the tube liner is allowed to extend forward of the metal tube the more materials you can tie into the fly. This is particularly advantageous for tying in multiple hackle collars for wing support on the "body-less" Shumakov tube. Shumakov's tubes limit you to tie basically an all wing fly but the machined grooves in the tubes can be painted with enamel to add some color to the body.

Comments: This Temple Dog style fly uses a Yuri Shumakov tube design that incorporates a Shumakov 1/2 inch Long Range brass tube. Shumakov is a world renowned fly tyer and Salmon fly fisherman from Sweden who passed away unexpectedly in 2006. He designed his short metal tubes for the classic long-winged Scandinavian or Temple Dog style flies.

His tubes come in brass or lighter aluminum tubes and are 1/2 inch long (he calls them "1/2-inchers"). They are available in various models including the Long Range, Heavy Long Range, Skittle and Summer Arrow. The rear of each tube is machined to allow a piece of soft silicon or stiffer vinyl junction tubing to be attached for hook connection. The aluminum versions are ideal for low water conditions and lightly dressed flies.

The Long range tube is designed for reaching deep steelhead lies without dragging bottom. The Long Range Heavy is for getting down even deeper to winter holding steelhead. The Skittle has great balance for a heavy tube. It has enough weight at the front to push the fly down and hold it firmly in very heavy current flows either horizontally or slightly nose down. The Summer Arrow is Shumakov's answer to using coneheads without the hollow inner surface inherent with a conehead which can make tying in a wing bothersome. is ideal for small ties and low water situations.

By machining the tubes in a weight forward design hook "hang-down" common in long-winged flies and short metal tubes is eliminated allowing the tube to swim level on the downstream swing. The Long Range and Skittle have four machining grooves (which can be painted) in the rear of the tube to accomplish this.

The upward slanting taper of the front part of Shumakov's tubes keeps the wing pointed up and prevents it from entangling with the hook. As stated earlier, tying the fly on the thin diameter plastic liner of the Shumakov tube minimizes tying bulk. This allows for a tiny finished head unlike when tying on larger diameter tubing which often results in bulky and unsightly heads. Indeed, Shumakov had designed the ultimate tube! The Irish Angler at www.irishangler.com carries Shumakov tubes, liner material, junction tubing as well as tube fly vise adapters.

Jack Cook of The Irish Angler has recently launched a 1/2 inch machined tube as part of Steelhead Anglers Tactical Tube System (TTS Tubes). The tube design is based on Jack's experience working with Yuri Shumakov, Mikael Frodin and Henrik Anderson fly designs as well as his own very successful steel-head fly design theory. The tubes are made in the USA in Portland, Oregon and are available in brass (.8 grams) and aluminum (.35 grams) with brass, nickel, copper and gun metal finishes. Various colored bodies are also available. They come complete with small diameter, hard plastic liner tubing.

After trying Shumakov and Cook TTS tubes on several Lake Erie tributaries for steelhead I was very impressed with the ease I could tie previously bulky flies on them (with small heads!) and the great level swimming action they had in various water flows. In addition to the Red, Black and Blue pattern I have come up with several of my own Scandinavian style winged patterns using these machined tubes including marabou speys, standard steelhead wets, leeches and various streamer patterns.

The Red, Black and Blue provides a large, dark silhouette that can be easily spotted by a steelhead during the low light conditions of early morning or late afternoon/evening as well as on overcast days. Larger and more heavily dressed versions can provide even larger profiles that are ideal for high, stained tributary flows. The blue and purple undertones of this fly also stand out well during low light conditions and the red guinea collar is a great strike trigger.

For detailed step-by-step instructions for tying Yuri Shumakov style tube flies by Shumakov himself visit the Racklehanen Fly Fishing Magazine website at: http://www.rackelhanen.se/eng/10265.htm

Sun Burst

Tyer: John Nagy, Pittsburgh, PA.
Thread: Uni-Thread, fire orange, 8/0 or Bennechi, 12/0.
Tube: Loop Tackle 1/2 inch or 5/8 inch (gold or silver) bottle tube. See Fly Plate XI for picture of Loop tube body.
Wing layers (from bottom to top): 4 strands of gold angel hair, yellow bucktail or calf tail, 4 strands of lime Krinkle Mirror flash, orange temple dog, 4 strands of gold angel hair, orange temple dog, 4 strands of gold angel hair, stiff orange saddle feather or cock neck feather, 4 strands of gold angel hair, yellow Russian silver goat or equivalent, 4 strands of red Fire Fly, 3 black ostrich herls. Fly finishes out at close to 3 5/8 inches long.
Wing tying notes: "Double" and "taper-cut" all flash material except for the red Fire Fly at the top of the wing (see Lake Erie Emerald Shiner tube pattern for details). The top temple dog wing layer should be approximately 3 1/2 inches long and slightly shorter than the longest flash material which should be around 3 3/4 inches. The ostrich feathers should extend to the length of the longest flash material.

Progressively build the wing from short to long starting from the bottom. The lower layer of bucktail (1 1/2 inches long) should have good width with the middle layers of temple dog (2 1/2 inches long) having most of the bulk of the wing. The top wing layer of silver goat (3 1/2 inches long) should be thin and long. Use a dubbing brush to remove under fur from temple dog and silver goat before tying in.
Cheeks: Jungle Cock slightly over 1 inch long and angled up along wing.
Head: Fire Orange thread wraps.
Hook: Gamakatsu #SL11-3H, size #8 standard bonefish hook (3X strong/carbon steel/tin plated) connected to the rear of Long Range brass tube with flexible silicon or vinyl junction tubing (fluorescent orange colored). Although not a standard, short shank tube hook, this very strong, medium length shank hook is ideal for picking up short-striking steelhead without bending and twisting during a fight (which can be a problem with longer shanked hooks). The "lever-action" of this hook is also minimal versus longer shanked hooks. Lengthening the junction tubing connection can locate hook even further back on long-winged flies also helping with "short-strikers". The light wire Partridge Nordic Single tube fly hook, # MM3STBN, size #8 is a good alternative.

Long-winged flies that use short 1/2 inch tube bodies and short shank hooks (affixed with short sections of junction tubing) can be prone to the hook tangling in the wing especially in fast water. Loop Bottle Tubes, which don't allow for wing support from a long, angled tail or body hackle (like in the Lake Erie Emerald Shiner tube pattern) can foster this problem even more. The solution is to use a "free-swinging" hook by disconnecting the junction tubing from the tube body and leaving the hook eye inserted into the rear of the junction tubing. The junction tubing will also keep hook riding straight behind the fly.
Tying notes: The neck of the Loop bottle tube does not leave a lot of room for tying multiple hackle collars for wing support and the large diameter neck (although smaller in diameter than most straight metal tubing) results in a somewhat bulky head. Using a small diameter, hard plastic tube liner to tie the fly on is an option for more tying room and a smaller finished head. See Lake Erie Emerald Shiner tube pattern for more details on constructing Temple Dog style wings.
Comments: I came up with this Temple Dog style tube as my answer to a spin fisherman I know who throws a medium size orange and gold spoon for steelhead on Conneaut Creek, OH and literally crushes them! The center of balance of the fast sinking Loop bottle tube is concentrated to the rear giving it action on the swing. Work's great on a swinging and stripping retrieve particularly on sunny days.

Lemon Lime

Tyer: John Nagy, Pittsburgh, PA.
Thread: Uni-Thread, fluorescent chartreuse or white, 8/0 or Bennechi, 12/0.
Tube: Eumer brass, 22mm (.866 inches) or 15mm (.590 inches), green Teardrop Tube and .07 inch (outside diameter.) stiff plastic tube liner. Leave at least 1/2 inch of plastic liner in front of the tube for tying the fly on. Prior to inserting liner into tube slightly melt one end of liner with flame to form lip. This end of liner will snug against rear of tube after insertion into tube. After fly is tied on exposed forward extension of liner, remaining liner in front of unfinished fly head is then cut to approximately 1/16 inch and then melted

to form lip. Final step is to finish head with thread up to lip of liner. Liner and tube can be mounted on a thread needle (secured in the vice jaws) that has a square eye to keep liner from rotating. HMH Vises, The Canadian Tube Fly Company, Veniard and Eumer offer inexpensive tube fly vice adapter tools that slip into the jaws of your vice and include metal pins or mandrels of different diameters for various size tubes. See Fly Plate XI for picture of assembled Eumer tube body.

Wing layers (from bottom to top): 4 strands of pearl green Angel Hair, chartreuse bucktail or calf tail, 4 strands of lime Krinkle Mirror Flash, stiff chartreuse saddle or cock neck feather, 4 strands of pearl green Angel Hair, chartreuse Russian silver goat or equivalent, 4 strands of pearl green Angel Hair, stiff chartreuse saddle or cock neck feather, 4 strands of lime Krinkle Mirror Flash, chartreuse Russian silver goat or equivalent, 4 strands of pearl green angel hair, natural teal flank feather ("folded" and wrapped to extend to end of tube), 4 strands of pearl green Angel Hair, chartreuse Russian silver goat or equivalent, 4 strands of pearl green Angel Hair, 4 black ostrich herls. Wing is tied completely on front plastic liner. Fly finishes out at close to 3 5/8 inches long.

Wing tying notes: "Double" and "taper-cut" all flash material except for Angel Hair at the top of the wing (see Lake Erie Emerald Shiner tube pattern for details). The top silver goat wing layer should be approximately 3 1/2 inches long and slightly shorter than the longest flash material which should be around 3 3/4 inches. Progressively build the wing from short to long starting from the bottom. The lower layer of bucktail (1 1/2 inches long) should have good width with the middle layers of silver goat (2 1/2 inches long) having most of the bulk of the wing. The top wing layer of silver goat (3 1/2 inches long) should be thin and long. Use a dubbing brush to remove under fur from temple dog and silver goat before tying in.

Cheeks: Jungle Cock slightly over 1 inch long and angled up along wing.

Head: Fluorescent chartreuse or white thread wraps. Head is not longer than 2mm.

Hook: Gamakatsu #SL11-3H, size #8 standard bonefish hook (3X strong/carbon steel/tin plated) connected to the rear of Eumer Teardrop Tube with clear, flexible silicon or vinyl junction tubing. Although not a standard, short shank tube hook, this very strong, medium length shank hook is ideal for picking up short-striking steelhead without bending and twisting during a fight (which can be a problem with longer shanked hooks). The "lever-action" of this hook is also minimal versus longer shanked hooks. Lengthening the junction tubing connection can locate hook even further back on long-winged flies also helping with "short-strikers". The light wire Partridge Nordic Single tube fly hook, # MM3STBN, size #8 is a good alternative.

Long-winged flies that use short 1/2 inch tube bodies and short shank hooks (affixed with short sections of junction tubing) can be prone to the hook tangling in the wing especially in fast water. Eumer Teardrop Tubes, which don't allow for wing support from a long, angled tail or body hackle (like in the Lake Erie Emerald Shiner tube pattern) can foster this problem even more. The solution is to use a "free-swinging" hook by disconnecting the junction tubing from the tube body and leaving the hook eye inserted into the rear of the junction tubing. The junction tubing will also keep hook riding straight behind the fly.

Tying notes: Tying the fly on the exposed forward extension of the thin diameter, hard plastic tube liner results in very little bulk in the tying process and small, finished heads. The longer the tube liner is allowed to extend forward of the metal tube the more materials you can tie into the fly. This is particularly advantageous for tying in multiple hackle collars for wing support on the "body-less" Eumer Teardrop Tube.

Comments: Eumer Teardrop tubes come in a variety of bright colors which makes dubbing a body optional. The chartreuse bucktail underwing of the Lemon Lime helps to support the wing in fast water. The Long teal flank collar gives the fly a spey action in the water. Very effective on a swinging and stripping retrieve particularly on sunny days

See Lake Erie Emerald Shiner tube pattern for more details on constructing Temple Dog style wings. For step-by-step instructions for tying Temple Dog style tube flies using Eumer tube bodies go to: www.eumer.com (look under "tying samples").

Fat Boy Slim

Tyer: Anthony L. DiBenedetto, Jr. of T Bone Fly Fishing, Poland, OH.

Tube: Large and small fluorescent orange Guideline FITS tube. Both tubes are 1 5/8 inches long.

Thread: Uni-Thread, black, 8/0 or Bennechi, 12/0.

Tag: Red or orange Antron yarn built up to angle tail up.

Tail: Orange Fluoro Fiber (2 inches long).

Rear body: Gold Gudebrod Electra Metallic Hologram Flat Braid tinsel or Lagartun holographic flat braid (3/4" inch length).

Front body: Black pearl Lite Brite Dubbing spun in a loop and teased out to approximately 3/4 inch long.

Hackle: Orange saddle hackle.

Ribbing: Medium oval gold tinsel ribbed through body over hackle.

Under-wing (from bottom to top): 5 strands of purple Gliss-n-Glow, purple temple dog (2 3/4 inches), 5 strands of purple Gliss-n-Glow, purple Russian silver goat or equivalent (3 1/2 inches long) and 5 strands of purple Gliss-n-Glow.

Collar: Orange schlappen or saddle hackle tied on the small tube after the under-wing is finished on large tube.

Over-wing layers (from bottom to top): 4 strands of purple ice angel hair, black temple (4 inches) dog, 4 strands of purple ice angel hair, black Russian silver goat or equivalent (4 3/4 inches), 4 strands of purple ice Angel Hair. Tie the over-wing in front of the collar on the small tube. Total length of the fly from the cone to the end of the wing is about 5 inches.

Secondary collar: Purple schlappen topped with 3 purple ostrich herls (4 3/4 inches).

Cheeks: Jungle Cock slightly over 1 inch long and angled up along wing.

Cone: Large silver FITS Turbo Cone.

Tying notes: When using a FITS Turbo Cone, collaring behind cone with schlappen, guinea or marabou feathers (secondary collar) will help fill the gap behind the cone and the wing. For detailed assembly instructions of this tube fly see Lake Erie Emerald Shiner tube fly pattern.

Hook: Hywell double tube hook, size #6 or Partridge Salar double tube hook, size #7 or #11. Tony prefers the Hywell double hook model for the close hook points and needle eye. Secure hook to fly by inserting hook eye directly into the end of large, flexible FITS tubing. The FITS tubing is designed with built in hook connection due to its semi-soft and flexible properties. No junction tubing connection is needed.

Comments: This big Temple Dog style fly uses the Mikael Frodin tube system and is Tony's high, muddy water fly. The dark colors, large size and flash stick out well in stained flows. The brass Frodin Turbo Cone has a concave scallop shape that creates an eddy of turbulence behind the fly that prevents the wing material from "flattening out" in faster current flows and keeps it "swimming." (This effect is much more pronounced than the turbulence created by a standard bullet shaped cone.) Turbo cones are especially advantageous for flies constructed of very soft materials like temple dog fur, arctic fox fur, marabou and ostrich feathers which have fantastic action in slow water but quickly lose volume and movement when surrounded by fast currents. They also can alert a steelhead when the tube fly is stripped in at the end of the swing by "pushing" water which sends out a disturbance in the water that a steelhead can sense with his lateral line.

Frodin Turbo Cones come in various colors and color combos as well as L, M, S and XS sizes. Larger size Turbo Cones are ideal for longer flies, since they create longer eddies behind them in the current flow. The actual formula for this is: Turbo eddy length = diameter of turbo multiplied by 10. This formula helps you to pick the correct Turbo cone size for the finished wing length in a tube fly pattern.

Tony ties his wing and tail angled high like a classic Temple Dog or Fatback design. Temple Dog originator Hakan Norling tied the wing on his Temple Dog tube patterns initially pointing forward and then folded it back toward the rear of the fly (the reverse-wing-technique) in order to maintain a high wing angle in the water and also end up with a smaller finished head. This tying step is really not necessary when using stiff hackle palmered over the front and rear bodies (in combination with collar hackle) which works quite well in supporting a high wing angle.

Steel Flamingo

Tyer: Anthony L. DiBenedetto, Jr. of T Bone Fly Fishing, Poland, OH.

Tube: Blue, transparent FlexTube from the Canadian Tube Fly Co. (1 inches long) attached to the rear of a medium, silver Wurm Tungsten Tube. Also smaller diameter (1/16 inch outside diameter) clear plastic tubing (1 7/8 inch long) inserted through Wurm tube and within the larger FlexTube tubing (approximately 3/4 inches to the rear of Wurm tube). Smaller tubing also secures Krinkle Mirror Flash material (see tail instructions). Leave enough tubing in front of the Wurm tube so as not to run out of plastic tubing and allow for finishing the wing and head. See Fly Plate XI for picture of assembled Wurm tube body.

Thread: Uni-Thread, hot pink, 8/0 or Bennechi, 12/0.

Tail (in tube body): 6 or 7 strands of pearl Krinkle Mirror Flash which extends 2 inches beyond end of FlexTube with "taper-cut" ends. Krinkle Mirror Flash is secured into tube body by feeding strands thru FlexTube tube (space evenly around inner diameter) and then inserting small diameter plastic tube (inserted into FlexTube 3/4 inch to rear of Wurm Tungsten Tube) to "pin-down" the Krinkle Mirror Flash. Add one or two drops of crazy glue to anchor small tube into FlexTube tube. Krinkle Mirror Flash strands do not interfere with the insertion of leader material into the tube body.

Tag: Hot pink Antron yarn built up to angle tail up.

Tail (on tube body): Hot pink Fluoro Fiber (1 1/4 inch long).

Body (back to front): Loop dub mixture of hot pink Serbrjanka Russian silver goat or equivalent (must have transparent/shiny properties) and pearl Angel Hair fibers on rear half of FlexTube body. "Cross-rib" over front body with loop dubbing leaving areas of colored FlexTube body exposed. Wraps of hot pink Crystal or Trilobal synthetic hackle over the tubing can be substituted for the dubbing although the transparent effect is less though. Loose wraps of these synthetic hackles will produce better transparency.

Under-wing (from bottom to top/tied on FlexTube): Baby blue T's Hair (2 inches), pearl Angel Hair (2-3 strands), hot pink temple dog (3 inches long), pearl Angel Hair (2-3 strands), Silver Doctor blue teal flank collar, baby blue temple dog (3 1/2 inches), pearl angel hair (2-3 strands), hot pink T's Fur or equivalent (4 inches), pearl Angel Hair (2 strands).

Front collar (wrapped in front of Wurm tube body on smaller front tubing): hot pink schlappen.

Over- wing (tied on smaller front tubing): pearl Angel Hair (2-3 strands), Caribbean blue T's Fur (4 1/2 inches),, pearl Angel Hair (2-3 strands), hot pink Serebjenka silver goat incorporated side-by-side with hot pink T's Fur (4 1/2 inches). Total length of the fly from the cone to the end of the wing is about 4 5/8 inches.

Cheeks: Jungle Cock slightly over 1 inch long and angled up along wing.

Head: Hot pink thread wraps. Finished head is no longer than 2mm in length.

Tying notes: Collar of blue teal flank is kept short to expose tube body color. For more detailed wing assembly instructions see Lake Erie Emerald Shiner tube fly pattern.

Hook: Hywell double tube hook, size #6 or Partridge Salar double tube hook, size #7 or #11. Tony prefers the Hywell double hook model for the close hook points and needle eye. Secure to fly by inserting hook eye directly into end of fly (tube). No junction tubing is needed. A larger/heavier hook is required to balance the weight of the Wurm Tungsten Tube especially when using larger size Wurm Tubes.

Comments: The Steel Flamingo tube pattern is based on one of the last tube designs Yuri Shumakov developed prior to his death in August 2006. It was Shumakov's answer to a fast-sinking conehead tube fly without the "unsightly" cone at the head of the fly (which he felt took away from the classic Scandinavian large wing/small head profile). A small diameter, "micro" Wurm Tungsten Tube is used in place of the cone (placed farther back on the fly) which is easily covered with dubbing and/or collar hackle. The Wurm Tube blends nicely into the FlexTube body due to its small diameter. This placement also balances the tube fly much better versus a conehead at the front. Finishing the fly on the small diameter, front tubing (in front of the Wurm Tube) allows for a small finished head.

Shumakov also felt that he could enhance the properties of transparent, colored tubing (like FlexTube or FITS tubing) by dubbing the tube with Serbrjanka Russian Silver goat and also inserting reflective flash material into the tubing itself. This transparent dubbing does not create a bulky/dense silhouette like other dubbings and the flash material does not interfere with the insertion of tippet material or the hook eye at the end of the tube. Wraps of Crystal or Trilobal synthetic hackle over the tubing can be substituted for the dubbing. Loose wraps of these hackles are better since it will produce better transparency.

For more detailed information on tying Shumakov colored tube body flies visit the Racklehanen Fly Fishing Magazine website at: http://www.rackelhanen.se/eng/10304.htm

Tony ties the wing and tail on the Steel Flamingo angled high like a classic Temple Dog or Fatback design. Temple Dog originator Hakan Norling tied the wing on his Temple Dog tube patterns initially pointing forward and then folded it back toward the rear of the fly (the reverse-wing-technique) in order to maintain a high wing angle in the water and also end up with a smaller finished head. This tying step is really not necessary when using a stiff base wing of T's Hair, collar hackle and a long, angled tail which all work quite well in supporting a high wing angle.

T Bone Fly Fishing distributes both T's Hair and T's Fur. T's Hair is a moderately stiff, very translucent and durable natural fiber ideal for structural support for tube fly wings. It is a superb substitute for bucktail due to its high translucency and long fiber availability. T's Fur is an extremely soft, semi-translucent and supple natural fiber material that is ideal for winging and dubbing. It dyes readily, has superb action in the current and is completely free of stiff guard hairs and excess under fur.

Witchy Woman

Tyer: Anthony L. DiBenedetto, Jr. of T Bone Fly Fishing, Poland, OH.

Tube: Yellow, transparent FlexTube from the Canadian Tube Fly Co. (1 1/4 inches long) with smaller diameter (OD equal to ID of the FlexTube) clear plastic tubing (3/4 inch long) to fit within the larger FlexTube tubing. Smaller tubing extends 3/8 inch forward of FlexTube for tying in wing and accommodating the cone. It is also used for securing in Gliss-N-Glow tail (see tail instructions below). FlexTube can be made longer to position the tube hook closer to the rear of the fly for "short-striking" steelhead.

Thread: Uni-Thread, black, 8/0 or Bennechi, 12/0.

Tail: 4 or 5 strands of pearlescent Gliss-n-Glow extending out of tube (4 1/2 inches long) with "taper-cut" ends. Gliss-N-Glow is secured into tube body by feeding strands thru FlexTube tube (space evenly around inner diameter) and then inserting small diameter plastic tube to "pin-down" the Gliss-n-Glow. Add one or two drops of crazy glue to anchor small tube into FlexTube tube. Gliss-n-Glow strands do not interfere with the insertion of leader material into the tube body.

Wing (from bottom to top): White Bucktail (2 inches long) with 2 strands of pearlescent Gliss-N-Glow on sides (5-6 inches long), yellow T's Hair (3 inches long), several fibers of fiery red brown T's Fiber (5-6 inches long), black Russian silver goat or equivalent (5-6 inches long).

Cheeks: Jungle Cock slightly over 1 inch long and angled up along wing.

Cone: Small gold cone set in place with gel type Crazy Glue.

Hook: Hywell double tube hook, size #6 or Partridge Salar double tube hook, size #7 or #11. Tony prefers the Hywell double hook model for the close hook points and needle eye. Hooks cannot be too heavy which can cause this light body fly to swim nose up and tail down. Bigger hooks require a larger cone for balance. Secure to fly by inserting hook eye directly into tube body. No junction tubing is needed.

Tying notes: After wing is tied put 1 or 2 drops of Crazy Glue just behind cone on wing fibers. Pull the wing fibers up (by tail) and toward the head of the fly for 30 seconds. Capillary action of natural hair fibers will pull the Crazy Glue into the fibers which will stiffen a few millimeters of fiber and "arch" the wing into place.

Comments: This is Tony's version of the eel like Sunray Shadow pattern. It was originally tied unweighted and fished fast and "square" across the surface current for sea trout and Atlantic salmon. Tony added a small cone to help it sink deeper on the swing and strip retrieve for bottom holding steelhead. The addition of strands of Gliss-N-Glow in the tubing adds eye-catching flash to the pattern. See Comments in Steel Flamingo tube pattern for description of T's Hair and T's Fur.

Liu Temple Dog Leech

Tyer: Guide Greg Liu of Pulaski, NY.

Tube: HMH 3/32 inch plastic tubing, 1 1/2 inches long. Aluminum tubes work also due to their light weight but avoid heavier brass or copper tubes.

Thread: Uni-Thread, black, 8/0.

Body: Black Polar Chenille or black Holographic Tri-Lobal synthetic hackle (1 1/4 in. size). Black Hackle Flash will work also.

Wing: Black Icelandic sheep hair (make approximately 4 inches long) or black E.P. Fibers. Any long fibers can be used as long as the material tapers to a point.

Collar: Red schlappen feather.

Hook: Daiichi #X510 tube fly hook (wide gap bend, 3X short, 3X strong, straight eye), size #8 with clear junction tubing.

Comments: Greg fishes this simplified Temple Dog style tube fly on the Salmon River in NY when water temperatures are in the 40's. The river gets a lot of pressure with small fly patterns so this large fly gets the attention of aggressive steelhead or "players." Using a light plastic or aluminum tube (versus a heavy copper or brass tube) in combination with a fast sink tip line, allows the fly to move in the current with an enticing darting action on the swing like a plug. When water flows are warm Greg starts swinging near the surface and then changes tips to progressively swim the tube deeper.

Pulaski Persecutor

Guide: Greg Liu of Pulaski, NY.

Tube: Orange beading tube (beading craft product that Wall Mart and Michaels Crafts stores carry) extending past wing length. Insert a metal pin or needle into the tubing to hold it in vice while tying.

Thread: Uni-Thread, orange, 8/0.

Collars (3): Estaz, Tri-Lobal or schlappen feathers in front of cones.

Wings (3): Orange artic fox tail. Secure wings in front of collars (cone is secured in front of each collar/ wing segment). Other good wing colors include blue/white with nickel front cone and black/chartreuse with chartreuse front cone. Total wing length is about 2 inches long.

Cones (3): One small fluorescent orange (front) and two small brass. Anchor all cones with tying thread and cement especially if spey casting. Leave short piece of tubing in front of orange cone and cut at a slight taper.

Hook: Daiichi #X510 tube fly hook (wide gap bend, 3X short, 3X strong, straight eye), size #8 inserted into rear of beading tube.

Comments: This tube pattern uses a segmented wing design and a multiple cone body (similar to Yuri Shumakov's Russian Silver Bullet tube fly). By securing each collar/wing segment in front of a cone it helps to flare the wing up in the "Fatback" or Temple Dog style. Greg says that by varying the number of cones on the tube (one, two or three) you can control the depth of the fly on the swing for the sink tip chosen. Multiple cone bodies, which concentrate the weight similar to a bottle tube design, sink extremely fast and are ideal for deep and fast flows. They can be made to be much heavier than most 1/2 inch bottle tubes. Shumakov liked to vary the size and weight of the cones and usually placed the heavier cone (when using multiple cones) toward the front of the tube body to help balance the fly.

Positioning the hook point up will reduce the chances of bottom snagging when fishing these heavy tubes deep. The long tubing on the Pulaski Persecutor helps locate the hook further back preventing hook tangling with the wing and also helping with "short-striking" steelhead. Greg also has found that placing the cones more on the body versus at the head of the tube results in better action on the swing.

Liu Snake Tube
Tyer: Guide Greg Liu of Pulaski, NY.
Tube: Blue, small diameter, soft Scoobies strand tubing or craft beading tubing extending roughly to wing length. Insert a metal pin or needle into the tubing to hold it in vice while tying. The Canadian Tube Fly Company markets a product called Wiggle Tube which is also ideal for tying snake tube bodies. T Bone Fly Fishing has a similar product called T's Tubing.
Thread: Uni-Thread, blue, 8/0.
Collar: Blue pearl Angel Hair tied in behind rear cone.
Cones: Two small brass. Anchor all cones with tying thread and cement especially if spey casting. Leave short piece of tubing in front and cut at a slight taper.
Top Wing: Blue pearl Angel Hair (4 inches long) topped with Blue Icelandic sheep hair or blue E.P. Fibers (3 1/2 inches long). Any long fibers can be used as long as the material tapers to a point.
Bottom Wing: Blue pearl Angel Hair (4 inches long).
Hook: Daiichi #X510 tube fly hook (wide gap bend, 3X short, 3X strong, straight eye), size #8 inserted into rear of beading tube.
Tying notes: Tie in points for both the top and bottom wing's is between the front and rear cones.
Comments: Snake flies with their slim profiles and highly flexible bodies are popular in Wales for sea trout. They are tied with long sections of soft, braided mono covered with woven Mylar tubing and typically use permanently attached hooks. Greg's snake tube pattern has all the benefits of a tube design while utilizing eye catching colored tubing that is soft, flexible and movable like the woven mylar.

The long tubing also helps locate the hook further back preventing hook tangling with the wing as well as helping with "short-striking" steelhead. Greg says that by varying the number of cones on the tube (one, two or three) you can control the depth of the tube on the swing for the sink tip chosen. More information on snake flies (including tube patterns) can be found at: www.seatroutfishing.net/flies.htm

Halebop
Tyer: Stuart Anderson of the Canadian Tube Fly Company, Edmonton, Alberta.
Thread: Uni-Thread, fire orange, 6/0.
Tube: Yuri Shumakov inch Long Range brass or aluminum tube and .07 inch (outside diameter.) plastic liner. Leave at least 1/2 inch of plastic liner in front of the tube for tying the fly. Prior to inserting liner into tube slightly melt one end of liner with flame to form lip. This end of liner will snug against rear of tube after insertion into tube. After wing is tied on exposed forward extension of liner, remaining liner in front of unfinished fly head is then cut to approximately 1/16 inch and then melted to form lip. Final step is to finish head with thread up to lip of liner. See Red, Black and Blue tube pattern for more details on Shumakov tube system.
Body: Fire orange enamel painted in grooves of tube.
Hackle (starting from rear): Orange, pink, purple hen or schlappen feather. Finished with blue teal flank feather.
Wing (from bottom to top): Purple bucktail, 8 strands of purple Flashabou, 2 purple cock feathers laid flat. Wing is approximately 1 3/4 inches long.
Hook: Talon #2A-8346, sizes #2-#6.
Comments: Although not tied in the Temple Dog style this feather wing tube pattern incorporates a Shumakov 1/2 inch, weight forward Long Range tube which balances the fly nicely on the swing. The purple bucktail underwing helps to support the wing in fast water. The long teal flank feather gives a spey look to the fly. Stuart got inspiration for this pattern from the famous Winter's Hope by Bill McMillan where the combina-

tion of three different hackles blend together into a stunning color pattern. Great fly to swing on overcast days.

Furabou 1/2-Incher
Tyer: John Nagy, Pittsburgh, PA.
Thread: Uni-Thread, white, 8/0 or Bennechi, 12/0.
Tube: Yuri Shumakov 1/2 inch Long Range brass or aluminum tube and .07 inch (outside diameter.)stiff plastic tube liner. The Jack Cook inch TTS brass tube and liner can also be used for the tube body. Leave at least 1/2 inch of plastic liner in front of the tube for tying the fly. Prior to inserting liner into tube slightly melt one end of liner with flame to form lip. This end of liner will snug against rear of tube after insertion into tube. After wing is tied on exposed forward extension of liner, remaining liner in front of unfinished fly head is then cut to approximately 1/16 inch and then melted to form lip. Final step is to finish head with thread up to lip of liner. See Red, Black and Blue tube pattern for more details on Shumakov tube system.
Wing: 3 or 4 wraps (going forward) of Roman Moser, white, short fiber Furabou on plastic tube liner. Stroke the Furabou fibers back prior to wrapping around plastic liner. Comb fibers backward after wrapping is complete forming 2 1/4 inch tapered wing. Top with 3 or 4 strands of olive Krinkle Mirror Flash and peacock Angel Hair (2 1/2 inches long). Color wing with permanent Prismacolor pens as follows: crimson red for gill plates, light cerulean blue for parr marks, black and canary for yellow back.
Eyes: 3/16 inch Mirage Eyes. Peel and stick, and then epoxy into place.
Hook: Gamakatsu #SL11-3H, size #8 standard bonefish hook (3X strong/carbon steel/tin plated) connected to the rear of Long Range brass tube with flexible silicon or vinyl clear junction tubing. Although not a standard, short shank tube hook, this very strong, medium length shank hook is ideal for picking up "short-striking" steelhead without bending and twisting during a fight (which can be a problem with longer shanked hooks). The "lever-action" of this hook is also minimal versus longer shanked hooks. Lengthening junction tubing connection can locate hook even further back on long-winged flies also helping with short-strikers. The light-weight Gamakatsu bonefish hook balances well with the weight forward, 1/2 inch Long Range brass tube. The light wire Partridge Nordic Single tube fly hook, # MM3STBN, size #8 is a good alternative.
     Long-winged flies that use short 1/2 inch tube bodies and short shank hooks (affixed with short sections of junction tubing) can be prone to the hook tangling in the wing especially in fast water. Shumakov's 1/2 inch tubes, which don't allow for wing support from a long, angled tail or body hackle (like in the Lake Erie Emerald Shiner tube pattern) can foster this problem even more. The solution is to use a "free-swinging" hook by disconnecting the junction tubing from the tube body and leaving the hook eye inserted into the rear of the junction tubing. The junction tubing will also keep hook riding straight behind the fly.
Comments: Although not tied in the Temple Dog wing style it incorporates a Shumakov 1/2 inch, weight forward Long Range tube which balances the fly nicely on the swing. Tying the wing on the thin diameter, plastic tube liner also reduces tying bulk at the front of fly. Probably the easiest and quickest way to tie a baitfish tube pattern. Has all the strike triggers including large eyes, red gill plates, dark back, flash and baitfish profile. Longer versions can be tied with long fiber Furabou. Prismacolor pens allow for an endless combination of colors and marking patterns.

*Tube Tying Materials and Accessories**
(See the Custom Fly Tyers and Flies section in Appendix D for tube pattern tyers.)

The following manufacturers, retailers and individuals supply tube tying materials and accessories for tying conventional and Scandinavian style tube flies. More sources can be found in the Fly Tying Materials (specialty items) section of Appendix D.

*Some foreign specialty tube manufacturers may not have distributors in the United States and require currency exchange and overseas shipping costs. Hopefully in the future, with the increasing popularity of tube flies, distributors and retailers in the US will pick up some of these innovative tube design systems.

HMH Vises
(starter tube tool kit, tube fly vise adapter tools, tube fly vise converter, conventional tubing assortments, tube hooks, junction tubing, coneheads, tube egg heads)
14 Maine Street,
PO Box 18,
Brunswick, ME 04011
(207) 729-5200
www.hmhvises.com

The Irish Angler
(TTS and Shumakov tubes, Frodin FITS, Wurm, Bidoz and Eumer tube systems, tube hooks and materials, Frodin Turbo cones, Veniard Slipstream tubes, Atlantic salmon and spey fly materials, Guideline products,
Frodin tube tying DVD)
32231 East Bird Street,
Carnation, WA 98014
(425) 333-6582
www.irishangler.com

The Fly Fishing Shop
(Shumakov and Frodin tubes, Loop Bottle tubes, tube hooks, tube fly vise adapter tool, tying materials)
PO Box 368,
67296 East Highway 26,
Welches, OR 97067
1-800-266-3971
www.flyfishusa.com

Canadian Tube Fly Company
(Shumakov tubes, Canadian Tube Fly Co. bottle tubes, Talon tube fly hooks, FlexTube tubing, Wiggle Tube,Lazer Wrap, tube fly vise adapter tool, jungle cock, tying materials, tube fly pattern kits)
4214 40 Avenue,
Edmonton, Alberta T6L 5T4
1-800-572-7493
www.canadiantubeflies.com/index.html
www.adiposflytying.com

Rooney Tube Works
(linerless brass tubes, plastic tubes)
1501 Libra Street,
Newberg, OR 97132
(503) 554-9839
www.rooneytubeworks.com

Anthony L. DiBenedetto, Jr.
T Bone Fly Fishing
(tube fly tying materials including T's Fur, T's Hair and T's Tubing, arctic fox fur, Wurm Tungsten Tubes and tubing, custom dyeing of temple dog fur, llama fur, arctic fox fur and ostrich feathers, fly fishing equipment and accessories, specializes in Scandinavian tube fly patterns)
7306 Yellow Creek Drive,
Poloand, OH 44514
(330) 757-3614
opus412@zoominternet.net
www.tboneflyfish.com

Rod Yerger
(plastic, aluminum and copper tubes with plastic liners, tapered vinyl hook sleeves, tube hooks, Yerger tube fly holder, also skittering, bead head, hot bead, cone head and micro tubes)
PO Box 294,
Lawrence, PA 15055
(724) 746-3511
rodyerger@yahoo.com
http://rodyerger.com/index.html

Tony Pagliei
(convertible tube flies)
T Pags Company, LLC
East Lansing, Michigan USA
info@tpagsco.com
www.tubeflies.com

Yuri Shumakov Tubes
(Swedish made Shumakov 1/2 inch tubes, Serebrjanka goat hair, tying instructions):
http://www.shumakovtubes.com/index.html

Partridge of Redditch
(Mikael Frodin tube flies)
http://www.partridge-of-redditch.co.uk/flies/mik_fr_fly.htm

Rainy's Flies
(Yuri Shumakov tube flies)
http://www.rainysflies.com/pages/flies.asp?page=shumakov

GuideLine
(Swedish made Frodin FITS tube system and cones)
www.GuideLineFlyFish.com

Wurm Tungsten Products
(German made tungsten bottle tubes, coneheads, beads and plastic tubes)
http://www.tungstenshop.de/

Loop Tackle
(Swedish made Loop bottle tubes and double tube hooks)
www.looptackle.se

Bidoz
(French made Joergensen bottle tubes, metal tube extensions)
www.Bidoz.com/tubes

Eumer Pro Fishing Accessories
(Made in Finland Eumer Teardrop, Tag, Conehead, Cone and Crayfish tubes, also plastic tubing, tube tying tool and tube fly box)
www.eumer.com

Hycreek
(Made in Finland Eumer Teardrop, Tag, Conehead, Cone and Crayfish tubes, also Eumer plastic tubing, tube tying starter kit, tube tying tool and tube fly box)
101 S. Main Street,
Ishpeming, MI 49849
(866) 459-4400
www.hycreek.com

Veniard Fly Tying
(Veniard Slipstream plastic and metal tubes, liner,
Scandi fluorescent tubing, silicon rubber tubing, bottle tubes)
www.veniard.com

The Fly Co
(Danish wholesale company that sells an extensive selection of tubes
including Shumakov, US and Morrum tubes as well as deep water and low water tubes)
www.flyco.dk/

White Tail Fly Tieing
(Atlantic salmon and tube fly materials,
fly tying instruction, catalog)
7060 White Tail Court
Toledo, Ohio 43617
(800) 579-5549
www.whitetailflytieing.com

Mike Martinek
(Mike Martinek's Electric Sashimi polyester body material)
15 Eastway
Reading, MA 01867
(781) 944-8744

E. Hille, The Angler's Supply House
(Roman Moser Furabou)
811 S. Market Street,
S. Williamsport, PA 17702
(570) 323-9995
www.anglersupplyhouse.com/shop/

Angler's Roost Enterprises
(jungle cock necks)
5820 Main Street,
Suite 308,
Williamsville, NY 14221
(716) 565-9838
anglersroostent@cs.com

Siskiyou Aviary
(source for specialty feathers including Rhea feathers)
2585 East Main Street,
Ashland, OR 97520
(541) 488-2835
www.siskiyouaviary.com

Saltwaterflies.com
(Polar Fiber, Icelandic sheep hair, artic fox, Fire Fly,
Krinkle Mirror Flash, Gliss-n-Glow, Angel Hair, Super Hair,
V ribbing)
PO Box 362,
Housatonic, MA 01236
(413) 274-6143
www.saltwaterflies.com

Creekside Fly Fishing Guides & Outfitters
(Atlantic salmon and spey fly materials)
345 High Street SE,
Salem, OR 97301
(877) 273-3574
www.creeksideflyfishing.com

Mad River Outfitters
(conventional tubing and accessories, coneheads, tube fly bead-heads)
813 Bethel Road,
Columbus, OH 43214
(614) 451-0363
1-888-451-0363
admin@madriveroutfitters.com
www.madriveroutfitters.com

The Oak Orchard Fly Shop
(conventional tubing and accessories, holographic Flashabou, HMH Egghead beads,
Bodi Works braid, marabou spey hackle, SLF dubbing)
5977 Main Street,
Williamsville, NY 14221
(716) 626-1323
info@oakorchardflyshop.com
www.oakorchardflyshop.com

Buffalo Outfitter's
(conventional tubing and accessories, coneheads, Loop bottle tubes, Shumakov tubes,
Angel Hair, Holo Eyes)
5655 Main Street
Williamsville, NY 14221
(716) 631-5131
www.buffalooutfittersflyshop.com

Grindstone Angling Specialties
(spey fly materials and hooks, Uninylon thread, Mega Hair)
P.O. Box 442,
24 Mill Street, North,
Waterdown, Ontario
LOR 2HO
(905) 689-0880
www.grindstoneangling.com
flyshop@grindstoneangling.com

English Angling Trappings
(spey fly materials and hooks, tube fly kits)
Box 8885
New Fairfield, CT
203-746-4121
Fax: 203-746-9929
alcoif@aol.com

"Shall I go to heaven or go a fishing?"

Henry David Thoreau

Most Common Mistakes Made by the Rookie Lake Erie Steelheader

Chapter 9

Every steelhead season, in the Lake Erie region, new fly fisherman come on the scene to experience catching migratory steelhead in the tributaries. Some seem to be naturals, quickly catching steelhead after some initial short instruction from a friend or guide, or just figuring it out on their own. These folks obviously have fly fished before (usually trout, bass, etc.) and seem to pick up the subtleties of the steelhead game fairly quickly, especially if they have some nymphing experience.

Others seem to struggle, not only with the seeming oddities of steelheading but the basics of fly fishing as well. More often than not, though, most are in between, needing some instruction on fly casting, dead-drifting and swinging techniques, equipment, leaders, steelhead behavior, tributary knowledge and reading surface water.

The uninitiated steelhead fly fisher certainly faces a challenge on the Lake Erie tributaries. To be successful he should first have a sound foundation in fly fishing skills and then obtain the necessary fly fishing equipment, tackle and flies needed for catching finicky Lake Erie steelhead.

Next, he should seek some instructional guiding, not only for the techniques needed to catch steelhead but also for other skills such as learning prime fishing locations and access points as well as characteristics of the tributaries themselves. Reading any books or articles related to Lake Erie steelheading, and surfing the net for stream reports, water flow data and weather conditions is also extremely helpful.

Finally "picking the brains" of your fellow steelheader on the tributaries is invaluable. If you do this in a gracious and appreciative way it can only open you up to a wealth of knowledge and experience.

The following is a list of the most common mistakes made by the rookie steelheader. The list is rather comprehensive and should also provide some beneficial pointers for the veteran steelheader as well.

Technique and Equipment—

1.) When short line nymphing (bottom-bouncing or the right-angle-floating indicator technique), *failure to drift the fly naturally and consistently along the stream bottom* where the steelhead are. The culprit is usually not enough, or too much split-shot.

2.) When swinging flies downstream, *failure to get fly down deep enough* to the steelhead. Using too long of a leader and /or too slow of a sink tip (or sinking leader) is usually the problem.

3.) *Holding the reel handle or fly line* after hooking a steelhead and…bing!…adios steelhead! Get the steelhead "on the reel" and use the drag of the reel to put steady pressure on the fish. Drag should be set light enough, though, to prevent breaking the tippet.

4.) Failure to *detect* a strike when bottom-bouncing. Strikes can be very soft, especially in the winter. Maintain a "tight" line during the drift to keep contact with the bottom and help detect any strikes. Detecting strikes when bottom-bouncing is part visual, feel and even a sixth sense. It takes time and experience to become proficient at it, but once you learn it you never forget the sensation!

5.) Failing to *set the hook* after getting a strike. This often requires a hard hook set, especially with a soft action fly rod.

6.) Failing to *play* steelhead properly. Reel in any slack line after initially hooking a steelhead and let the steelhead run. Keep the rod high to absorb sudden surges and to steer line around obstacles. Then, wear the fish down by pumping the rod with a side-to-side movement. Don't point the rod directly at the fish or you'll lose the shock absorbing action of the rod. Also "run" along the stream with the fish to avoid excessive fly line getting into the water which causes more drag and break-offs.

7.) Making *poor knot connections.* Knot failure is a major cause of losing fish. Tie knots carefully. Practicing the more difficult knots at home makes it much easier on the stream.

8.) The failure to use the *correct* floating indicator size and placement, tippet size, split-shot amount, split-shot-to-fly distance and fly pattern for the current water conditions (high, low, stained or clear) and water types (pools, runs, pocket water). This requires constant on-stream adjustments.

9.) The failure to *mend and check* the floating indicator. This will keep the fly from being pulled off the bottom and drifting faster than the bottom current and results in a drag-free, natural drift.

10.) The failure to *adjust* the floating indicator to the depth of the water (water surface to just above the streambed). This keeps the fly on the "noses" of the steelhead (important for lethargic winter steelhead) and eliminates most unintentional snagging and hang-ups.

11.) Using *too short* of a fly rod and leader when short line nymphing. Fly rods 9 ft. and longer allow for longer leader usage, which gets your fly quickly on the stream bottom. They also are superior for line control and mending.

12.) *Failing* to select fly patterns appropriate for the conditions encountered on the tributary. Use big, bright flies for high stained water, small and natural colored flies for lower clearer conditions.

13.) Lacks pre-trip *preparation* (leaders, flies, split-shot, indicators, appropriate clothing and dry waders). Remember, a successful steelhead trip often starts at the local fly shop and your fly tying bench!

Locating Steelhead—

14.) Failing to *read variations in surface water texture* (seams, riffles, etc.) in order to locate steelhead holding areas This is vital in stained water. Using your Polaroid sunglasses to cut down on surface glare helps tremendously.

15.) Failing to take *water temperatures* to locate *seasonal* steelhead holding areas in the fall, winter and spring. This helps locate the type of water where the bulk of the steelhead are holding such as pocket water, heads of pools, runs, mid-pool, tail-outs, eddies and spawning gravel.

Weather and Stream Conditions—

16.) The failure to get pre-trip *weather and stream reports* in order to predict *"prime water conditions"* for a particular tributary. Knowing the "run-off" rates of the tributaries is fundamental for predicting stream conditions on a day to day basis.

17.) The failure to *predict and avoid* high murky water, extremely low/clear flows, peak fall leaf drop, stream slush and ice flows, stream ice-over, smolt stocking areas, spring suckers and crowds.

Tributaries—

18.) The failure to *know* the high probability tributaries that are either smolt stocked by fishery departments or are sleeper "stray" steelhead tributaries.

19.) The failure to *know* local road systems and tributary access points. Obtain a variety of map sources and start studying!

20.) The failure to *locate* the "hot" tributary with the *best numbers* of steelhead or a specific section of a tributary with the *highest concentration* of fish. Steelhead are highly migratory in nature, so "following" a run upstream over a period of days is a good tactic.

21.) Lacking *mobility* on a tributary and fishing only easy access areas. Take a hike to find solitude and unmolested steelhead! Be sure, though, to ask for permission before entering private lands.

Philosophy—

22.) Failing to value the "total" steelhead experience over the concept that a successful steelhead trip is determined by high hook-up days or continual harvesting of steelhead. When the steelheader removes these pressures upon himself, he finds he is able to enjoy himself more on the tributaries. Adhering to some catch and release philosophy also allows steelhead to be caught multiple times during a season and protects developing wild steelhead fisheries.

Steelheader's Tip

Fly brightness and size is more important than fly color, especially in low light and stained water conditions.

Steelheader's Quiz*

So you think you are a "hard-core" Lake Erie tributary steelheader? Take this multiple choice quiz to really find out. Each question has five possible responses with the letter A worth ten points, B eight points, C six points, D four points and E zero points. At the end of the quiz are five scoring categories that you can fall into depending on your total score.

How often do you watch weather reports to predict run-off conditions?

A. I live right on my favorite tributary stream and don't need a weather forecast.

B. On my way to the steelhead tributaries I have a mobile internet connection that shows weather radar displays for the Lake Erie Region and "real-time" USGS tributary river gage data.

C. My baby boy knows all the names of the weather forecasters on the Weather Channel which I play continuously during the steelhead season.

D. I look at the seven day forecast in my Sunday paper if I can get away from football on the tube.

E. I never watch weather reports and usually go fishing "hell or high water!"

How many fishing licenses do you purchase during the course of the steelhead season?

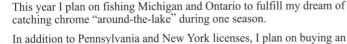

A. I buy fishing licenses for Ohio, Pennsylvania and New York every year on the internet.

B. This year I plan on fishing Michigan and Ontario to fulfill my dream of catching chrome "around-the-lake" during one season.

C. In addition to Pennsylvania and New York licenses, I plan on buying an Ohio license this year to give the spring Little Manistee run a try.

D. Pennsylvania fulfills all my needs for steelhead fishing!

E. I may buy a fishing license this year if the runs are good this fall. Licenses are too expensive these days. I now get my fishing thrills playing fishing video games.

How far are you willing to travel to catch a steelhead?

A. My buddies and I drive from Key West every fall to hook up with fall running "chrome bullets." It's an easier trip than driving to the Kenai River in Alaska for kings!

B. It's not a problem to chase "chrome" in Ohio, Pennsylvania and New York in one day!

C. Sometimes I sneak up from Pennsylvania in the fall to fish the "Cat" in New York to hook-up with some "wild steelies."

D. An Erie local recently called me one of the "uppers" (up from Pittsburgh). I can see Interstate 79 North in Pennsylvania becoming a second home to me in the future!

E. I can't afford the gas prices to drive to Erie!

The concept for the the Steelheader's Quiz came from the Steelheader's Test by Dave Vedder that appeared in the December-January 1994 issue of Salmon, Trout, Steelheader Magazine.

How often do you fish for steelhead during the steelhead season?

A. Since I live right in the middle of "steelhead alley", I try to get out everyday during the steelhead season to get my "steelhead fix."

B. The words "winter steelhead fishing" do not bring chills down my spine but conjure thoughts of big "metal-bruisers" and fishing in practical solitude.

C. I live for fall steelheading and "silver bullets" becoming airborne!

D. 25 years ago my dad and uncle took me up to Erie for the famed Coho salmon run. I caught a fish that the locals called a "rainbow" casting at night with a glow-in-the-dark Little Cleo spoon. Never been back since!

E. If I can get my "honey-do-list" done I may give it a try this fall!

How many steelhead rods do you own?

A. I addition to all my production steelhead rods I plan on building at least 3 new fly rods this year for steelhead fishing. I also consult with several of the major rod manufacturers on designing Great Lakes Steelhead rods.

B. I have more steelhead rods than golf clubs.

C. In addition to my "high-stick" nymphing rod and my "single-handed" fly rod for swinging flies, I plan on buying my first "double-handed" spey rod this fall.

D. My indestructible St. Croix fly rod has served me well over the years!

E. I decided to buy a new bowling ball instead of a steelhead rod.

Do you tie your own steelhead flies?

A. My custom steelhead flies are so "hot" that Orvis and Umpqua want to carry them.

B. In addition to tying egg and nymph patterns I just started tying my own traditional spey and Scandinavian tube flies for steelhead.

C. All I ever use are my own egg pattern ties. My "chrome-buster" is a killer!

D. I try to get to the fly shop early in the steelhead season before all the locally tied steelhead flies are gone!

E. I plan on using some of my old trout flies when I go steelheading someday!

In what kind of weather are you willing to fish for steelhead?

A. I usually don't consider it a true "steelhead experience" unless I have to break stream ice to drift my fly.

B. Since I usually ice fish all winter anyway, winter steelheading is a welcome break!

C. I bought a new SUV specifically for driving in lake effect snow!

D. I make it a point to watch the weather report and only steelhead fish when air temperatures are above 32 degrees F.

E. If I can't fish in short sleeves I stay home!

How many steelhead techniques can you do?

A. I only nymph for steelies if I have to. Traditional fishing for steelhead with a spey rod is the pinnacle of the sport!

B. I can dead-drift flies with or without an indicator and have just started to learn how to swing a fly for steelhead. My next goal is to catch some chrome on a dry fly!

C. I don't go anywhere without my floating indicators!

D. I once hooked a steelhead when my line was accidentally in the water while I was talking to my fishing buddy. Fish on!

E. I read on a fishing discussion board on the internet that you can catch steelhead by working your fly like a crab on the bottom. Or was that bonefish? Besides, I can't wait to try that when I make that trip north for steelhead someday!

Do you know how steelhead got their name?

A. I have been so busy catching "chrome" I never took the time to find out!

B. Steelhead have a characteristic blued-steel color on their heads and backs.

C. Pacific Northwest commercial fisherman found that it was much easier to dispatch a salmon over the head with a club versus a steelhead which has a head like hard steel.

D. I am still trying to find out if a steelhead is a fresh or saltwater fish!

E. Weren't they named after that rock band from the late 60's?

How has your personal life been affected by steelhead fishing?

A. All my friends are "metal-heads" and regrettably I got a divorce and lost my job this past year because I was always away "chasing chrome." My new girlfriend, though, ties awesome steelhead egg and nymph patterns and is thinking about selling them to some of the shops.

B. My kids' middle names are "Oncorhynchus" and "Mykiss."

C. I take a family vacation to "steelhead alley" every fall!

D. One time I called in sick to fish a fresh "chrome-run."

E. My wife may let me go steelhead fishing this fall if I finish painting the house.

Scoring

80 to 100 points: Nice going, you're officially a "hard-core" Lake Erie tributary steelheader. It's amazing you had the time to take the quiz. It's probably mid-summer and the 10 month tributary steelhead season is over. To ease withdrawal symptoms though you have booked a bunch of charter boat trips on the big Lake to catch some "chrome!"

60 to 79 points: At this level you are not quite a hard-core steelheader and balance your steelhead addiction well in your life. Your life's responsibilities are important to you but if "fresh chrome" is in you are gone!

40 to 59 points: Even with all your multiple interests like archery, deer hunting, spring turkey and trout fishing you are making time for more steelhead fishing.
If you purchase that new steelhead fly rod you always wanted and book a trip or two with a tributary steelhead guide, you could have a great steelhead season this year!

20 to 39 points: You are more of an "outsider" in the sport of steelhead fishing and consider it both a mysterious and "cult-like" sport. Try not to read magazine articles on steelheading, watch steelhead fishing DVD's or read John Nagy's Steelhead Guide Book or your life could be changed forever by the steelhead bug!

0 to 19 points: More than likely you never took the test and were just interested in how the scoring worked. You have heard of the "steelhead fish" before but never caught one. Hopefully the "metal-heads" and "chrome-chasers" of the sport won't scare you away!

UNHOOKED ®

Additional Steelheader's Tips

Bright, neon colored egg patterns are not only effective in stained water but also during the low light of early morning and the fading light of late afternoon and evening, particularly when the water is clear.

A good rule of thumb when dead-drifting, whether bottom bouncing or indicator fishing, is to fish the "bubble or foam lines" of the water surface that run adjacent to the main current flow. These lines indicate slower current areas below the water surface that steelhead prefer to use for resting and holding. Watch the bubble lines carefully though, they have a tendency to ebb and flow back and forth as the current flow fluctuates.

A good strategy is to target steelhead that are located below spawning beds by dead-drifting egg patterns. These fish are usually "unpaired" and are opportunistically feeding on eggs drifting down from the beds.

Using small egg patterns and nymphs, size #14 and smaller, can result in hook "tear-outs" when excessive pressure is applied when playing a steelhead. This is due to the minimal hook penetration of smaller hooks and can be remedied by using softer action fly rods and more patient fish fighting skills. Tear-outs can also be reduced by tying small fly patterns on larger hook sizes which provide deeper hook penetration.

Some steelheaders use round, oval or tear-shaped floating indictors with fluorescent colored tops and white bottoms. The bright colored tops are ideal for spotting indicators in the surface currents, especially during low-light periods, and the white bottoms blend into the sky and surface bubbles when viewed from underneath to help prevent spooking steelhead in clear water.

When tributary temperatures drop into the mid to low 30's steelheaders need not hit their favorite steelhead hole at the crack of dawn. Better to sleep in and try from late morning to early afternoon when water temperatures have nudged up enough to activate lethargic steelhead into biting. Don't worry about the crowds. Solitude is the norm in winter steelheading.

Accidentally dunking your fly reel in the water is a no-no for the winter steelheader. The reel can quickly freeze-up and bind in sub-freezing air temperatures. Your windshield heater blower comes in handy to quickly thaw and dry frozen reels although a complete drying will be required later to remove all the water in the reel.

Felt bottom wading boots can quickly build up with snow making hiking along your favorite tributary in the winter difficult. Companies like Korkers, Simms and Patagonia offer rubber soled wading boots that are ideal for hiking in the snow without snow buildup. The Korker and Simms models also come studded.

Lethargic winter steelhead can be very finicky and fussy and develop a "condensed" strike zone where they will rarely move more than 6 inches for a fly. The key is to perform multiple dead-drift presentations with down-sized flies of various patterns and colors and cover the drift completely and precisely. The difference of a couple inches in your presentation can result in a bonus hook-up that you would have otherwise missed.

Dead-drifting flies like egg patterns, nymphs and small wooly buggers is deadly in the ice-water tributary flows of winter as long as you keep them close to the stream bottom (where winter steelhead hold) drifting at or slightly slower than the bottom current. Incorporating brass, tungsten or glass beads, as well as wire ribbing into these fly patterns ensures that they stay near the bottom and allows for less shot usage.

During a severe winter cold snap, steelhead will forgo overhead cover and hold in slower pools and runs that have moderate depth of 4 feet or less and dark bottoms. These locations energize steelhead since sunlight penetration warms the stream bottom as well as the backs of the steelhead. Fish them before they freeze over or, if the surface is frozen, break the ice and return later when the fish have "settled." During milder winter periods look for steelhead to hold in deeper bend pools, pool tail-outs, pool back eddies and runs as well as faster, broken water areas which all provide good cover from predators without "super-chilling" the steelhead.

The steelhead's reaction to color is an important consideration for the steelheader. In stained flows, with reduced light penetration, egg patterns and nymphs that have bright fluorescent or neon colors in chartreuse, orange and red, stick out well while large, dark colored streamers in black, brown and purples provide a big, blocky profile in murky flows that a steelhead cannot miss.

During the low light of early morning, and fading light of late afternoon, try blue and purple flies which stay much more visible to a steelhead versus red and oranges due to their shorter wavelength absorption in the water. This effect is also holds true in deep, clear flows where light penetration decreases with water depth.

Increased fishing success on a tributary stream often boils down to simply keeping your fly in the water as much as possible. By tying good knots, watching your back cast (trees!), patiently getting snags out (you may have to wade upstream or to the opposite side to loosen them) and playing fish properly (don't horse them!) unnecessary break-offs and lost flies are eliminated and you will spend more time fishing than tying on flies!

Avoid the temptation of initially casting a long line when swinging flies in a large run or pool. Steelhead often hold close up at the heads of pools and runs and can be easily reached with a short-line swing presentation or just dangling the fly just below you.

Early morning steelheader's on the Grand River, ON at Caledonia in late October.
(Peter Charles photo)

Ontario and Michigan Lake Erie Tributaries

Chapter 10

Southern Ontario Lake Erie tributaries

The southern Ontario tributary streams draining the northern shore of Lake Erie (see Ontario Tributary Streams map and Tables 9, 10, 11 and 12 on pages 237-243) are dominated by the Norfolk sand plain in the Long Point Bay area. This sand plain is a massive deposit of sand that is over a 100 feet deep in places that allows for clear and cold groundwater seepage (on a steady basis) into many of these sandy and gravel bottom streams. The result is tributaries such as Big Creek and Young's Creek have prime habitats for natural reproduction of both resident stream trout, lake-run brown trout and steelhead.

According to Al Murray, Management Biologist for the Lake Erie Management Unit of the Ontario Ministry of Natural Resources, 90% of the steelhead runs in southern Ontario are naturally reproduced. This percentage is based on recent angler's logs and studies of returning steelhead at fishways located on Big Creek and the Grand River. Because all hatchery steelhead stocked in southern Ontario by the Ontario MNR have a left pectoral fin clip they can be easily distinguished from wild steelhead and any unclipped hatchery "strays" of other Lake Erie agencies. The percentage of stray hatchery fish is unknown but the Ontario MNR do not consider it to be a large percentage overall.

The Grand River has a huge watershed (200 miles long) with the first impassable dam 60 miles from the lake at Paris. The upper reaches of the Grand in the Fergus and Elora areas is well known as a trophy, resident brown trout fishery. The lower reaches of the river has developed into an excellent wild steelhead fishery ever since the Lorne dam at Brantford was removed in 1988.

October steelhead drift (near York) on the Grand River, Ontario.
(Larry Halyk photo)

Migratory steelhead now have access to groundwater fed stream flows and gravel beds above the Lorne dam that provide ideal spawning and rearing habitat for steelhead. The Ontario MNR now estimates that 10,000 steelhead run annually on the Grand River.

Whiteman's Creek, a tributary of the Grand River (it enters a few miles upstream of the Wilkes dam in Brantford), has also benefited from the removal of the Lorne Dam. According to Larry Halyk, Lead Management Biologist for the Lake Erie Unit of the Ontario MNR, wild steelhead have been running into Whiteman's Creek for only about 5 years. He believes that after the removal of the Lorne dam in 1988 it took a number of years for the steelhead to find the tributary and start naturally reproducing in it.

Although closed from October 1 to April 23 to protect trout and steelhead natural reproduction, Whiteman's Creek has great dry fly fishing for wild steelhead in September and in the spring after the opener. There is also a special regulation section on Whiteman's Creek at App's Mill Nature Center between Robinson Road and Cleaver Sideroad that also boasts a wild population of resident brown trout. Regulations for this 3.7-mile section include artificial lure and barbless hooks only with a catch and possession limit of 1 brown and rainbow trout (minimum size 19.7 inches).

The normal open season for brown trout and steelhead in southern Ontario is April 24 (last Saturday) to September 30. There is an extended season of April 24 (last Saturday) to December 31 allowed on sections of several important southern Ontario steelhead tributaries including Big Otter Creek, Little Otter Creek, Big Creek, North Creek, Grand River and Young's Creek.

Southern Ontario's steelhead fishing season may seem too short at first glance due to the closed winter and early spring seasons, which are meant to protect natural steelhead reproduction. But John Valk, guide and owner of Grindstone Angling Specialties in Waterdown, Ontario, says the spring months of late April, May and June provide plenty of opportunity for the fly fisherman. Valk also says that steelhead in a cold water year are still in the Grand River as late as the first week of July.

Ontario MNR Steelhead Management Policy

According to Larry Halyk, of the Ontario MNR, their agency has always placed a high value on sustainable, naturally reproduced fish populations. Their management approach over the years has been always to stock far less steelhead than other agencies and to emphasize protection and rehabilitation of steelhead habitat. Presently the Ontario MNR is reviewing how they manage steelhead on Lake Erie by doing population genetics work, tributary assessment, tagging and diet studies. The

John Valk with client on the Grand River, Ontario. (John Valk photo)

Wild fall steelhead caught on the Grand River, ON. (Ken Chandler photo)

goal is to come up with a plan to maximize the abundance of wild steelhead in their tributaries.

The Ontario MNR is also leading an international review of steelhead manage-ment with the other agencies bordering Lake Erie in the U.S. The goal here, through agency consensus, is to minimize potential conflicts in management policies. One example would be the impact of large numbers of hatchery "stray fish" on a stream being managed for wild steelhead.

The Ontario MNR stocks very few steelhead juveniles into their tributaries when compared to other agencies of the Lake Erie region (see Appendix E, Table 6.1). Big Creek has been stocked over the last few years (see Introduction to the Second Edition) with wild Ganaraska-strain steelhead only as a rehabilitation strategy. The Ontario MNR now believes that it may be doing more harm than good in helping the wild steelhead runs of Big Creek recover based on ongoing genetic analysis studies.

Fly Patterns

The wild steelhead of the Grand River system (including Whiteman's Creek and the Nith River) have a juvenile history of feeding on various stages of aquatic insects such as mayflies and especially caddis flies. As returning adult steelhead they quickly revert back to this behavior taking dead drifted caddis larvae and nymphs and traditionally swung spey and soft hackles (imitating emerging caddis.) Dead-drifting mayfly duns and swinging adult caddis imitations on the surface are also very effective in taking these wild steelhead. Most opportunities for dry fly fishing for steelhead on the Grand and it's tributaries will occur during the warmer water conditions of early fall (September) and the spring months of late April, May and June.

The very fertile Whiteman's Creek has a variety of aquatic insect hatches that can coax both fresh-run steelhead in the fall and drop-back steelhead in the spring to the surface. These include the October Caddis or Great Orange Sedge (size #8-#10) which hatches in the mornings from mid September to the end of October. It can be imitated by using orange and brown bombers and stimulator patterns. The Giant Drake mayfly (size #8) or "Hex" hatch comes off on Whiteman's from early August-mid September throughout the day. In the spring, from late April to early May, the Hendrickson mayfly hatch (size #12-#16) becomes prevalent on Whiteman's, usually hatching in the afternoon hours.

Farther west of the Grand River, in the Norfolk Sand Plain area, caddis flies are not as common on tributaries such as Big Creek, Big Otter Creek and Young's Creek. Even so, wild steelhead entering these streams will actively take dead-drifted nymphs such as stoneflies, swung wet fly patterns as well as standard egg patterns, wooly buggers and streamers.

Guide Ken Collins with steelhead caught on the Grand River, ON
(Ken Collins photo)

*Rick Whorwood with large hen caught on the Grand River, Ontario.
(Rick Whorwood photo).*

Grand River Float

A very effective and pleasant way to fish the Grand River is by drift boat or canoe. Canoe rentals are available in Brantford, Paris and Caledonia. John Valk of Grindstone Angling and Ken Collins of Grand River Troutfitters both offer drift boat service on the Grand River. Easy one day drifts (with time for fishing) on the Grand include: Bean Park (Paris) to Brant Park (Brantford), Brant Park to Erie Avenue, Caledonia Dam or Seneca Park to York, York to Kinsman's Park.

Steelheader's Tip

*At the end of a traditional wet fly swing
hold your fly stationary for a few seconds. Steelhead will
frequently follow the fly and take it after it stops.*

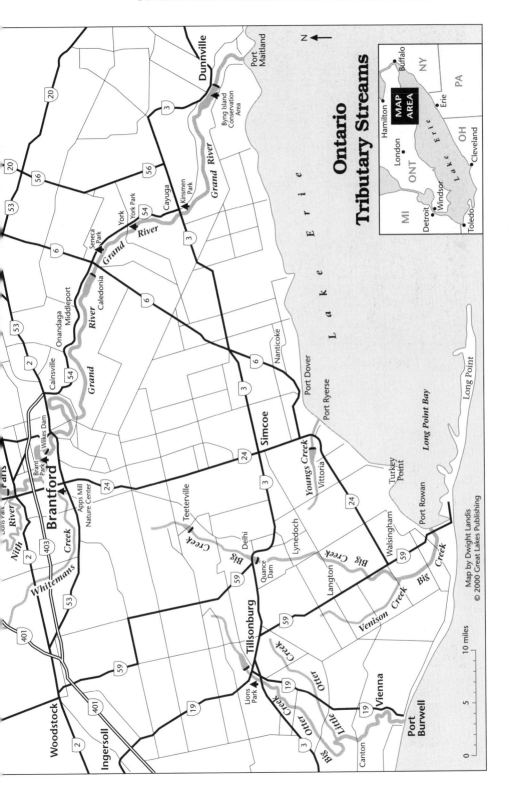

Ontario
Tributary Streams

Map by Dwight Landis
© 2000 Great Lakes Publishing

Table 9: Ontario Tributary Information

Tributary	Watershed Size & Type	Run-off Rate*	Steelhead Source	Surrounding Terrian	Important Feeders
Big Otter Creek	Medium; sand & gravel bottom	2-3 days	Wild, stray	Rural, farmland, wooded	Little Otter Creek
Big Creek	Medium; gravel & sand bottom; abundant spring seepage	1-2 days	Wild, stocked	Rural, farmland, wooded	Venison Creek, Stoney Creek, North Creek, Trout Creek, Deerlick Creek
Venison Creek	Small & brushy; gravel & sand bottom; abundant spring seepage	Less than one day	Wild	Rural, farmland, wooded	
Young Creek	Small & brushy; gravel & sand bottom; abundant spring seepage	Less than one day	Wild	Rural, farmland, wooded	
Grand River	Very large; gravel, rubble, & limestone bottom	2-3 days	Wild, stray	Urban parkland, Rural farmland, wooded	Nith River, Whitemans Creek
Nith River	Large; gravel, rubble, boulder, and limestone bottom	3-4 days	Wild, stray	Rural, some urban, farmland, wooded	Alder Creek, Washington Creek, Cedar Creek
Whitemans Creek	Medium, gravel & sand bottom; abundant spring seepage	2-3 days	Wild	Rural, farmland, wooded	

* run- off rates not directly comparable to south shore Lake Erie streams. Ontario streams require much more rain (usually 1.5 inches or more) before becoming unfishable, and even then many do not get muddy, just tea coloured. This is due to the porous soils that prevent run-off.

This table is courtesy of Larry Halyk of the Ontario Ministry of Natural Resources.

Table 10: Ontario Tributary Information

Tributary	Average Width (feet)	Total Stream Length (miles)	Steelhead Access (miles)*	Average Stream Flow (cubic feet per second)		
				April	August	November
Big Otter Creek	30 - 50	60	25	425	75	150
Big Creek	30 - 50	55	35	350	100	175
Venison Creek	15 - 20	16	12	62	23	35
Young Creek	15 - 20	13	3	40	17	24
Grand River	200 - 300	185	60	5000	1000	1500
Nith River	80 - 100	100	50	935	150	300
Whitemans Creek	25 - 40	50	20	350	60	120

* length of stream that steelhead have access to (generally the length of stream to the first impassable barrier)

This table is courtesy of Larry Halyk of the Ontario Ministry of Natural Resources.

Table 11
Ontario Tributary Access Points

Tributary	Major Access Points
Grand River (Cayuga)	**Kinsmen Park:** On East side of river just south (downstream) of highway 3 (Talbot Road). There is a boat launch (can be used by canoes & drift boats).
Grand River (York)	**York Park:** Regional Road 54 parallels the east bank of the river and connects Cayuga with Caledonia. York is a small village about 1/2 way between the two towns. The municipal park is immediately downstream of a bridge across the river.
Grand River (Caledonia)	**Seneca Park:** A municipal park is located on the east bank of the south edge of town off Regional Road 54 (turns into Caithness St.). **Caledonia Dam:** Can be accessed on both sides of the river upstream of Argyle St. There is lots of parkland on both sides of the river for some distance downstream of the dam.
Grand River (Brantford)	**Erie Ave. (Cockshut Bridge):** South end of town. Park at the old road allowance on the east side of the road and walk upstream. **Gilkison Flats Park:** On west side of river off Gilkison St. **Fordview Park:** Moving upstream (north) on Gilkison St. **D'Aubigney Creeks Park:** On west side of river about 1/2 mile upstream of Fordview park. Access via Colborne St. West (highway 24). **Waterworks Park:** On east side of river off Grand River Ave. This is a huge park that runs from Wilkes Dam downstream to a point across the river from D'Aubigney Cr. Park. **Brant Park:** Located at Wilkes Dam on the west side of the river. Camping available.

This table is courtesy of Larry Halyk of the Ontario Ministry of Natural Resources.

Table 11
Ontario Tributary Access Points (cont.)

Tributary	Major Access Points
Grand River (Paris)	**Bean Park & Optimist Park:** Both parks are located on the west bank of the river at the south end of town. Access via residential streets that parallel the river south of Dundas St. (highway 5). **Penmans Dam:** Located near the downtown core. Best access is via a park located on the east side of the river.
Nith River	1. **Lions Park, Paris:** Located on Laurel St.- turn north off King St. (highway 2). 2. **Canning Road:** Take highway 2 west of Paris and turn north on Canning Road.
Whitemans Creek	3. **Apps Mill Nature Centre:** Turn west on to Robinson Road off Rest Acres Road (highway 24). This section has artificals only/catch and release regulations in place.
Big Creek	4. **Quance Dam, Delhi:** Where Big Creek crosses highway 3 (can follow park down stream for several street crossings in Delhi). 5. **Dalton Road:** Just south of Delhi. Turn west off highway 3. Park at dead end road and walk to creek along road allowance. 6. **Regional Road 16:** Southwest of Lynedoch.
Venison Creek	7. **Regional Roads 21 & 45:** There is only one publicity owned land tract (located at Rd 45). However, the farmers in this area are very good about access to the creek and all of the concession roads between Regional Roads 21 & 45 are commonly used by anglers.

Table 11
Ontario Tributary Access Points (cont.)

Tributary	Major Access Points
Big Otter Creek	8. **Lions Park, Tillsonburg:** Old Vienna Road. Access via Vienna Road (highway 19) north of highway 3. 9. **Baynor Road:** Turn west off highway 19 south of Tillsonburg.
Youngs Creek	10. **Port Ryerse:** Take port Ryerse Road (Regional Road 57) off highway 24 south of Simcoe). 11. **Highway 24:** Access to creek directly from highway crossing. 12. **Vittoria/Sowden Tract:** Public park down stream of the dam. Take Vittoria Road west of Highway 24 south of Simcoe.

Peter Charles with early October steelhead taken at Caledonia on the Grand River, ON. (Peter Charles photo).

Table 12
*Tributary Ideal Water Flow Data Table
(for southern Ontario tributaries)

Tributary	Ideal Flow (cubic meters per second)	Watershed Size (square kilometers)
Grand River (at Brantford or Caledonia)	18-60 cms (Fishes best between 25-40 cms. Weeds can be a problem during low flows in September but are usually gone by the middle or end of the month.)	5210
Whitemans Creek (lower river)	3-7 cms (Ideal at 5 cms, gets quite stained over 8-10 cms.)	383
Nith River (lower river from Ayr to Paris using Canning flow gage)	3-15 cms (Can be stained at flows of 15 cms.)	1030
Big Creek (Walsingham flow gage)	4.1-4.9 meters (In the early fall, irrigation withdrawal can mean stage below 3.545 meters, making for tough fishing.)	591
Big Otter Creek (Calton flow gage)	9.982-10.353 meters (In the early fall, irrigation withdrawal can mean stage below 9.631 meters, making for tough fishing. Runs slightly more colored than Big Creek.)	676

*Real time water flow data (cubic meters per second) is available for the Grand River, Nith River and Whitemans Creek at the **Grand River Conservation Authority** web site: www.grandriver.ca/ or (519) 621-2761, ext 519.

Real time water stage/gage height data (meters) is available for Big Creek and Big Otter Creek at the **Canada Water Survey** web site: http://scitech.pyr.ec.gc.ca/waterweb/formnav.asp?lang=0

This table is courtesy of Larry Halyk of the Ontario Ministry of Natural Resources.

Sources of information
for Southern Ontario Tributaries
Tackle shops and guide services

Grindstone Angling Specialties
(specializing in steelhead, salmon,
streambred trout, smallmouth bass, fly
fishing retail, fly fishing schools, fly
fishing and light tackle guide service and
drift boat service on the Grand and upper
Saugeen Rivers, also fishing reports,
river conditions and accommodation
recommendations.)
P.O. Box 442,
24 Mill Street, North,
Waterdown, Ontario
LOR 2HO
(905) 689-0880
www.grindstoneangling.com
flyshop@grindstoneangling.com

Grand River Troutfitters & Archery Shop
(fly fishing retail, fly fishing courses and
workshops, guiding, drift boat service on
the Grand and upper Saugeen Rivers)
9-105 Queen St. W. (Fergus Market),
Fergus, Ontario
N1M 1S6
(519) 787-4359
trout@grandrivertroutfitters.com
www.grandrivertroutfitters.com

Natural Sports-The Fishing Store
(largest full service fishing store in
Ontario including fly fishing equipment,
fly tying supplies, custom flies, Certified
FFF fly casting instructor, rod building
and center-pin tackle)
1572 Victoria Street North,
Kitchener, Ontario N2B 3E5
(888) 629-3474
mail@naturalsports.ca
www.naturalsports.ca

Joe Penich
(guiding on Grand, Niagra and Saugeen
Rivers, fly tying)
Contact at Grindstone Angling Specialties

Skinners
50 King Street, East,
Toronto, Ontario
M5C 1E5
(416) 863-9701

Hook, Line and Sinker
(steelhead tackle, equipment, guiding,
custom flies, fly tying supplies, center-pin
tackle and accessories)
380 Eramosa Road,
Guelph, Ontario
N1E 0R2
(519) 766-Hook (4665)
www.hooklineandsinker.ca/

Angling Specialties
(fly fishing retail, guide service)
2104 Hwy 7 Unit #15,
Concord, ON
L4K 2S9
(905) 660-9707

Wilson's
(fly fishing retail, guiding, custom flies,
fly tying supplies, custom rods, casting
lessons)
199 Queen St. E. @ Jarvis
Toronto, Ontario M5A 1S2
(877) 347-4460
www.wilsonstoronto.com

Rick Whorwood
(guiding, FFF masters certified casting
instructor, speaker, fly tying instruction)
4 Brae Crest Ct.,
Stoney Creek, ON L8G-3A6
(905) 662-8999
whorwood@cogeco.ca
www.flycastingschool.com

Ken Chandler
Ken Chandler Fly Fishing Adventures
RR #1 554428
Markdale, Ontario NOC-1H0
(wade and float trips for steelhead, bass,
muskie and pike, single-handed
and spey fly casting lessons, steelhead
and spey clinics)
www.ontariodriftboatgides.com
(519) 820-8506

Ian Colin James
(guiding, professional fly tyer, writer)
P.O. Box 48034,
Pond Mills,
London, Ontario N6M 1K5
(519) 681-4796
ianjames@sympatico.ca
www.ianjames.on.ca

Ontario Ministry of Natural Resources

Ontario Ministry of Natural Resources
Information Center: 1-800-667-1940
http://www.mnr.gov.on.ca/MNR/fishing/

Lake Erie Management Unit
659 Exeter Road,
London, Ontario N6E 1L3
(519) 873-4612

Organizations

Grand River Conservation Authority
www.grandriver.ca/

The Casual Dress Fly Fishing Club
Guelph, Ontario
(519) 836-6424

**Ontario Federation of Hunters
and Fisherman**
http://www.ofah.org/flash.cfm?Dim=1024

Canada Weather
http://weatheroffice.ec.gc.ca/index.html

Steelheader's Tip

*In clearer tributary flows, a subtle change in water color,
such as a deeper tint or hue, is a good indication of
slightly deeper water which steelhead are keen to take
advantage of for cover and holding purposes.*

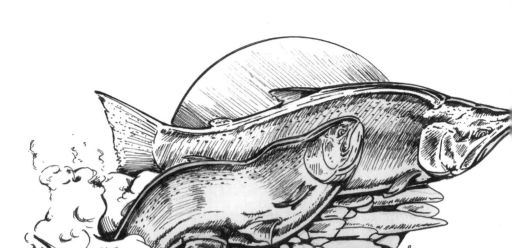

Province of Ontario fishing regulations (as of 2007)

Rainbow (steelhead) and brown trout regulations: Normal open season is April 24 (last Saturday) to September 30, extended season is April 24 (last Saturday) to December 31 on sections of the following Southern Ontario Lake Erie tributaries (check Ontario MNR Regulation Summary for specific sections): Big Otter Creek, Little Otter Creek, Big Creek and North Creek, Grand River and Young's Creek. The following southern Ontario tributary stream mouths are open year round: Big Creek and Young's Creek.

Standard catch and possession limit is 5 rainbow and brown trout/day (no minimum size) with conservation catch and possession limit 2 rainbow and brown trout/day (no minimum size). The Grand River from October 1 to December 31 (82 ft. downstream of Wilkes dam in the City of Brantford to Lake Erie) has a standard catch and possession limit of 1 rainbow and brown trout (no minimum size) and a conservation limit of 0 rainbow and brown trout.

In 2002 the Ontario Ministry of Natural Resources opened an 8-km fish sanctuary for all species (including steelhead) between Paris and Brantford on the Grand River. Regulations for this section include no fishing from March 1-April 27 (last Saturday), catch and release only, single/barbless hook and artificial lure only.

A special regulation section is located on Whiteman's Creek (a tributary of the Grand River) at App's Mill Nature Center between Robinson Road and Cleaver Sideroad. Regulations for this 3.7-mile section include artificial lure and barbless hooks only with a catch and possession limit of 1 brown and rainbow trout (minimum size 19.7 inches). Whiteman's Creek is closed from October 1 to April 23.

License Year: January 1 to December 31

License Fees (Canadian funds): annual resident, $29.00; annual resident conservation license, $19.50; resident 1 day, $10.00; annual non-resident, $64.00; annual non-resident conservation license, $39.00; non-resident 8 day license, $41.00; non-resident 8 day conservation license, $24.00; non-resident 1 day, $17.00.

Additional Map Sources

Ontario Topographic Maps: Energy, Mines and Resources, Canada Map Office, 615 Booth Street, Ottawa, Ontario K1A 0E9.

Ontario Road Maps: Map Art Publishing Corp., 70 Bloor St. E., Oshawa, Ontario L1H 3M2, (905) 436-2525, (www.mapart.com).

Steelheader's Tip

When spring steelhead fishing starts to become marginal on the smaller to mid-size Lake Erie tributaries due to low flows and warm water temperatures switch to some of the bigger tributaries like the Grand River, OH, or Cattaraugus Creek, NY which can hold up into early May or the Grand River, ON, which fishes well as late as early July.

Huron River of Michigan

The Huron River, which drains into the western end of Lake Erie near Rockwood, Michigan, is the only important Lake Erie steelhead tributary of Michigan. Set in both a rural and urban setting (see Table 12 on page 250), an impassable hydroelectric dam at Belleville Lake (25 miles from the lake) blocks any upstream migration of steelhead. It is a large tributary, encompassing a total watershed of 75 miles, which averages 3-6 feet in depth below Belleville Lake. Public access is very good on the Huron with numerous city and metro parks located along its banks (see Huron River map and Table 13 on pages 249 and 250). Below Flat Rock only 10% of the river is accessible by foot and is better done by boat.

Hydroelectric dams at Belleville and Ford Lakes (Ford Lake is above Belleville Lake) do not allow water flows in the river to fluctuate dramatically, like most Erie tributaries, but off-color water is not unusual. Ice up on the Huron normally doesn't occur below Belleville dam to the Flat Rock dam due to the steady hydroelectric releases. It can freeze up, though, below Flat Rock dam (an over-flow dam) down to the lake in cold winters.

After the construction of a fishway at the Flat Rock dam in 1996 and an increase in steelhead smolt stockings from 20,000 (in 1995) to 59,200 (in 1996) the steelhead runs have greatly improved. Jeff Brouncheidel of the Michigan DNR has observed the runs increase by 5 to 10 fold with estimates of 3,000-5,000 fish running in the spring of 1999. Interestingly, during the spring of 1999, 90% of the steelhead surveyed at the fishway in Flat Rock had a right pectoral fin clip (indicating a steelhead of the Michigan steelhead program).

Since 1996, the Michigan DNR has been averaging about 60,000 steelhead smolt plantings every year with 60,300 smolts stocked in 1998 (see Appendix E, Table 6.1). These steelhead are of the wild Little Manistee variety obtained by the Michigan DNR from the Little Manistee River in Michigan.

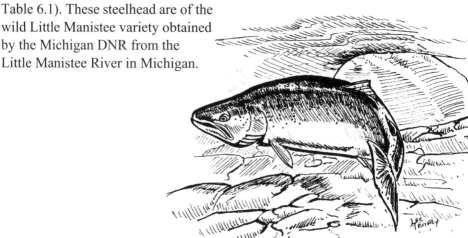

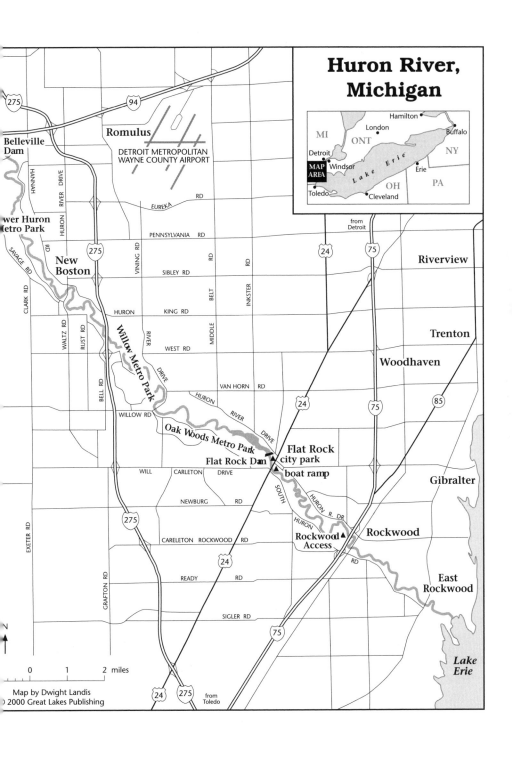

Huron River, Michigan

Map by Dwight Landis
© 2000 Great Lakes Publishing

Table 12
Huron River Tributary Information

Watershed Size Streambed Type	Run-off Rate	Steelhead Source	Surrounding Terrain	Important Feeders
Large, Broken rock and gravel (clay banks)	Does not fluctuate dramatically (dependent on dam releases)	Stocked	Urban below Flat Rock, wooded in Metro Parks	None

Table 13
Huron River Public Access Points

Public Access Points
Rockwood City Access, Flat Rock City boat ramp, Flat Rock City Park, Flat Rock dam (fishway), Oakwoods Metro Park, Willow Metro Park, Lower Huron Metro Park, Belleville dam (impassable).

Sources of Information for the Huron River

Tackle Shops

Bottom Line Bait & Tackle
32660 West Jefferson,
Rockwood, Michigan 48173
(734) 379-9762

Little Dipper Bait & Tackle
26464 West Huron River Dr.,
Flat Rock, Michigan 48134
(734) 782-4277

Useful Contacts and Websites

Huron River Fishing Association
(Huron River fishing club and conservation organization, river clean-ups, flat rock fish ladder surveys)
(734) 654-8058

Huron River Watershed Council
http://www.hrwc.org/

Lower Huron River Watershed
http://www.lowerhuronriver.net/index.html

Quest Outdoors
http://www.questoutdoors.net/locs/michigan/huron_mi/

Huron River Net
http://huronriver.pinckneymich.net/

The Steelhead Journal (eMagazine dedicated to the Great Lakes Steelheader):
www.steelheadjournal.com

Guide Services

Michigan River Works, LLC
(Michigan guided fly fishing trip
outfitter for
steelhead, trout, bass and pike)
www.miriverworks.com
(248) 895-3858

Eric Zadorecky Guide Service
(float trips on the Huron and
Muskegon Rivers in Michigan)
http://www.questoutdoors.net/fishing-
guides/zadorecky/guide.html
ericz@questoutdoors.net

Mike Shultz
mike@miriverworks.com
(734) 546-1723

Joe Cyrek
joe@miriverworks.com
(248) 895-3858

Kevin Feenstra
Feenstra Guide Service
(float trips on the Muskegon River)
PO Box 640,
Newaygo, MI 49337
(231) 652-3528
http://www.feenstraguideservice.com/

Michigan Department of Natural Resources

Michigan Department of Natural Resources
http://www.michigan.gov/dnr

Lake Erie Management Unit
2600 West 8 Mile Road,
Southfield, Michigan 48034
(248) 359-9040

Weekly Fishing Report
http://www.michigan.gov/dnr/0,1607,7-153-10364-34956—,00.html

State of Michigan Fishery Regulations (as of 2007)

Steelhead Regulations: Open year round, daily limit 5, minimum length 10
inches (no more than 3 fish larger than 15 inches).

License Year: Beginning March 1st to March 31st of the following year.

License Fees (all species): Annual resident, $27.00; annual non-resident, $41.00;
resident and non-resident 24 hour license, $7.00.

Angler practicing catch and release philosophy on Raccoon Creek, PA.

Closing

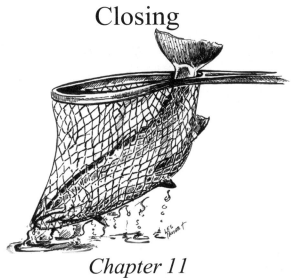

Chapter 11

Lake Erie steelheading has become very popular over the last five years. Since it is close to major population areas, Lake Erie offers an economic alternative to the more aesthetically pleasing, but more expensive Alaskan and British Columbia trips.

Due to its popularity, Lake Erie steelheading can not always be the peaceful experience that most fly fisherman are seeking. This can be especially true on the Pennsylvania tributaries where some crowding can be expected early in the fall particularly closer to the lakeshore. This problem is usually remedied with fall and winter rains and snow melt which helps migrating steelhead move farther upstream, creating more fishing opportunities.

The sport's popularity has also resulted in stream access problems on some of the tributaries especially in Pennsylvania where 99% of all steelhead stream fishing is dependent upon property owners allowing public fishing. In 1996 the Pennsylvania Steelhead Association was organized to educate fisherman to respect landowners and their streamside property as well as to address landowner concerns and needs so as to encourage them to continue to allow public fishing on their lands.

The Pennsylvania Steelhead Association (PSA) has over the years has had a positive impact on Pennsylvania steelhead fishery. The Walnut Creek Stream Enhancement Project has brought fantastic steelhead fishing opportunities to the general public where they previously did not exist. By creating and enhancing pools in the shale bottom of the stream, the lower section of Walnut Creek provides holding water for running steelhead and produced the new state record steelhead in 2001. It was over 20 pounds.

During the summer of 2002, the PSA undertook a bank stabilization project on Crooked Creek. The project ensured that this section of stream, which was at one time posted, remained open for public fishing. Six log deflectors were installed

Ken Seremet fishing Four-Mile Creek, PA near the Lake Erie shoreline.

creating quality cold water habitat for returning steelhead. With the help of local TU chapter members, a wild steelhead presence in the watershed was found and photographed. Future stream enhancement projects are in the works.

Every year, the PSA works with 3-C-U Trout Association in the raising of 50,000 steelhead fry at the Cooperative Bay Front hatchery. Fertilized eggs are hatched and the newly hatched fish are fed until they are transferred to 3-C-U raceways located throughout Erie County. With diminishing numbers of steelhead stocked by the Pennsylvania Boat & Fish Commission, this work becomes more important on a yearly basis.

The Pennsylvania Steelhead Association takes an active role in promoting and educating the public about the Pennsylvania fishery through sport show seminars, meetings, and PF&BC related fishing programs. Through their work with local landowners, municipalities, state and federal agencies, and local conservancies, they hope to continue the improvement and growth of Pennsylvania's steelhead fishery.

PSA is a non-profit organization dedicated to the growth, enhancement, and protection of Pennsylvania's steelhead fishery. Individual memberships are available for $15.00 per year, $5.00 for junior members. They can be contacted at:

Pennsylvania Steelhead Association
P.O. Box 8892
Erie, PA 16505
www.pasteelhead.org/index.html

The Ohio Central Basin Steelheaders (OCBS) is a similar organization to the PSA. It was formed in 1984 and is dedicated to the protection and promotion of steelhead sport fishing in Ohio and the Great Lakes Region.

The OCBS has financially supported the Grand River Conservatory for the purchase of land rights in the Grand River watershed. This has helped ensure continued access to the Grand River and prevented possible future development. They have also worked with the Ohio Department of Natural Resources and other clubs to have Conneaut Creek designated as a wild and scenic river. Each spring they conduct on stream steelheading seminars in conjunction with the Lake County Metro Parks. OCBS annual memberships for individuals cost $25 per year, $35 for families. They can be contacted at:

Ohio Central Basin Steelheaders
P.O. Box 29577
Parma, Ohio 44129
www.ohiosteelheaders.com/
steelie2000@cs.com

Catch and Release Philosophy

I'd like to add a final note about applying the catch and release philosophy to Erie steelhead fishing. Because of the generous regulations of the fishery for creel sizes and daily limits in the tributaries, the temptation exists to over-harvest steelhead during the course of a season. Even though the fishery is supported mostly by smolt stocking programs (the exception is the Northern shore tributaries of the Province of Ontario which are almost exclusively based on natural steelhead reproduction) and most adult steelhead have a life span of three to four years, catch and release should be practiced more often than not to ensure an ample supply of adult steelhead in the streams for that particular season. Catch and release also promotes the growth of the developing wild steelhead fisheries on certain tributaries and it shows tremendous respect for what has to be the most spectacular of all freshwater sport fish.

Steelheader's Tip

*Use the longest leader that is manageable
in order to minimize fly line
interference on a drag-free fly drift.*

APPENDIX A
Local tackle shops

(Tackle shops located near or are very familiar with a specific tributary stream(s) have the tributary listed in parentheses. Other tackle shops listed are familiar with several tributaries and/or specialize in steelhead related products and services).

OHIO

Mad River Outfitters
(OH, PA and NY tributaries, steelhead fly fishing equipment, accessories, fly tying supplies, guiding, custom flies, Mad River Media steelhead fly fishing videos, destination fly fishing trips and a wide variety of fly fishing classes)
813 Bethel Road,
Columbus, OH 43214
(614) 451-0363
1-888-451-0363
admin@madriveroutfitters.com
www.madriveroutfitters.com

Grand River Tackle
(Grand River, Chagrin River and other OH tributaries, steelhead tackle, equipment, fly tying supplies, guiding and custom flies)
1250 High Street,
Fairport Harbor, OH 44077
(440) 352-7222
www.grandrivertackle.com
grandrivertackle@sbcglobal.net

Angler's Mail
(Rocky River, steelhead tackle, equipment, fly tying supplies and custom flies)
6495 Pearl Road
Cleveland, OH 44130
(440) 884-7877

Chagrin River Outfitters
(North East Ohio and PA tributaries, fly fishing equipment, fly tying supplies, custom flies, uiding, fly tying and casting lessons, fly fishing schools, PA trout trips, saltwater excursions)
100 North Main Street,
Chagrin Falls, OH 44022
(440) 247-7110
www.chagrinriveroutfitters.com

Erie Outfitters
(Rocky, Vermillion, Black and other west side tributaries of OH, steelhead tackle, equipment, fly tying supplies, guiding, custom flies and also steelhead/walleye lake charters)
5404 Lake Road,
Sheffield Lake, OH 44054
(440) 949-8934
www.erieoutfitters.com

Backpackers Shop of Ohio Canoe Adventures
(Vermillion, Rocky, Chagrin and Grand Rivers, Conneaut Creek, steelhead fly fishing equipment, fly tying supplies, fly tyers club, guiding, custom flies)
5128 Colorado Avenue (Exit 151 off I-90 on Rt. 611),
Sheffield Village, OH 44054
(440) 934-5345
1-888-303-3307
http://www.steeliesonthefly.com/
http://www.backpackersshop.com

Snug Harbor Bait Shop
(Conneaut Creek, steelhead tackle, equipment, guiding and custom flies, daily recorded lake and stream conditions report)
1021 Broad Street,
Conneaut, OH 44030
(440) 593-3755

D&W Bait and Tackle
(Grand River, steelhead tackle, equipment, fly tying supplies and custom flies)
786 Richmond Street,
Painesville, OH 44077
(440) 354-8473

TMF Sports Shop
(Rocky, Chagrin, Grand and Conneaut Creek, steelhead tackle, equipment, fly tying supplies and custom flies)
4081 Sandy Lake Road,
Ravenna, OH 44266
(330) 296-2614
http://www.bright.net/~tmfsportshop/

Getaway Outfitters
(steelhead tackle, equipment, fly tying supplies,
fly casting and fly tying classes,
guiding and custom flies)
2552 Schneider's Crossing Road, NW
Dover, OH 44620
(330) 364-4471
http://web.tusco.net/getaway/

Rodmakers Shoppe
(all major OH steelhead tributaries, steelhead
tackle, equipment, fly tying supplies, rod
building supplies, rod and reel repair, guiding
and custom flies)
20884 Royalton Road,
Strongsville, OH 44149
(440) 572-0400

Karran Shop
(Conneaut, Cowles, Wheeler and Arcola Creeks,
Ashtabula River, steelhead tackle and equipment)
413 South Ridge East,
Geneva, OH 44041
(440) 466-3561

Geneva Bait and Tackle
(Arcola, Cowles, Wheeler and Indian Creeks,
steelhead tackle and equipment)
4140 North Broadway Street (Rt. 534),
Geneva, OH 44041
(440) 466-7683

Kame's Sports
(steelhead tackle, equipment, fly tying supplies
and custom flies)
8516 Cleveland Avenue,
North Canton, OH 44720
(330) 499-4558
www.kamessports.com

L & D Bait & Tackle
(Rocky River)
18508 Detroit Ave.,
Cleveland, OH (Lakewood) 44107
(216)226-3474

PENNSYLVANIA

Elk Creek Sports
(Elk Creek and West Side tributaries of PA,
steelhead tackle, equipment and custom flies)
10543 Old Lake Road,
Lake City, PA 16423
(814) 774-8755
http://www.elkcreekarea.info/fishing

Poor Richard's Bait & Tackle Shop (West)
(Walnut Creek and West Side tributaries of PA,
steelhead tackle, equipment, fly tying supplies
and custom flies)
5821 West Lake Road,
Erie, PA 16415
(814) 474-5623
www.fisherie.com/poorrichards/

Poor Richard's Bait & Tackle Shop (East)
(16-Mile Creek and East side tributaries of PA,
steelhead tackle, equipment, fly tying supplies
and custom flies)
11150 East Lake Road,
North East, PA 16428
(814) 725-8483
www.fisherie.com/poorrichards/

Flies & More
(steelhead flies, fly rods, leaders, guiding,
casting lessons)
8 N. 4th St., Youngwood, PA
(724) 925-1428
kenseremet@lcsys.net

Folly's End Campground Fly & Tackle Shop
(located on Elk Creek, steelhead tackle, fly
fishing equipment and fly tying supplies)
RD #2 8600 Avonia Road,
Girard, PA 16417
www.follysend.com/
(814) 474-5730

B.A.C. Inc.
(Trout Run and West side tributaries of PA,
steelhead tackle, equipment, fly tying supplies
and custom flies)
7490 West Lake Road,
Fairview, PA 16415
(814) 474-3992

FishUSA.com
(steelhead fly, float/center pin and conventional
tackle, equipment and fly tying supplies)
901 West 12th Street,
Erie, PA 16501
800-922-1219
www.FishUSA.com
FishUSA owns and hosts two regional fishing
sites: www.FishErie.com
and www.FishSalmonRiver.com

Neshannock Creek Fly Shop
(steelhead fly fishing equipment, fly tying
supplies and lessons, guiding and custom flies,
female angler's school)
Main Street,
Volant, PA 16156
(724) 533-3212
info@ncflyshop.com
www.ncflyshop.com
(724) 533-3212

Hoey's Fly Fishing Shop
(steelhead fly fishing equipment, custom flies,
fly tying supplies and lessons)
970 Perry Hwy.,
Pittsburgh, Pa. 15237
(412) 364-2850
www.hoeysflyshop.com

Lake Erie Ultimate Angler
(OH, PA and NY tributaries, steelhead tackle,
equipment, fly tying supplies, guiding,
custom flies, steelhead/trout/bass fly fishing
schools, fly tying schools, mail order service)
3737 W. 12th St.,
Erie, PA 16505
(814) 833-4040
http://www.LakeerieUltimateAngler.com/

Transues's Tackle
(steelhead fly fishing equipment, authorized
St. Croix and Cortland shop,
fly tying supplies, custom flies)
321 Butler Road,
Kittanning, PA 16201
(724) 543-2971

International Angler
(steelhead fly fishing equipment, fly tying a
nd rod building supplies,
guiding and custom flies)
2 locations:
501 Freeport Road,
Pittsburgh, PA 15215
1-800-782-4222
(412) 782-2222
www.internationalangler.com (both stores)
internationalangler@comcast.net

5275 Steubenville Pike,
Pittsburgh, Pa. 15205
(412) 788-8088
ia2@internationalangler.com

Fly Fisher's Paradise
(steelhead fly fishing equipment, fly tying
supplies, custom flies, full line catalog)
2603 East College Avenue,
State College, PA 16801
(814) 234-4189
www.flyfishersparadise.com

Indiana Angler
(steelhead fly fishing equipment, rod building/
repair, Mark DeCarlo guide trips, wade and float
trips for trout, steelhead and smallmouth)
218 Grandview Avenue,
Indiana, PA 15701
(724) 463-2011
indianaangler@yourinter.net

The Contented Angler
Joe & Amy Gablick
(steelhead tackle, equipment, fly tying materials,
fly fishing instruction,
custom flies including classic Atlantic Salmon
Featherwings and Spey and Dee flies)
147 Jefferson Avenue,
Lower Burrell, PA 15068
(724) 337-0437
joeamy@content-angler.com

Orchard View Angling
(steelhead tackle, equipment, fly tying materials,
rod building supplies, guiding, seminars and
custom flies)
3540 Washington Road (Rt.19),
McMurray, PA 15317
(724) 942-5485
zoogfish@adelphia.net
www.orchardviewangling.com

Ligonier Outfitters
(steelhead tackle, equipment, fly fishing and
tying lessons, fly tying supplies, custom flies)
127 West Main Street,
Ligonier, PA 15658
(724) 238-4900
www.ligonieroutfitters.com

NEW YORK

Buffalo Outfitter's
Western NY tributaries of Lake Erie and
Lake Ontario including Niagara River and
Cattaraugus Creek. Steelhead fly fishing
equipment, fly tying supplies, guiding,
fly fishing schools, fly tying classes,
fly casting lessons.)
5655 Main Street
Williamsville, NY 14221
716) 631-5131
www.buffalooutfittersflyshop.com

Orleans Outdoor
Western NY tributaries of Lake Erie, Lake
Ontario tribs as well as the Niagra River,
steelhead tackle, equipment, fly tying supplies,
guiding, private water, lodging and custom flies.
Located on the Oak Orchard River)
1764 Oak Orchard Road (Route 98),
Albion, NY 14411
585) 682-4546
www.orleansoutdoor.com

The Oak Orchard Fly Shop
Western NY tributaries of Lake Erie as well as
Lake Ontario tribs, fly fishing equipment,
spey rods and equipment, fly tying supplies
including traditional materials, locally tied flies,
guiding, steelhead/trout/spey schools)
5977 Main Street,
Williamsville, NY 14221
(716) 626-1323
info@oakorchardflyshop.com
www.oakorchardflyshop.com

Bill's Hooks
(Western NY tributaries of Lake Erie, steelhead
tackle, equipment, guiding, custom flies and
center-pin tackle and accessories)
5139 West Lake Road (Route 5),
Dunkirk, NY 14048
(716) 366-0268
billshooks@adelphia.net
www.billshooks.com

Miller's Bait & Tackle
(Cattaraugus Creek near break wall, steelhead
tackle and equipment)
12707 Alleghany Road & Route 20,
Irving, NY 14081
(716) 934-2477

Carl Coleman's Fly Shop
(Lake Ontario tributaries, steelhead tackle,
equipment, fly tying supplies, guiding and
custom flies)
4786 Ridge Road West (Route 104),
Spencerport, NY 14559
(585) 352-4775
www.colemansflyshop.com

Dave's Bait & Tackle
(18-Mile Creek and other Western NY
tributaries, steelhead tackle, equipment)
6798 Wellington Drive,
Derby, NY 14047
(716) 947-5990

Bill's Bait & Tackle
(Cattaraugus Creek at Springville Dam,
steelhead tackle and equipment)
26 West Main Street,
Springville, NY 14141
(716) 592-2111

NEW JERSEY

Sportsmen's Center
(steelhead tackle, fly fishing equipment and
fly tying supplies,
also out of state fishing licenses)
US Highway 130,
Bordentown, NY 08505
(609) 298-5300

Guide Services
(also see Local Tackle Shop list for Guide Services)
OHIO

Jerry Darkes
(specializes in Great Lakes steelhead videos and seminars)
Angling Consulting Services
13098 Tradewind Drive,
Strongsville, OH 44136
(440) 781-3906
jdacs55@aol.com
www.guidepatterns.com

Greg Senyo
(Orvis Endorsed Fly Fishing Guide
Field Staff Ohio Country Anglin' Magazine)
Jag Fly Company & Steelhead Alley Outfitters
(419) 466-9382
info@jagflyco.com
www.steelheadalleyoutfitters.com
www.jagflyco.com

Will Turek
(specializes in single and two handed spey casting instruction)
Great Lakes Guide N' Travel
6165 Stow Road,
Hudson, OH 44236
(330) 653-5128
willturek@alltel.net

Bob Tomlinson
(guided fly fishing trips in "steelhead alley")
Roaming River Guide Service
19756 Lorain Road #3,
Fairview Park, OH 44126
(440) 895-0278
RT1steelheader@WebTV.net

Larry Rummel
(also Lake Ontario tributaries, north central and central PA trout fly fishing trips, Labrador retriever training, custom portable fly tying desks and OH/PA spring turkey guiding)
Larry's Fishing Excursions
7229 W. Broad,
Galloway, OH 43119
(614) 679-1049

John Rochus
(also steelhead schools, fly tying, fly casting and PA trout trips)
Ohio Fly Fishing Excursions
2925 Blake Avenue N. W.,
Canton, OH 44718
(330) 456-8731
(330) 280-0208

Bob Schmidt
Bob's Steelhead Guide Service
216 255 7302
stealhed@hotmail.com

Marion Graven
(also offers drift boat trips with 16 ft. Clackacraft on the Grand River, OH and Huron River, MI)
North Coast Salmon & Steelhead
North Olmsted, OH
(440) 779-5270
mfgiv@aol.com
www.northcoastsalmonsteelheadguide.com

G. Ara Hamamjian
(Rocky River, also offers feather wing Atlantic salmon flies and teaches fly tying at Cleveland Museum of Natural History)
19046 Old Detroit Road,
Rocky River, OH 44116
(440) 331-8406

Monte Casey
One-on-One River Steelhead Adventures
(also offers seminars and fly tying video)
24659 Framingham Drive,
Westlake, OH 44145
(440) 734-0689
(440) 773-8064
flyfishing@steelheadguide.com
http://www.steelheadguide.com/

Craig Lewis
(also steelhead/walleye lake charters)
Erie Outfitters
5404 Lake Road,
Sheffield Lake, OH 44054
(440) 949-8934
www.erieoutfitters.com

Bill German
(also smallmouth trips)
Steely Guide Service
8311 Stoney Brook,
Chagrin Falls, OH 44023
(440) 667-7822
steelyguides@yahoo.com
www.steelyguides1.com

OHIO, cont.

Don Mathews
Dfishinfool's Guide Service
3357 Rt. 422,
Southington, OH 44470
(330) 898-5894
(330) 565-5457
don@dfishinfool.com
www.Dfishinfool.com

Bob Williams
Screaming Reels Guide Service
3691 Traynham,
Shaker Hts., OH 44122
(440) 487-8111
steelheader1@sbcglobal.net
www.screamingreels.net

Lenny Pitts
Fresh Run Inc.
(also offers fly tying instruction,
spey flies)
4415 Janell Court,
Canfield, OH 44406
(330) 797-9717

Mad River Outfitters
(OH, PA and NY tributaries)
813 Bethel Road,
Columbus, OH 43214
(614) 451-0363
1-888-451-0363
www.madriveroutfitters.com

Chagrin River Outfitters
(also PA steelhead tributaries, PA trout trips and
saltwater excursions)
100 North Main Street,
Chagrin Falls, OH 44022
(440) 247-7110

Grand River Tackle
(Grand River, Chagrin River and other OH
tributaries)
1250 High Street,
Fairport Harbor, OH 44077
(440) 352-7222
www.grandrivertackle.com
grandrivertackle@sbcglobal.net

Backpackers Shop of Ohio Canoe Adventures
5128 Colorado Avenue,
Sheffield Village, OH 44054
(440) 934-5345
1-888-303-3307
http://www.steeliesonthefly.com/
http://www.backpackersshop.com

Ken Seremet
8 N. 4th St., Youngwood, PA
(724) 925-1428
kenseremet@lcsys.net

The Prowler Charters
(Lake charters for Lake Erie walleye and perch,
Lake Ontario salmon)
Captain Brian Selai
86968 Briar Road,
Jewett, Ohio 43986
1-888-ON PROWL
(740) 946-1076
http://www.theprowlercharters.com/
theprowler18@hotmail.com
(814) 336-7000

PENNSYLVANIA

John Nagy
Steelhead Guide Service
(Offers instructional steelhead guide trips in
steelhead nymphing and traditional swinging
techniques, float trips, steelhead seminars, fly
tying and casting instruction, custom "noodle"
fly rods, Solitude fly reels, custom flies and
leaders, Scandinavian style tube flies. Also
Pennsylvania Laurel Highland's wild brook trout
fishing, outdoor digital photography, landscape
photography fine art prints, self-publishing
consulting.)
606 Crysler Street,
Pittsburgh, PA 15226
(412) 531-5819
steelheadguide@hotmail.com
http://groups.msn.com/
JohnNagySteelheadGuide/

Mark DeCarlo
Erie Steelhead Outfitters
(Steelhead guide for all PA, NY and OH
tributaries, also offers wade and float trips on
inland waters for trout and smallmouth)
204 Huckleberry Road,
Indiana, PA 15701
(724) 349-8742
flyfishinguide@yahoo.com

Karl N. Weixlmann
Fly Fish Erie
(PA and NY licensed guide, also offers slide
programs, fly fishing trips for smallmouth,
largemouth and pikeon Presque Isle Bay)
4050 Canterbury Drive,
Erie, PA 16506
(814) 836-8013
Flyfisheriekarl@aol.com
www.fisherie.com/flyfisherie

Neshannock Creek Fly Shop
(steelhead tackle, equipment, fly tying supplies
and lessons, guiding and custom flies, female
and young angler schools)
Main Street,
Volant, PA 16156
(724) 533-3212
info@ncflyshop.com
www.ncflyshop.com

Steve Young
Steelhead Alley Guide Service
2665 Weinman Road,
Wexford, Pa. 15090
(724) 816-0700
(724) 935-1779
http://www.northforkflies.com/pages SHGuide.html

John Bodner
Fish Man Guide Services
(also offers Lake Erie tributary map & access
guides)
P.O. Box 8367
Erie, PA 16505
(412) 269-1285
(814) 392-7856
jbfish1@comcast.net
www.thefishman.com

Michael Hilf
(724) 766-7235
www.steelheadtrips.com

Mark Sikora
International Angler
501 Freeport Road,
Pittsburgh, PA 15215
(412) 782-2222
angler@sgi.net
www.int-angler.com

Greg Hines
Get Hooked Guides
662 S. Geary Street,
Mt. Pleasant, PA 15666
(724) 547-8812
gregoh72@aol.com

Ken Nulph
(fly tying instruction, also guides for Alagnak
River Lodge in Alaska)
Iron Head Fishing Expeditions
259 Rt. 908,
Natrona Heights, PA 15065
(724) 294-2450
(412) 607-6495
ironhed@hotmail.com

Lake Erie Ultimate Angler
(OH and PA tributaries)
3737 W. 12th St.,
Erie, PA 16505
(814) 833-4040
www.lakeerieultimateangler.com/

Steven Brugger
(also Presque Isle for warm water species and
Oil Creek area in Titusville, PA)
(814) 440-4725
Portaledge@aol.com
www.lakeerieultimateangler.com

Doc Wally's Steelhead Guide Service
Walter J. Myslewski, M.D.
320 Elm Drive,
Greensburg, PA 15601
(724) 837-2200
(724) 309-7501
www.PASteelheadguide.com

Steelheader's Tip

*Instead of waiting for the "back-side" or downward
trend of tributary run-off to occur, traveling steelheaders
should head to the Erie tributaries at peak run-off and
plan on fishing some smaller tributaries initially.
These small tribs run-off so fast that by the time you get
there they will more than likely be fishable.*

NEW YORK

Vince Tobia
Cattaraugus Creek Outfitters
(specializes in traditional techniques as well as
nymphing on Cattaraugus Creek and other Lake
Erie tributaries, provides streamside lodging on
Cattaraugus Creek also specializes in trips to
Montana, British Columbia, the Bahamas and
Mexico)
266 Troy Del Way
Williamsville, NY 14221
(716) 479-2327
vtobia@aol.com
www.cattarauguscreekoutfitters.com
(website has updated stream reports, including
Cattaraugus Creek)

Michael Prairie
(also Lake Ontario tributaries, trout trips on PA
spring creeks, NY's Delaware system and
Adirondacks)
727 Sweethome Road,
Amherst, NY 14226
(716) 835-5956

Brian Slavinski
Flies Only Guide Service
(specializes in traditional techniques for
steelhead, also offers inland trout trips and
organizes trips to the Gaspe Peninsula in Quebec
for Atlantic salmon)
56 Huth Road, Cheektowaga, NY 14225
(716) 834-4331

Ron Bierstine
Orleans Outdoor
(also Lake Ontario tributaries including Oak
Orchard River)
1764 Oak Orchard Road (Route 98),
Albion, NY 14411
(585) 682-4546
www.orleansoutdoor.com

Jay Peck
(NY Registered Guide, Lake Ontario tributaries
for steelhead, brown trout and salmon, specializes
in spey casting and traditional presentations as
well as nymphing)
(585) 352-4710
(585) 352-4775
jay@jaypecksguides.com
http://www.jaypeckguides.com/main/

Ed Luba
Cattaraugus Creek Outfitters
(716)-648-9732
(716)-523-7650
lelbows@aol.com

Dave Guest
Steelhead Alley Guides
P.O.Box 112
Angola, NY 14006
(716)-880-6104
http://www.steelheadalleyguides.com/
steelheadalleyguides@yahoo.com

Buffalo Outfitter's
5655 Main Street,
Williamsville, NY 14221
(716) 631-5131
www.buffalooutfittersflyshop.com

Greg Liu's Oswego Outfitters
(steelhead, salmon, brown trout on the Salmon
River, specializes in traditional techniques as
well as nymphing)
PO Box 86,
Pulaski, NY 13142
(315) 298-6349
Gregaliu@aol.com

Bill's Hooks
5139 West Lake Road (Route 5),
Dunkirk, NY 14048
(716) 366-0268
billshooks@adelphia.net
www.billshooks.com

Carl Coleman's Fly Shop
(Lake Ontario tributaries for steelhead, brown
trout and salmon)
4786 Ridge Road West (Route 104),
Spencerport, NY 14559
(585) 352-4775
www.colemansflyshop.com

Dejon Hamann
(Progressive techniques for catching trout both
steelhead and inland including European
nymphing and Stillwater techniques. "Fish-With-
The-Guides" expert guided trips annually to the
West Branch of the Delaware, Ausable, and
Grand River's)
(716) 834-4331
www.ChromeOnChrome.com

Lodging and Dining

(Nearest Lake Erie tributary is listed in parenthesis. Businesses are listed going from west to east on Lake Erie Shoreline and are generally priced moderate to inexpensive.)

MICHIGAN

Sleep Inn
(Huron River)
29101 Commerce Dr. (off Rt. 75 & Gibraltor Rd.),
Flat Rock, MI 48134
(734) 782-9898

Riverfront Family Restaurant
(Huron River)
22825 Huron River Dr (Rt. 24),
Rockwood, MI 48173
(734) 379-3444

OHIO

Amherst Motel 6
(Vermilion River)
704 North Leavitt Road (Rt. 58),
Amherst, OH 44001
(440) 988-3266

Motel Plaza
(Vermilion River)
4645 Liberty Ave. (Rt. 6),
Vermillion, OH 44089
(440) 967-3191

Salvatore's Ristorante
(Vermilion River)
4560 Liberty Ave. #C (Rt. 6),
Vermilion, OH 44089
(440) 967-0777

Ponderosa Steakhouse
(Vermilion River)
4415 Liberty Avenue (Rt. 6),
Vermilion, OH 44089
(440) 967-1615

Super 8
(Black River)
910 Lorain Blvd. (Rt. 57 & I 80/I 90),
Elyria, OH 44035
(440) 323-7488

Mr. D's Restaurant
(Black River)
1825 Lorain Blvd. (Rt. 57 & I 80/I 90),
Elyria, OH 44035
(440) 233-7465
Nick's Family Restaurant
(Black River)
1005 E. Broad St.,
Elyria, OH 44035
(440) 365-2099

Days Inn of Lakewood
(lower Rocky River, near mouth)
12019 Lake Ave.,
Lakewood, OH 44107
(216) 226-4800

Days Inn-Cleveland Airport
(upper Rocky River, near Cedar Point Bridge)
24399 Lorain Rd. (Rt. 10),
North Olmstead, OH 44070
(440) 777-4100

John's Diner
(Rocky River)
18260 Detroit Ave.,
Lakewood, OH 44107
(216) 228-0871

Café Stratos
(upper Rocky River, near Cedar Point Bridge)
23642 Lorain Rd. (Rt. 10),
North Olmstead, OH 44070
(440) 734-9431

Pacers
(Rocky River near Lakewood)
14600 Detroit Ave.,
Cleveland, OH 44107
(216) 226-2000

West End Tavern
(Rocky River)
18514 Detroit Ave.,
Cleveland, OH (Lakewood) 44107
(216) 521-7684

Red Roof Inn
(Cuyahoga River)
6020 Quarry Ln. (Rt. 77),
Independence, OH 44131
(216) 447-0030

Eddie's Creekside Restaurant
(Cuyahoga River)
8803 Brecksville Rd. (Rt. 21),
Brecksville, Ohio (Independence) 44141
(440) 546-0555

Super 8 Motel
(Lower Grand and Chagrin Rivers)
7325 Palisades Parkway (Routes 2 & 306),
Mentor, Ohio 44060
(440) 951-8558

Red Roof Inn
(Chagrin River)
4166 State Rt. 306,
Willoughby, OH 44094
(440) 946-9872

Courtyard by Marriot
(Chagrin River)
35103 Maple grove Rd. (off I 90),
Willoughby, OH 44094
(440) 530-1100

Inn of Chagrin Falls
(Lodging and food, upper Chagrin River)
87 West St.
Chagrin Falls, OH 44022
(440) 247-1200

Villa Rosa Motel
(Lower Grand River)
2140 North Ridge Road (Rt. 20),
Painesville, OH 44077
(440) 357-7502

Comfort Inn
(upper Grand River)
1860 Austinburg Rd., (off Rt. 45 & I 90),
Austinburg, OH 44010
(440) 275-2711

Mr. C's Family Restaurant
(upper Grand River)
2346 State Rt. 45 (off I 90),
Austinburg, OH 44010
(440) 275-9911

Chop's Grill & Tap House
(upper Grand River)
1752 State Rt. 534 (south of I 90
and Harpersfield Dam)
Geneva, OH 44041
(440) 466-4638

Cedars Motel
(Ashtabula River)
2015 W. Prospect Rd. (Rt. 20),
Ashtabula, OH 44004
(440) 992-5406

Covered Bridge Pizza
(Ashtabula River, Conneaut Creek)
1461 Northridge West (Rt. 20),
Ashtabula, OH 44004
(440) 969-1000

Days Inn
(lower Conneaut Creek)
600 Days Blvd. (Rt. 7 & I 90),
Conneaut, OH 44030
(440) 593-6000

Dav-Ed Motel
(upper Conneaut Creek)
5750 State Route 193 (Rt. 193 & I 90),
Kingsville, OH 44048
(440) 224-1094

Kay's Place Restaurant
(upper Conneaut Creek)
5552 State Route 193 (Rt. 193 & I 90),
Kingsville, OH 44048
(440) 224-2104

Beef and Beer
(lower Conneaut Creek)
57 Underridge Road (Rt. 7 & I 90),
Conneaut, OH 44030
(440) 593-3667

Biscotti's Restaurant
(lower Conneaut Creek)
186 Park Ave.,
Conneaut, OH 44030
(440) 593-6766

PENNSYLVANIA

Sunset Motel
(Raccoon and Crooked Creeks)
13825 Ridge Rd. (Rt. 20),
West Springfield, PA 16443
(814) 922-3550

Elk Creek Lodge
(lodging on middle Elk Creek)
209 E. Main St.,
Girard, PA 16417
(814) 774-8755 (Elk Creek Sports)
(814) 774-0011 (Lodge)
www.elkcreeksports.com

PENNSYLVANIA, cont.

Gudgeonville Lodge
(lodging on upper Elk Creek)
8322 Gudgeonville Road,
Girard, PA 16417
http://www.gudgeonvillelodge.com/
admin@gudgeonvillelodge.com

Green Roof Inn
(Elk Creek)
3790 Meadville Road (Rt. 18),
Girard, PA 16417
(814) 774-7072
www.thegreenroofinn.com

Best Western Presque Isle Country Inn
(lodging and food, Elk and Walnut Creeks)
6467 Sterrettania Rd. (Rt. 832 & I 90),
Fairview, PA 16415
(814) 838-7647

Crowley's Restaurant
(Elk Creek)
8844 Route 18,
Cranesville, PA 16410
(814) 774-8450

Girard Dinor
(Elk Creek)
222 Main St. W. (Rt. 20),
Girard, PA 16417
(814) 774-4888

Hunter Jacks
(Elk Creek)
10100 Ridge Rd. (Rt. 20),
Girard, PA 16417
(814) 774-8643

Elk Creek Inn
(food and drinks, Elk and Walnut Creeks)
6886 Sterrettania Rd. (Rt. 832),
Fairview, PA 16415
(814) 474-2013

Vernondale Motel
(Walnut Creek)
5422 W. Lake Rd. (Rt. 5),
Erie, PA 16505
(814) 838-2372

El Patio Motel
(Walnut Creek)
2950 W. 8th St. (Alt. Rt. 5),
Erie, PA 16505
(814) 838-9772

Riviera Motel
(Walnut Creek)
3107 W. Lake Rd. (Alt. Rt. 5),
Erie, PA 16505
(814) 838-1997

Lake Erie Lodge
(Walnut Creek)
1015 Peninsula Dr. (Rt. 832),
Erie, PA 16505
(814) 833-9855

Avonia Tavern
(Trout Run, Walnut Creek)
7321 W. Lake Rd. (Rt. 5),
Fairview, PA 16415
(814) 474-5347

Taki's Restaurant
(Walnut Creek)
2933 W. 12th St. (Rt. 5),
Erie, PA 16505
(814) 833-1798

Colonial Motel
(16-Mile Creek)
11329 E. Lake Rd. (Rt. 5),
North East, PA 16428
(814) 725-5513

Red Carpet Inn
(16-Mile Creek)
12264 East Main Rd. (Rt. 20 & I 90),
North East, PA 16428
(814) 725-4554

Waterfall Restaurant
(7-Mile Creek)
5735 E. Lake Rd. (Rt. 5),
Erie, PA 16511
(814) 899-8173

Freeport Restaurant
(16-Mile Creek)
Rt. 5 & Rt. 89,
North East, PA 16428
(814) 725-4607

NEW YORK

Pines Hotel
(20-Mile Creek)
6207 Shortman Rd (Rt. 20 & I 90),
Ripley, NY 14775
(716) 736-7463

Holiday Motel
(Chautauqua Creek)
223 N. Portage St. (Rt. 394 & I 90),
Westfield, NY 14787
(716) 326-3741

Westfield Main Diner
(Chautauqua Creek)
40 E. Main St. (Rt. 20),
Westfield, NY 14787
(716) 326-4351

Best Western Inn
(Canadaway Creek)
3912 Vineyard Dr. (Rt. 60 & I 90),
Dunkirk, NY 14048
(716) 366-7100

Dunkirk Motel
(Canadaway Creek)
310 Lake Shore Dr. W. (Rt. 5),
Dunkirk, NY 14048
(716) 366-2200

Four Seasons Family Restaurant
(Canadaway Creek)
1190 Central Ave.,
Dunkirk, NY 14048
(716) 366-0362

Vince Tobia
(streamside lodging on Cattaraugus Creek)
266 Troy Del Way
Williamsville, NY 14221
(716) 479-2327
vtobia@aol.com
www.cattarauguscreekoutfitters.com

Light House Inn
(lower Cattaraugus Creek)
965 Main Rd. (Rt. 5/20),
Irving, NY 14081
(716) 934-3877

Palm Garden Motel
(middle Cattaraugus Creek)
212 Buffalo St.,
Gowanda, NY 14070
(716) 532-9764

Tee Pee Bed & Breakfast
(middle Cattaraugus Creek)
14396 State Route 438,
Gowanda, NY 14070
(716) 532-2168

Microtel Inns
(upper Cattaraugus Creek)
270 S. Cascade Dr. (Rt. 219),
Springville, NY 14141
(716) 592-3141

Oasis Bed & Breakfast
(upper Cattaraugus Creek)
619 E. Main St,.
Springville, NY 14141
(866) 56-OASIS
(716) 592-0333

Aunt Millie's Kitchen
(lower Cattaraugus Creek)
Rt. 5/20,
Irving, NY 14081
(716) 934-2525

Seneca Hawk Restaurant
(lower Cattaraugus Creek)
Rt. 5/20,
Irving, NY 14081
(716) 934-4219

Wulff Run Service Station and Sandwich Shop
(lower Cattaraugus Creek)
Rt. 438, Versailles, NY

Olympia Restaurant
(middle Cattaraugus Creek)
2 Jamestown St.,
Gowanda, NY 14070
(716) 532-5303

Country Deli
(upper Cattaraugus Creek)
405 S. Cascade Dr. (Rt. 219 S.),
Springville, NY 14141
(716) 592-7011

Angola Motel
(Cattaraugus and 18-Mile Creeks)
9159 Erie Rd. (Rt.5),
Angola, NY 14006
(716) 549-9866

Red Roof Inn
(18-Mile Creek)
5370 Camp Rd. (Rt. 75 & I 90),
Hamburg, NY 14075
(716) 648-7222

Comfort Inn
(18-Mile Creek)
3615 Commerce Place (Rt. 75 & I 90),
Hamburg, NY 14075
(716) 648-2922

NEW YORK, cont.

Camp Road Diner
(18-Mile Creek)
S5564 Camp Rd. (Rt. 75 & I 90),
Hamburg, NY 14075
(716) 648-2028

Broadway Motel
(Cayuga and Buffalo Creeks)
3895 Broadway St. (Rt. 130),
Cheektowaga, NY 14227
(716) 683-2222

ONTARIO

Grand Retreat Bed & Breakfast
(Grand River)
340 St. Andrew St. East,
Fergus, ON N1MR1
(519) 843-1851
www.grandretreat.com

Three Bears Bed & Breakfast
(Grand River)
0568 S. River Rd.,
Elora, ON N0B1S0
(519) 843-5556
1-866-457-7770
www.the3bears.com

Breadalbane Inn
(Grand River, also lodging)
487 St. Andrew St. West,
Belwood, ON N1M 1P2
(519) 843-4770
(888) 842-2825
www.breadalbaneinn.com

The Highlander Inn
(Grand River)
280 Bridge St.,
Fergus, ON N1M 1T6
(519) 843-3115

Grindstone Angling Specialties
(contact for more Ontario lodging and dining info
P.O. Box 442,
24 Mill Street, North,
Waterdown, Ontario
LOR 2HO
(905) 689-0880
www.grindstoneangling.com
flyshop@grindstoneangling.com

Weather Web Sites and Phone Numbers

The Weather Channel
1-900-WEATHER
(including 3 and 10 day weather forecasts)
www.weather.com

Intellicast
(including regional radar)
www.intellicast.com

National Weather Service
(including 24 hour observed precipitation amounts in map/text form
and advanced hydrologic river predictions for limited rivers)
www.nws.noaa.gov/

Weather Underground
www.wunderground.com

United States Weather Pages
www.uswx.com/us/wx/pa/keri/

Lake Erie Surface Water Temperatures
www.landbigfish.com/watertemps/erie.cfm

Ohio
Cleveland Weather Forecast: (216) 931-1212

Pennsylvania
Erie Weather Forecast: (814) 453-2211

New York
Buffalo Weather Forecast: (716) 844-444

Useful Web Sites

Steelhead Site (Great Lakes tributary reports, fly patterns, discussion boards, guide database, real-time water flow data): www.steelheadsite.com

Fish Erie (Lake Erie tributary fisherman reports, weather information, guide and tackle shop lists, PA tributary descriptions and maps, discussion boards, Pennsylvania Fish & Boat Commission WCO fishing reports for Erie County, Pa., weekly tributary photos): www.fisherie.com

Pennsylvania Fly Fishing (Pennsylvania stream reports, weather information): http://www.paflyfish.com/

The Fly Guys (Ohio and Pennsylvania tributary reports): www.geocities.com/kibarg

Elk Creek Sports (Pennsylvania tributary reports): http://www.elkcreekarea.info/fishing

Pennsylvania Fish & Boat Commission Waterway's Conservation Officer Reports for Erie County, PA: http://sites.state.pa.us/PA_Exec/Fish_Boat/eriewco.htm

Cattaraugus Creek, NY: www.geocities.com/cattaraugusfishery/main.html, http://www.newyorkfishingforums.com/hotspots/west/cattaraugus.shtml

NYSDEC Western New York fishing report: www.dec.state.ny.us/website/dfwmr/fish/hotline.html

Cleveland Metroparks (fishing report for Rocky and Chagrin Rivers): http://www.clemetparks.com/recreation/fishing/fishingreport.asp

Ohio Department of Natural Resources fishing report: http://www.onlineerie.com/pages/fishing_page

Great Lakes Sports Fishing Council (Great Lakes tributary reports, weather): http://www.great-lakes.org" www.great-lakes.org

Great Lakes Fishery Commission (Great Lakes fisheries research, management and lamprey control): http://www.glfc.org/

Great Lakes Temperature Information: www.coastwatch.msu.edu/

Fly and Float (up-to-date info on Great Lakes fly fishing, float fishing, steelhead, trout including discussion forums and OH High Water Access Rights Data Base sign-up): http://www.flyandfloatfishing.com/

Fish weight calculation (calculates fish weight based on length and girth): http://www.fishdreams.com/calculator.all_species.html

Online fishing licenses: http://www.cattaraugusflyshop.com/archive/cat_online_fishing_licenses.html

Animated Fishing Knots: http://www.animatedknots.com/

Fishing Knots: http://www.netknots.com/html/fishing_knots.html

Steelheadquarters.com (weekly reports for the Grand and Chagrin Rivers in Ohio): www.steelheadquarters.com

Great Lakes on the Fly (Great Lakes fly fishing websites): http://www.greatlakesonthefly.com/

Ohio Department of Natural Resources River Access Points: http://www.ohiodnr.com/watercraft/boat/nerivers.htm

Online Erie (your everything Erie site): http://www.onlineerie.com/pages/fishing_page

Rules for the River: http://www.uky.edu/%7eagrdanny/flyfish/rules.htm

Midwest Fly Fishing Magazine: http://www.mwfly.com/contents.html

Quest Outdoors (Great Lakes Fishing Resource): http://www.questoutdoors.net/index.html

Fish Lake Erie (Lake Erie tributary reports, weather information, tackle shops, lodging, guides): www.FishLakeErie.com

Erie area convention and visitors bureau: http://www.visiteriepa.com/

Dana's Spey Pages (spey casting resource): www.speypages.com

Fly and Float (Great Lakes steelhead, salmon and trout fishing information, fly tying patterns, custom built rods, fly fishing and center pinning forum): http://www.flyandfloatfishing.com/

Salmonfly.net (salmon and steelhead fly tying guide): http://www.angelfire.com/wa/salmonid/

Fly Anglers Online (step by step Atlantic, Spey and Dee fly tying instructions): www.flyanglersonline.com

Information on Scandinavian Shooting Head Systems for the Great Lakes by Ontario's Peter Charles: http://home.mountaincable.net/~pcharles/scando-2.html

The Global Fly Fisher (Denmark's Martin Joergensen helped develop this cutting edge international fly fishing site): www.globalflyfisher.com

Real Time Water Flow Data Sources

(Stage and discharge data can be greatly impacted by cold weather and ice effects.)

United States Geological Survey (real time water flow and stage data in cubic feet per second and feet): http://water.usgs.gov/realtime.html

Grand River Conservation Authority (real time water flow data in cubic meters per second for Grand River, Ontario): (519) 621-2761, ext 519 or www.grandriver.ca/

Canada Water Survey (real time water stage data in meters): http://scitech.pyr.ec.gc.ca/waterweb/formnav.asp?lang=0

Hot Line Numbers

Pennsylvania Fish & Boat Commission Walnut Creek Access Area (Lake Erie and Walnut Creek water conditions, fishing reports May through October): (814) 833-2464

New York DEC Lake Erie Fishing Hot Line (Fishing reports on Western New York tributary streams): (716) 679-ERIE

Ohio Division of Wildlife Lake Erie Fishing Hot Line (Fishing reports on Ohio tributary streams): 1-888-HOOKFISH

Poacher Numbers (for reporting fishing violations)

Michigan DNR: 1-800-292-7800

Ohio DNR: 1-800-Poacher

Pennsylvania F&BC: (814) 572-0066 (central Erie County), (814) 572-0078 (eastern Erie County), (814) 566-7869 (western Erie County), (814) 337-0444 (PF&BC Bureau of Law Enforcement, NW Region Office).

New York DEC: 1-800-(Tipp-DEC)

Ontario MNR: 1-800-222-Tips-8477

Organizations

Pennsylvania Steelhead Association: http:/www.pasteelhead.org/index.html

Pennsylvania 3-C-U Trout Association: http://www.fisherie.com/3CU/main.htm

Ohio Central Basin Steelheaders: www.ohiosteelheaders.com/

Northwest PA Chapter of Trout Unlimited: www.fisherie.com/nwpatu/

Emerald Necklace Chapter of Trout Unlimited (Cleveland area): www.tucleveland.org/

Western New York Chapter of Trout Unlimited: http://wnytu.org/home.html

North Coast Fly Fishers: http://www.ncff.net/" www.ncff.net/

Gem Cities Fly Tyers Club: http://gcocflytiers.com/Index.html

Ohio's Remedial Action Plan Program (Black, Cuyahoga, Ashtabula and Maumee Rivers: http://www.epa.state.oh.us/dsw/rap/rap.html

Chagrin River Watershed Partners, Inc.: www.crwp.org

Grand River Partners Inc. (OH): http://www.grandriverpartners.org/

Rocky River Watershed: http://www.myrockyriver.org/

Eco City Cleveland (overviews of North East Ohio Rivers): http://www.ecocitycleveland.org/smartgrowth/watershed/rivers/rivers.html

Friends of Conneaut Creek: http://www.friendsofconneautcreek.com/

Cleveland Museum of Natural History Trout Club: http://www.cmnh.org/site/GetInvolved_ClubsandSocieties_TroutClub.aspx"

Great Lakes Council of the Federation of Fly Fishers: http://www.fffglc.org/clubs.html

Great Lakes Restoration: http://www.restorethelakes.org/index.html

Canoe Rentals

(Before floating any river make sure water levels are safe for the craft being used, wear a floatation device and inquire about possible hazards to avoid)

Raccoon Run Canoe Rental
(canoe & kayak rentals and shuttles on the Grand River, OH)
1153 State Rd.,
Geneva, Ohio
(440) 466-7414
http://raccoonruncanoerental.com/

Zoar Valley Canoe & Rafting Co.
(canoe rentals and shuttles on Cattaraugus Creek, NY,
recommended portages exist above and below S. Branch of Cattaraugus Creek confluence)
PO Box 695,
Dunkirk, NY 14048
(716) 679-RAFT
http://www.zoarvalleyrafting.com/index.php3

Grand Experiences
(canoe rentals and shuttles on the Grand and Nith Rivers, ON,
guided steelhead and smallmouth float trips on the middle Grand and Nith Rivers)
113 Grand River St. N.,
Paris, ON N3L 2M4
1-888-258-0441
http://www.grand-experiences.com/

APPENDIX B
State Fishery Departments and Regulations (1), (2)

OHIO

Ohio Department of Wildlife, Fairport Harbor Fisheries Research Unit
412 High Street,
Fairport Harbor, Ohio 44077
(440) 352-4199

http://www.dnr.state.oh.us/wildlife/fishing/fairport/steelhead.htm

Steelhead Regulations: September 1 through May 15, daily limit 2, minimum length 12 inches. May 16 through August 31, daily limit 5, minimum length 12 inches.

License Year: March 1 through February 28

License Fees: resident (season), $19.00; non-resident (season), $40.00; non-resident (3-day), $19.00; non-resident and resident (1-day), $11.00.

PENNSYLVANIA

Pennsylvania Fish & Boat Commission Division of Research
Lake Erie Research Unit
2000 Lohrer Road,
P.O. Box 531,
Fairview, Pa. 16415
(814) 474-1515

www.fish.state.pa.us

Steelhead Regulations: 8 a.m. April 14 through September 3, daily limit 5, minimum length 9 inches. September 4 through April 13, daily limit 3, minimum length 15 inches.

License Year: December 1 to December 31 of the year following, inclusive.

License Fees: resident, $21.00; non-resident season, $51.00; 7-day tourist, $33.00; 3-day tourist, $25.00; 1-day tourist (not valid April 1-April 30), $25.00; trout/salmon permit, $8.00; Lake Erie permit, $8.00; combination trout/salmon/Lake Erie permit, $14.00.

NEW YORK

New York State Department of Environmental Conservation
Lake Erie Fisheries Unit
178 Point Drive North,
Dunkirk, NY 14048
(716) 366-0228

www.dec.state.ny.us

1) As of 2007.
2) Specific tributary streams may have special regulations concerning seasons and nursery waters.

Steelhead Regulations: All year, daily limit 3, minimum length 9 inches.

Special Regulations: The use of more than one hook is prohibited, except for multiple hooks attached to floating lures. Also, the distance between the hook, artificial fly or lure and any weight attached to the line or leader, whether fixed or sliding, shall not exceed 48 inches.

Special year round catch and release regulations for Chautauqua Creek and Eighteen Mile Creek (both Lake Erie tributaries): Catch and release only (trout and salmon), artificial lures only, seasonal regulations regarding hooks, leaders and weights for Great Lakes tributaries shall apply (see above and pages 7, 21-23 of New York State freshwater fishing regulations book for details). Chautauqua Creek location: from the bridge on South Gale Street upstream 1.3 miles to the upper dam used by the village of Westfield for water intake. Main Branch of Eighteen Mile Creek (Erie County, excluding S. Branch) location: contained within Eighteen Mile Creek County Park.

License Year: October 1 to September 30.

License Fees: resident, $19; non-resident season, $40; non-resident 7-day, $25; non-resident and resident 1-day, $15.

Cattaraugus Indian Reservation*

The Seneca Nations of Indians
William Seneca Building
1490 Route 438, Irving, NY 14081
(716) 532-4900
www.sni.org/

Steelhead Regulations: All year, daily limit 5, minimum length 9 inches. All New York State fishing regulations apply on the reservation.

License Year: January 1 to December 31.

License Fees: non-Indian season, $35; non-Indian minor (10-16 yrs.), $20; Senior citizen (65 yrs. or older), $10.

Reservation fishing licenses are available at the following locations:

Cattaraugus Indian Reservation,
William Seneca Building (Clerks Office),
1490 Route 438,
Irving, NY 14081
(716) 532-4900
(open 8-5 during the week only)

Seneca-One-Stop
(open 24 hours)
11150 Routes 5 & 20,
Irving, NY 14081
(716) 934-9524

Allegany Indian Reservation
G. K. Plummer Building (Clerks Office),
3582 Center Road,
Salamanca, NY 14779
(716) 945-1790
(open 8-5 during the week only)

Seneca-One-Stop
(open 24 hours)
745 Broad Street,
Salamanca, NY 14779
(716) 945-5400

*****Cattaraugus Indian Reservation** surrounds Cattaraugus Creek between Lake Erie and Gowanda, except for the south bank of the stream (between Lake Erie and 1/2 mile north of I 90) as well as the Versailles area. The reservation also surrounds most of Clear Creek except for upstream of Taylor Hollow Rd. Fishing is prohibited from Jan. 1 to March 31 on Spooner creek and the N. Branch of Clear Creek (from Taylor Hollow Rd. upstream to Jennings Rd.)*

APPENDIX C
Additional Map Sources, Videos and DVD's
MI, OH, PA, and NY Delorme Atlas & Gazetters

Delorme
Two Delorme Drive,
P.O. Box 298,
Yarmouth, ME 04096
1-800-452-5931
www.delorme.com

State Fishery Department Maps

Ohio Department of Wildlife (Ohio tributaries): http://www.dnr.state.oh.us/ wildlife/fishing/fairport/steelhead.htm

Pennsylvania Fish & Boat Commission (Pennsylvania Tributaries): http://www.fish.state.pa.us/water/lakes/erie/00erie.htm

New York DEC (Public Fishing Rights Access for Western NY tributaries of Lake Erie including Chautauqua Creek, Cattaraugus Creek and 18 Mile Creek): http://www.dec.ny.gov/outdoor/32426.html

State Township & County Maps

PA Department of Transportation
Publication Sales Store,
P.O. Box 2028,
Harrisburg, PA 17105
(717) 787-6746

Ohio Department of Transportation
Map Sales Room 118,
P.O. Box 899,
Columbus, Ohio 43216-0899
(614) 466-3220

NY Department of Transportation
State Campus Bldg. 4,
Room 105
Albany, NY 12232-0415

Pennsylvania State Parks

Erie Bluffs State Park
http://www.dcnr.state.pa.us/stateparks/parks/eriebluffs.aspx

Pennsylvania Steelhead Association

(Offers maps showing public fishing easements obtained on several Pennsylvania tributaries through the Lake Erie Access Improvement Program.)

Pennsylvania Steelhead Association
PO Box 8892,
Erie, PA 16505
www.pasteelhead.org/index.html

Ohio Park and Metro Maps

Cleveland Metroparks
(Rocky and Chagrin Rivers)

Cleveland Metro Parks
4101 Fulton Parkway,
Cleveland, OH 44144
(216) 351-6300
http://www.clemetparks.com/

Michael Durkalec
Aquatic Biologist,
Cleveland Metroparks,
4550 Valley Parkway,
Fairview Park, OH 44126
(440) 331-8017
http://www.clemetparks.com/recreation/fishing/
fishingreport.asp
md@clevelandmetroparks.com

Lake County Metroparks
(Grand River, Chagrin River and Arcola Creek)

Concord Woods Nature Park
11211 Spear Road,
Concord Township 44077
(800) 227-PARK
http://www.lakemetroparks.com/default.asp

Geneva State Park
(Wheeler and Cowles Creeks)

Geneva State Park
P.O. Box 429,
Padanarum Road,
Geneva, OH 44041
(440) 466-8400
http://www.dnr.state.oh.us/parks/parks/
geneva.htm

Lorain County Metroparks
(Black and Vermillion Rivers)

Lorain County Metroparks
12882 Diagonal Road
LaGrange, Ohio 44050
1-800-LCM-PARK
http://www.loraincountymetroparks.com/

Cuyahoga Valley National Park
(Cuyahoga River)

Cuyahoga Valley National Park
15610 Vaughn Road,
Brecksville, OH 44141
(440) 546-5991
http://www.nps.gov/cuva/

New York State DEC

*(Offers maps of Public Fishing Rights lands and
parking areas on Cattaraugus Creek, Chautauqua Creek and 18 Mile Creek.)*

New York State DEC
102 E. Union St., Suite 2,
Allegany, NY 14706
(716) 372-0645
http://www.dec.ny.gov/outdoor/32426.html

Lake Erie Fisherman's Map & Access Guides (OH & PA)

John Bodner,
Fish Man Guide Services,
118 Shippen Drive,
Coraopolis, PA 15108
(412) 269-1285 or (814) 392-7856
www.fishman.com
jbfish1@aol.com

FishUSA Map Source

FishUSA (Pennsylvania tributaries): www.fishusa.com/FishErie/Maps.asp

SGC Maps

Stream Guide Companion Maps/Steelhead Alley Series (CD map reference
guides for Ohio, Pennsylvania and New York steelhead tributaries):
http://sgcmaps.com/

Videos/DVD's

Mad River Media (Chasing Silver, Steelheading Made Simple, Cool Flies for Hot Fish and other fly fishing videos): www.madrivermedia.net or Mad River Outfitters at 1-888-451-0363.

Fishdog Films (Great Lakes Steelhead Chronicles and Guide Patterns for Steelhead): www.guidepatterns.com

In-Fisherman (Steelhead Strategies/DVD and Great Lakes Salmon & Trout/DVD): www.in-fisherman.com

Quest Outdoors (Spey Fishing/Great Lakes Style, Center pin 101): http://www.questoutdoors.net/episodes/sk3001/

Hooked on Fly Tying (Intro to Tube Flies I and Tube Fly Patterns and Techniques II by Dick Talleur): http://dicktalleur.com/publ.htm

T Pags Company, LLC (Tying Convertible Tube Flies, Volumes 1 and 2): www.madriveroutfitters.com

GuideLine (Mikael Frodin's Modern Salmon Flies-Tying on Tubes): www.irishangler.com

APPENDIX D

Fly Rods, Fly Reels, Accessories, Fly Tying Materials, Rod Builders and Fly Tyer Sources.

Fly Rods

Diamondback Inc.
3736 Kellog Road,
Cortland, NY 13045
(607) 756-2851
www.diamondbackflyrods.com

CND, The Spey Underground
(exclusively manufactures spey rods and lines)
http://www.cndspeyusa.com/Pages/about.html

Redington Inc.
(also fly reels)
12715 Miller Road NE #101,
Bainbridge Island, WA 98110
(800) 253-2538
www.redington.com
Sage
(also fly reels)
8500 Northeast Day Road,
Bainbridge Island, WA 98110
(800) 533-3004
www.SAGEflyfish.com

Scott Fly Rod Company
2355 Air Park Way,
Montrose, Colorado 81401
(800) 728-7208
www.scottflyrod.com

St Croix Rod
P.O. Box 279
856 4th Avenue North,
North Park Falls, WI 54552
(800) 826-7042
www.stcroixrods.com

Thomas & Thomas Rodmakers, Inc.
627 Barton Road,
Greenfield, MA 01301
(413) 774-5436
www.thomasandthomas.com

R.L. Winston Rod Company
PO Box 411,
500 South Main Street,
Twin Bridges, MT 59754
(406) 684-5674
www.winstonrods.com

Quarrow
(Alliance Sport Group)
602 Fountain Parkway,
Grand Prairie, TX 75050
(800) 255-6061
www.Quarrow.com

Orvis Company
(also fly reels and accessories)
Route 7-A,
Manchester, VT 05254
(800) 333-1550
www.orvis.com

Echo
(fly rods and reels by Tim Rajeff)
7113 NW 25th Avenue,
Vancouver, WA 98665
(866) 347-4359
www.rajeffsports.com

Fly Reels

Nautilus Reels
1549 NW 165th Street,
Miami, FL 33169
(888) 397-7355
www.nautilusreels.com

Galvan Fly Reels, Inc.
17425 Overland Trail,
Sonora, CA 95370
(209) 588-2813
www.galvanflyreels.com

Bauer Premium Fly Reels
PO Box 747,
Ashland, OR 97520
(888) 484-4165
www.bauerflyreel.com

Solitude Reels
14508 Ovenell Road,
Mount Vernon, WA 98273
(360) 424-6600
www.solitudereels.com

Ross Reels
1 Ponderosa Court,
Montrose, CO 81401
(970) 249-1212
www.rossreels.com

Waterworks/Lamson
(800) 435-9374
www.waterworks-lamson.com

Loop Tackle
(888) 566-7872
www.looptackle.com

Abel Reels
165 Aviador Street,
Camarillo, CA 93010
(805) 484-8789
www.abelreels.com

Scientific Anglers
(also fly lines)
3M Center Bldg.,
St Paul, MN 55144-1000
(888) 364-3577
www.scientificanglers.com

Teton Fly Reels, Inc.
924 Church Hill Road,
San Andreas, CA 95249
(800) 831-0855
www.tetonflyreels.com

Accessories

Fishpond, Inc.
(chest packs, fishing vests, tools, bags, luggage)
863 Otter Creek Road,
Silverthorne, CO 80498
requests@fishpondusa.com
www.fishpondusa.com

SR Trout Supply
(Ashima fluorocarbon line, hooks)
39 Sunrise Street,
Worthington, WV 26591
(866) SRTROUT
www.srtroutsupply.com/ashima.html

Oregon Fishing
(pontoon boats and accessories, fishing gear)
691 E. Vilas Road,
Central Point, Oregon 97502
(877) 694-0856
www.oregonfishing.com

Water Skeeter
(pontoon boats and accessories)
2701 E. Hammer Lane,
Suite 101,
Stockton, CA 95210
(800) 339-7261
www.waterskeeter.com

Optronics
(Firepod pocket and muff-style handwarmers)
www.optronicsinc.com

Flambeau Fly Fishing
(Blue Ribbon waterproof fly boxes)
www.flambeauoutdoors.com

Lasava Unique Fishing Clothing
(Polartec under-wader liner layers)
www.fishwithra.com

Float Master Company
(innovative strike indicators, fly fishing accessories)
1167 Potomac Drive,
Brunswick, OH 44212
www.floatmasterco.net
info@floatmaster.net

The Adventure Fly Fishing Company
(waterproof vest and vest-jackets)
(877) 435-9347
www.TheAdventureFlyfishingCo.com

Angling Designs Incorporated
(Dry Tech MRT fly boxes)
(303) 288-7888
www.anglingdesigns.com

Feather-Craft Fly Fishing
(Toobies Shot System)
8307 Manchester Road,
PO Box 19904,
St. Louis, MO 63144
www.feather-craft.com/index.html

Flow Tek, Inc.
(Monic fly lines, AquaGlo glow dressing)
P.O. Box 2018,
Boulder, CO 80306
(303) 530-3050
www.monic.com

Brodin
(landing nets and magnetic net releases)
P.O. Box 9898,
Asheville, NC 28815
(800) 336-8738
http://www.brodin.com/

Michigan River Works, LLC
(mesh landing mitt)
www.miriverworks.com
(248) 895-3858

Royal Wulff Products
(Triangle Taper fly lines with J3 coating, fluorocarbon tippet, GSP ultra-thin backing, Wulff
School of Fly Fishing)
7 Main Street,
Box 948,
Livingston Manor, NY 12758
(845) 439-4060
(845) 439-5020 (Fly Fishing School)
www.royalwulff.com

Yakima Bait Company
(Little Corkie floating indicators)
P.O. Box 310,
Granger, WA 98932
(509) 854-1311
www.yakimabait.com

Rio Products
(fly lines, leaders, tippet and accessories)
5050 South Yellowstone Hwy,
Idaho Falls, ID 83402
(800) 553-0838
www.rioproducts.com

Airflo
(fly lines, leaders, tippet and accessories)
7113 NW 25th Avenue,
Vancouver, WA 98665
(866) 347-4359
www.flylines.com

GuideLine
(offers specialty fly lines,
as well as fly reels and rods)
www.GuideLineFlyFish.com

Teeny Nymph Company
(fly lines, flies and fly rods)
P.O. Box 989
Gresham, OR 97030
(503) 667-2917
www.jimteeny.com

Angler's Roost Enterprises
(A.R.E. Roto-Vise and fly reels, hooks,
fly rods, flies)
5820 Main Street,
Suite 308,
Williamsville, NY 14221
(716) 565-9838
anglersroostent@cs.com

Fisherman's Shack
(Slinky Drifter components)
9465 Airlie Road,
Monmouth, OR 97361
(503) 838-6395
www.fishermanshack.net/index.htm

Cortland Line Company
(fly lines)
P.O. Box 5588
3736 Kellog Road,
Cortland, NY 13045
www.cortlandline.com

William Joseph
(chest packs, creels, back packs,
chest waders, wading jackets,
digital and infrared thermometers)
1700 South 753 West,
Salt Lake City, Utah 84104
1-800-269-1875
www.williamjosephfishing.com

Chota Outdoor Gear
(wading shoes and breathable waders)
PO Box 31137,
Knoxville, TN 37930
877-GO-CHOTA toll free
www.chotaoutdoorgear.com

Simms
(wading shoes, breathable waders, jackets and vests)
101 Evergreen Drive,
Bozeman, MT 59715
(406) 585-3557
www.simmsfishing.com

Korkers
(convertible wading boots)
1239 SE 12th Avenue,
Portland, OR 97214
1-800-524-8899
www.korkers.com

Patagonia
(wading shoes, breathable waders, vests, jackets and insulating underwear)
8550 White Fir Street,
PO Box 32050,
Reno, NV 89523
1-800-638-6464
www.patagonia.com

Mad River Outfitter's
(B. K. Weigh Nets, Stanley's Ice Off paste,
Midstream Landing Hand, Rio Shock Gum,
Pop-Top indicators, glue gun kits, Split-Shot
Companion, Dropper Rig Fly Box)
813 Bethel Road,
Columbus, OH 43214
(888) 451-0363
www.madriveroutfitters.com

Glacier Glove
(neoprene and fleece fishing gloves, waders)
4890 Aircenter Cir. #210,
Reno NV 89502
1-800-728-8235
www.glacierglove.com

FishUSA.com
(Toggs Hellbender stocking foot waders,
Redington fly rods,
Okuma and Bauer fly reels, Chota wading boots,
Korkers wading sandals)
901 West 12th Street,
Erie, PA 16501
800-922-1219
www.FishUSA.com
FishUSA owns and hosts two regional fishing sites: www.FishErie.com
and www.FishSalmonRiver.com

Lindy Little Joe
(Thill floats and shot)
(218) 829-1714
www.lindylittlejoe.com

Redwing Tackle
(Blackbird shot, floats and Phantom fluorocarbon)
55 Mills Road #8,
Ajax, Ontario L1S 2H2
(905) 683-8989
www.redwingtackle.com

Gamma Technologies
(Frog Hair, Deep Blue and Frog Hair fluorocarbon tippet materials,strike indicators,
Great Lakes steelhead leaders)
200 Waterfront Drive,
Pittsburgh, Pa. 15222
(800) 437-2971
info@froghairfishing.com
www.froghair.com

P.A. Lures
(Glo-Bob foam floats)
132 S. Pine Street,
PO Box 585,
Ellsworth, PA 15331
(724) 239-2302
http://palures.tripod.com

Dan Bailey's Fly Shop
(Sunset Amnesia fluorescent red monofilament running line, Boga Grip,
breathable waders)
209 West Park Street,
PO Box 1019,
Livingston, MT 59047
1-800-356-4052
www.dan-bailey.com

Maxima America
(Maxima Chameleon and Ultragreen leader material)
3301 S. Susan St.,
Santa Ana, CA 92704
(714) 850-5966
www.maxima-lines.com

Fly Tying Materials (specialty items)

HMH Vises
(starter tube tool kit, tube fly vises, tube assortments, tube hooks, junction tubing,
coneheads, tube egg heads)
14 Maine Street,
PO Box 18,
Brunswick, ME 04011
(207) 729-5200
www.hmhvises.com

The Irish Angler
TTS, Shumakov and Frodin tube systems, tube
hooks and materials, Frodin Turbo cones,
Veniard Slipstream tubes, Atlantic salmon and
spey fly materials, Guideline products,
Michael Frodin tube tying DVD)
32231 East Bird Street,
Carnation, WA 98014
(425) 333-6582
www.irishangler.com

Yuri Shumakov Tubes
(Shumakov tube flies, tubes, Serebrjanka goat
hair, tying instructions):
http://www.shumakovtubes.com/index.html

Canadian Tube Fly Company
(Shumakov and Frodin tubes, tube hooks, tying
materials)
http://www.canadiantubeflies.com/index.html

Wurm Tungsten Products
(tungsten bottle tubes, coneheads, beads and
plastic tubes)
http://www.tungstenshop.de/

Bidoz
(Joergensen bottle tubes, metal tube extensions)
www.Bidoz.com/tubes

GuideLine
(offers Frodin FITS tube system)
www.GuideLineFlyFish.com

Loop Tackle
(Loop bottle tubes and double tube hooks)
www.looptackle.se

Anthony L. DiBenedetto, Jr.
T Bone Fly Fishing
(tube fly tying materials including T's Fur, T's
Hair and T's Tubing, arctic fox fur, Wurm
Tungsten Tubes and tubing, custom dyeing of
temple dog fur, llama fur, arctic fox fur and
ostrich feathers, fly fishing equipment and
accessories, specializes in Scandinavian tube
fly patterns)
7306 Yellow Creek Drive,
Poloand, OH 44514
(330) 757-3614
opus412@zoominternet.net
www.tboneflyfish.com

Blue Ribbon Flies
(premium soft hackle, bird skins and feathers)
PO Box 1037
West Yellowstone, MT 59758
(406) 646-7642
www.blueribbonflies.com

Jay's Sporting Goods
(custom dyed egg yarn)
8800 South Clare Avenue,
Clare, MI 48617
(989) 386-3475

Mad River Outfitters
(Tube fly tying supplies)
813 Bethel Road,
Columbus, OH 43214
(614) 451-0363
1-888-451-0363
admin@madriveroutfitters.com
www.madriveroutfitters.com

Jann's Netcraft
(fly tying, rod building, lure making supplies,
tackle)
3350 Briarfield Blvd.,
Maumee, Ohio 43537
(800) NETCRAFT
www.jannsnetcraft.com/

White Tail Fly Tieing
(Atlantic salmon and tube fly materials, fly tying
instruction, catalog)
7060 White Tail Court
Toledo, Ohio 43617
(800) 579-5549
www.whitetailflytieing.com

Rod Yerger
(plastic, aluminum and copper tubes with plastic
liners, tapered vinyl hook sleeves, tube hooks,
also skittering, bead head, hot bead, cone head
and micro tubes, McMurray ant kits)
PO Box 294,
Lawrence, PA 15055
(724) 746-3511
rodyerger@yahoo.com
http://rodyerger.com/index.html

DougSwisher.com
(Rub-A-Dub, Peacock Plus and Generation X
Dubbing, Rub-A-Dub and Generation X
Wigglys, Incredible Legs, Congo and Gator Hair,
Flash Enhancers)
PO Box 725,
Hamilton, MT 59840
(406) 961-4416
www.dougswisher.com
dsflyfisher@aol.com

Mike Martinek
(Mike Martinek's Electric Sashimi polyester
body material)
15 Eastway
Reading, MA 01867
(781) 944-8744

Angler's Roost Enterprises
(jungle cock necks)
5820 Main Street, Suite 502,
Williamsville, NY 14221
(716) 565-9838
anglersroostent@cs.com

Chagrin River Outfitters
(Australian opossum skins for sculpin patterns)
100 North Main Street,
Chagrin Falls, OH 44022
(440) 247-7110
www.chagrinriveroutfitters.com

Schmidt Outfitters
(Crystal Egg Balls)
918 Seaman Road,
Wellston, MI 49689
(888) 221-9056
www.schmidtoutfitters.com

Folly's End Fly & Tackle Shop
(Steel-Ed's Laser Yarn and Laser Tail material)
RD #2 8600 Avonia Road,
Girard, PA 16417
http://www.follysend.com/
(814) 474-5730

Badger Creek Fly Tying
(Mike Hogue carries many specialty fly tying
itemsincluding Tarantula Legs, Polar Chenille
and many types of soft hackle)
622 West Dryden Road,
Freeville, NY 13068
(607) 347-4946
www.eflytyer.com

The Contented Angler
(steelhead fly tying materials including Spirit
River Humpback Beads)
147 Jefferson Avenue,
Lower Burrell, PA 15068
(724) 337-0437
joeamy@content-angler.com

Feather-Craft Fly Fishing
(Jelly Rope, Hot beads, Lite Brite, Ice Dub,
Crazy Legs, McFly Foam,
Estaz, ostrich and, emu feathers)
8307 Manchester Road,
PO Box 19904,
St. Louis, MO 63144
www.feather-craft.com/index.html

Saltwaterflies.com
(Polar Fiber, Icelandic sheep hair, artic fox, Fire
Fly, Krinkle Mirror Flash, Gliss n Glow, Angel
Hair, Super Hair,V ribbing)
PO Box 362,
Housatonic, MA 01236
(413) 274-6143
www.saltwaterflies.com

Grand River Tackle
(Hackle Flash, Ice Yarn)
1250 High Street,
Fairport Harbor, OH 44077
(440) 352-7222
www.grandrivertackle.com
grandrivertackle@sbcglobal.net

The Oak Orchard Fly Shop
(steelhead fly tying materials including
holographic Flashabou, Egghead beads,
Bodi Works braid, marabou spey hackle,
SLF dubbing)
5977 Main Street,
Williamsville, NY 14221
(716) 626-1323
info@oakorchardflyshop.com
www.oakorchardflyshop.com

Lake Erie Ultimate Angler
(H2O Fuzzy Bug Chenille)
3737 W. 12th St.,
Erie, PA 16505
(814) 833-4040
http://www.LakeerieUltimateAngler.com/

Buffalo Outfitter's
(E-Z Bug chenille, Artic Runner, rams wool,
SLF dubbing hanks, DNA Holo Fusion, spey fly
materials and hooks, Yuri Shumakov tubes and
tube hooks)
5655 Main Street
Williamsville, NY 14221
(716) 631-5131
www.buffalooutfittersflyshop.com

Carl Coleman's Fly Shop
(spey fly materials and hooks, tube fly kits,
lazer wrap, edge brite)
4786 Ridge Road West (Route 104),
Spencerport, NY 14559
(585) 352-4775
www.colemansflyshop.com

Grindstone Angling Specialties
(spey fly materials and hooks, Uninylon thread,
Mega Hair)
P.O. Box 442,
24 Mill Street, North,
Waterdown, Ontario
LOR 2HO
(905) 689-0880
www.grindstoneangling.com
flyshop@grindstoneangling.com

English Angling Trappings
(spey fly materials and hooks, tube fly kits)
Box 8885
New Fairfield, CT
203-746-4121
Fax: 203-746-9929
alcoif@aol.com

Creekside Fly Fishing Guides & Outfitters
(Atlantic salmon and spey fly materials)
345 High Street SE,
Salem, OR 97301
(877) 273-3574
www.creeksideflyfishing.com

Orleans Outdoor
(Petite Estaz)
1764 Oak Orchard Road (Route 98),
Albion, NY 14411
(585) 682-4546
www.orleansoutdoor.com

Orchard View Angling
(Salmon/Steelhead Sponge, Slinky Fiber,
Gudebrod Electra Metallic Hologram Braid and
tying threads)
3540 Washington Road (Rt.19),
McMurray, PA 15317
(724) 942-5485
zoogfish@adelphia.net
www.orchardviewangling.com

Siskiyou Aviary
(source for specialty feathers)
2585 East Main Street,
Ashland, OR 97520
(541) 488-2835
www.siskiyouaviary.com

Michael's, The Arts & Crafts Store
(Tulip Fabric Paint, Textured Yarn, Nylon Plus
Yarn, glue gun kits, glass beads)
1-800-Michaels

Rod Builders, Blanks and Components

John Nagy
Steelhead Guide Service
(offers custom made "noodle" fly rods for Lake
Erie steelhead fishing as well as other custom
fishing rods)
606 Crysler Street,
Pittsburgh, PA 15226
(412) 531-5819
steelheadguide@hotmail.com
http://groups.msn.com/JohnNagySteelheadGuide/

Rod Makers Shop
20884 Royalton Rd.,
Strongsville, Ohio 44149
(440) 572-0400

Shelbyville Rod Co.
1103 Brooks Road,
Hastings, MI 49058
(269) 948-0396
www.shelbyvillerodco.com

Terry Palmer Custom Rods
413 East Main Street,
Conneaut, Ohio 44030
(440) 593-2714, (440) 576-7575
(Also specializes in custom rod weaving designs.)

John DiMartino Custom Rods & Tackle
PO Box 67935,
Rochester, NY 14617
(585) 756-8777
www.customfishingtackle.com

Orchard View Angling
Richard Zoog
3540 Washington Road (Rt.19),
McMurray, PA 15317
(724) 942-5485
zoogfish@adelphia.net
www.orchardviewangling.com

Indiana Angler
(also rod repair)
218 Grandview Avenue,
Indiana, PA 15701
(724) 463-2011
indianaangler@yourinter.net

R. B. Meiser Fly Rods
(limited production and custom rod building,
specializes in rods and blanks for the worlds
two handed fly rod community)
Medford, OR
(541) 770-9522
www.meiserflyrods.com

REC Components
(quality reel seats, grips, rod cases and rod
building supplies)
17 Middle River Drive,
Stafford Springs, CT 06076
(860) 749-3476
www.rec.com

Pacific Bay International, Inc.
(fly rod blanks as well as reel seats, guides, grips)
165 Business Park Loop,
Sequim, WA 98382
(800) 272-2229
www.fishpacbay.com

Custom Fly Tyers and Flies

John Nagy
Steelhead Guide Service
(offers custom steelhead flies as well as
Scandinavian style tube flies)
606 Crysler Street,
Pittsburgh, PA 15226
(412) 531-5819
steelheadguide@hotmail.com
http://groups.msn.com/JohnNagySteelheadGuide/

Jim Winger
1212 Plum Street,
Steubenville, Ohio 43952
(740) 282-1304
jmwng312@sbcglobal.net

Anthony L. DiBenedetto, Jr.
T Bone Fly Fishing
(custom Scandinavian style tube flies and tube
materials)
7306 Yellow Creek Drive,
Poland, OH 44514
(330) 757-3614
opus412@zoominternet.net
www.tboneflyfish.com

Steven Wascher
(specializes in tube fly patterns and bass flies,
NY State licensed guide)
PO Box 178,
Greenhurst, NY 14742
(716) 664-7698
stevenwascher@gmail.com

The Irish Angler
(Yuri Shumakov and Michael Frodin tube flies,
also spey and Atlantic salmon flies)
32231 East Bird Street,
Carnation, WA 98014
(425) 333-6582
www.irishangler.com

Prime Flies
2507 Wigwam Road,
Aliquippa, PA 15001
(724) 601-7061
www.primeflies.net

Eggman Flies
Dan Walker
48 Maple Drive,
Belleville, MI 48111
(734) 699-8113
dh.walker@yahoo.com

Kopczyk's Fly Sales
777 N. Pleasant Way,
Milford, MI 48380
(248) 431-7761
www.kopczyksflysales.com/index.html
admin@kopczyksflysales.com

Mark DeFrank
Chestnut Ridge Flies
19 Crawford Street,
Uniontown, PA 15401
(724) 437-3546
(724) 317-8582
(724) 984-8886
www.chestnutridgeflies.com
www.DeFranksFlies.com
defranksflies@yahoo.com

Jim Guida
(innovative steelhead, trout and bass flies,
Signature Fly Designer for Umpqua Feather
Merchants)
(716) 684-8645
jimguida@hotmail.com

Jeff "Bear" Andrews
(fly designer for Umpqua Feather Merchants)
jbearfly@aol.com
www.bearandrews.com

Tony Pagliei
(convertible tube flies)
T Pags Company, LLC
East Lansing, Michigan USA
info@tpagsco.com
www.tubeflies.com

Bill Ingersoll
(Rainy's, Inc. Innovator Tyer, specializes in
steelhead and trout soft hackles, nymphs and
streamers)
1227 Orr Street Ext,
Jamestown, NY 14701
(716) 664-6872

Dave Schmezer
(Custom fly tying, original fly designs
and tying instruction)
RD 4 Box 100 D,
Latrobe, PA 15650
(724) 532-1393
smtzrfly@earthlink.net

Gary Selig
(Also offers hand tied freshwater, saltwater and
spey knotted leaders, Atlantic salmon trips to
Mirimichi River, New Brunswick at Upper Oxbow
Lodge.)
363 Chestnut Street,
Mertztown, Pa. 19539
(610) 682-6255

Greg Senyo
Jag Fly Company & Steelhead Alley Outfitters
(419) 466-9382
info@jagflyco.com
www.steelheadalleyoutfitters.com
www.jagflyco.com

The Contented Angler
Joe & Amy Gablick
(custom steelhead flies including classic Atlantic
Salmon Featherwings and Hairwings,
as well as contemporary Spey and Dee flies)
147 Jefferson Avenue,
Lower Burrell, PA 15068
(724) 337-0437
joeamy@content-angler.com

Tony Evangelista
7105 Bridlewood Drive,
Concord, OH 44077
(440) 352-8378

Fresh Run Inc.
Lenny Pitts,
4415 Janell Court,
Canfield, OH 44406
(330) 797-9717

Rod Yerger
Large selection of Atlantic Salmon flies plus
unique flies for steelhead, trout, smallmouth and
saltwater, also tube flies and extensive fly catalog)
PO Box 294,
Lawrence, PA 15055
(724) 746-3511
rodyerger@yahoo.com
http://rodyerger.com/index.html

Chris Helm
(also fly tying instruction)
White Tail Fly Tieing
7060 White Tail Court
Toledo, Ohio 43617
(800) 579-5549
www.whitetailflytieing.com

Ian Colin James
P.O. Box 48034,
Pond Mills,
London, Ontario N6M 1K5
(519) 681-4796
ianjames@sympatico.ca
www.ianjames.on.ca

Joe Penich
(Grindstone Angling Specialties)
P.O. Box 442,
24 Mill Street, North,
Waterdown, Ontario
LOR 2HO
(905) 689-0880
grindsto@cgocable.net

Partridge of Redditch
(Mikael Frodin tube flies)
http://www.partridge-of-redditch.co.uk/flies/
mik_fr_fly.htm

Rainy's Flies
(Yuri Shumakov tube flies)
http://www.rainysflies.com/pages/
flies.asp?page=shumakov

Yuri Shumakov Tubes
(Shumakov tube flies)
http://www.shumakovtubes.com/index.html

Canadian Tube Fly Company
(Yuri Shumakov tube flies)
http://www.canadiantubeflies.com/index.html

Mark DeCarlo
Erie Steelhead Outfitter's
204 Huckleberry Road,
Indiana, PA 15701
(724) 349-8742
flyfishinguide@yahoo.com

Miscellaneous

Les Troyer
(Artist specializing in wildlife art, original
paintings, ink renderings and illustration. Did
many of the drawings for the Steelhead Guide
Book by John Nagy.)
www.natureartists.com/les_troyer.asp
(330) 497-3493 (home)
(330) 877-4685 (work)

Marni Cayro
(Graphic Designer who did the layout and
design work for the Steelhead Guide Book by
John Nagy. Fantastic!)
(717) 790-5477
(717) 802-5478
marnilyn@aol.com

APPENDIX E
Lake Erie Fishery Reports and Studies

**Pennsylvania Fish and Boat Commission (PF&BC) Lake Erie Steelhead
Fishing and Angler Survey (April 17, 1993-April 15, 1994).**

In March, 1995, Charles Murray and Rickalon Hoopes of the PF&BC,
Division of Research, Lake Erie Research Unit, Fairview, PA completed a study (of
the above title). The study used data collected from an angler survey conducted
from April 17, 1993-April 15, 1994 to determine the level of angler use, angler
catch and release, document changes since a similar 1982 survey and make
recommendations for the future management of the Pennsylvania steelhead fishery.

The length frequency and age composition of harvested steelhead figures that
follow are taken from the study with permission of the authors and the PF&BC.
They point out some of the important trends of the data collected during the angler
survey. Persons interested in reviewing the entire study (including management
recommendations) should contact the PF&BC Lake Erie Research Unit. See
Appendix B for the address.

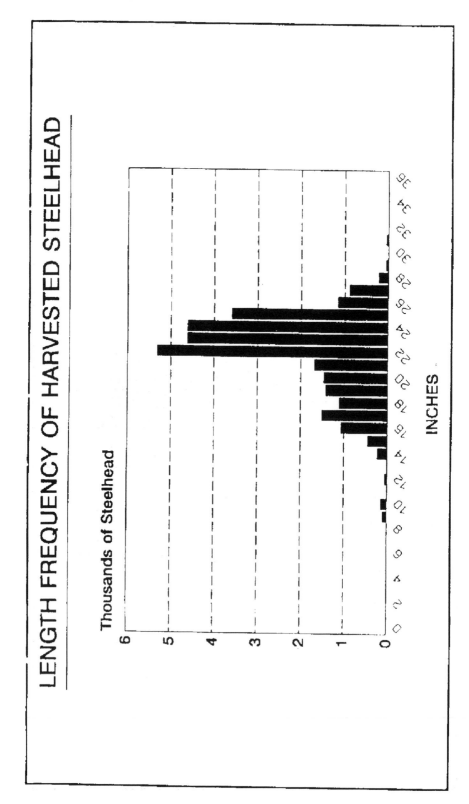

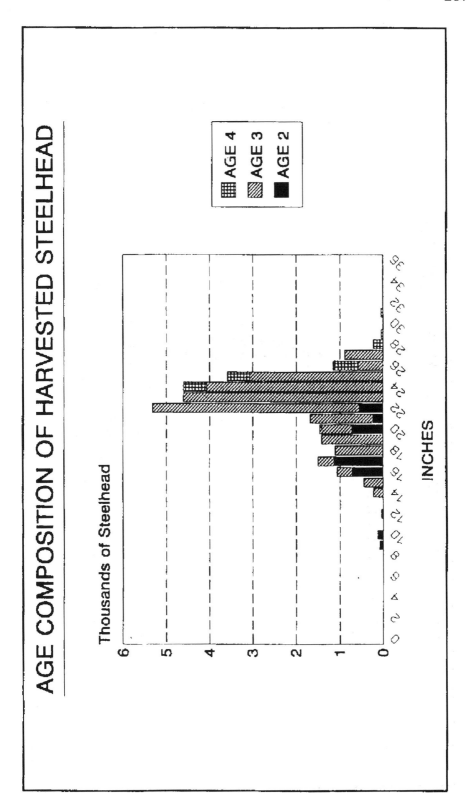

Table 12 was taken from the Brad Thompson thesis, "Population Biology of Steelhead in Pennsylvania's Lake Erie Tributaries." Mr. Thompson used this thesis to complete his master's degree in wildlife and fisheries science from Penn State University in August 1999.

Tributary (State/Prov.)	Lake/ Ocean	Percent Wild	Sex ratio (F:M)	Repeat Spawners (%)		Age Composition (%) Lake years 1	2	3	4	Length (mm) at age Lake years 1	2	3	4	References
PA study streams	Erie	6-14	39:61	4-37	Females	14	62	18	6	478	615	661	709	This study
				2-15	Males	69	24	6	0	465	623	681	-	
Huron River (MI)	Erie	0	36:64	22		36	49	15	1	425	600	700	-	Seelbach et. al. 1994
Conneaut Creek (OH)	Erie	-	-	-		25	60	8	5	480	600	720	750	Kayle 1996
Little Manistee River (MI)	Michigan	100	54:46	21-27		5	24	58	13	443	646	732	783	Seelbach 1993
Betsie River (MI)	Michigan	24-43	-	10-18		-	-	-	-	-	-	-	-	Harbeck 1999
Grand River (MI)	Michigan	10-22	45:55	15		2	35	56	6	440	630	720	690	Seelbach et. al. 1994
Bothwell Creek (ON)	Huron	100	53:47	65		12	25	37	20	-	-	-	-	Dodge and MacCrimmon 1970
Huron (MI)	Superior	86	-	54	Females	0	19	67	14	362	509	617	678	Seelbach and Miller 1993
					Males	78	10	10	2					
Kalama River (WA)	Pacific	59	53:47	5-20		5	55	31	-	555	699	831	-	Leider et al. 1986
Alsea River (OR)	Pacific	90	50:50	3-17		5	66	26	3	-	-	-	-	Chapman 1958
Chilliwack River (BC)	Pacific	-	60:40	-		<1	50	49	<1	472	701	813	879	Maher and Larkin 1955 (fork lengths)
Frasier River Tribs. (BC)	Pacific	-	66:34	5-31		2	52	38	8	-	-	-	-	Withler 1966

Table 12. Population statistics, including relative contribution of wild fish, sex ratio, age structure, repeat spawning, and observed mean length at age of steelhead spawning runs throughout the Great Lakes and in the the Pacific northwest.

289

Pennsylvania Fish & Boat Commission (PF&BC) Creel Analysis and Economic Impact study of Pennsylvania's Lake Erie tributary fisheries (2003/2004).

In October, 2004, Charles Murray of the PF&BC, Division of Research, Lake Erie Research Unit, Fairview, PA and M. Shields of the Center for Economic and Community Development, The Pennsylvania State University, completed a study (of the above title).

Table 13 and Figure 3 are taken from the study (with the permission of the authors and the PF&BC) and point out some of the important trends of the data collected during the study. Persons interested in reviewing the entire study (including management recommendations) should contact the PF&BC Lake Erie Research Unit, Fairview, Pennsylvania. See Appendix B for the address.

Table 13: Steelhead angler directed effort statistics including number of interviews (N), percent success, catch per angler hour and harvest per angler hour by fishery and total from the 2003 Lake Erie Tributary Creel Survey.

Fishery	N	% Success	Catch Rate	Harvest Rate
Elk Creek	1,488	48%	0.565	0.114
Godfrey Run	101	52%	0.531	0.187
Trout Run	178	50%	0.680	0.273
Walnut Ck	697	55%	0.624	0.166
Fourmile Ck	91	59%	0.820	0.219
Sevenmile Ck	64	67%	1.075	0.151
Twelvemile Ck	116	56%	0.878	0.224
Sixteenmile Ck	92	49%	0.823	0.084
Twentymile Ck	276	45%	0.665	0.174
Overall	3,103	50%	0.630	0.150

Figure 3: Total estimated steelhead angler trips, steelhead catch and steelhead harvest by month from the 23 survey sites from the Lake Erie Tributary Creel Survey October 1, 2003 – April 30, 2004.

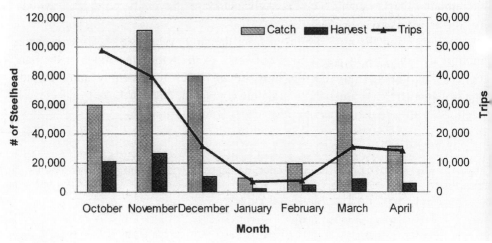

Report(s) of the Coldwater Task Group to the standing technical committee of the Lake Erie Committee, Great Lakes Fishery Commission.

The Coldwater Task Group was formed under the Lake Erie Committee (represented by personnel from the Ohio DOW, Michigan DNR, New York DEC, Ontario MNR, Pennsylvania F&BC and the US Fish and Wildlife Service) to address specific charges related to the Lake Erie cold water fish community. Two of those charges address maintaining an annual interagency electronic data base of Lake Erie salmonid stocking and to report on the status of rainbow trout (steelhead) in Lake Erie, including stocking numbers, strains being stocked, academic and resource agency research interests, and related population parameters, including growth, diet and exploitation.

The following data (Tables 6.1/2005 stocking, 6.1/2006 stocking, 6.3, 5.02, 5.03 and Figures 6.2, 6.3 and 8.5) was taken from the 1999, 2003, 2006 and 2007 Task Group reports with the permission of the Cold Water Task Group.

ble 6.3   Estimated rainbow trout density (number of individuals per ha) for selected Ontario and New York tributaries of Lake Erie sampled in 1997 and 1998

TARIO TRIBS	1997		1998	
Grand River Tribs.	0+ /ha	1++/ha	0+ /ha	1++/ha
Alder Cr.			196	513
Whiteman's Cr.			2400	1300
Landon's Cr.			6316	3996
Big Cr. Tribs.				
Big Cr.	196	35	536	416
Brandy Cr.			4297	0
Trout Cr.	722	429	726	726
Cranberry Cr.			443	0
Deerlick Cr.	1122	89	4644	899
Short Cr.			351	0
Stoney Cr.	2919	1545	3622	1092
North Cr.	500	97	358	177
Outlet Cr.			2208	183
South Cr.	408	408	486	0
Central Basin Tribs				
Cultus Cr.	648	0	268	0
Condie Dr.	12879	4437	16916	3618
L. Otter Cr.			191	69
L. Otter Trib #1			6096	0
L. Otter Trib #2			1642	0
Arthur Beck			13486	2206
Long Point Bay Tribs.				
Fishers's	2465	352	2084	608
Young's Cr.	1000	435	2100	850
Young's Trib #1			6763	0
Young's Trib #2			2627	0
W YORK TRIBS.				
Spooner Creek	6153	301	3446	837
Derby Brook	3875	83	3121	1819
North Br. Clear Cr.	893	41	891	

Note: mean #/ha is shown for streams with multiple stations

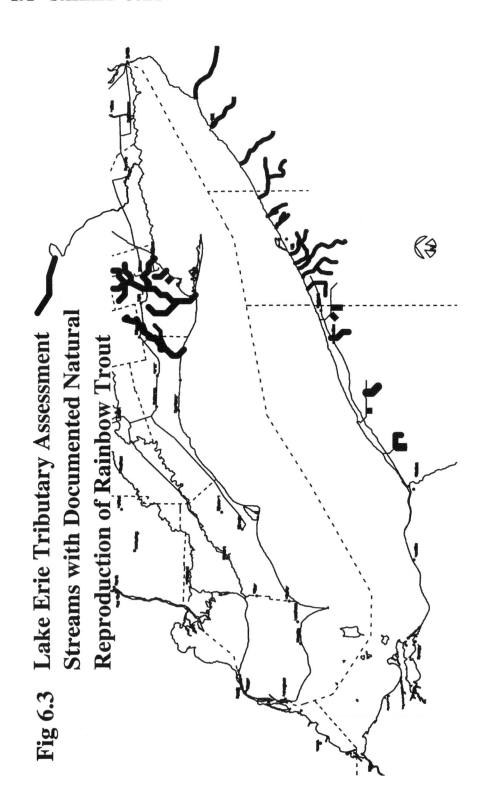

Fig 6.3   Lake Erie Tributary Assessment Streams with Documented Natural Reproduction of Rainbow Trout

Table 5.02

Diet items (by frequency of occurrence) for steelhead recorded in a pilot study conducted in the Central Basin from July to September 2002 (Ohio DOW).

Item	% Occurrence (N=310)	% with food (N=230)	% with fish (N=117)
Bythotrephes cederstroemi	49.4	66.5	--
Smelt	23.9	32.2	63.2
Emerald Shiners	8.1	10.9	21.4
Unidentified fish remains	3.9	5.2	10.3
Asian Lady Beetles	2.3	3.0	--
Freshwater Drum	1.6	2.2	4.3
White Perch	1.6	2.2	4.3
Alewife	1.0	1.3	2.6
Chironomid larvae	1.0	1.3	--
Round Goby	1.0	1.3	2.6
Fingernail Clams	0.6	0.9	--
Dreissena Mussels	0.6	0.9	--
Yellow Perch	0.3	0.4	0.9
empty	25.8	--	--

Table 5.03

Proportions of biomass (by dry weight) of prey items recorded in stomachs of steelhead from a pilot study conducted in the Central Basin from July to September 2002 (Ohio DOW).

Item	% Dry Weight (N=230)
Smelt	37.7 %
White Perch	24.6
Emerald Shiners	16.3
Freshwater Drum	8.7
Alewife	7.0
Unidentified fish remains	2.6
Round Goby	1.7
Yellow Perch	1.4
Bythotrephes cederstroemi	0.1
Asian Lady Beetles	< 0.1
Chironomid larvae	< 0.1
Fingernail Clams	< 0.1
Dreissena sp. mussels	< 0.1

Coldwater Task Group Report 2006

Table 6.1. Rainbow trout /steelhead stocking by jurisdiction for 2005.

Agency	Location	Strain	Fin Clips	Number	Life Stage	Yearling Equivalents
Michigan	Flat Rock	Manistee River, L. Michigan	No	30,900	Yearling	30,900
		Manistee River, L. Michigan	RP	30,000	Yearling	30,000
						60,900 Sub-Total
Ontario	Mill Creek	Mill Creek (wild), L. Erie	RP	13,500	Yearling	13,500
	Mill Creek	Ganaraska River, L. Ontario	RP	35,000	Yearling	35,000
	Erieau Harbour	Ganaraska River, L. Ontario	RP	6,500	Yearling	6,500
						55,000 Sub-Total
Pennsylvania	Conneaut Creek	Trout Run & Godfrey Run, L. Erie	No	75,002	Yearling	75,002
	Crooked Creek	Trout Run & Godfrey Run, L. Erie	No	52,875	Yearling	52,875
	Elk Creek	Trout Run & Godfrey Run, L. Erie	No	269,490	Yearling	269,490
	Fourmile Creek	Trout Run & Godfrey Run, L. Erie	No	14,511	Yearling	14,511
	Godfrey Run	Trout Run & Godfrey Run, L. Erie	No	71,580	Yearling	71,580
	Presque Isle Bay	Trout Run & Godfrey Run, L. Erie	No	58,019	Yearling	58,019
	Raccoon Creek	Trout Run & Godfrey Run, L. Erie	No	48,355	Yearling	48,355
	Sevenmile Creek	Trout Run & Godfrey Run, L. Erie	No	19,340	Yearling	19,340
	Trout Run	Trout Run & Godfrey Run, L. Erie	No	161,797	Yearling	161,797
	Twelvemile Creek	Trout Run & Godfrey Run, L. Erie	No	38,687	Yearling	38,687
	Twentymile Creek	Trout Run & Godfrey Run, L. Erie	No	154,520	Yearling	154,520
	Walnut Creek	Trout Run & Godfrey Run, L. Erie	No	219,070	Yearling	219,070
						1,183,246 Sub-Total
Ohio	Chagrin River	Manistee River, L. Michigan	No	90,017	Yearling	90,017
	Conneaut Creek	Manistee River, L. Michigan	No	74,042	Yearling	74,042
	Grand River	Manistee River, L. Michigan	No	93,773	Yearling	93,773
	Rocky River	Manistee River, L. Michigan	No	89,781	Yearling	89,781
	Vermillion River	Manistee River, L. Michigan	No	55,214	Yearling	55,214
						402,827 Sub-Total
New York	Buffalo Creek	Chambers Creek, L. Ontario	No	15,000	Yearling	15,000
	Buffalo River	Chambers Creek, L. Ontario	No	5,000	Yearling	5,000
	Canadaway Creek	Chambers Creek, L. Ontario	No	20,000	Yearling	20,000
	Cattaraugus Creek	Chambers Creek, L. Ontario	No	90,000	Yearling	90,000
	Cattaraugus Creek	Skamania, L. Ontario	ADLV	15,000	Yearling	15,000
	Cayuga Creek	Chambers Creek, L. Ontario	No	15,000	Yearling	15,000
	Chautauqua Creek	Chambers Creek, L. Ontario	No	40,000	Yearling	40,000
	Dunkirk Harbor	Chambers Creek, L. Ontario	No	10,000	Yearling	10,000
	East Br. Cazenovia Cr.	Chambers Creek, L. Ontario	No	10,000	Yearling	10,000
	Eighteen-Mile Creek	Domestic	No	5,000	Yearling	5,000
	Eighteen-Mile Creek	Chambers Creek, L. Ontario	No	40,000	Yearling	40,000
	Silver Creek	Chambers Creek, L. Ontario	No	5,000	Yearling	5,000
	Walnut Creek	Chambers Creek, L. Ontario	No	5,000	Yearling	5,000
						275,000 Sub-Tota

1,976,973 Grand T

Coldwater Task Group Report 2007

Table 6.1. Rainbow trout /steelhead stockings by jurisdiction for 2006.

Jurisdiction	Location	Strain	Fin Clips	Number	Life Stage	Yearling Equivalents	
Michigan	Flat Rock	Manistee River, L. Michigan	No	66,514	Yearling	66,514	Sub-Total
Ontario	Young's Creek	Young's Creek (wild), L. Erie	No	550	Yearling	550	
	Mill Creek	Ganaraska River, L. Ontario	LP	21,000	Yearling	21,000	
	Erieau Harbour	Ganaraska River, L. Ontario	LP	22,800	Yearling	22,800	
						44,350	Sub-Total
Pennsylvania	Bear Creek	Trout Run & Godfrey Run, L. Erie	No	9,500	Yearling	9,500	
	Conneaut Creek	Trout Run & Godfrey Run, L. Erie	No	75,000	Yearling	75,000	
	Crooked Creek	Trout Run & Godfrey Run, L. Erie	No	58,800	Yearling	58,800	
	Elk Creek	Trout Run & Godfrey Run, L. Erie	No	277,590	Yearling	277,590	
	Fourmile Creek	Trout Run & Godfrey Run, L. Erie	No	15,790	Yearling	15,790	
	Godfrey Run	Trout Run & Godfrey Run, L. Erie	No	92,100	Yearling	92,100	
	Presque Isle Bay	Trout Run & Godfrey Run, L. Erie	No	58,800	Yearling	58,800	
	Raccoon Creek	Trout Run & Godfrey Run, L. Erie	No	49,007	Yearling	49,007	
	Sevenmile Creek	Trout Run & Godfrey Run, L. Erie	No	21,260	Yearling	21,260	
	Trout Run	Trout Run & Godfrey Run, L. Erie	No	123,500	Yearling	123,500	
	Twelvemile Creek	Trout Run & Godfrey Run, L. Erie	No	40,270	Yearling	40,270	
	Twentymile Creek	Trout Run & Godfrey Run, L. Erie	No	156,794	Yearling	156,794	
	Walnut Creek	Trout Run & Godfrey Run, L. Erie	No	226,792	Yearling	226,792	
						1,205,203	Sub-Total
Ohio	Chagrin River	Manistee River, L. Michigan	No	109,310	Yearling	109,310	
	Conneaut Creek	Manistee River, L. Michigan	No	87,334	Yearling	87,334	
	Grand River	Manistee River, L. Michigan	No	108,116	Yearling	108,116	
	Rocky River	Manistee River, L. Michigan	No	106,598	Yearling	106,598	
	Vermillion River	Manistee River, L. Michigan	No	80,585	Yearling	80,585	
						491,943	Sub-Total
New York	Buffalo Creek	Chambers Creek, L. Ontario	No	15,000	Yearling	15,000	
	Buffalo River	Chambers Creek, L. Ontario	No	10,000	Yearling	10,000	
	Canadaway Creek	Chambers Creek, L. Ontario	No	20,000	Yearling	20,000	
	Cattaraugus Creek	Chambers Creek, L. Ontario	No	90,000	Yearling	90,000	
	Cattaraugus Creek	Skamania, L. Ontario	No	15,000	Yearling	15,000	
	Cayuga Creek	Chambers Creek, L. Ontario	No	10,000	Yearling	10,000	
	Chautauqua Creek	Chambers Creek, L. Ontario	No	40,000	Yearling	40,000	
	Dunkirk Harbor	Chambers Creek, L. Ontario	No	10,000	Yearling	10,000	
	East Branch Cazenovia	Chambers Creek, L. Ontario	No	10,000	Yearling	10,000	
	Eighteen-Mile Creek	Domestic	No	5,000	Yearling	5,000	
	Eighteen-Mile Creek	Chambers Creek, L. Ontario	No	40,000	Yearling	40,000	
	Silver Creek	Chambers Creek, L. Ontario	No	5,000	Yearling	5,000	
	Walnut Creek	Chambers Creek, L. Ontario	No	5,000	Yearling	5,000	
						275,000	Sub-Total
						2,083,010	Grand Total

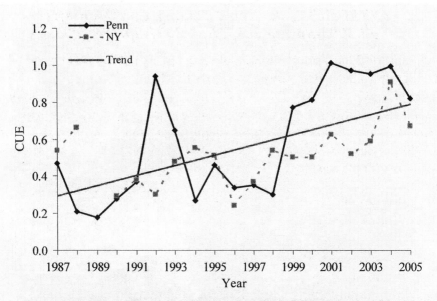

Figure 6.2. Targeted salmonid catch rates in Lake Erie tributaries by Pennsylvania and New York angl
diary cooperators, 1987-2005. A fitted linear trend line is presented from mean interagenc
catch rates by year.

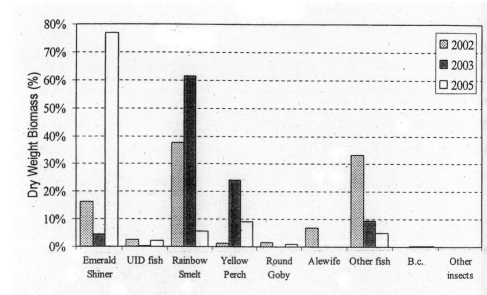

Figure 8.5. Dry weight biomass (by % of total) of diet items found in steelhead stomachs collected
during the summer in Ohio's portion of the central basin of Lake Erie in 2002, 2003, and
2005. Note: UID fish is unidentified fish species from incomplete samples.

New York State Department of Environmental Conservation (NYSDEC), Lake Erie Tributary Creel Survey: Fall 2003-Spring 2004, Fall 2004-Spring 2005.

In January, 2006, James Markham of the NYSDEC, Lake Erie Fisheries Unit, Dunkirk, NY completed a study (of the above title).

Figures 6a, 6b, 7a, 7b, 7c and 7d are taken from the study (with the permission of the author and the NYSDEC) and point out some of the important trends of the data collected during the survey. Persons interested in reviewing the entire study (including discussion) should contact the NYSDEC Lake Erie Research Unit. See Appendix B for the address.

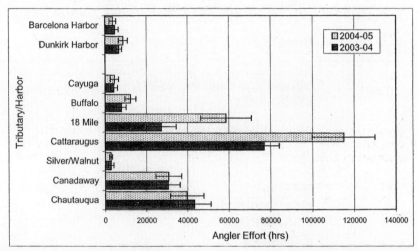

Figure 6a. Total angler effort (angler hrs.) directed at salmonids in major tributaries and harbors of New York waters of Lake Erie, 10 September 2003 - 15 May 2004 and 16 September 2004 - 15 May 2005. Error bars show 2 standard errors of the total effort.

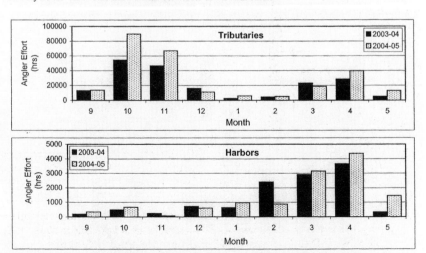

Figure 6b. Total angler effort (angler hrs.) directed at salmonids by month in major tributaries and harbors of New York waters of Lake Erie, 10 September 2003 - 15 May 2004 and 16 September 2004 - 15 May 2005.

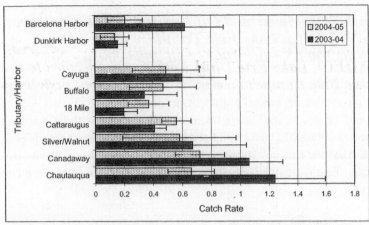

Figure 7a. Targeted catch rates of salmonids by anglers fishing the New York tributaries and harbors of Lake Erie, September 2003 - May 2004 and September 2004 - May 2005. Error bars show 2 standard errors of the catch rate.

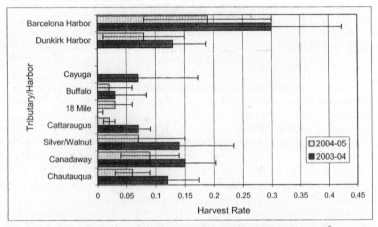

Figure 7b. Targeted harvest rates of salmonids by anglers fishing the New York tributaries and harbors of Lake Erie, September 2003 - May 2004 and September 2004 - May 2005. Error bars show 2 standard errors of the harvest rate.

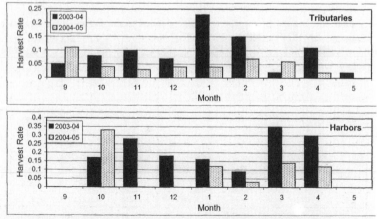

Figure 7d. Monthly targeted harvest rates of salmonids by anglers fishing the New York tributaries and harbors of Lake Erie, September 2003 - May 2004 and September 2004 - May 2005.

New York State Department of Environmental Conservation (NYSDEC), Lake Erie Unit, 2005 Annual Report to the Lake Erie Committee and the Great Lakes Fishery Commission, March 2007.

Tables J.1, J.2 and J.3 were taken from the above annual report. Persons interested in reviewing the entire study (including recommendations) should contact the NYSDEC Lake Erie Research Unit, Dunkirk, NY. See Appendix B for the address.

YSDEC Lake Erie Annual Report 2006

able J.2. Assigned values of the Reproductive Potential (RP) Index used for each sampled stream to ndicate its potential for producing wild steelhead trout. The index is based upon the abundance of YOY teelhead, instream habitat, water flow, canopy, and water temperature.

RP = 0: Adult steelhead do not have access to run this stream.

RP = 1: Spawning potential is very low. Few if any YOY trout are found. Limited habitat for spawning nd rearing available. Drainage reaches high summer temperatures due to lack of canopy and/or poor vater flow.

RP = 2: Moderate spawning potential. Good spawning and rearing habitat in small parts of the stream. 'OY steelhead are present but are only found in specific habitats. Stream is probably still limited by anopy, water flow, and/or water temperature.

RP = 3: Average spawning potential. Stream possesses adequate spawning and rearing habitat in larger ections of the creek. Good numbers of YOY steelhead and maybe a few holdovers (age 1) are present. tream may be limited in terms of water temperature, canopy, or water flow that hinders it full potential.

P = 4: Good spawning potential. Large numbers of YOY and some holdovers are present. Stream ossesses adequate canopy, water flow, and temperature for yoy production and survival. However, some her factor, such as a barrier, limits overall production to a reduced area.

P = 5: High spawning potential. Large numbers of YOY and holdovers present. Stream is not limited by y factor and has the potential to produce large numbers of naturally produced fish in a large portion of its ach.

able J.3. List of Lake Erie tributaries sampled for wild steelhead production in 2006. The general undance of young-of-year (YOY) steelhead, instream habitat, and water quality were graded for each ream. The RP Index, an index of reproductive potential (Scale range = 0 - 5), was assigned to each stream dicating its potential for producing wild steelhead trout.

Stream	Stream Code	Last Sampling Date	YOY Steelhead Abundance	Spawning Habitat	Canopy	Water Temp	Water Flow	RP Index
Point Peter Brook	E.23-19	10-6-2006	-----	Poor	Average	-----	Average	1
N. Branch Clear Creek	E.23-6-4	10-10-2006	Good	Excellent	Good	Good	Good	3
Doty Creek	E.65	10-16-2006	Poor	Poor	Good	Poor	Poor	1
Bournes Creek	E.61	10-16-2006	Poor	Poor	Average	Poor	Poor	1
Kelley Brook	E.23-24	10-10-2006	Poor	Poor	Excellent	Average	Poor	1

NYSDEC Lake Erie Annual Report 2006

Table J.1.   Tributaries to Lake Erie known to have adult steelhead runs in the fall and/or spring. Most of these streams will be evaluated for trout habitat and spawning potential to develop an inventory of streams that will support wild rainbow/steelhead trout populations. Sampled streams were assigned a RP Indice (Range = 0 - 5), which is an index of reproductive potential to indicate its potential for producing wild steelhead trout.

Stream	Stream Code	County	Year Sampled	RP Index
Buffalo Creek	E.1	Erie		
Beaver Creek	E.37-2	Chautauqua	2002	1
Beaver Creek (2nd Gulf)	E.31	Chautauqua	2002	2
Big Indian Creek	E.23-5	Cattaraugus	-----	1
Big Sister Creek	E.20	Erie	2002	1
Bournes Creek	E.61	Chautauqua	2006	1
Canadaway Creek	E.37	Chautauqua	2004	1
Cayuga Creek	E.1-6	Erie		
Cazenovia Creek	E.1-4	Erie		
Chautauqua Creek	E.68	Chautauqua	2001	2
Clear Creek	E.23-6	Erie	2004	2
Connoisarauley Creek	E.23-27	Cattaraugus	2002	3
Coon Brook	E.23-25	Erie	2005	3
Corell Creek	E.51	Chautauqua	2002	1
Crooked Brook	E.36	Chautauqua	2002	1
Delaware Creek	E.21	Erie	2002	1
Derby Brook	E.23-28	Erie	2004, 2005	4
Doty Creek	E.65	Chautauqua	2006	2
Eighteen Mile Creek	E.13	Erie		
Grannis Creek	E.23-18	Erie	2005	2
Half Way Brook	E.24	Chautauqua	2005	1
Kelly Brook	E.23-24	Erie	2006	0
Little Canadaway Creek	E.43	Chautauqua	-----	1
Little Chautauqua Creek	E.68-1	Chautauqua	2001	4
Little Indian Creek	E.23-5-1	Cattaraugus	-----	1
Little Sister Creek	E.19	Erie	-----	1
Morton=s Corner	E.23-28-3	Cattaraugus	2005	3
Muddy Creek	E.22	Erie	2002	1
Nigh Creek	E.23-27-1	Cattaraugus	2005	1
N. Branch Clear Creek	E.23-6-4	Erie	2006	3
Point Peter Brook	E.23-19	Cattaraugus	2006	1
Reiter Creek	E.30	Chautauqua	2002	2
Scott Creek (1st Gulf)	E.32	Chautauqua	2002	1
Silver Creek	E.25	Chautauqua	-----	1
Slippery Rock Creek	E.50	Chautauqua	2002	1
Smokes Creek	E.2	Erie	-----	1
S. Branch Cattaraugus Creek	E.23-20	Cattaraugus	2004	1
S. Branch Eighteen Mile Creek	E.13-4	Erie		
Spooners Creek	E.23-30	Erie	2001	5
Thatcher Brook	E.23-17	Cattaraugus	2005	1
Twenty Mile Creek	E.96	Chautauqua	2006	*
Utley Brook	E.23-23	Cattaraugus	1996	1
Walnut Creek	E.25-1	Chautauqua	-----	1
Waterman Brook	E.23-21	Cattaraugus	2004	1

* 20 Mile Creek was sampled by Region 9 inland fisheries in 2006 and no RP index was determined. Significant numbers of steelhead were sampled in this stream.

References

Bashline, James. Atlantic Salmon Fishing, Harrisburg, Pa., Stackpole Books, 1987.

Behnke, Robert. Steelhead Trout, Trout Magazine, Winter, 1984.

Brouncheidel, Jeff. Fisheries Survey (February 26 to April 25, 2000) on the Huron River @ FlatRock, Wayne County, MI. Michigan Department of Natural Resources, Livonia, Michigan, January 7, 2003.

Combs, Trey. Steelhead Fly Fishing, New York, NY, Lyons & Burford Publishers, 1991.

Cornelius, Floyd. Wild Steelhead of Cattaraugus Creek (E.23) Below Springville Dam, Dunkirk, NY, NY State DEC, Lake Erie Fisheries Unit, Region 9, June 1997.

Culligan, Bill. NYSDEC Lake Erie Unit 2002 Annual Report to the Lake Erie Committee and the Great Lakes Fishery Commission, Albany, NY, New York State Department of Environmental Conservation, February, 2003.

Filkins, Kenn. Fly Fishing for Salmon and Steelhead of the Great Lakes, Chelsea, Michigan, Wilderness Adventure Books, 1998.

Frodin, Mikael. Make them swim! Trout and Salmon (a UK publication), December, 2006.

Grooms, Steve. Best Bets for Steelheading, Great Lakes Fisherman, March, 1986.

Haig-Brown, Roderick. A River Never Sleeps, New York, Crown Publishers, 1946.

Halyk, Larry (Lead Management Biologist for the OMNR, Lake Erie Management Unit.) Lake Erie Steelhead Fly Fisheries, Characterization of Lake Erie and Lake Erie Tributaries, 1999.

Halyk, Larry (Lead Management Biologist, Ontario Ministry of Natural Resources, Lake Erie Management Unit.) Steelhead Management Summary Province of Ontario, August 30, 1999.

Herzog, Bill. The Steelheader's Key to Success, Reading Water, Salmon Trout Steelheader, Vol 28, August-September 1994.

Kageyama, Colin. What Fish See: Understanding Optics and Color Shifts for Designing Lures and Flies, Portland, Oregon, Frank Amato Publications, 1999.

Kustich, Rich and Jerry. Fly Fishing for Great Lakes Steelhead-an Advanced Look at an Emerging Fishery, Grand Island, NY, West River Publishing Company, 1999.

Landis, Dwight. Trout Streams of Pennsylvania, Bellefonte, Pa., Hempstead-Lyndell, 1995.

Linesenman, Bob and Nevela, Steve. Great Lakes Steelhead, A Guided Tour for Fly Anglers, Woodstock, VT, The Countryman Press, 1995.

Linesenman, Bob. Best Streams for Great Lakes Steelhead, Woodstock, Vermont, The Countryman Press, 2005.

Lorentz, Jim. Niagra Frontier Steelhead, Wild Steelhead and Salmon, Autumn 1996.

Mandell, Mark and Johnson, Les. Tube Flies: A Tying, Fishing & Historical Guide, Portland, OR, Frank Amato Publications, 1995.

Mann, Chris. Hairwing & Tube Flies for Salmon & Steelhead, Mechanicsburg, PA, Stackpole Books, 2004.

Mandell, Mark and Kenly, Robert. Tube Flies Two: Evolution, Portland, OR, Frank Amato Publications, 2007.

McClane, A.J. McClane's Game Fish of North America, NY, NY, Times Books, 1984.

Meyer, Deke. Advanced Fly Fishing Techniques for Steelhead, Portland, OR, Frank Amato Publications, 1992.

Modrzynski, Mike. Great Lakes Steelhead Guide, Portland Oregon, Frank Amato

Winter wonderland at lower end of Twenty-Mile Creek, PA.
(Kathie Shore photo)

Tributary Steelhead Log

Date: **Time period fished:**

Tributary: **Tributary section:**

Weather (sunny, cloudy, rain, drizzle, snow, moon phase):

Temperatures (air, tributary water, lakeshore water):

Water conditions (rising/falling/steady, dirty/clear/prime, high/medium/low, cfs flow/ft. stage, slush/ice, leaves, smolts/suckers, crowded/light pressure):

Water type fished (pool, run/riffle, tail-out, pocket water, eddy, gravel, lakeshore):

Technique used (bottom-bouncing, indicator fishing, tandem fly rig, chuck-n-duck, swinging streamers, stripping wooly buggers, dry flies):

Equipment used (rod and reel type, fly line type and taper, leader design and length, tippet length and size, indicator size, shot amount, sink rate and length of sinking leader/sink tip):

Flies used (pattern, color, hook size and type, weighted, beads, tube fly):

Steelhead caught (number, size, males/females, fresh run/dark, pre-spawn/spawner/drop-down, jacks, bonus salmon or brown trout):

Special notes:

Ordering information for additional books

Additional copies of **Steelhead Guide, Fly Fishing Techniques and Strategies for Lake Erie Steelhead** (Updated and Expanded 4th edition) can be ordered directly from Great Lakes Publishing for $32.95 each, plus $4.00 shipping and handling per order. Residents of Pennsylvania please add 7% sales tax ($2.59). Send order along with check or money order made payable to:

Great Lakes Publishing
606 Crysler Street
Pittsburgh, Pa. 15226

Ordering information for custom
Lake Erie steelhead flies

To order 1 dozen effective Lake Erie steelhead flies tied by guide and author John Nagy, send $24.95 plus $4.00 shipping and handling to Great Lakes Publishing (see address above). Residents of Pennsylvania please include 7% state sales tax ($2.03).

Custom steelhead fly orders, custom Lake Erie noodle fly rods, Solitude fly reels, custom leaders and floating indicator kits can also be ordered by contacting John Nagy at (412) 531-5819 or steelheadguide@hotmail.com